LYTTON STRACHEY

Lytton Strachey

HIS MIND AND ART

by Charles Richard Sanders

NEW HAVEN: YALE UNIVERSITY PRESS, 1957

London: Oxford University Press

ACKNOWLEDGMENTS

IT IS A PLEASURE here to acknowledge my indebtedness to Lytton Strachey's publishers, Chatto and Windus, and Harcourt, Brace and Company, for permission to quote from his books; to his sisters and brother, Miss Phillipa Strachey, Mme Bussy (née Dorothy Strachey), Miss Marjorie Strachey, the late Miss Joan Pernel Strachey, and Mr. Oliver Strachey, for pictures, information, and criticism; and to Strachey's friends, Mr. Saxon Sydney-Turner, Mr. and Mrs. Ralph Partridge, Mr. Leonard Woolf, and Mrs. Nicholas Bagenal, for similar help; to H. Wilson Harris, late editor of the *Spectator,* for permission to use a marked file through which Strachey's unsigned contributions to the *Spectator* were identified and for permission to quote from these writings; to the editors of *Philological Quarterly, Modern Language Quarterly, Modern Language Notes, Emory University Quarterly, College English, Modern Philology,* and *PMLA* for permission to republish my articles on Strachey which have appeared in these journals; to Professor Fred B. Millett, who read the complete manuscript, for valuable criticism; to my colleagues, Professors William H. Irving, Benjamin Boyce, and Charles E. Ward, and to my friend, Professor LeRoy Smith, for reading the chapter on the eighteenth century; to Edward Dowden for the subtitle; to Dr. Paul M. Gross, Dr. Walter M. Nielsen and the Duke University Research Council, the Carnegie Foundation, Mr. John Marshall and the Rockefeller Foundation for encouragement and financial assistance; and chiefly to Mr. James Strachey, Brother and literary executor of Lytton Strachey, and to Mrs. James Strachey for their unreserved cooperation in putting the pertinent materials, both published and unpublished, at my disposal and for their kindly but penetrating insight into both the subject of this book and the difficult problems encountered by the author in writing it.

C.R.S.

May 10, 1957

CONTENTS

LIST OF ILLUSTRATIONS
(between pages 34–35)

The picture of Ham Spray House on the title page is from a letter-head designed by Carrington.

Sutton Court, near Pensford, Somerset. Used by permission of *Country Life*.

Rook's Nest, in Surrey, country home of the first Sir Henry Strachey in the eighteenth century. Used by permission of Lord Strachie.

Stowey House, Clapham Common, London, where Lytton Strachey was born. Used by permission of Misses Philippa and Marjorie Strachey.

General Sir Richard Strachey. Photograph by Hollyer. Used by permission of Misses Philippa and Marjorie Strachey.

Jane Maria Lady Strachey. Used by permission of Misses Philippa and Marjorie Strachey.

The first Earl of Lytton ("Owen Meredith") in Viceroyal regalia. From a painting by Prinseps in possession of Mr. Ralph Brown, of B. F. Stevens & Brown, and used with his permission.

Lytton Strachey at the age of three. Used by permission of Misses Philippa and Marjorie Strachey.

Family of Sir Richard and Lady Strachey posing to form a medallion, with Sutton Court in background. Used by permission of Misses Philippa and Marjorie Strachey.

Sons and daughters of Sir Richard and Lady Strachey, with Sutton Court in background. Used by permission of Misses Philippa and Marjorie Strachey.

ix

Ham Spray House as it faces the down. From a photograph by C. R. Sanders.

Another view of Ham Spray House showing the weeping ilex tree. From a photograph by C. R. Sanders.

"The Lacket," cottage belonging to Hilton Young (later Lord Kennet) at Lockeridge, near Marlborough, Wiltshire. From a photograph made by Ralph Partridge and used with his permission.

"The Mill House," Tidmarsh, Pangbourne. From a painting by Carrington. Used by permission of Mr. and Mrs. Ralph Partridge.

Strachey's study at Ham Spray House. Used by permission of Mr. and Mrs. Ralph Partridge.

Close-up view of the Voltaire picture. Used by permission of Mr. and Mrs. Ralph Partridge.

Strachey's writing desk in his study at Ham Spray House and the view. Used by permission of Mr. and Mrs. Ralph Partridge.

Teatime at Ham Spray House. Used with permission of Mr. and Mrs. Ralph Partridge.

Lytton Strachey, Carrington, and James Strachey. Used by permission of James Strachey.

Lytton Strachey and Virginia Woolf about 1918. Used by permission of James Strachey.

A study of Strachey's face and hands by Carrington. Used by permission of Mr. and Mrs. Ralph Partridge.

A group at Garsington Manor. Used by permission of Mrs. Nicholas Bagenal.

The bedroom at Ham Spray House in which Strachey died. Used by permission of Mr. and Mrs. Ralph Partridge.

LYTTON STRACHEY

Biographical Sketch

LYTTON STRACHEY was born on March 1, 1880, at Stowey House, Clapham Common, London, the fifth son and the eleventh child of Lieutenant General Sir Richard and Jane Maria Strachey. He was named Giles Lytton after an early sixteenth-century Gyles Strachey and the first Earl of Lytton (the poet "Owen Meredith"), who had been a friend of the Richard Stracheys when he was viceroy of India in the late 1870's. The Earl of Lytton was also Lytton Strachey's godfather. Pamela Lady Lytton, wife of the second earl, was a relative of Strachey's mother through the Plowden family.

Although the neighborhood of Clapham had in the early nineteenth century been the center of activities of a famous group of Evangelicals, the "Clapham Sect," to which Lytton Strachey's paternal grandmother had belonged, the influence of Evangelical religion in the family had pretty well spent its force before Strachey was born. Stowey House, large and comfortable, with trees and a pleasant garden, was named after the pretty little village of Stowey on the Strachey estate of Sutton Court in Somerset. Located near Pensford and about fifteen miles south of Bristol, the estate had come into the possession of the Stracheys in the middle of the seventeenth century. Since then its ancient stone manor house has been to members of the family the symbol of rich cultural associations. The earliest parts of the house are Norman and were built by the Suttons, who held the land at the time of the Domesday survey. The St. Loes owned the estate in the fifteenth century, and in the Tudor period important additions were made to the house by Elizabeth Hardwicke—affectionately called "Building Bess" by the Stracheys—after she had married Sir William St. Loe, her third husband. By her fourth marriage she became the Countess of Shrewsbury. But her second husband had been a Cavendish, and it was to her son Charles Cavendish that she left Sutton Court. From the descendants and heirs of Charles Cavendish, Elizabeth, the third wife of William Strachey of Camberwell, purchased the estate in 1642. She left it to her son John Strachey, and it has belonged to the Stracheys ever since.[1]

The Strachey family rose to prominence in Essex and Middlesex in the middle of the sixteenth century. Previously Stracheys had been sheriffs of Somerset and Dorset in the reigns of Henry III and his four successors; in the fourteenth century Sir John Strachie had been knighted with other companions of the Black Prince; and another John Strachie, who died in 1427, had kept a court at Oxborough in Norfolk. But the history of the family did not really become noteworthy before the time of the Stracheys of Saffron Walden, Essex, in the reign of Queen Elizabeth. One of these, a William Strachey who died in 1598, owned a brewhouse and wharf in Westminster and other valuable property there and on Fish Street Hill; he contributed £50 to the fund for defeating the Spanish Armada. His son, another William Strachey, traveler, writer, and friend of Ben Jonson, John Donne, Thomas Campion,[2] and many other men of letters of his day, is the subject of articles in both the *Dictionary of National Biography* and the *Dictionary of American Biography*. He was in the great storm which wrecked the fleet of Sir George Somers off the Bermudas in July, 1609, and in the opinion of many scholars it was his description of this storm in a letter sent to England from Jamestown that Shakespeare used when he wrote *The Tempest*. This Strachey became the first Secretary of the Colony of Virginia and helped to draw up its first laws. He compiled a dictionary for the Chesapeake Indian language and

1. For additional information on Sutton Court and the Strachey family, see my article, "The Strachey Family, Sutton Court, and John Locke," *Virginia Magazine of History and Biography*, 59 (July 1951), 275–96, which provides some pictures.

2. Campion wrote a Latin sonnet, "Ad Gulielman Strachaeum," in praise of this William Strachey. It is to be found in his *Epigrammatum* (1629). Lytton Strachey's copy and translation of it have been preserved among his papers.

wrote one of the best early histories of Virginia.[3] His son, still another William Strachey, married Elizabeth, daughter of William Cross and widow of Samuel Jepp. It was she who bought Sutton Court in 1642 and left it to her son John Strachey at her death.

John Strachey was the intimate friend of John Locke, and much of the correspondence between him and Locke has been preserved. His son, another John Strachey, became an antiquarian and geologist of considerable note. He was elected a member of the Royal Society in the early eighteenth century and has been given credit for being the first to give a genuinely scientific explanation for the earth's stratification. In the late eighteenth century his grandson, the first Sir Henry Strachey, was the secretary and friend of Lord Clive. He went with Clive to India and was the first in four generations of Stracheys to serve there. He was also active in helping to negotiate the treaty with the United States at the end of the American Revolution. His brother, John Strachey, was Archdeacon of Norwich and Chaplain in Ordinary to King George III.

The history of the Stracheys in the nineteenth century becomes so full and important that it can be merely suggested here. It has much to tell us about the second Sir Henry Strachey, who had, despite his many eccentricities, a reputable career in India and was the admired friend of Walter Savage Landor; and about his brother, Edward Strachey (Lytton Strachey's grandfather), for some time a judge at Bengal and later an examiner in the India House, a lover of Persian poetry and of Chaucer, who knew James and John Stuart Mill and was the close friend of Thomas Love Peacock and Thomas Carlyle. He married Julia Kirkpatrick, a woman often praised by Carlyle as the best friend he ever had. All of the eight sons and daughters of Edward and Julia Strachey were remarkable; at least half of them achieved distinction in their Victorian world. The oldest of these, Sir Edward Strachey, was a disciple of Coleridge, a friend of Carlyle, F. D. Maurice, and

3. Members of the family have justifiably been proud of this Strachey who could well have been Shakespeare's friend. For further information concerning him, see my article, "William Strachey, the Virginia Colony, and Shakespeare," *Virginia Magazine of History and Biography*, 57 (April 1949), 115–32.

Edward Lear, a Shakespearean scholar, and a literary critic who, like his father, throughout his life took great delight in the Persian poets and in Chaucer. He married Mary Isabella Symonds, sister of the critic and historian John Addington Symonds.

Three of Sir Edward's younger brothers, John, Henry, and Richard, distinguished themselves in India, and one of these, Sir John Strachey (1823–1907), became lieutenant governor of the Northwest Provinces in 1874. In the face of great difficulties he pushed through important reforms: first, the removal of the Inland Customs line or Salt Barrier; and second, the abolition of the import duties on cotton. He commanded the complete confidence and was an intimate friend of the first Earl of Lytton, viceroy of India from 1876 to 1880. It has been said that his knowledge of the intricate involutions of Indian finance surpassed that of anyone else of his day. He also wrote books on India and has been described as "the literary expositor of the domestic and financial policy of three successive Viceroys." He spent much of his old age in Florence, giving his time to the study of architecture and Dante.

Another brother, Lieutenant Colonel Henry Strachey, was one of the earliest Englishmen to explore northwestern Tibet, where, according to the *Encyclopedia Britannica*, he reached Mansarowar Lake in 1846. He was given the Gold Medal of the Royal Geographical Society in 1852. An ardent mathematician, he possessed a lifelong enthusiasm for architecture and helped to build the Grand Trunk Road and the Katubdia Lighthouse in India.

Probably the most brilliant, however, of the three brothers who went to India was Lytton Strachey's father, Lieutenant General Sir Richard Strachey (1817–1908). Those who knew him spoke of the various and complex facets of his mind and described him as one who distinguished himself as a soldier in the Sikh War, as an engineer in the construction of railways and irrigation canals, as an administrator, and as a scientist with achievements in the fields of geography, geology, meteorology, and botany. In 1848 and 1849 he and J. E. Winterbottom gathered from the dangerous mountains of northern India and Tibet the large botanical collection which was given their name—over two thousand specimens, all carefully ticketed with notes of localities and elevations at which they were found.[4] Thirty-two of the plants, one of them a new genus, now bear the name Strachey. Sir Richard was elected a fellow of the Royal Society in 1854 and president of the Royal Geographical Society in 1887. He served as a member of the Indian Council from 1876 to 1889.

He was married twice. By the first marriage there were no children. His second wife, the mother of Lytton Strachey, was Jane Maria, daughter of Sir John Peter Grant (1807–73), who belonged to another noteworthy Anglo-Indian family, the Grants of Rothiemurchus, a large estate on the River Spey in the Scottish Highlands. The Grants, marrying into the Plowden, Ironside, Raper, and Gordon families, go back to John Grant, Chief of Grant, who in 1539 married Lady Majorie Stuart. The Grants were a people of many achievements and extensive culture, strongly attached to their ancestral seat in the Highlands and to the traditions which had been handed down to them. For generations before the birth of Jane Maria, the family had cultivated a special interest in the French language and literature. Lady Strachey also found great delight in English literature, particularly in the Elizabethans and Milton. She edited her aunt's memoirs, which gave much information about Rothiemurchus and the Grants. Her *Lay Texts for the Young, in Both English and French* appeared in 1887; her *Poets on Poets* in 1894; and her *Recollections of a Long Life,* selections which Leonard Woolf made from her memoirs, in the *Nation and Athenaeum* from January 5 to August 24, 1924. She also wrote poems, many of them in French patterns, from time to time throughout her life. A number of these have been published. Her verse for children is excellent.[5] We may be certain that her son Lytton Strachey, in his knowledge and enjoyment of both English and French literature, owed much to her.

4. The specimens in this collection were distributed in 1852–53. Some went to the Hookerian Herbarium at Kew Gardens; others to the British Museum, to the Linnean Society, and to some of the Continental museums.

5. See her *Nursery Lyrics* (London, Bliss, Sands, and Foster, 1893), with illustrations by G. P. Jacomb Hood.

The world in which Lytton Strachey grew up also contained a number of cousins and other relations who made a name for themselves. Sir Edward Strachey's oldest son Edward, who in 1911 became the first Lord Strachie, was from 1912 to 1915 paymaster general of Great Britain and for many years an influential leader in the movement to bring about agricultural reform. His wife, born Constance Braham, became the editor of Edward Lear's works. Their son Edward, who became the second Lord Strachie, now lives at Sutton Court and is the head of the family. Sir Edward's younger son, St. Loe Strachey, was the proprietor and gifted editor of the *Spectator* from 1898 to 1925. Still another son of Sir Edward, Henry Strachey, was an artist and for many years an art critic for the *Spectator*. Lionel Strachey, son of Lytton Strachey's Uncle George, had a career as a man of letters in New York. Sir Arthur and Sir Charles Strachey were talented sons of another uncle, Sir John. St. Loe Strachey's wife, born Amy Simpson, granddaughter of the Victorian economist Nassau W. Senior, was distinguished both for her writings and for her work in taking care of children and wounded soldiers during both World Wars. Her daughter, Mrs. Amabel Williams-Ellis, wrote a number of noteworthy books, and her son, John Strachey, was author of many leftist books and articles, officer in the R.A.F., and member of the British Labor Cabinet after the second World War.

More important, however, as an influence on Lytton Strachey were his own brothers and sisters. The oldest, Elinor, married James Meadows Rendel. According to her brothers and sisters, she was next to Lytton in her possession of literary talent but was extremely shy about displaying her writings. The oldest brother, Richard John, carried on the family tradition and had a military career in India. Another sister, Dorothy, married the French artist, Simon Bussy. She has written a number of books and has translated others from the French, including many by her friend André Gide. Next to her was Ralph, who was brilliant in mathematics and who became chief engineer of the East Indian Railway. Still another sister, Philippa, O.B.E., became Secretary of the London and National Society for Women's Suffrage and has been active during wartime in hospital and relief work in

London. A brother, Oliver, C.B.E., has served with the East Indian Railway, written a book dealing with Indian history, and done distinguished work in the Foreign and War Offices during the two World Wars.[6] A sister, Joan Pernel, was principal of Newnham College, Cambridge, from 1923 to 1941 and an authority on Old French. These were the brothers and sisters older than Lytton. After him came Marjorie Colville and James Beaumont.[7] Marjorie became a teacher and writer. James became a psychoanalyst of distinction. He studied with Freud in Vienna, has translated a large number of his works into English, and is editor of the new and definitive edition of his works now being translated.

Through the centuries Strachey's family had produced a comparatively large number of talented individuals and had handed down cultural traditions which made an important contribution to his mind and work. One of the most striking characteristics of his writings is the equilibrium which they maintain between independence of mind and group consciousness.[8]

When Lytton was just four years old, the family moved from Stowey House to 69 Lancaster Gate, just north of Kensington Gardens. This was their home until Sir Richard Strachey retired over twenty years later. Throughout his life Lytton Strachey was peculiarly susceptible to the spell of places and houses, and the big house at Lancaster Gate, in which he spent most of the years of his childhood and youth, was a major influence in his life. In an unpublished essay, "Lancaster Gate," written in 1922, he discusses the nature of this influence. The influences

6. Oliver Strachey's second wife, born Rachel ("Ray") Costello, wrote a number of books. Her mother was the sister of Logan Pearsall Smith. Her sister married Adrian Stephen, son of Sir Leslie and brother of Virginia Woolf. Alice, another sister of Logan Pearsall Smith, married Bertrand Russell.

7. There were thirteen children in all, three of whom—Caroline, Olivia, and Roger—did not grow up. The name Olivia suggested the title *Olivia by Olivia,* a book by Dorothy Strachey (Mme Bussy) (New York, William Sloane associates, 1949), based on Mlle Souvestre's school at Fontainebleau.

8. I have studied the history of the family in its relation to British culture in *The Strachey Family: Their Writings and Literary Associations* (Durham, N.C., Duke University Press, 1953).

of houses on their inhabitants might well be the subject of a scientific investigation. Those curious contraptions of stones or bricks, with all their peculiar adjuncts, trimmings, and furniture, their specific immutable shapes, their intense and inspissated atmosphere, in which our lives are entangled as completely as our souls in our bodies—what powers do they not wield over us, what subtle and pervasive effects upon the whole substance of our existence may not be theirs? Our fathers, no doubt, would have laughed at such a speculation; for to our fathers the visible conformations of things were unimportant. . . . We find satisfaction in curves and colors, walls and windows fascinate us, we are agitated by staircases, inspired by doors, disgusted by cornices, depressed by chairs, made wanton by ceilings, entranced by passages, and exacerbated by a rug.

Admitting that he is a "confirmed dreamer," Strachey writes that he often dreams that the family is back at Lancaster Gate. Then a feeling of "intimate satisfaction" comes over him, even though, awake, he would be disgusted if the family should return there. "Apart from my pleasure at it, no doubt it is hardly surprising that Lancaster Gate should haunt me. For it was a portentous place, and I spent in it the first twenty-five years of my conscious life. My remembrances of Stowey House are dim and sporadic—Jim Rendel with a penny in a passage—a miraculous bean at the bottom of the garden—Beatrice Chamberlain playing at having tea with me, with leaves and acorns, under a tree. But my consecutive existence began in the nursery at Lancaster Gate—the nursery that I can see now, empty and odd and infinitely elevated, as it was when I stood in it for the first time at the age of four with my mother, and looked out of the window at the surprisingly tall houses opposite, and was told that this was where we were going to live."

At Lancaster Gate in the 1880's and 1890's Lady Strachey and her children wrote verse in great abundance and variety. Much of this was collected in an unpublished book which the family made, entitled "Our Rhymes: or Five Minutes with the Worst Authors." One poem by Lytton bears the date 1885: if the date

is right, he wrote it when he was five years old. The concluding
stanza reads:

> Dorothy, Dorothy,
> Where were you last?
> Feeding the piggies
> That gobble so fast.

"Our Rhymes" also contains his poem "To Janie," dated 1886,
of which the last of three stanzas reads:

> The evening blossoms wither,
> The old oak tree does fall,
> But she's the prettiest girl I know
> Beside the garden wall.

At the age of seven he wrote a fairly long, complex, and ingenious
poem called "Songs of Animals, Fishes, and Birds."

Preserved among his papers is a commonplace book, dated 1886,
in which he laboriously copied lyrics from Shakespeare, Marlowe,
Blake, and others—poems which his mother had taught him to
love. One of his favorites was a song from Ben Jonson's *Oberon:*

> Buz, quoth the blue-fly,
> Hum, quoth the bee;
> Buz and hum they cry,
> And so do we.
> In his ear, in his nose,
> Thus, do we see
> He eat the dormouse,
> Else it was he.

This he soon knew by heart. Often he and his mother would say
it together, the one giving one line, the other the next. The words
became a kind of private password between them. They appeared
also in their letters to one another as a bond and sign of affection.
Even after Lytton Strachey became famous, many of the letters in
this correspondence began with or were signed by such expressions
as "Buz," "Hum," or other snatches of words from Jonson's lyric.

By 1887 he had begun the study of French. His mother succeeded admirably in conveying to him her enthusiasm for that language and its literature. Still preserved is a letter from her to him, dated May 12 of this year, in which she says: "I am very glad you like French; the further you go the more exciting you will find it. There are beautiful stories and books of all sorts in it." He was delighted on his tenth birthday when his mother gave him a book of French songs and a copy of La Fontaine's fables. Mlle Marie Souvestre, who had had some of Lytton's older sisters in her school at Fontainebleau, had now moved to Allenswood, Wimbledon. She was frequently in the Strachey home; and there was much going back and forth between Lancaster Gate and Allenswood, where some of the younger girls were in school and where Dorothy taught. Mlle Souvestre embodied the best that French culture had to offer. Her influence on Lytton Strachey was important.

One of Lytton's favorite pastimes was making little books of verse, much of it in French, usually in collaboration with his sister Marjorie. These little books were as attractive as possible in every detail, the children frequently supplying illustrative sketches. Some of the French verses made very little sense; the important thing in them was the appeal to the ear when the lines were read aloud.

Possibly the most interesting early poem written by Strachey was "Rival Flowers," composed when he was seven. In it the larkspur and the thistle are the rivals; the rose is appointed judge between them, and the concluding stanza runs:

> "The thistle," the rose answered blushing,
> "The thistle is rough, but he's kind;
> The larkspur is gentle, but silly,
> And that's what I've got in my mind."

One is tempted to find here a strange prophecy of a life and a literary career of which the kind thistle would be a not inappropriate symbol—a rough exterior of personal eccentricity and prickly satire, with a dislike of silly, larkspur sentimentalism, and a capacious interior filled with warm humanity, kindness, and talent for friendship. The child is father of the man.

Having recognized early her son's special talent, Lady Strachey put him in private schools where he would receive, she hoped, as much sympathetic individual attention as possible. The first of these schools was that conducted by Henry Forde at Luscombe, Parkstone, in Dorsetshire. After several years there, Strachey was in 1893 sent to the New School, Abbotshohme, Rocester, Derbyshire—with almost tragic consequences. The school was run by an oddly individualistic Mr. Reddy who had many extreme ideas about education. One of these was that each student should do a great deal of manual work every day, and in attempting this, Lytton Strachey collapsed. He was then entered at Leamington College, where he was subjected to the most savage kind of bullying.[9] We know that while here he played, at the age of sixteen, the role of Charon in the *Frogs* of Aristophanes and that a woman in the audience exclaimed loudly, "What terribly thin arms he's got!" At Leamington the other boys gave him the nickname "Scraggs." Finally, for the last two years before he entered Cambridge in 1899, he was at Liverpool College. His stay here was pleasant and successful, chiefly because of the friends he made. The most important of these was Professor Walter Raleigh, who consistently took a personal interest in him and who gave a series of lectures on Elizabethan poetry which delighted Strachey. His cousin, Sir Charles Strachey, had married Raleigh's sister Ada.

Perhaps his happiest days as a boy were those spent at Rothiemur-

9. The following letter from Bishop E. J. Bidwell to the *Times* (London), Jan. 25, 1932, p. 17, throws interesting light on Strachey when he was a student at Leamington: "It is stated in his obituary notice that Lytton Strachey was educated 'privately.' As a matter of fact, he was a pupil of mine when I was chaplain and a form master at old Leamington College, which then ranked as one of the minor public schools. I never saw or heard from him after he left till upwards of two years ago, when, seeing my name and address in a communication to your columns, he wrote me a most delightful letter, of the sort that gladdens the heart of an old schoolmaster. He said that he had been wanting to express his gratitude (I am afraid little deserved) for years, but had lost track of me when I went abroad. He describes himself as my 'somewhat wayward pupil.' He certainly was, as I quickly perceived, different from the average boy, but my recollections of him as a boy are entirely pleasing, and I deeply regret his premature passing." Strachey's letters written while he was at Leamington praise Bidwell.

chus in the Scottish Highlands, the home of his mother's people, the Grants. For many years Lady Strachey would take her children there for a month or two each summer. Intermittently all through life Strachey began new diaries, and he kept one during July and August of 1890 in which he recorded the various pleasures of Rothiemurchus. Here he tells about playing on the grass with his cousin Pat, eating strawberries fresh from the garden, riding the pony, walking beside the River Spey, vaulting with a pole across smaller streams, hiking to Loch-An-Eilan and getting caught in a shower, climbing up the slopes of the mountains, visiting the churchyard where the Grants were buried, joining his brother Oliver in teasing the peacock, playing cricket, musical chairs, and robber band, buying whistles and blowing them all over creation, listening to his mother as she read parts of the *Iliad* from time to time and to his sister Dorothy read from Scott's *The Abbot,* being photographed, dancing, listening to the bagpipe, and making sketches of the mountain scenery. As a boy Strachey was completely fascinated by puzzles, much more so, even, than the average boy. His father, mother, brothers, and sisters were hard put to keep him supplied.

During the winter of 1890–91 he was at Mr. Forde's school, but the following July and August, while he was at home on vacation, he resumed his diary. Now he tells of being taken by his father to see the Royal Naval Exhibition where he beheld a panorama of the Battle of Trafalgar, with Nelson done in wax works, an artificial Aurora Borealis, and a "rather foolish" iceberg. He also tells of going with his father to the Crystal Palace to see "The Wonderful Performance of Wild Beasts"—12 lions, three tigers, two bears, and other animals. He remarks that all the animals seemed drowsy, as if they had been drugged. But he is impressed by a lion with a crown on his head who rides in a chariot. This summer he also plays dominoes and enjoys going to plays.

In October, 1891, his mother wrote to him: "I have been reading Uncle John's new book in the proof sheets . . . written in vindication of a very great Indian statesman, Warren Hastings." Thus at this time, if not even earlier, his attention was called to one of the most vigorous Strachey traditions—that which defended Clive and Hastings against all comers. He would soon contribute his full share to this defense.

Unquestionably, both the sense of humor and the sense of style appeared in him extremely early. That even at the age of twelve he had a reputation for humor within his family is reflected by a passage in a letter to him from his mother, dated November 15, 1892: "When I read James [his five-year-old brother] the superscription of your letter, he said, 'I know that's from Lytton, he's always so absurd'; and when he had heard the contents he exclaimed, 'He *is* a funny little creature!' " Very significant are the observations on young Strachey made by his unusually wise and discerning teacher, Mr. Forde, in a letter to General Strachey dated March 17, 1892:

> It would not at all surprise me if he were to become literary; I do not mean merely fond of letters—that he is sure to be—but a contributor to them, a writer. He has an ear for, and knack of hitting off queer and picturesque phrases and turns of expression, and I could quite easily fancy his developing a marked style of his own in the future and one that would stand out. He is a distinctly unusual and original kind of boy; and I should think had best be let develop in his own way; his education should be chiefly directed to giving him help to evolve himself, not to forcing him into ordinary moulds. Owing to his biddable-ness and—one must at present say—timidity, he might be easily moulded after the average standard, with the result, I believe, of docking and thwarting what is special in him.

Slight hints of the budding sense of style appear in a long diary, begun December 23, 1892, in which he records his thoughts and experiences on a voyage to Gibraltar, Egypt, and the Cape of Good Hope. On board the *Coromandel* with his sister Dorothy, he sails out into a sea which is "simply exquisite." At first he is seasick, but soon he recovers, takes champagne, eats an apple, and as the ship approaches the coast of Spain admires the "lovely" sea. In view of Gibraltar he notes that "All the houses were like

toy houses scattered about the rock" and that "The water became filled with toy boats." He is impressed by the mountains, the
blue sky and sea, and the white towns. He goes on shore to
spend a month and notes that January 1 is a beautiful day in
Spain, "like Sunday in the Summer in Hyde Park." He attends a
children's dance, for which he gets a haircut and buys a pair
of white kid gloves. He visits a bull ring and a lighthouse, watches
a spectacular military parade, and in mid-January he finds thousands of narcissuses in bloom and picks some. On January 30 he
sails away on the *Himalaya,* bound for Egypt, where he is over-
joyed to be joined by his cousin Pat. Together they see the sights
of Alexandria and Cairo. He climbs to the top of one of the Pyra-
mids; he visits the Sphinx and is completely fascinated. Apostro-
phizing it, he speaks of "that sublime expression" on its face and
exclaims, "An exquisite face it is—how solemn, how majestic!"
One wishes that a photograph had been made of the twelve-year-
old Lytton Strachey facing the Sphinx. Surely the wise Sphinx
realized that it was confronted by the larger enigma. On the other
hand, the Sphinx symbolized perfectly what always interested
Strachey most—complexity and the enigmatical in character. He
sees much else, including mummies and a mirage. He and Pat
work with great industry to bring out an illustrated magazine, the
Comet, which he declares "a great success, with poems and stories."
Its contents include a "double acrostic all in verse" and a sensational poem on "Buffalo Bill."

On February 29 he is back on the *Himalaya,* headed for the
Suez Canal. He is delighted to catch sight of the old *Coromandel*
once more. On March 1 he exclaims: "My birthday today—how
odd—a birthday in the Suez Canal!" In the Gulf of Suez he suffers
much from the intense heat but nevertheless enjoys watching divers
go down for sixpences. On April 1 he reaches Cape Town, where
he rides in a Cape-cart, which he describes with amusing ambiguity as "a delightful vehicle drawn by two horses on two wheels."
Pat is with him here also, and they enjoy swimming together,
particularly the water fights. He tells us of another sport which
they find highly amusing—"Pat and I have bull fights every morning. We squat on the ground and charge against each other." The

word "sweet" appears again and again on the last pages of the
diary. He has picked it up, as boys do pick up such words, to be
used in the slang sense of "really nice, altogether pleasing." The
diary ends on April 21, which was about the time he sailed for
England.

Back at home and in school, he must have been impressed
by a passage in a letter which his mother, always a great lover
of music, wrote to him on December 12: "Pippa and I went last
night to the St. James Hall Concert to hear the pianist Paderew-
sky play; he is a great favorite, and was recalled several times,
after which a voice in the gallery shouted out, 'One cheer more
for the color of his hair!' which is of a vivid red and plenty of it."

Throughout his life Strachey was extraordinarily fond of plays
—of seeing them, of writing them, of acting in them. He never
missed a chance to participate in the amateur theatricals in which
his family and friends were constantly engaging. It is interesting
to consider in this connection an amusing story told of him when
he was an awkward, decidedly odd-looking lad of fifteen. He was
taking a walk with his older sister Pippa, when a strange man
approached and began making alarming advances toward her.
Lytton immediately dropped into the role of an idiot and began
to jabber and gesticulate wildly. The frightened stranger lost no
time in leaving the scene.

On March 3, 1898, now at Liverpool College, he began a new
diary, even though, he says, "My previous attempts have always
been drowned with failure." His mother was then editing and
putting through the press her aunt's autobiography, *Memoirs of
a Highland Lady,* dealing delightfully with Rothiemurchus and
the Grants. In his diary Strachey praises it highly: "My great-
Aunt Eliza must have been a wonderful woman to have been able
to describe with so vivid a minuteness the life she had lived 50
or 60 years before." Turning his attention in upon himself, he
finds himself mystified by his own nature—as he would always be.
"My character," he says, "is not crystalized. So there will be little
recorded here that is not transitory, and there will be much here
that is quite untrue. The inquisitive reader, should he peep between the covers, will find anything but myself, who perhaps

after all do not exist but in my own phantasy." Then, seeking a precedent, he asks: "Had Shakespeare any character? of His own, that is to say?" He answers that Shakespeare had not and that Shakespeare was "a cynic in his inmost heart of hearts." The comment which he adds is significant: "It is better so. There are quite sufficient of the other sort." He hopes that his diary will at least act as "a safety valve to my morbidity." Probably it did, for it enabled him to turn his sense of humor, now well developed, on himself. He writes: "When I consider that I am now 18 years of age, a shudder passes through my mind, and I hardly dare look at the creature those years have made me. Well, perhaps I had better not. It will save a scene."

Some days later he writes: "As I walk through the street I am agonized by the thought of my appearance. Of course it is hideous, but what *does* it matter? I only make it worse by peering into people's faces to see what they are thinking. . . . The truth is I want *companionship*."

But he also discovers that personal eccentricity has advantages as well as disadvantages. Scheduled to defend in debate the use of slang, he is filled with apprehension up to the very last minute. Yet when he rises to speak, he finds that all goes well. "Fortunately for me I have come to be considered a funny man, so that the audience began to laugh even before I spoke. Perhaps my appearance accounted for this." His side lost by a narrow margin, 20-18.

Nor was he entirely without companionship. He was very fond of both Professor Walter Raleigh and Mrs. Raleigh, and they lost no opportunity to be kind to him. He also took bicycle trips with a Miss Coombe, whose sister, he discovered to his great delight, had married the artist Roger Fry, a friend of his brother Oliver. At a dinner party he met and enjoyed talking with the Dean of Ely, who "turned out to have been an intimate friend of Papa's and the tutor of Charlie and Arthur." [10]

During this period he read a great deal, and his opinions concerning books were already definite and vigorous. On March 11,

10. Sons of his uncle, Sir John Strachey.

1898, he wrote in his diary that he had just had a friendly argument with his landlord, a Dr. Stookes (promptly nicknamed "Spooks" by young Strachey), about Ruskin. "He said today that my taste was not sufficiently catholic, chiefly, I believe, because I averred that I could not put up with Ruskin. He appeared astonished when I told him that I had been a devout Christian up to the age of 16." After he had borrowed and read *Sesame and Lilies*, he was willing to grant that Ruskin was clear. His great faults were "wrong-headedness and a lack of a sense of proportion." He was not, young Strachey felt sure, to be compared with Stevenson. His other reading in the Liverpool period included Shelley's lyrics, which delighted him; Boswell's *Johnson*, "the best biography ever written"; Byron (although he exclaims, "Quel homme, ce Byron!" in his diary, he never had great admiration for Byron's poetry); and Meredith. On March 19 he wrote: "I have just finished *The Ordeal of Richard Feverel*. It is excellent. But it needs re-reading, so I have begun again." He added, however, that perhaps the novel lacked unity. The Liverpool diary came to an end on April 21, 1898. But letters written during the early months of the same year show that he was enjoying other authors: Beaumont and Fletcher, Trollope, Mrs. Ritchie, and Ben Jonson. Jonson's plays he read with great avidity, and in one letter to his mother he exclaimed, "What plays for acting!"

From time to time throughout his life Strachey studied Italian, German, and French, and in the summer of 1898 he went to France in order to become more familiar with the language, returning to Liverpool College in the fall. He now had to face the problem of determining what university he should enter. Several years before, he had taken the Oxford and Cambridge Lower Certificate Examination and had passed seven subjects, with First Classes in arithmetic and English. It had been assumed that he would go to Cambridge, but after it had been decided that he should prepare himself for the Civil Service, his mother and others believed that Balliol College, Oxford, was the best place for the purpose. He failed, however, to be admitted at Balliol and so turned again to Cambridge. He was admitted as Pensioner at

Trinity College, Cambridge, on September 30, 1899, with Mr.
Duff as tutor. He became an Exhibitioner in 1900 and a Scholar
in 1902. He won the Chancellor's Medal for English Verse in
1902 and was given his B.A. degree after he had won a second-
class in the History Tripos in June 1903. He did not, however,
take final leave of Trinity but remained there until October 1905
to work on a thesis which he hoped would gain him a Fellowship.

The Cambridge period was an extremely happy and productive
one in Strachey's life. Among those who influenced him there
were G. Lowes Dickinson, Bertrand Russell, and G. E. Moore.
Moore's philosophy, with its assumption that the *summum bonum*
lies in achieving a high quality of humanity, in experiencing
delectable states of mind, and in intensifying experience by con-
templating great works of art, was a particularly important influence. Roger Fry, a friend of both Dickinson and Oliver Strachey,
he had come to know by this time. In his reading he developed
a great enthusiasm for John Donne, for Swinburne (he bought
and devoured all of Swinburne that had been published), and
for Sir Thomas Browne. He also read Pope, for whom he already
had great admiration. In a letter to his mother, dated March 11,
1900, he wrote: "I fear the world in general does not appreciate
Pope and the Classicists enough. Don't you think the R. of the
Lock the most perfect poem (of its length) in the English language?" Another of his favorites was Henry James, constantly
being read and talked about by his mother and her whole family
in these days.

It was also a period in which he made many lifelong friends:
Leonard Woolf, Saxon Sydney-Turner, Henry T. J. Norton, John
Maynard Keynes, Clive Bell, Walter Lamb (brother of Henry
Lamb, who was to paint the best-known portrait of Strachey),
Lumsden Barkway (later Bishop of St. Andrew's), whom he had
come to know at Liverpool, J. T. Sheppard (later Provost of King's
College), and George Mallory (who perished upon the slopes of
Mt. Everest). One of Lady Strachey's little jokes was that her son
had among his friends a Lamb, a Sheppard, and a Woolf.

He was a member of the Midnight Society, founded in the
autumn of 1899, and of the "Conversazione Society," the famous

"Cambridge Apostles" to which Tennyson, Hallam, Maurice, and Sterling had once belonged. Participation in the discussions of this society at its weekly meetings on Saturday night was of incalculable value to Strachey, as it had been to many other Apostles. Some idea of the traditional way in which the meetings of the Apostles were conducted may be gained from the biography of one who belonged to the society in the third quarter of the century and who later as a Fellow and holder of a professorship at Cambridge was influential at the university until his death in 1900. The following passage is from *Henry Sidgwick: A Memoir* (1906): [11]

> The meetings were held every Saturday at 8:30 in the rooms of the "Moderator," that is to say, the man who was to read the essay. The business began with tea, to which anchovy toast was an indispensable, and perhaps symbolic, adjunct; and then the essay was read, the "brethren" sitting round the fire, the reader usually at the table. Next came the discussion. Every one who was there stood up in turn before the fire, facing the circle, and gave his views on the subject, or on the essay, or on the arguments used by previous speakers, or, indeed, on anything which he was pleased to consider relevant to any one of these. The freedom both of subject and of handling was absolute; and not only did no one ever dream of violating this freedom or suggesting any limit to it, but every member would have regarded such an attempt as an attack on the ark of the covenant.

11. This biography did not please Keynes. He wrote to B. W. Swithinbank on March 27, 1906: "Have you read Sidgwick's life? . . . He never did anything but wonder whether Christianity was true and prove that it wasn't and hope that it was. . . . The last part is all about ghosts and Mr. Balfour. I have never found so dull a book so absorbing." R. F. Harrod, *The Life of John Maynard Keynes* (New York, Harcourt, Brace, 1951), pp. 116–17. According to Clive Bell, the Midnight Society was the real foundation of Bloomsbury. Its original members were Saxon Sydney-Turner, Leonard Woolf, Lytton Strachey, Thoby Stephen, A. J. Robertson, and Clive Bell. See "Recollections of Lytton Strachey," *Cornhill Magazine, 165* (Winter 1950–51), 11.

When the discussion was over the moderator replied, usually answering opponents, but in no way bound to do so, since he enjoyed the same absolute freedom of presentment as the rest. The society then proceeded to put the question. But the question as put was by no means necessarily in the same terms, and often not on the same issue, as the subject of the essay; it was always formulated afresh. An attempt was usually made to pick out the deepest, or the widest, or the most interesting of the points raised (by moderator or speakers) during the evening; but the statement of it was often so epigrammatic, cryptic, ironical, or bizarre that the last state of that question was (to the outward eye) far indeed from the first. When it was at last formulated, presenting some simple alternative issue, every member signed, as on one side or the other, or as refusing to vote, in the page of the society's book where the meeting was recorded. Each member had the right to add a note to his signature, explaining, or further specifying his view, or modifying the apparent meaning of his vote. The notes often contained the most luminous or interesting suggestion, couched usually in humorous or ironic form.

The subjects were chosen as follows:—At the end of each meeting, the man whose turn it was to "moderate" next week was bound to produce four subjects, from which the members chose one. It was usual, possibly in humorous imitation of the Greek drama, to have three serious questions, and the fourth playful. But the choice might as legally fall on the last one as on any of the others. The choice would generally turn on what each voter thought would produce the best discussion, though it was not at all necessary for the essayist to explain what line he would take, or even what the questions meant.

The subjects of the essays which Lytton Strachey read suggest that the brothers frequently selected his fourth subject—the humorous one. He read papers on "Ought the Father to Grow a Beard?," on "Dignity, Romance, and Vegetarianism," and on "Does Absence Make the Heart Grow Fonder?" But he also dealt with more serious questions in "When Is a Drama Not a Drama?,"

"Do Two and Two Make Five?" (on mysticism), "Ought Art to Be Always Beautiful?," "Shall We Be Missionaries?" (on imperialism), and "Christ or Caliban?" (a Swinburnian essay in which Caliban symbolizes freedom from all restraint).

The basic assumption of the society was the belief that one *could* learn much from opinions opposite to one's own and that one *should* make the effort to do so. The Coleridgeans, Maurice and Sterling, had established the principle when the society was first organized in the late 1820's. The complementary principle was that one should not be satisfied with intellectual relativism but should work one's way toward standards, and standards were likely to be trustworthy only when they had been subjected to the liberal method which required that all ideas participate in a conflict in which they were challenged by opposite ones. In the liberal Apostolic atmosphere Strachey rapidly found his own mind and began to exert an influence, intellectual as well as literary, which persisted years later as the spirit of the Bloomsbury group and which lasted the rest of his life.

He also was a member of the Sunday Essay Society, an organization which met every week in Professor Bevan's rooms at Trinity College. To this society he read such essays as "Conversation and Conversations," a thoughtful consideration of conversation as an art; "The Historian of the Future"; and "The Ethics of the Gospels." One of these essays, "Shakespeare's Final Period," read before the society on November 29, 1903, was published in the *Independent Review* for August 1904, and is to be found among his collected works.

The Cambridge period was also one in which Strachey was highly prolific in writing verse, much of which has been preserved and some of which was published at the time. Some of the verse is serious; much of it has the abandonment and ribaldry of a young satyr. In the lines entitled "I like the maiden of the Farm" (dated October 24, 1899) one stanza runs:

> She cannot hear me when I speak,
> She thinks that I'm absurdly weak;
> She thinks that I'm a dreadful fright
> On all occasions—and she's right.

His parody "After Herrick" was written about the same time:

> Whenas I walk abroad by Night,
> And Heavens-ward cast up my sight,
> The Luminaries of the Skies
> Make me think on Julia's Eyes.
>
> But when I take my walks by Day
> In flower-deckt field or garden gay,
> I see the flaming of the rose,
> And straightway think on Julia's Nose.[12]

Another poem of this time is important not only because it strongly suggests the influence of Swinburne but also because it is an antecedent of the famous passage in the preface to *Eminent Victorians* in which he declares that the literary artist must be able to enjoy individual freedom. In the last stanza of this poem, "Ningamus Serta Rosarum," he writes:

> We live a shackled life; and I,
> Ere the dim voice of winter call,
> As in a Roman carnival
> Would gladly feel the blossoms fall
> And fall and fall and cover all,
> And laugh, and kiss them, and so die.[13]

One of the poems, "The Cat," suggests that he found that enigmatical and amusing animal fascinating, as some of his ancestors had. Here the cat ("Dear creature by the fire a-purr") finally disappears in a mystic vision!

> With tail erect and pompous march,
> The proudest puss that ever trod,
> Through many a grove, neath many an arch,
> Impenetrable as a God,

12. Published in the *Cambridge Review*, Supplement, June 12, 1902, p. 388. Still earlier, on February 14, 1901, he had published a poem entitled "The Monk. 600 A.D." in the same journal, possibly his first published piece of writing if we except his contributions to *Our Rhymes*. It is signed "Selig," anagram for Giles.

13. *Cambridge Review*, June 5, 1901, p. xiii.

> Down many an alabaster flight
> Of broad and cedar-shaded stairs,
> While over us the elaborate night
> Mysteriously gleams and glares! [14]

Years later, at Ham Spray House, he found great delight in observing the capricious conduct and antics of his favorite cat, Tiber ("Tiberius").[15]

The most ambitious and the best of Strachey's Cambridge poems was "Ely: An Ode," with which he won the Chancellor's Medal for English Verse in 1902. The poem is cast in the difficult Pindaric mold, with strophes, antistrophes, and epodes. The subject is the neighboring cathedral of Ely. The final epode deals with the gorgeous procession of Cambridge poets:

> Here, in the rapture of our mortal gaze,
> We hold the immaculate vision which has drawn
> Through centuries the eyes of bard and seer
> Towards its loveliness; their most gracious lays
> Have breathed some inspiration from the peace
> Of eve around it or the joy of dawn;
> Their souls perchance first spread their pinions here.
> For here a troup, unparalleled since that hour
> Which saw the immortal glory of old Greece,
> Have passed along: Spenser, whose voice divine
> Resounds for ever with enchanted power
> Of purest melody through all human ears;
> Greene, sweetest harbinger of mightiest song,
> And Marlowe the young God, flushed with immortal wine.
> Here saintly Herbert dropped some gentle tears,
> And Jonson threw his laugh out, loud and long;
> Here Suckling wandered, Crashaw, lost in thought,
> Lingered, and Herrick gathered daffodils.

14. *Ibid.* Also in *Euphrosyne: A Collection of Verse* (Cambridge, Elijah Johnson, 1905), p. 11.
15. The name may have been inspired by the lines:
> "So Tiberius would have sat
> Had Tiberius been a cat."

Here Waller, dreaming of immortal bays,
Saw Thyrsis crowned with Sacharissa's praise;
Beneath these moving branches Cowley sought
To fly the weary coil of mortal ills,
Enwrapped in friendship; Marvell trod this ground;
The deepest voiced of all the eternal choir,
Milton, chief lord of contrapuntal verse,
Here smiled before he frowned;
And Dryden glowed with the impassioned fire
Stirring within him strong and fierce,
Knew noble loathing, felt contempt sublime,
And first essayed the two-edged sword of rhyme.
Nor was Gray absent; Wordsworth, calm and deep,
Unknowing crossed the footsteps of that Friend
Whose name shall live with his till Time have end;
And Byron followed with his mockery;
Last, in the quiet of the evening, he
Whom most beloved, our brother, still we weep.[16]

In the Cambridge years Strachey amused himself and sharpened his style by formulating aphorisms. Some samples are as follows: "A witty thing is sometimes said by accident, but never a stupid one"; "We find it easier to reflect on the actions we have performed than to act on the reflections we have made"; "The worst and best parts of us are the secrets we never reveal"; "The excitement in conversation which is given by champagne is present of its own accord in the most exciting conversations"; "We are so unimportant that whether we think we are or not hardly matters"; "Civilization loves the truth, and Barbarism tells it"; and "There are few things more difficult than to write a good aphorism; and one of them is to write a true one."

In September 1901 he finished a long essay on Warren Hastings. It is in excellent style and follows eloquently in the tradition of his family. The blackest of villains in the Great Trial, Strachey says, was Hastings' enemy, Philip Francis, who "could boast of a

16. In *Prolusionae Academicae* (Cambridge, Cambridge University Press, 1902), pp. 9–15. The last member of the "unparalleled troup" is Tennyson.

great reserve of malignity, of meanness, and of unscrupulous ambition," who was "crafty, false, arrogant, selfish," and who was guilty of "relentless cruelty." The passionate orations of Burke and Sheridan arose out of the grossest ignorance. It was greatly to be deplored that Hastings' reputation had suffered so much from the misrepresentations in Byron's "Monody on Sheridan," James Mill's history of India, and Macaulay's essays.

In the summer of 1903 Strachey applied for a position in the Education Department of the Civil Service. The letters of recommendation written for him by those under whom he had studied show, after all allowances are made for the good will, generosity, and spirit of helpfulness usually motivating such testimonials, that he was held in high esteem. Walter Raleigh, who had left Liverpool College and had taken a position at the University of Glasgow, wrote:

> I have known Mr. Strachey for years, and I cannot think of anyone among my numerous past pupils whom I should prefer to him for work requiring ability, tact, and judgment. He has a mind of rare power and distinction, a character of great decision, and a temper so reasonable and gentle that it is a delight to work with him. I hope that he may be successful in obtaining the appointment that he seeks, where I am sure he would quickly gain the confidence and esteem of all who should have to do with him.

Stanley Leathes, Fellow and Lecturer of Trinity College, Cambridge, wrote:

> Mr. Giles Lytton Strachey was under my charge for two years of his University Course, and I examined him for both parts of the Historical Tripos. He obtained a second class in each part: much to my disappointment, as his abilities deserved a higher place. He is a man of unusually wide culture, of considerable originality, and unusual literary gifts. An essay on Warren Hastings which he wrote for a College prize was the best piece of work of the kind which I have seen. I think it likely that his wide range of interests and literary predilec-

tions prevented him from directing his attention so exclusively
to his university studies as might have been desired. But
he is in every sense a well-educated man, and worthy to rank
with first-class men, as is shown by his being elected to a
Scholarship at Trinity. I think that his intelligence, wide
reading, versatility, and cultivation would render him a good
public servant in the Education Department. His intellectual
capacity is far above his University degree.

J. D. Duff, Fellow and Tutor of Trinity College, Cambridge,
wrote:

I have known Mr. Strachey well during his four years of
residence. His character has always been excellent; and in
point of intellect I consider him not inferior to any among
the two hundred men who have been my pupils during the
last four years.

Yet he failed to get the appointment and decided to try for a
fellowship in Trinity College. He returned to the subject of Warren Hastings and began to gather additional materials concerning
him. The 400-page thesis on Hastings which he wrote from 1903 to
1905 is a thoroughgoing piece of scholarship dealing with an extremely complex and difficult subject. Even so, it did not earn
him the fellowship. For one thing he met with unusually stiff
opposition from the scientists at this time. For another, although
in general he never lost his faith in Hastings, as he accumulated
more and more facts relating to the question a doubt did grow in
his mind as to whether he could altogether succeed in what he had
undertaken—to complete through irrefutable scholarship the vindication of Hastings toward which Sir James Stephen and Sir John
Strachey had already made great progress.[17] On the other hand,
despite the disappointment which the thesis brought him, he
gained from his efforts here an intellectual discipline and a knowl-

17. Particularly in Stephen's *The Story of Nuncomar and the Impeach-
ment of Sir Elijah Impey* (1885) and Sir John Strachey's *Hastings and the
Rohilla War* (1892).

edge of the methods of scholarship which would be invaluable to him as a biographer.

Naturally at times his disappointment and dejection were almost unbearable. He wrote to one of his friends in October, 1905: "You don't know what it is to be 25, dejected, uncouth, unsuccessful—you don't know how humble and wretched and lonely I sometimes feel." But he was becoming a name at Cambridge, as a correspondent there assured him a little later, after he had established himself in London: "I see that you are rapidly becoming a kind of distant, eminent brilliant wicked Mephistophelian myth."

When in the autumn of 1905 he cleared out of Staircase K in the Great Court at Trinity College (and his younger brother James immediately moved in), his mother assigned him a bed-sitting room at 69 Lancaster Gate. After the family moved to 67 Belsize Gardens in Hampstead and later to another house in the same street, he was again assigned bed-sitters. In these rooms he did most of his writing for a number of years after he left Cambridge. But family life irritated him, and when his brother James left Cambridge in 1909 there were many plans for the two to set up housekeeping together. These came to nothing. Strachey managed, however, to get away from London on visits frequently. The big houses in the country which the family usually rented in the summer during this period also provided welcome relief. About 1910–11 he spent some time in the summers at Saltsjöbaden, near Stockholm, in Sweden. In this period he also lived for a while in a cottage on Dartmoor and about 1911–12 spent a whole winter at East Ilsley on the Berkshire Downs. He also grew his beard in April and May of 1911, when he was staying at Corfe Castle and while he was recovering from the mumps. On May 9 he wrote to his mother: "The chief news is that I have grown a beard! Its color is very much admired, and it is generally considered extremely effective, though some ill-bred persons have been observed to laugh. It is a red-brown of the most approved tint, and makes me look like a French decadent poet—or something equally distinguished."

There is a curious analogy between Strachey and an earlier

Apostle, Tennyson, who was parodied by Strachey in the Swinburnian manner and who represented the kind of Victorianism
which both fascinated him and provoked his most lively satire.
Both men achieved, almost it would seem without effort, early
leadership and dominance which they never lost over those who
knew them best; both seem to have enjoyed a self-confidence which
asserted itself early; and yet both had to wait long years before
they achieved fame. One of Strachey's friends, Francis Birrell,
has written: "Je n'ai jamais recontré quelqu'un qui dominât la
vie comme lui. Souvent silencieux et morose, généralement en
proie à quelque malaise, il était constamment environné d'une
atmosphère de déférence." [18]

But if, like Tennyson, Strachey displayed his talent early and
reaped his fame late, he was also like Tennyson in not wasting
his time in the long interval. The seven years from 1905 to 1912,
when his first book, *Landmarks in French Literature,* was published, are to Strachey what the Horton period was to Milton and
what the period which Swift spent as Temple's secretary at Moor
Park was to him. Strachey used his time in writing critical articles
for the *Independent Review,* a periodical which in its short lifetime attracted some of the most brilliant literary talent then
available; [19] in making various contributions to the *New Quarterly;*
in writing reviews of books and critical articles on the drama for

18. "Lytton Strachey," *Revue Hebdomadaire,* July 23, 1932, p. 405.
19. The contributors included Desmond MacCarthy, Hilaire Belloc, H. N.
Brailsford, G. K. Chesterton, G. Lowes Dickinson, E. M. Forster, G. M.
Trevelyan, H. G. Wells, Bertrand Russell, Ramsay MacDonald, Wilfrid
Blunt, and Lascelles Abercrombie. The first issue was that of October 1903.
After the name was changed to the *Albany Review* in April 1907, the con-
tributors also included William Archer, G. W. E. Russell, Thomas Hardy,
Gilbert Murray, Andrew Lang, Sidney Webb, and A. C. Bradley. Under
both names the journal ran from October 1903 to March 1908 (fourteen
volumes). Lionel Trilling in his *E. M. Forster* says that Nathaniel Wedd,
G. L. Dickinson, and G. M. Trevelyan had much to do with founding it.
According to Forster, it was to combat aggressive imperialism, protection,
and Joe Chamberlain, and to advocate constructive domestic policies. (Norfolk, Conn., New Directions, 1943), pp. 30–1. Strachey wrote to his mother
on March 3, 1903: "I have taken 5 shares in Trevelyan and Co's Review. . . .
They haven't yet thought of a name."

the *Spectator,* which his cousin St. Loe Strachey then owned and edited; in discovering and eliminating flaws in his style; in gradually developing his theory of biography as he read and reviewed many biographies written by others; and in reading the best books that he could find in Elizabethan literature, in eighteenth-century English and French literature, and in the literature of the Victorian period. No one enjoyed reading more. In this period and during the rest of his life it was very unusual to find him, seated or in bed, without a book in his hand. He had a little book in which conscientiously and with obvious pleasure he entered the title of each work after he had read it.

From first to last, his taste in reading was far more catholic than it has been represented as being. He found intense delight not only in Molière, Racine, Voltaire, Horace Walpole, Gibbon, and Boswell but also in Marlowe, Shakespeare, Jonson, Browne, Beddoes, Lockhart, William Barnes, and Dostoievski. Writers of the past and present he read with equal discrimination. For some weeks in the autumn of 1919 he completely lost himself in Chaucer as he did "absolutely nothing but read the Canterbury Tales." Always an admirer of Fielding, he was greatly pleased when he acquired "a charming little Joseph Andrews with the most delectable cuts." He once said that when in his youth he read *Tristram Shandy* there was not in it an asterisk that he did not adore. He was highly enthusiastic, too, about Charles Lamb's letters: "They are indeed divine—perhaps the best in the world. They give such a notion of character—and so perfect a character! Some of them, too, really make me laugh out loud, they're still so amusing." Jane Austen was another writer in whom he could become entirely absorbed, as he once did in 1906 when she stole the time that he was supposed to be giving to *Spectator* reviews. Rereading *Pride and Prejudice* many years later, he lamented the fact that the story so swiftly swept to its end. Among the Victorians he could read Charles Darwin purely for pleasure, not merely because he was a great scientist but also because he admired his style. He spoke of Darwin's "high nobility and infinite charm." He also read and enjoyed the writings of William Cobbett. Much of Carlyle was to Strachey mere twaddle, but he was nonetheless "A psalm-singing

Scotchman with a power of observation and description which
knocks you flat." *The Education of Henry Adams* he read in
1919 and thought it "a most remarkable book." He read *Madame
Bovary*, as early as 1902, with great pleasure. He even read J. W.
Vandercook's novel *Black Majesty*—about Negroes in Haiti after
the French Revolution—and found it good, except that it was
unluckily written "in that almost incomprehensible and quite
intolerable language—American." Although in his youth he had
read *The Ordeal of Richard Feverel*, with admiration, when he
tried to read Meredith's letters in 1912 he found them "nauseating"
and so tainted with Victorianism that he vowed: "Nothing will
induce me to read another word the man wrote." Edith Sitwell's
verse he dismissed as "absurd stuff" and was once extremely bored
when he had to listen to her read some of it aloud at Arnold
Bennett's home. Conrad, on the other hand, was superb; *Lord
Jim* was "full of splendid things."

It is safe to predict that when Strachey's reviews and critical
articles published before *Eminent Victorians* (1918) become better
known, his rank among English literary critics will be considerably elevated. Even his earliest piece of published prose, "Two
Frenchmen," which appeared in the *Independent Review*, October 1903, has great brilliance of style. It was this essay which
recommended him some years later to those who asked him to
write *Landmarks in French Literature*. Dealing not only with
two Frenchmen, La Bruyère and Vaugenargues, but a third, La
Rochefoucald, it begins significantly: "The greatest misfortune
that can happen to a witty man is to be born out of France." There
are also many admirable passages—excellent in style and as criticism—in the uncollected reviews (about ninety of them) which
Strachey contributed to the *Spectator* from 1904 to 1914. In these
we find noteworthy observations concerning Shakespeare, Spenser,
Molière, Macaulay, Milton, Coleridge, Thomson, Wordsworth,
T. E. Brown, Henley, Barrie, Yeats, Fitzgerald, Boileau, Bacon,
Barnes, Hardy, Swift, Galsworthy, Pope, Marvell, Donne, Carlyle,
Tolstoi, Dostoievsky, and many others. But Strachey felt some-
what cramped in writing these reviews and always shook his head
at the idea of collecting them. Although he was aware in writing

them that the editor of the *Spectator,* St. Loe Strachey, would not think of imposing restrictions on him and furthermore had the highest opinion of him as a critic, nevertheless the "Spectatorial policy," a sinister something which he intuitively sensed and which he felt was in some mysterious and vague way related to the hundreds of country clergymen among the subscribers to this periodical, was constantly whispering in his ear as he wrote. Much of this work, accordingly, is the normal product of the talented journeyman of letters. But, even so, when one goes from the reviews which others contributed to the *Spectator* during these years to his, one immediately discerns the touch of his style even in the most uninspired passages, and one is again and again surprised and delighted by other passages which have burst brilliantly into flame.

His dreams of what the future might bring to himself and to others who were close to him are indicated in a letter written to Keynes on March 11, 1906:

> Oh dear me! When will my Heaven be realized?—My Castle in Spain? Rooms, you know, for you, Duncan, and Swithin, as fixtures—Woolf of course, too, if we could lure him from Ceylon; and several suites for guests. Can you conceive anything more supreme! I should write tragedies; you would revolutionize political economy; Swithin would compose French poetry; Duncan would paint our portraits in every conceivable combination and permutation, and Woolf would criticize us and our works without remorse.[20]

But all was not dreams, drudgery, and disappointment in the period from 1905 to 1912 when Strachey was trying to make a living by writing for the *Spectator* and other periodicals. There was always a gaiety and playfulness in his mind which could not for long be suppressed. In these long years when he seemed to be making so little progress he was continuing to write verse, much of which was humorous. For instance, after hearing McTaggart lecture on good and evil at Cambridge, he wrote:

20. Harrod, *Keynes,* pp. 114–15. Duncan is Strachey's cousin, the artist Duncan Grant. Swithin is short for B. W. Swithinbank.

McTaggart's seen through God,
And put him on the shelf;
Isn't it rather odd
He don't see through himself.

And he also amused himself by writing the following lines on Spurgeon:

Dr. Spurgeon
—Fat old sinner!—
Ate a sturgeon
For his dinner.

When the surgeon
Came to save him,
Purge on purge on
Purge he gave him.

Rash!—to urge on
What's o'erloaded.
Dr. Spurgeon
Just exploded.

The interesting story of how Strachey came to write his first book has been put on record by H. A. L. Fisher, onetime president of the British Academy and of the Board of Education. He writes that the editors of the Home University Library in casting about to find a competent person to write a short, one-volume survey of French literature, had first thought of Edmund Gosse, then "an established oracle" on the subject. Fisher, however, had another candidate.

They were kind enough, however, to concede to my earnest request that the volume should be entrusted to the unknown author of this short review [Strachey's "Two Frenchmen," *Independent Review* (1903)], whom I had ascertained to be a young man, and a recent graduate of Cambridge. . . . I well remember my first interview with Strachey, a sensitive ungainly youth; awkward in his bearing, and presenting an appearance of great physical debility, as if he had recently risen from the bed of an invalid. His voice was faint and squeaky. His pale face was at that time closely shaven. The long red beard of Lamb's portrait, which has made him so familiar, was a thing of the future. He was very silent, but uncannily quick and comprehending. I told him that I wanted him to write a sketch of French literature in fifty thousand words, and showed him J. W. Mackail's *Latin Literature,* with which he was not then acquainted, as a model which he might be content to follow. He assented to my proposal with rare economy of speech, and with none of the usual expressions of diffidence, which an editor is accustomed to hear from an untried author to whom he has offered a task of exceptional difficulty. In a very few months the manuscript of the outlines of French literature was in my hands. It was a masterpiece of imaginative and scholarly appreciation, and an extraordinary achievement for so young a writer.

It was Fisher's opinion that Strachey was "one of those rare Englishmen who know French from the inside." [21]

Landmarks in French Literature, appropriately dedicated to "J[ane] M[aria] S[trachey]," his mother, was published on January 12, 1912. Despite its very great merits, the fact that the *Times Literary Supplement* on February 1 accorded it almost a full column of praise, and the remarkable fact that by April 1914 it had sold nearly 12,000 copies in the British Empire and America, the book did not bring Strachey either the fame or the money which he so badly needed.

Yet he was finding himself. In a significant letter written on February 6, 1912, Strachey said: "For the last year I have been going through a Spiritual Revolution—which has been exciting and on the whole pleasant. I had feared that after 30 one didn't have these things." His signature on his publications through *Landmarks* had been "G. L. Strachey"; with the appearance of "Madame du Deffand" in the *Edinburgh Review* for January 1913 he became "Lytton Strachey," almost a symbolic change. The time

21. "The Subtle Strachey," *Saturday Review, 8* (March 26, 1932), 613–14.

for writing *Eminent Victorians* was not far away; and Strachey was now fully conscious in himself of the peculiar gifts which were to go into the making of that book.

In both his outward appearance and his inward ripeness he had become the man that later generations would remember. Clifford Bower-Shore has described him as a tall, slender, red-bearded figure with exquisite hands and with "a small quiet voice, touched with elfin-satanism." On his walks in the country he usually carried a stick. When in repose, his usual state, he suggested perfect calm and equanimity. His eyes were sardonic, "flashing with a mystic brilliance." [22] His closest friends point out that he actually had two voices: a high, piping voice which he used when excited, when he wanted to point his statement, or when he wished to produce a comic effect—the only voice which strangers usually heard; and a much lower, rich baritone voice which he used when reading or talking seriously with his friends and which was capable of conveying great emotion and meaning. He had a trick of sucking in his breath just at the moment when he wished to say something emphatic. Doubtless many of the peculiarities of his voice were simply an accentuation of those belonging to the "Strachey voice," familiar to all who have known the various members of Sir Richard Strachey's family. [23]

22. *Lytton Strachey: An Essay* (London, Fenland Press, 1933), p. 19. For other pen portraits of Strachey, see [Sir] Max Beerbohm, *Lytton Strachey,* the Rede Lecture at Cambridge for 1943 (New York, Alfred A. Knopf, 1943), p. 7; André Maurois, *Prophets and Poets,* trans. Hamish Miles (New York and London, Harper, 1935), pp. 241–2; *London Mercury, 25* (Feb. 1932), 322–4; Prince (D. S.) Mirsky, "Mr. Lytton Strachey," *London Mercury, 8* (June 1923), 175–84; Vincent Sheean, "Lytton Strachey: Cambridge and Bloomsbury," *New Republic, 70* (Feb. 17, 1932), 19–20; and Frank Swinnerton, *The Georgian Scene* (New York, Farrar and Rinehart, 1934), pp. 360–8.

23. Mr. Ralph Partridge, certainly one of those who knew Strachey best, has said: "Those two voices of his were not an affectation but a natural gamut of expression—and the top notes were an echo of Voltaire's 'high cackle' from the eighteenth century." For further comment on Strachey's voice, see Beerbohm, *Lytton Strachey,* p. 11, where Strachey's voice is likened to Benjamin Jowett's; Leonard Woolf, "Lytton Strachey," *New Statesman and Nation, 3* (Jan. 30, 1932), 118–19; and Desmond MacCarthy, "Lytton Strachey," *Sunday Times,* Jan. 24, 1932, p. 8.

Norman tower and Tudor addition of Sutton Court, family seat of the Stracheys since 1642. Used with permission of *Country Life*.

Rook's Nest, Surrey, one of the homes of the first Sir Henry Strachey in the eighteenth century. The original picture hangs at Sutton Court.

Stowey House, Clapham Common, London, where Lytton Strachey was born

General Sir Richard Strachey

Jane Maria Lady Strachey
when young

The first Earl of Lytton ("Owen Meredith") in Viceroyal regalia.
Strachey was named for Lord Lytton, who was his godfather.

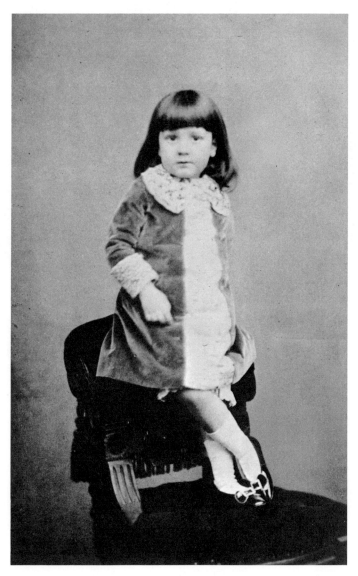

Lytton Strachey at the age of three

Family of Sir Richard and Lady Strachey posing to form a medallion. Left to right: James, Lytton, Oliver, Ralph, Dick, Sir Richard, Lady Strachey, Elinor, Dorothea, Philippa, Joan Pernel, Marjorie

Sons and daughters of Sir Richard and Lady Strachey. Left to right: Marjorie, Dorothy, Lytton, Joan Pernel, Oliver, Dick, Ralph, Philippa, Elinor, James

A view of Ham Spray House as it faces the down. Strachey bought Ham Spray soon after his success with *Queen Victoria*.

Another view of Ham Spray House showing the weeping ilex tree

"The Lacket," a cottage at Lockeridge, near Marlborough, Wiltshire, where Strachey lived when he wrote most of *Eminent Victorians*

A painting by Carrington of the "Mill House," Tidmarsh, Pangbourne, on the upper Thames, where much of *Queen Victoria* was written

Lytton Strachey's study at Ham Spray House. Over the fireplace hangs a picture of Voltaire in the midst of his friends and disciples.

Close-up view of the Voltaire picture in Strachey's study, showing the monkey face and the upraised hand of benediction

Strachey's writing desk in his study at Ham Spray House and the view through the windows across the valley to the down

Teatime on a summer day at Ham Spray House, showing Carrington, Ralph Partridge, and Lytton Strachey

Lytton Strachey, Carrington (an elusive subject for the camera), and James Strachey

Lytton Strachey and Virginia Woolf about 1918 in a spontaneous pose

A study of Strachey's face and hands by Carrington

A group at Garsington Manor, country home of Lady Ottoline Morrell, near Oxford. Left to right: Lady Ottoline Morrell, Mrs. Aldous Huxley, Lytton Strachey, Duncan Grant, and Vanessa Bell

The bedroom and bed at **Ham Spray House** in which Strachey died. Note Carrington's decorations around the fireplace.

Soon after the publication of *Landmarks,* Strachey's mother and his friend Harry Norton [24] each provided him with £100 which, together with earnings from the *Edinburgh Review* (to which he had now become a contributor) and from other periodicals, made it possible for him to rent a small, romantic-looking thatched cottage called "The Lacket" outside the village of Lockridge, near Marlborough in Wiltshire. Here he established himself comfortably, and here he remained until 1916. Here also he wrote the first three parts of *Eminent Victorians.* Rapidly now he discovered that he was becoming emancipated—from bed-sitters, from routine writing of reviews for the *Spectator,* and from the notions of those who had written fat, two-volume Victorian biographies. The preface to *Eminent Victorians* and the spirit of the whole book reflect this emancipation.

His theory of biography was now fully developed and mature. This is not the place for a thorough discussion of it, but it is important here to note the extremely important influence on it of Dostoievsky, whose novels Strachey had been reading and reviewing as they appeared in Constance Garnett's translation. He was greatly impressed by the Russian novelist's remarkable psychological insight and by his conception of human beings as highly complex—a mixture of many heterogeneous elements. On the other hand, there is very little of Freud in *Eminent Victorians* or in *Queen Victoria.* (It is known, however, that Freud read all of Strachey's books and enjoyed them very much.) The influence of Freud would manifest itself later, chiefly in *Elizabeth and Essex.* Strachey's brother James, as we know, became an authority on Freud.

In 1916 Lytton Strachey was back in London living with his mother at 6 Belsize Park Gardens, Hampstead, whence she had now moved. Here he finished the "General Gordon." In the late autumn of 1917, however, another place in the country was found for him. His brother Oliver and his friends Harry Norton, John Maynard Keynes, and Saxon Sydney-Turner agreed to pay the rent on "The Mill House" at Tidmarsh, near Pangbourne, Berk-

24. Henry Tertius James Norton, the "H.T.J.N." to whom *Eminent Victorians* is dedicated. Strachey later paid back the money.

shire. Here he was installed, nominally as a caretaker. After the success of *Eminent Victorians,* published on May 9, 1918, he needed no help from the outside. He continued to live at Tidmarsh until the proceeds from *Queen Victoria* (1921) made it possible for him to buy Ham Spray House near Marlborough, Wiltshire, to which he moved in July 1924, and which was his home for the rest of his life.[25]

When Strachey first conceived the idea of *Eminent Victorians* he planned twelve or more portraits of Victorians—some to be admired and some to be ridiculed. The portraits to be admired would deal with scientists. The others would deal with nonscientists. In Strachey's reaction against Victorianism there was no revolt against father and mother such as one finds in Gosse's *Father and Son* (1907). The proper objects of Lytton Strachey's satire were not people like his father, a scientist and a levelheaded administrator; or his father's friends, Galton, Huxley, and Darwin; or his own grandfather, Edward Strachey, a mathematician and a Utilitarian.[26]

During the first World War Strachey was a conscientious ob-

25. Tidmarsh, in later years, had a very special place in Strachey's memory. Possibly his happiest days were spent there. On January 1, 1924, just a few months before he left, he wrote: "Old age, I suppose, but, for whatever reason, the solid calmness of Tidmarsh exactly suits me." One night in July 1928 he almost wept as music on a phonograph record suggested memories of Tidmarsh. "Among others, there was a string quartet by Schubert, which brought back Tidmarsh to me with extraordinary vividness. I felt the loss of that old regime very strongly, and in fact . . . nearly burst into tears. I hope and pray that our new grandeur . . . won't alter anything in any way—it would be wretched to lose our native simplicity!"

26. The comments and suggestions of Strachey's old friend and former teacher, Sir Walter Raleigh, to be found in letters written at this time are full of interest. On May 8, 1918, Raleigh wrote to Strachey: "Pass a person through your mind, with all the documents, and see what comes out. That seems to be the method. Also, choose them, in the first place, because you dislike them. Well, it gives a queer and strange result. . . . There is some kind of creed at the back." In a letter of May 13, Raleigh advised Strachey to apply the method next to "the great Panjandrum—Victoria Herself" and later to Jowett, Tennyson, and Disraeli. *The Letters of Sir Walter Raleigh* (1879–1922), ed. Lady Raleigh and David Nichol Smith (London, Methuen, 1926), 2, 479–82. Raleigh was probably the first to suggest the subject of Queen Victoria to Strachey. Note, however, these sentences from two letters

jector. In general, he had little respect for diplomacy and diplomats, both of which he believed would become extinct once the age of intense nationalism had worn itself out. He had no confidence in either Asquith or Churchill. Woodrow Wilson had admirable ideals but was primarily a Presbyterian preacher much too slow-minded and inexperienced to deal successfully with Clemenceau and the agile, worldly Lloyd George. "Ultimately," he wrote in May, 1918, "the world is governed by moderate men." The voice of wisdom was that of his friend John Maynard Keynes, but Keynes was so far advanced in his thinking that the politicians would not listen to him. The heroism of Rupert Brooke was both unwise and tragic. Strachey could not possibly have passed the physical examination, but for the sake of principle he wished to assert himself in support of his friends, most of whom were pacifists. In his written statement as a conscientious objector, still preserved in manuscript, he says flatly: "My opinion in general has been for many years strongly critical of the whole structure of society." One wonders whether the second World War would have caused him to change his mind. If Strachey had had his way, however, there might never have been a second World War. He believed even the comparatively easy terms which his friend Keynes would have imposed on Germany in 1919 to be too harsh and wrote to him on December 16, "To my mind the ideal thing would be to abolish reparations altogether—but of course that is not practical politics —at any rate just yet; perhaps in the end it will become so."

The years following the publication of *Eminent Victorians* were in general happy ones for him. He was now famous—in Great Britain, on the Continent, and in America. He enjoyed the continued friendship of those who had been most devoted to him at Cambridge—of John Maynard Keynes, of Desmond MacCarthy, of Harry Norton, of Saxon Sydney-Turner, of G. Lowes Dickenson, of Clive Bell, and of Leonard Woolf. He did not lose his friends but possessed in large degree the Strachey talent for preserving as well as forming friendships. There were other

---

dated December 9 and December 11, 1917: "All the Victorians are now neatly bound in their red cases, ready to be taken off to the publishers— whoever they may be"; "I am now reading Victoria's diary, when a young maid—most absorbing, but not long enough."

friends whom he had acquired through the years—Max Beerbohm,
T. S. Eliot,[27] Virginia Woolf and her sister Vanessa (Mrs. Clive
Bell),[28] Roger Senhouse, and Lady Ottoline Morrell.[29] The Clive

27. In letters dated May 12 and 14, 1919, Strachey wrote: "A long and
interesting conversation with Eliot in the morning. He's greatly improved—
far more self-assured, decidedly intelligent, and, so far as I could see, nice.
I hope to see more of him." "Poet Eliot had dinner with me on Monday—
rather ill and rather American: altogether not quite gay enough for my
taste. But by no means to be sniffed at."

28. Strachey had met Virginia and Vanessa many years before Bloomsbury
flourished; they were old friends by that time. In a letter dated April 12,
1907, he raised the interesting question as to which was most beautiful:
"It's difficult to say, but I suppose most people would vote for Vanessa." On
February 25, 1909, he wrote: "The people I see and like most are two women
—viz. Vanessa and Virginia." He warmly praised Virginia's *The Voyage Out*
soon after it appeared in 1915. "I read it with breathless pleasure the minute
it came out." He spoke of its wit, its exquisiteness, its solidity, the fact that
its characters were more than mere satirical silhouettes, its secular sense,
its eighteenth-century absence of folly combined with the color and amusement of modern life. She praised his "General Gordon": "How you weave
in every scrap—my God, *what* scraps!—of interest to be had, like (you must
pardon the metaphor) a snake insinuating himself through innumerable
golden rings. . . . I don't see how skill could be carried further." She liked
Queen Victoria even better than *Eminent Victorians*. She was naturally
jealous of his fame at times, but there was no one whose opinions concerning her work she respected more highly, and his praise was pure gold to her.
She wrote in her diary on June 18, 1925: "No, Lytton does not like *Mrs.
Dalloway*, and, what is odd, I like him all the better for saying so, and don't
much mind. . . . It's odd that when . . . others (several of them) say it is
a masterpiece, I am not much exalted; when Lytton picks holes, I get back
into my working fighting mood, which is natural to me." *A Writer's Diary*,
ed. Leonard Woolf (London, Hogarth Press, 1954), pp. 78–9; also pp. 31,
33, 35, 240, 306. See also Virginia Woolf, "The Art of Biography," *Atlantic
Monthly, 163* (April 1939), 506–10, and *Virginia Woolf and Lytton Strachey:
Letters* (New York: Harcourt Brace, 1956).

29. Lady Ottoline Morrell, niece of the Duke of Portland, often entertained
artistic and literary friends at her country house, Garsington Manor, near
Oxford. Garsington was not far from the Earl of Asquith's country home,
The Wharf, Sutton Courtney. Asquith's Romanes Lecture at Oxford on June
8, 1918, which Strachey heard, gave influential praise to *Eminent Victorians*,
recently published. Keynes was a frequent visitor at both Garsington and
The Wharf. It was Lady Ottoline who called Asquith's attention to Strachey's
book. See Harrod, *Keynes*, pp. 171, 211.

Bells owned a country place at Charleston, Sussex, where he was frequently a guest. And he saw much of his cousin Duncan Grant, who had become an artist of acknowledged distinction. These were the days of "Bloomsbury," a group made up of Strachey and these friends. It was given its name by someone on the outside because many of its members now lived in the Bloomsbury District of London—in the general neighborhood of the British Museum, Bloomsbury Square, and Gordon Square.[30] In September 1921 Lady Strachey and some of her daughters had moved from Hampstead to 51 Gordon Square; and James Strachey lived at 41 Gordon Square. Various members of the group were often together in an informal way. Sometimes they went to the country —to Ham Spray or to Charleston. In later years at Ham Spray amateur theatricals were always in order. Among Strachey's manuscripts there are many plays (he was nearly always working on one) written for such occasions.

Particularly important were two new friends acquired during the war years: Ralph Partridge and his wife. Mrs. Partridge had been Dora Carrington before her marriage and preferred to go by the name of "Carrington." She was an artist and a decorator who had studied at the Slade School of Art. The Partridges became greatly devoted to Strachey, and their friendship was of incalculable value to him. They kept house for him at Tidmarsh and at Ham Spray. They did their best to see that nothing was lacking conducive to his comfort and to a milieu which would enable him to do his very best literary work. Mr. Partridge was affable, friendly, and highly practical. He served admirably as Strachey's secretary. Mrs. Partridge used her skill as a decorator to make the houses in which they lived as attractive as possible. Under her hand Ham Spray House became in every room and in the smallest detail a delight to the eye, and it has been preserved today very much as she left it. (Her death occurred in early 1932, two months after Strachey's.) But the Partridges did more than this for Lytton Strachey. As he progressed with his writing, he

30. The fullest and most helpful study of Bloomsbury so far is J. K. Johnstone's *The Bloomsbury Group* (London, Secker & Warburg, 1954). See also Sheean and Harrod.

made it his habit to read aloud to them what he had just written; they were his first audience. Mr. Partridge, an Oxford man, was himself a talented man of letters. Mrs. Partridge's opinions combined a gleeful, Puckish sense of humor with the uncanny, intuitional, frequently illogical but nevertheless convincing insight of an artist. The three would meet for reading and discussion of the manuscripts in front of the fire in the downstairs front sitting room. The writing had been done in the study upstairs, where Strachey must have been often conscious of the picture over the chimney piece—a picture with Voltaire in the center, seated at a table with a group of his friends, his hand raised in perpetual benediction above his friends and above the little group at Ham Spray. For these three Voltaire was the patron saint.[31]

Queen Victoria was written, in the main, at Tidmarsh. When Lady Strachey heard that he had undertaken this biography she protested gently. "I don't much fancy your taking up Queen Victoria to deal with," she wrote to him in January 1919. "She could not help being stupid, but she tried hard to do her duty, . . . highly to her credit. What about taking up Disraeli?" When he persisted, however, her intimate knowledge of many famous Victorians and the Victorian world was a great help to him. Lady Lytton, wife of the first earl, who had been one of Queen Victoria's ladies-in-waiting and who was quite fond of Lytton Strachey, was also a great help. Much of the "private information" referred to in the footnotes of the biography came from her. The book, dedicated to Virginia Woolf and published in early April 1921, was acknowledged to be a classic almost immediately. To this writer it is Strachey's masterpiece.

Strachey next gathered some of his fugitive essays—selecting the ones he liked best—from the many reviews and articles which he had written since his Cambridge days. His style, as we have seen, had matured early, and these required only minor revisions before they were republished in Strachey's fourth volume, *Books*

31. Strachey collected books by Voltaire and other eighteenth-century writers. His will bequeathed all books published before 1841 to his friend Roger Senhouse.

and Characters (May 1922).[32] This book, dedicated to John Maynard Keynes, contains some of Strachey's best criticism, including the admirable essay on Racine. The high quality of the criticism was recognized in reviews at the time; *Books and Characters* went far toward establishing Strachey among those few English critics whose opinions no student of literature can afford to neglect.

In the years after he had written his thesis on Hastings at Cambridge he had not lost sight of his family traditions or an inbred sense of loyalty to them. Their influence on him has not been altogether overlooked by critics. André Maurois has written: "But the conquest of Lytton Strachey by Queen Victoria was easy. It counted for something that Strachey sprang from one of the great Whig families. He could depict with true understanding those solid, silent characters, seemingly proof against all enthusiasms, whose sound sense ensures the permanence of England and saves her from all freakish dangers." [33] The best comment on the subject so far, however, has been made by Strachey's friend Raymond Mortimer in "Mrs. Woolf and Mr. Strachey," an essay which gives attention to the cultural traditions of not only the Stracheys but also the Stephens and the Sackvilles. Mortimer writes that Virginia Woolf and Lytton Strachey, "related to half the most scholarly families in England," used the very weapons on the Victorians which had been "forged in Victorians' homes." Furthermore, "The mastery of a mass of detail, the solid and admirably proportioned architecture of Mr. Strachey's books are an inheritance from generations of civil servants." He adds that what Virginia Woolf and Lytton Strachey have in common "has some relation to a voice that is never too loud, a skepticism that remains polite, a learning that is never paraded, and a disregard, that never becomes insulting, for the public taste. It is a quality of inherited culture." [34]

32. For a list of these revisions and a discussion of them, see my articles: "Lytton Strachey's Revisions in *Books and Characters*," *Modern Language Notes*, April 1945, pp. 226–34; and "Lytton Strachey Improves His Style," *College English*, 7 (Jan. 1946), 215–19.

33. *Prophets and Poets*, pp. 240–1.

34. *Bookman* (London), *68* (Feb. 1929), 625–9.

Strachey's last years were crowded with work and with plans for more work. Some of his most brilliant writing is in the miniature pen portraits which he wrote during this period, most of which he collected in *Portraits in Miniature* (1931). One of these, "Charles Greville" (*Nation and Athenaeum*, August 11, 1923), is important not only because of its intrinsic merits but because it is a delightful by-product of what had become a major interest to him—the study of the *Greville Memoirs*.[35] He had used the complete manuscript of this fascinating work in the British Museum when he was writing *Queen Victoria*—had reveled in it— but had been filled with disgust when he discovered that all printed editions of it were badly expurgated. Much earlier he had protested again and again against the bowdlerizing of Horace Walpole's letters. Throughout his whole life he waged war for the principle of the unexpurgated text. About 1928 he obtained permission from the authorities of the British Museum to publish an edition of the complete *Greville*. By the time of his death in 1932 the work had been carried far, and he had written most of the notes. His labors were completed by Roger Fulford with the help of Ralph Partridge and the second Mrs. Partridge. The complete memoirs were published in eight large volumes in 1938.[36]

In June 1925, his provocative essay on "Pope" appeared. It had been the Leslie Stephen Lecture at Cambridge for that year. In August, 1925, there were two performances at the Scala Theater of *The Son of Heaven*, Strachey's play dealing with the Boxer War in China, with Gertrude Kingston in the leading role. Proceeds went to the London Society of Women's Service, in which Lady Strachey still took a great interest and of which Lytton Strachey's sister Philippa was secretary. The play was not a great success, partly because it was written many years before and did not represent the mature Strachey and partly because it was badly

35. This essay on Greville has been collected in Lytton Strachey's *Biographical Essays*, one volume of the new, highly attractive six-volume edition of Strachey's works edited by James Strachey (London, Chatto and Windus, 1948). All the other writings in this new edition have been collected previously.
36. *The Greville Memoirs, 1814–1860* (London, Macmillan, 1938).

cut by those who produced it. Strachey himself would not witness it but fled to France during its performance.[37] Yet this play fared very well and ran for three weeks when it was revived at the New Lindsey Theatre in London in the spring of 1949.

He visited Denmark in August 1928. Although he liked much that he saw there, he could not admire the people altogether and in a letter commented thus on them: "The inhabitants are pleasant, but oh! so lacking in temperament! Duty seems to guide their steps, and duty alone."

Elizabeth and Essex, his second full-length biography, was published, with omissions, in the *Ladies' Home Journal* from September to December, 1928, and in England as a book in December of that year. It was dedicated to Strachey's brother James and his wife Alix. Almost from the beginning this book has been underrated. The statement which has echoed again and again is that as biography it is chiefly guesswork—that Strachey did not know the Elizabethan Age. Actually, as his *Spectator* reviews and much other evidence indicate, he was well read in the period. The book has great merits: it has a consummately beautiful style sustained throughout; it has delicately and delightfully balanced architectonics; again and again it shows a sure sense of the dramatic; it deals with highly complex characters—Elizabeth, Bacon, Essex—with firmness, justice, and astonishing insight; and it is probably the most thoroughly fused piece of art which Strachey produced.

Portraits in Miniature, published in 1931, was dedicated to Max Beerbohm "with Gratitude and Admiration." The last of Strachey's six books, *Characters and Commentaries,* another collection of fugitive pieces, some of which had been written quite early, was edited by James Strachey and published in 1933, after the author's death.

Lytton Strachey hoped to be able to write his masterpiece after he reached his sixties. He had various subjects in mind, including Benjamin Jowett, General Booth, and George Washington. In the meantime he amused himself with shorter pieces, both poetry

37. For reviews, see the *Times* (London), July 14, 1925, p. 12, which gives the complete cast; Desmond MacCarthy in the *New Statesman,* July 18, 1925, p. 394; and J. C. Squire in the *London Mercury, 12* (August 1925), 422–3.

and prose in a great variety of forms. These include light, satirical dialogues, in imitation of Voltaire, between such people as Cleopatra and Mrs. Humphrey Ward,[38] Sennacherib and Rupert Brooke,[39] and Catullus and Lord Tennyson.

From time to time honors were bestowed upon him. The Royal Society of Literature gave him its medal in 1923. The University of Edinburgh awarded him the Order of Merit in the department of letters in July 1926. Many literary critics assumed without question that he was not only the father of the new school of biography but the best writer in this school.

Writing *Elizabeth and Essex* greatly reduced his physical strength. Strachey never enjoyed good health; even when young, he had had to learn how to husband all his strength in order to energize his mind. In his most characteristic sitting posture his body was completely relaxed all the time that his mind was working with the vigor of a dynamo. In the summer of 1931, however, he seemed in better health than usual. The *Weekend Review* that summer ran a contest offering a prize of two guineas for the best profile of Strachey himself. Playfully, Mrs. Partridge, signing

38. Mrs. Ward, niece of Matthew Arnold, made an angry attack on Strachey in the *Times Literary Supplement* soon after the publication of *Eminent Victorians*.

39. Strachey met Brooke during his Cambridge days and saw him from time to time later; his comments on him through the years show mixed feelings. September 1905: "He has rather nice—but you know—yellow-ochreish hair, and a healthy young complexion. . . . He talked about Poetry and Public Schools as decently as could be expected. . . . I wasn't particularly impressed. . . . He's damned literary, rather too serious and conscientious, and devoid of finesse." April 1908: "Rupert Brooke—isn't it a romantic name?—with pink cheeks and bright yellow hair—it sounds horrible, but it wasn't." August 1914: "Rupert also intends to go to Belgium. I cannot see the use of intellectual persons doing this, as long as there are enough men in any case, and the country is not in danger. Home defense is another matter, and I think I should certainly train if I had the strength." April 25, 1915: "The news [of Brooke's death] came yesterday: apparently it was owing to some illness or other. . . . The meaningless[ness] of fate is intolerable; it is all muddle and futility. After all the pother of those years of living, its effects are simply nothing. It is like a confused tale, just beginning, and then broken off for no reason, and for ever."

herself "Mopsa," submitted a fictitious obituary notice of him which easily won the prize.[40] When Strachey actually died just a few months later, she felt with rather weird intuition that she had somehow killed him with her obituary notice. She never forgave herself.

In early September 1931, Strachey spent a fortnight in France. Here he kept the last of his diaries. Seemingly he was still in very good health, yet in the diary he wrote: "More than once my visionary existence has seemed more real than reality—a state of affairs that should not last too long." One day as he walked down a street in Rheims, he suddenly found himself "jumping skyhigh at one moment before the startled gaze of an elderly inhabitant" and commented, "an attack of the Strachey twist." Again he wrote: "I forgot to mention an incident in the Rue St. Honoré yesterday. Looking at myself in a shop-window mirror, I saw for the first time how completely gray my hair was over my temples. So that has come at last! I was beginning to think it never would. Do I feel like it? Perhaps I do a little—a very little. A certain sense of detachment declares itself amid the agitations that continue to strew my path. . . . That dreadful abysmal sensation in the pit of the stomach is absent. What a relief!" A little later: "My mind is interrogative"; and still later: "In this wretched world unkindness is out of place."

After returning to Ham Spray he soon realized that he was very ill and late in November took to his bed. Through the weeks that followed there were days when he seemed better. He wanted very much to live and fought hard. But the general drift was downward. He could retain no food; his body wasted away almost to nothing before his death. He died at 1:30 in the afternoon of January 21, 1932. At the time of his death the weather was fair —intensely still, as it had been for many days. If he had lived until March 1, he would have been fifty-two years old.

While he was alive his illness was diagnosed as ulcerative colitis and paratyphoid. The post-mortem, however, showed that his stomach had been practically eaten up by cancer. The body was

40. Published on July 18, 1931, p. 79.

cremated, and a bronze plate commemorating him was placed in
the Strachey Chapel at Chew Magna Church, Somerset.

When his friends met from time to time in the weeks following
his death they were bewildered, very much at a loss for the right
thing to say. Many observed quietly: "He gave us a standard. Who
will now show us how to live?" One friend said, "There are things
one would like to say and never will say now." Others said: "He
was an inexhaustible fountain of mirth; laughter has departed
from us." And another said, "I wake in the night with the sense
of being in an empty hall." Still others lamented: "For us a light
has suddenly gone out; our lives can never be the same again."
And though they were still gay, their gaiety took on a new poignancy, for they all knew that no one could take the place of Lytton.[41]

41. One of those who knew Strachey most intimately said at the time of
his death that he was best described in a poem which he himself loved,
Cowley's "On the Death of Mr. William Hervey."

CHAPTER 2

Writing from a "Point of View"

WHAT did Lytton Strachey mean when he insisted in the preface to *Eminent Victorians* and elsewhere that the biographer should have a clear and definite point of view? When we have answered this question we are certain to encounter another: was Strachey right? Should biography be written from a fixed point of view? Is there a danger that the biographer with a rigid point of view will treat his subject as a victim forced to lie upon the bed of Procrustes?

It is reasonable to assume that Strachey meant at least two things. First, he meant that for the sake of both art and truth the biographer must employ selection, proportion, and emphasis in dealing with the facts relating to his subject. Only thus could he achieve the perspective which a good portrait must always have. Second, Strachey meant that biography should be critical and evaluative. The biographer should seek to determine the extent to which his subject lived in accordance with true values or was misled by false values—the extent to which his subject succeeded in living the good life. He must discover the extent to which his subject practiced wisdom or fell into stupidity.

But here other questions arise. What, after all, is wise and what is stupid? What system of values may a biographer justifiably employ in judging the complex behavior of human beings? And, most important, did Strachey himself in writing his biographies make consistent reference to any system of values which informed, thoughtful readers could accept as valid? Was he guided by willful and specious preconceptions or by conclusions resting upon the evidence and by sound, steady judgment?

47

Some critics have contended that he did not have a clear sense of values. In 1922 Lloyd R. Morris wrote, "Mr Strachey is fundamentally an idealist, but he is desperately uncertain as to what ideals he should give his allegiance." [1] On the other hand, the chief tribute which his friends paid to him was expressed quite simply in their words, "He gave us a standard," and by a standard they meant something to live by and something to think by. These were words which they used often and which represented a consistent attitude toward Strachey. What were the elements of Strachey's mind and character which for them served to clarify and stabilize life and thought?

He was not fond of the word "ideal" and rarely used it. For him it was a word which had hazy and questionable ethical and religious associations and which often carried with it the naive assumption that there would be a future which would somehow manage to be better than the present. Living was a day-by-day matter for Strachey, and the good life could be grasped only at the present moment. Idealism as one might connect it with Galahad was for him simply ridiculous. His was a secular mind in the very best sense; and he made for himself a world insulated against the disturbing and confusing things which were nonsecular in order to establish his premises and formulate his creed. Selection counted for fully as much in the method by which he arrived at values and determined a philosophy of life as it did in the method by which he wrote his books.

He knew very well what he believed in. Perhaps no one, not even Lord Macaulay, has been more sure about the values to which he would yield allegiance. This is not to say that he attempted to work out for himself a completely logical and systematic scheme of thought and philosophy of life. He was always highly suspicious of systems of thought. But there were basic beliefs which established themselves as fixed points around which the movements of his mind could pivot. His confidence in these and his consistent awareness of them gave his mind the stability which impressed his friends and which counts for much in his books.

1. *Outlook,* August 23, 1922, pp. 681–2.

It is not really difficult for the reader of these books today to discover the things in which he believed, for he holds them up for admiration whenever they appear upon his pages, and he heaps ridicule upon the heads of those who do not know their value. What he liked was a way of life characterized by unaffected simplicity, by individual freedom, by that highest exercise of intelligence which he often calls "sanity," by a sensitiveness to beauty in both nature and art, by an intense interest in people and a proper respect for the high potentialities of humanity, and by the glorification of the quality of experience made possible by friendship and love.

In letters and art Strachey admired simplicity without losing his sense of the value of the complex. His taste was catholic. He admired the Gothic almost as much as the Greek, Sir Thomas Browne's prose almost as much as Swift's. In reviewing Swinburne's *The Age of Shakespeare* in 1908, he wrote:

> It is sometimes said that great art is always simple. This is untrue; for art cannot be bounded by definitions, and some of the most elaborate of man's creations have been the most beautiful. But it is true that simplicity is often the surest test of an artist's power. A bad artist must fail when he is simple; but whoever is simple and succeeds must be great. How constantly, amid all the complexity and the rhetoric of the Elizabethan dramatists, do we come upon passages of triumphant simplicity! And nowhere more often than in Webster.[2]

Although good art might be either simple or complex, the good life was almost always simple. The essential Strachey is clearly revealed in a little poem which he composed for Mr. and Mrs. Ralph Partridge on his fortieth birthday (1920), after he had won fame with *Eminent Victorians* and while he was working on *Queen Victoria*. A few stanzas follow:

2. *Spectator, 101* (Oct. 3, 1908), 502–3. This and other unsigned contributions to the *Spectator* I have been able to identify as Strachey's partly through the help of James Strachey, his brother and literary executor (who has generously given me permission to quote from them and from unpublished manuscripts), and partly through access to a marked file of the *Spectator*, kindly granted to me by the late editor, H. Wilson Harris.

Suppose the kind gods said, "Today
You're forty. True: but still, rejoice!
Gifts we have got will smooth away
The ills of age. Come, take your choice!"

What should I answer? Well, you know
I'm modest—very. So, no shower
Of endless gold I'd beg, nor show
Of proud-faced pomp, nor regal power.

No; ordinary things and good
I'd choose: friends, wise and kind and few;
A country house, a pretty wood
To walk in; books both old and new

To read; a life retired, apart,
Where leisure and repose might dwell
With industry; a little art;
Perhaps a little fame as well.[3]

Moderation was the key to his mind and character. After telling
us that Prince Albert cultivated the strenuous life until he could
not relax and finally worked himself to death, Strachey inter-
prets: " 'In nothing be over-zealous,' says an old Greek. 'The due
measure in all the works of man is best. For often one who
zealously pushes towards some excellence, though he be pursuing
a gain, is really being led utterly astray by the will of some Power,
which makes those things that are evil seem to him good, and
those things seem to him evil that are for his advantage.' "[4] The
irresistible force in Florence Nightingale which drove her to
serve mankind was also a demon that forced her to become the

3. From the manuscript. Note Strachey's Wordsworthian comment on
Rousseau after he had gone through intense mental suffering: "The perplexed and tortured spirit could still find rest among the simple vegetable
things he loved so well,—the flowers, and the mosses, and the humblest
offspring of the earth." "Three Frenchmen in England," *Spectator, 100*
(May 30, 1908), 866–7.
4. *Queen Victoria* (New York, Harcourt, Brace, 1921), pp. 287–8.

enemy of her friends and of her own human nature. Moderate men, Strachey felt sure, would inherit the earth, not those wildly frenzied men who were driven hither and thither by inordinate ambition. Like Wordsworth, he realized the great danger of having the world too much with us and of laying waste our powers in busyness. He worked out the idea once in the form of a parable:

"For the last six months," said Cleanthes, "I have been very busy. I have written four more chapters of my history of Cos. I have converted three Boeotians from Polytheism to Democracy, and I have found two shipwrecked mariners a comfortable home; I have given several lectures, and I have attended countless numbers of committees, boards, and syndicates; I have walked from Athens to Corinth and from Corinth to Athens twenty-five times; I have had a most interesting conversation with Xenophon; I have taken a great deal of exercise, and done a great deal of work, and a great deal of talking, and a great deal of good; and tomorrow I am going to be married."

"And when," I inquired, "did you last see Socrates?"

"Would you believe it?" he answered; "for the last six months I have been so extraordinarily busy that, though he lives upon the next staircase, I have not had time to speak to Socrates once." [5]

The ordinary idealist aiming at "practical," extrinsic goals would naturally find Strachey totally lacking in ideals. The wife of Socrates had her doubts about him.

5. From the manuscript. One of the eighty-eight "aphorisms" probably written when Strachey was at Cambridge. Compare the following passage which Strachey wrote with the first World War in mind: "Ultimately the world is governed by moderate men. Extremists and fanatics and desperadoes may make a noise or a disturbance, they may even at times appear to control the course of events; but in reality they are always secondary figures— either symptoms or instruments; whatever happens, the great mass of ordinary, stolid, humdrum, respectable persons remains the dominating force in human affairs." "Militarism and Theology," *War and Peace*, May 1918, p. 223. There is much here to suggest Arnold's dislike of "Jacobinism," particularly its fierceness and its way of going to extremes.

When in the preface to *Eminent Victorians* Strachey insisted that the biographer should enjoy freedom of mind and spirit, he was speaking of something which had been bred in his bones. Stracheys for generations before him had been independent-minded individuals. Lytton Strachey grew up in a household dominated by a mother who greatly admired Milton, John Stuart Mill, George Eliot, and Browning and who never hesitated to defy the social conventions of her day. At Cambridge, too, he had given himself up completely to Swinburne, and he never quite outgrew the Swinburnian influence. Like Swinburne, he suffered from the feeling that he was an extremely peculiar individual and that perfectly normal people could never understand him. There were times when he naturally rebelled, as Swinburne had done, against a world seemingly made for ordinary, common-place people. But as Strachey grew older he acquired a quiet wisdom which Swinburne never had. He learned how to escape from the complaining, protesting ego. He learned that it was much better to laugh at the world than to rebel against it. He also learned that there were times when he could win a complete victory over it simply by ignoring it.

There could be no doubt in his mind that in art and life freedom was the only way. Strachey was delighted with the freedom which he found at Cambridge, a freedom which he said was in the very architecture and the landscape of the place.

> Cambridge, like so many English things, grew to be itself almost casually, and as it were by accident. . . . If one were to try to define the particular fascination of Cambridge architecture, one would have to take into account this characteristic of waywardness and spontaneity. How different is the impression produced by Oxford, with her solemn and noble masses, her wide perspectives, and her imposing domes. In spite of Trinity, in spite even of King's Chapel, Cambridge, as a whole, lacks grandeur. . . . The real enchantment of Cambridge is of the intimate kind; an enchantment lingering in nooks and corners, coming upon one gradually down the narrow streets, and ripening year by year. The little river

amid its lawns and willows, the old trees in the old gardens, the obscure bowling-greens, the crooked lanes with their glimpses of cornices and turrets, the low dark doors opening out on to sunny grass,—in these, and in things like these, dwells the fascination of Cambridge.[6]

Strachey found very little to admire in Matthew Arnold the critic. Particularly objectionable to him was Arnold's assumption that there were objective standards by which art could be evaluated and that authority could sit in judgment on artists and their work. Arnold had looked longingly toward France, where the authority of the National Academy and a national theater counted for much. To Strachey, an artist was first of all a free individual. His work would partake of his own freedom and could be appraised only in terms of its own indwelling laws. Of no art was this more true than that of the drama. Strachey wrote:

> "The State shall be my governors, but not my critics," wrote a greater than Matthew Arnold. . . . We should do well to remember Milton's weighty words. . . . Drama is not a science; it is an art. It is not a dead thing to be pinned down and classified and docketed; it is a living creature, winged and wondrous, hovering inexplicably over magical flowers, and amenable to no laws but those of fancy. Such a phenomenon, it is easy to imagine, would not stay for long in the keeping of public trustees . . .
>
> Even in France—under far more favorable conditions— the history of the Comédie Française has been marked by a succession of internecine struggles and intrigues, of mon-

6. "Cambridge," *Spectator, 99* (Nov. 2, 1907), 668–9. Compare this passage from a letter written in 1928: "Never have I seen anything more beautiful than Cambridge this morning—a delicious warm sun, lighting up everything, and the trees in every variety of colour. In fact, I was so much rapt in admiration that, as I stood looking at the Senate House, an individual accosted me with—'Do you want a guide, sir?'" Such passages show how peculiarly susceptible Strachey was to the charm of places. He liked to speculate upon a "philosophy of places." He would not have agreed with Milton's "The mind is its own place" but has something in common with Thomas Hardy here.

strous pretensions, and of violent revolts. And in England neither our art nor our character has any natural inclination towards authority. . . . Who can limit the number of ways in which it is right to act Shakespeare? . . . [The English drama] must be allowed, like La Fontaine's wolf, to "run where it likes"; it must be given the fresh air of freedom.[7]

Freedom in the arts and in criticism was important; the very principle of life which gave vitality to the arts demanded freedom. The art of living as practiced by an intelligent human being presupposed the same need for freedom. The need was particularly great in the educational process, where the growth of the mind and spirit of the individual was a matter of primary concern. Strachey had suffered much from unintelligent authoritarian education before he entered Liverpool College. He never quite forgot or forgave those who had persecuted him in the name of education. In writing of J. A. Froude, he asserted the opinion that "old Mr. Froude" denied his son the freedom of mind and spirit that would have made him one of the greatest historians.[8] And he clearly sympathized with Edward VII in his refusal to conform to the strict Victorian moral code. Edward VII, he said, "was typical of his age in discovering that in order to be conscientious it was not necessary to be restricted and repressed. He showed that it was possible for a King of England to enjoy himself and to do his duty at the same time." [9] Voltaire had had many personal faults, Strachey conceded, but his main gospel, based on freedom and good sense, would in the end prevail. "Short of some overwhelming catastrophe, the doctrine which he preached—that life should be ruled, not by the dictates of tyranny and superstition, but by those of reason and humanity—can never be obliterated from the minds of men." [10] Humanity had the best chance to fulfill itself in a world where freedom and toleration walked hand

7. "L'Art Administratif," *Spectator*, *99* (Dec. 28, 1907), 1093–4.
8. "One of the Victorians" (republished as "Froude" in *Portraits in Miniature*), *Saturday Review of Literature*, Dec. 6, 1930, pp. 418–19.
9. "A Frock-Coat Portrait of a Great King," *Daily Mail*, Oct. 11, 1927, p. 10.
10. "Voltaire," *Athenaeum*, Aug. 1, 1919, pp. 677–8.

in hand as they were guided by the light of reason. Authority might produce grandeur, as it had at Versailles in the time of Louis XIV, but there was something better than grandeur, something which satisfied a higher need of the human spirit. At the very time when the spirit of Versailles shone forth with greatest brilliance, another spirit, which "dwelt somewhere among the grimy streets of the city of London," awakened. And the future belonged to this spirit. "It was with Somers and with Montagu, with Newton and with Locke—the apostles of science and toleration—that the future lay." [11]

Strachey was not a Christian, but in his secular mind as in Christianity it was the truth that made men free. The allegiance which Voltaire and the Enlightenment gave to reason and the confidence which Newton and his successors had in science were both part of a great tradition of independent-minded thinkers who lived in the air of freedom. They embodied and exemplified what was truly an ideal—an ideal of sanity which might in the end save the world. Reason and sanity were closely associated in his mind with common sense and science. All of these had to do with a way of thinking which was disassociated from the emotional and the vague and which steadfastly considered the world just as it is. Strachey owned something here to his scientist father and and to his father's father, who to his friend Carlyle was a good fellow but a "logic-chopper." He also owed much to Cambridge, "whose cloisters," he said, "have ever been consecrated to poetry and common sense." [12] He was indebted, furthermore, as we know, to G. E. Moore's *Principia Ethica* with its insistence that the thinker's first step was to formulate clear questions in order to make it possible to formulate clear answers.[13] He sometimes used the word "worldly" to mean a highly civilized state of mind in which the spirit of the world succeeded in shutting out terrors and

11. "The Age of Louis XIV," *Spectator, 100* (April 11, 1908), 577–8.
12. *Eminent Victorians*, p. 13.
13. See J. M. Keynes, *Two Memoirs* (London, Rupert Hart-Davis, 1949), pp. 88–9. See also the valuable treatment of Bloomsbury and its values in R. F. Harrod, *The Life of John Maynard Keynes* (New York, Harcourt, Brace, 1951), pp. 172–94 and *passim*.

mysteries and in a concentrated light considered "unhindered the mind of man—of man, not rapt aloft in the vast ardors of speculation, nor involved in the solitary inspection of his own breast; but of man, civilized, actual, among his fellows, in the bright light of the world." [14] Strachey was delighted with "that positive spirit of searching and unmitigated common sense which has given French prose its peculiar distinction." [15] It was the greatness of Wordsworth that "his egotism, his introspection, and his love of freedom had been bounded and controlled by a profound sanity." [16] Johnson's greatness also, "apart from his mastery of English," lay in "the breadth and sanity of his outlook upon life." [17] Likewise the chief merit of most of the major English novelists was that they could write about life "with sanity, with breadth, with humor." [18] Even love—whether love between man and woman or love of country—profited from sanity. Near the end of the first World War Strachey wrote that "nothing sweetens love—even love of one's country—so much as a little common sense." Queen Elizabeth's love for her country was just the right kind, "for it was a patriotism which paid a very strict attention to disagreeable facts; which was never agitated and never sentimental; which did not deal in pompous platitudes; and which—a most important detail—was always ready to explore every avenue to peace." [19] The modern world began when science gained for itself a position of respect. "If one were asked to choose a date for the beginning of the modern world, probably July 15, 1662, would be the best to fix upon. For on that day the Royal Society was founded, and the place of Science in civilization became a definite and recognizable thing." [20] Harold Nicolson is justified in considering extremely important Strachey's "calm conviction that thought and reason

14. *Landmarks in French Literature,* p. 70.
15. *Ibid.,* p. 201.
16. "Wordsworth's Letters," *Spectator, 100* (March 21, 1908), 460–1.
17. "Shakespeare on Johnson," *Spectator, 101* (Aug. 1, 1908), 164–5.
18. "Dostoievsky," *Spectator, 109* (Sept. 28, 1912), 451–2.
19. "The Claims of Patriotism," *War and Peace,* July 4, 1918, pp. 292–3.
20. "John Aubrey," *Nation and Athenaeum, 33* (Sept. 15, 1923), 741–2.

are in fact the most important elements in human nature; a respect, ultimately, for man's unconquerable mind." [21]

As strongly as Strachey disapproved of Matthew Arnold, he could devote himself to one of Arnold's highest ideals. For both believed that the surest manifestation of a life lived in accordance with reason was a habit of thought governed by detachment. Strachey's emotions were deep and powerful, and he realized clearly that emotion as well as reason was important in both living and thinking. The enemy was not emotion itself but rather emotion dominated by the clamoring and fretting ego—an ego which through agitated emotion sought to influence both behavior and judgment. In the realms of both behavior and judgment Strachey had come to grips with this ego many years before. As far as his personal behavior was concerned, lapses from conformity and conventionality could disturb him not at all; he had no desire to conform. But nothing was more characteristic of him than the distress which he felt at the mere suggestion of a lapse into selfishness. And in his literary judgments, whether he wrote as a biographer or a critic, the evidence is overwhelming that he assiduously cultivated detachment, impartiality, and justice.

When he found detachment in others, he gave it high praise, as he does in the following passage on Hume.

> In what resides the most characteristic virtue of humanity? In good works? Possibly. In the creation of beautiful objects? Perhaps. But some would look in a different direction, and find it in detachment. To all such David Hume must be a great saint in the calendar; for no mortal being was ever more completely divested of the trammels of the personal and the particular, none ever practiced with a more consummate success the

21. *The Development of English Biography* (London, Hogarth Press, 1933), p. 150. The personality, ideas, and idealism of G. Lowes Dickinson became another potent influence on Strachey and his Cambridge friends. It is clearly reflected in a letter from Strachey to Keynes written in late 1905. Professor Walter Raleigh, Strachey declared, had "consummate brilliance"; nevertheless, he belonged to "the age before the flood—the pre-Dickinsonian era, which is really fatal. . . . He might be one's father." Harrod, *Keynes, 3.*

divine art of impartiality. And certainly to have no axe to
grind is something very noble and very rare. It may be said to
be the antithesis of the bestial.[22]

One of the great faults of the Victorian age, on the other hand,
was "its incurable lack of detachment." [23] Victorian biographies
suffered from precisely this fault.[24] Sir Desmond MacCarthy has
pointed out that an important reason why Strachey disliked most
types of ambition was that they "took control of personal relations
and destroyed detachment." [25]

As Strachey's successive books came from the press, more than
one critic was impressed by the quality of detachment to be found
in them. There were accusations of unfairness and of misrepresentation too—some of them perhaps deserved—in appraisals of
Strachey's Dr. Arnold, his Florence Nightingale, and his Lord
Cromer; but the remarkable thing to discerning critics of Strachey's
books was that they displayed so little unfairness, so little misrepresentation. The critic who reviewed *Eminent Victorians* for
the *Times Literary Supplement* on May 16, 1918, said that there
was "something almost uncanny in the author's detachment." The
book had only one fault: it was too amusing; "the Victorian age was
something more than a joke." Yet it was the work of an author who
was "urbane, impartial, detached, and full of observation and
curiosity" and who made "a very sincere and scholarly attempt to
understand the generation which preceded his own." [26] Writing for
the *Nation and Athenaeum,* April 25, 1925, Edwin Muir asserted
that impartiality was one of Strachey's chief virtues. "Every stroke
of irony in his books is weighed not for its effectiveness but for its
justice; and accordingly every stroke tells." [27] Just a few days after
Strachey's death, Arthur Waugh made very much the same point in
the *Spectator.* "If to these other gifts he added in a double measure
an air of irony and detachment, his was an irony that was never far

22. "Hume," *Nation and Athenaeum, 42* (Jan. 7, 1923), 536–8.
23. "A Victorian Critic," *New Statesman,* Aug. 1, 1914, 529–30.
24. See the preface to *Eminent Victorians.*
25. "Lytton Strachey," *Sunday Times* (London), Jan. 24, 1932, p. 8.
26. "Megatheria," *Times Literary Supplement,* May 16, 1918, p. 230.
27. "Lytton Strachey," pp. 102–4.

removed from pity, and a detachment that held his subject at arm's length, only to place him, with a gesture of discreet propriety, in his true relation to the world around him." [28]

Two reviewers of *Books and Characters* (1922) went further than this. They declared that Strachey not only attempted to practice justice himself but also was quick to go to the rescue of whoever or whatever had suffered from the injustice of others. The critic for the London *Times* was particularly impressed by the essay on Racine.

> Mr. Lytton Strachey has cleared the honor of the nation. He has repaired past sacrileges by publishing the finest essay upon Racine which has ever been written in English. . . . Mr. Strachey's is perhaps the finest critical intelligence at work in English literature today, and it has this admirable peculiarity that it operates most securely in the presence of misunderstanding. Nothing stimulates him so much as a judgment, whether of a particular critic or of a tradition, which seems to him to miss the essential individuality of a character or of a work. His most intense delight is to reveal the hidden quality of things that we have forgotten how to understand." [29]

J. Middleton Murry, writing for the *National and Athenaeum,* was in complete agreement:

> The real Mr. Strachey is neither iconoclast nor hero-worshipper. He is a man with a critical intelligence of the first order, whose delicate insight is tempered and subtilized by a catholic sympathy. Esteeming individuality of mind or temperament above all else, he goes about redressing the injustices of time. He removes the dust of neglect from forgotten faces; he stretches out a kindly hand to the creatures of oblivion. None know so well as he that there is an oblivion of memory as of forgetfulness. Men and books (those faithful mirrors of men) are as often buried beneath reputation as contempt. Mr.

28. "Mr. Lytton Strachey," a letter to the *Spectator, 148* (Jan. 30, 1932), 146. Compare a letter from Strachey's cousin, Miss Edith Plowden, published in the London *Times* on January 28, 1932, p. 6.

29. May 18, 1922, p. 16.

Strachey would like to save them from both calamities. . . .
Justice, the finest of all virtues, is the least popular. Mr. Strachey has more of it than any other critic living today. . . . A
misunderstanding is the keenest spur to Mr. Strachey's sympa-
thies. No nuance of inclination can stand against his desire to
right an injustice.[30]

But for Strachey the detached mind was not necessarily the
coldly judicious mind or the intellectually dry mind. Such minds
suggested dullness and inadequacy. Life and thought without excitement would be a very poor thing. In his diaries Strachey re-
minds one of the medieval knight who day after day went out to
seek adventures and who assumed that plenty of them would turn
up. Expectation and a delight in surprises were characteristic of
him from earliest childhood to the end of his life. His temperament, as many have pointed out, was in considerable part romantic. In him as usually in Wordsworth the vision of delight would
suddenly burst upon his sight. He and his friends at Cambridge
consciously sought for what was truly important, which, for them,
meant what was truly interesting. As far as they could, they excluded the rest. Significantly, "intensity" and "passion" are two of
Strachey's favorite words. The objects to be chosen—the objects of
highest value—were always those which possessed the power to
intensify and impassion the mind and emotions. Here again
Strachey and his Cambridge friends owed much to the teachings
of G. E. Moore. Lord Keynes recalled in some detail the nature of
this influence. "Nothing mattered except states of mind, our own
and other people's, of course, but chiefly our own. These states of
mind were not associated with action or achievement or with consequences. They consisted in timeless, passionate states of contemplation and communion, largely unattached to 'before' and 'after.' "
And what objects had the power to produce these delightfully
intensified states of mind? Keynes and the other disciples of Moore
had no doubt as to what they were. "The appropriate subjects of
passionate contemplation and communion were a beloved person,
beauty and truth, and one's prime objects in life were love, the

30. June 3, 1922, pp. 346–7.

creation and enjoyment of aesthetic experience and the pursuit of knowledge." [31]

Thus both as a disciple of Moore and as the son of a distinguished and enthusiastic scientist, Strachey found the search for truth full of excitement. It is characteristic of his style that it seizes upon a biographical or historical fact with as much zest and fervor as an entomologist displays when he finally succeeds in impaling a rare insect. The world which his mind made for itself—a sane, common-sense world teeming with facts from which one could always select the most interesting ones—was far indeed from being dull. Strachey would have agreed fully with G. M. Harper, who said brilliantly in the very midst of a romantic context: "There is no fire more intense than the flame of pure intelligence." [32] To read Strachey is to consider facts which have been bathed in the light and warmed by the heat of this flame.

A belief in the power of beauty and art to intensify thought and experience is likewise characteristic of Strachey and is implicit in all that he wrote. For him the groundwork of this belief required no argument. It strongly influenced all his judgments as a literary critic, and it was the shaping force of his various writings. The superiority of whatever had achieved the high perfection of art over whatever had almost achieved it or over whatever was not art at all was to him infinite. The following passage from his review of Granville Barker's production of Galsworthy's *Strife* in 1909 shows how clearly he realized the difference and also shows how alertly, vigorously, and sensitively he responded to art when he came into the presence of it, even when it was an art about which he knew very little—music. After conceding that the play was well produced and well acted and that Galsworthy had definite gifts as a dramatist, he declared that this play was a failure because in it the playwright had not been able to reconcile his purpose of showing the struggle between the prejudices and ideals of two classes with his desire to give a picture of conflicting persons. Although we get interested in the individual persons, the dramatist never tells us enough about them:

31. Keynes, *Two Memoirs*, p. 83.
32. *William Wordsworth* (London, John Murray, 1929), p. 186.

It almost seems as if Mr. Galsworthy himself was not quite sure of what he was aiming at. He has hesitated between his principles and his persons, and it is only too true that, in the drama, he who hesitates is lost. . . . One was left with a sense of confusion and dissatisfaction; how different from the feelings aroused by truly great art! It chanced that at the Haymarket the contrast was actually pointed in an unexpected way,—by the exquisite music of Mozart, which, somewhat injudiciously, was played between the acts. As one listened one forgot the difficulty, the discord, the ambiguity of Mr. Galsworthy's drama; one had come, quite simply and suddenly, into the heart of perfect beauty and the intimate glories of heaven.[33]

Likewise personal relationships—friendship and love—could be an invaluable vitalizing and intensifying power. Individuality realized itself at its best and fullest in the midst of a group; art was most likely to thrive there. Strachey had little respect for the anarchistic type of individualism which sought to realize itself in a social vacuum—in the desert place, in the cave, or in the remote recesses of an esoteric intellectual labyrinth. He believed that to thrive the artist needed the critical loyalty of his friends. Both at Cambridge and at Bloomsbury he was in a circle—a circle of friends full of faith in one another, loyal to one another, and yet freely exercising all the prerogatives of individualism and freely critical of one another. To outsiders they appeared to be a formidable clique of highly unconventional and eccentric intellectuals. Within the group there were often moments of friction when the sparks flew. Periods of turbulence were inevitable among such free individuals. But, everything considered, the truly remarkable quality of the friendships which bound this group together was their stability. Many of the friendships had begun back in the days when Strachey, Keynes, Woolf, and Sydney-Turner were active Apostles at Cambridge, and they lost no strength through the years. The stability involved not merely the meeting of mind with mind but the complex adjustment and readjustment of personalities to one another.

33. "Mr. Galsworthy's Plays," *Spectator, 102* (March 27, 1909), 498–9.

The impact of Strachey's personality on his friends was, from first to last, tremendous. Leonard Woolf, who was certainly in a position to know, has written: "I think that the most significant thing about Lytton Strachey both as a person and as a writer is that his writing came so directly from himself, from the very core of his character, that years before he had achieved anything or had become famous he was impinging (as he would have said himself) upon practically everyone with whom he came in contact in exactly the same way in which he impinged upon the reading public by his books." [34] He did much to help the group realize the zest for living, the excitement, the joy, the optimism which true disciples of G. E. Moore sought. Six years after Strachey's death, Keynes wrote: "It was exciting, exhilarating, the beginning of a new renaissance, the opening of a new heaven on a new earth, we were the forerunners of a new dispensation, we were not afraid of anything. Perhaps it was because we were so brought up that even at our gloomiest and worst we have never lost a certain resilience which the younger generation seem never to have had." [35]

But the excitement, the intense pleasure, produced by friendship was mild compared with that produced by love. To deny love, Strachey said, as the medieval monk or as Florence Nightingale had denied love, was to deny "the most powerful and the profoundest of all the instincts of humanity." [36] One of the best stories about Strachey is that which André Maurois tells concerning an occurrence at a meeting of celebrities at the Abbey of Pontigny in the spring of 1922. A subject for discussion—"The Meaning of Honor" —had been announced. During most of the long and heated debate upon the subject, Strachey, apparently bored, listened for a time and then went to sleep. The rest of the story must be given in Maurois's words: " 'And what in your opinion, Monsieur Strachey, is the most important thing in the world?' Paul Desjardins asked

34. "Lytton Strachey," *New Statesman and Nation, 3* (Jan. 30, 1932), 118. See also Vincent Sheean's excellent article on the same group, "Lytton Strachey: Cambridge and Bloomsbury," *New Republic, 70* (Feb. 17, 1932), 19–20.

35. *Two Memoirs*, p. 82.

36. *Eminent Victorians* (London, Chatto and Windus, 1926), p. 119.

suddenly. There was a long silence. Then from the sleeping beard of Strachey issued a tiny falsetto voice: 'Passion,' he said finally with suave nonchalance. And the solemn circle, relieved for an instant, broke into laughter." [37]

Actually, Strachey was simply saying what he believed. He knew that passion could be a wild, savage, dangerous thing; but he also believed that properly realized and controlled it was the *summum bonum*. In a review written in early 1909, years before the Pontigny conference which he attended, he had said: "It was not the sophisms but the charms of Cleopatra which led Antony to ruin. There is only one thing which could have blinded a man in Antony's position so completely as we now know he actually was blinded, and that thing is passion. The world might be lost if he fled to Egypt, but it would be well lost; it would be lost with Cleopatra." [38] And the truly impressive thing about the letters of Mademoiselle de Lespinasse is their passion; these letters are "the most complete analysis the world possesses of a passion which actually existed in a human mind. Thus, when one thinks of Mademoiselle de Lespinasse, it is towards passion, and all the fearful accompaniments of passion, that one's imagination naturally turns." [39] Among the eighty-eight aphorisms which he wrote at Cambridge were these two: "Our best and most beautiful pleasure is love"; and "To love is second nature to some men; to all women it is nature itself." [40] In *Elizabeth and Essex* much of the interpretation of Elizabeth's behavior depends on the assumption that she had "a special cause for a neurotic condition; her sexual organization was seriously warped." [41] Likewise, Macaulay might have been a better historian —a better stylist even—if he could have known what love was:

> The stout square man with the prodigious memory and the inexhaustible capacity for conversation, was apparently a

37. *I Remember, I Remember* (New York and London, Harper, 1942), pp. 140–2.

38. "A New History of Rome," *Spectator, 102* (Jan. 2, 1909), 20–1.

39. "Mademoiselle de Lespinasse," *Independent Review, 10* (Sept. 1906), 345 ff.

40. From the manuscript.

41. (New York, Harcourt, Brace, 1928), p. 20.

normal human being, except in one direction: he never married, and there seems no reason to suppose that he was ever in love. An entertaining essay might perhaps be written on the sexlessness of historians; but it would be entertaining and nothing more: we do not know enough either about the historians or sex. Yet, in Macaulay's case, one cannot resist the conclusion that the absence from his make-up of intense physical emotion brought a barrenness upon his style. His sentences have no warmth and no curves; the embracing fluidity of love is lacking.[42]

The letters of the Carlyles to one another suffered from a similar deficiency: "This correspondence seems remarkable mainly for its sanity; it is, as Mr. Alexander Carlyle observes in his preface, the record of a courtship eminently Scotch. . . . Intense passion is never wordy; and the feelings of the Carlyles spread themselves over sheets and sheets." [43]

On the other hand, the presence of real passion in Pope's poetry makes amends for many deficiences. Strachey tells us that Pope had "a power of affection as unmistakable as his power of hate." He asks:

How is it possible that verse so regular, so ordered, so scrupulously exact, so "smooth," as the eighteenth-century phrase went, should be the language of passion? Every one knows that passion is a rough, disordered, fitful thing, chafing at artificial rules, and bending the stiff conventions of verse-making to its own vigorous and unexpected purposes; the true vehicle for passion is the varied blank verse of the Elizabethans, not the even couplet of Pope. . . . He succeeded in expressing passion, not by means of his medium, but in spite of it.[44]

42. "Macaulay," *Nation and Athenaeum, 42* (Jan. 21, 1928), 596–7. Compare this early comment on the style of Sidney Lee: "After all, is not even the most succulent of meats liable to be tasteless without a pinch or two of salt? In other words, Mr. Lee, in his hatred of rhetoric, of sentimentalism, and of 'gush,' is sometimes carried too far towards the opposite extremes of the frigid and the commonplace." "Mr. Sidney Lee on Shakespeare," *Spectator, 97* (Dec. 1, 1906), 887–8.

43. "Some New Carlyle Letters," *Spectator, 102* (April 10, 1909), 577–8.

44. "Alexander Pope," *Spectator, 103* (Nov. 20, 1909), 847–8.

In John Donne, always a great favorite with Strachey, an intensely passionate soul triumphed gloriously in the midst of stylistic difficulties very different from those which are associated with Pope. In Donne passion brought great art into being in the midst of the grotesque and unruly eccentricity.

> Donne really has achieved the impossible. The ardors of his passionate soul transfuse his antiquated mannerisms, his contorted and remote conceptions, and fill them with an intensely human significance. . . . To him God and Heaven were blazing and palpitating realities, and the human soul was a miracle about which no exaggeration of statement was possible. . . . For that strange nature rhetorical eccentricity seems to have been the sincerest expression of mystical ravishment, just as dialectical quibbling was the natural language of his most passionate love.[45]

Another very important conception played a large part in determining Strachey's judgments relating to people and books. It is "best described," as Strachey himself once wrote, "by the fine old-fashioned word 'humanity.' " [46] It has been stated that he "did not waste his sympathy upon that vague thing called humanity"; [47] but actually Strachey knew that humanity, like some of the other finer qualities of men, was vague in definition only and that it was something quite easy to recognize as clear and definite when it manifested itself in the lives and characters of people. He who lacked it, however gifted he might be, was an incomplete person; the book which lacked it might have very great merits, but it could never be thought of as altogether adequate; it could never claim praise as supreme art. Even the white light of absolute sanity, as admirable as that was, could never be accepted as a substitute for it. *Elizabeth and Essex* contains a remarkable passage in which the soul of Francis Bacon, immediately after his intellect has been shown functioning at its clearest and best in the trial of Essex, is weighed

45. "The Poetry of John Donne," *Spectator, 110* (Jan. 18, 1913), 102–3.
46. "Music and Men," *Spectator, 101* (Dec. 19, 1908), 1059–60.
47. Clifford Bower-Shore, *Lytton Strachey: An Essay* (London, Fenland Press, 1933), p. 92. I find this in the main an excellent piece of criticism.

in the balance and found wanting, because what is really needed
for the occasion is humanity; superior logic is not enough.

> Never had his intellect functioned with a more satisfactory,
> a more beautiful, precision. The argument was perfect; there
> was, in fact, only one mistake about it, and that was that it had
> ever been made. A simpleton might have done better, for a
> simpleton might have perceived instinctively the essentials of
> the situation. It was an occasion for the broad grasp of com-
> mon humanity, not for the razor-blade of subtle intelligence.
> Bacon could not see this; he could not see that the long friend-
> ship, the incessant kindness, the high generosity, and the
> touching admiration of the Earl had made a participation in
> his ruin a deplorable and disgraceful thing. Sir Charles Davers
> was not a clever man; but his absolute devotion to his bene-
> factor still smells sweet amid the withered corruptions of his-
> tory.[48]

Hence follows Strachey's distrust of mystics and mysticism. The
typical mystic ran counter to both common sense and humanity.
He might experience a delightful intensity as he beheld his vision
and dreamed his dream, but in him something essential was still
missing. Even Blake, whose poetry contained many qualities which
Strachey admired, had the shortcomings of the mystic, and he de-
servedly suffered accordingly both as a man and as an artist. "Be-
sides its unreasonableness, there is an even more serious objection
to Blake's mysticism—and indeed to all mysticism: its lack of humanity." [49]
But where humanity was found, especially when it was found in
the company of talents of a high order, it was to be esteemed as
priceless. Strachey found such a combination of humanity and talent in Rabelais and in the French caricaturist Caran D'Ache.

48. P. 250. Although Strachey's conception of humanity included far more
than mere *humaneness* or kindness, this quality was extremely important to
him. "You are right," a friend wrote to him in December 1918, "there's
nothing so crushing and wretched as hard human beings without feelings."
49. "The Poetry of Blake," *Books and Characters* (New York, Harcourt,
Brace, 1922), p. 229.

"Those rapid, preposterous, good-humored, and somewhat scurrilous drawings," he wrote of Caran D'Ache, "call up before the
mind the image of one imbued through and through with some
of the most marked characteristics of the French race." Behind the
pencil of the artist is laughter which is "neither malignant nor
meaningless, but eminently human. At its best, as in Rabelais, it is
elemental,—the golden and eternal laughter of the gods." [50] Even
classicism with its lofty artistic aims was inadequate and unsatisfy-
ing without humanity. Strachey admired the precision, the restraint, the careful and judicious selection, and the impeccable
form of classicism but insisted that these by themselves were not
enough. When these appeared, however, as they did in Molière,
joined with the high quality of humanity, the world could then
behold an art certain to fill it with wonder and delight: "The
weakness of the classical ideal lies in its tendency towards the
narrow and the confined,—towards a perfection which is only perfect because it has excluded and ignored so much. Pushed to its
extremity, it produces a Voltaire, the most consummate of artists,
dancing in a vacuum on the tight-rope of his own wit. . . . The
marvelous achievement of Molière was to combine the polished
brilliance of the classic with the romantic sense of humanity." [51]

Thus the world in which Lytton Strachey wanted to live was an
idealistic world, and the ideals were lofty ideals. Nothing could be
more positive than his values and his philosophy were. No one
could have attempted to live in accordance with what he believed
more consistently than Strachey did. He was a courageous man, and
he was fortunate to have courage in the kind of world in which he
had to live—a world in which formidable forces constantly threatened to destroy completely all that he believed in. In his effort to
repel these forces he had more than courage: he had literary art;

50. "Caran D'Ache," *Spectator, 102* (March 6, 1909), 371-2. Strachey
also wrote that "in the wonderful pages on Friendship one sees in all its
charm and all its sweetness that beautiful humanity which is the inward
essence of Montaigne." *Landmarks in French Literature* (New York and
London, Henry Holt and Thornton Butterworth, 1912), p. 41.

51. "Molière," *Spectator, 99* (Oct. 26, 1907), 612-13.

he had intellectual swiftness; he had imagination; he had a profound sense of irony; and he had a remarkable quickness in discovering the ridiculous and pouncing upon it. His satire, like all other good satire, has a positive basis. It is aimed at whatever challenges his ideals or at, what is perhaps worse, that which falsely pretends to embody one of those ideals. Much of Strachey's best satire —most of the passages in which he successfully exploits the uses of irreverence—spring from his delight in stripping the mask off the enemy or in exposing pure humbug. He was not therefore a cynic in the true sense, for a cynic doubts even the best and is usually devoid of courage. Actually, Strachey had little respect for "the kind of easy-going cynicism which . . . has been no uncommon characteristic of the second-rate man of letters." [52]

But there can be no doubt that he enjoyed the battle. Frail though his body always was, his sense of intellectual firmness, strength, and dominance gave him a confidence in victory which made him almost gleeful in the presence of his enemies. Rarely did he wait to fight defensively; instead he ferreted out his victims from their secret hiding places and, as they fled, pursued them with reckless hilarity. Jubilation rode upon his sword; his thrust was not only deadly but accompanied by exultation and laughter.

Sometimes there were cases of mistaken identity among his victims, but usually he attacked the right foes—the true enemies of his world and his philosophy. We know, for instance, that he believed in simplicity and moderation as a way of life. We know too that he believed in acting like a civilized person—that he believed in good manners. But good manners were not affected, artificial, elaborate, or highly conventionalized. Good manners were characterized by simplicity and moderation. Only stupid people acted as if they were otherwise:

> The precise domain of the gentleman lies in that region of the
> soul where morals seem to melt into aesthetics; it is bounded

52. "John Milton," *Spectator, 101* (Dec. 5, 1908), 933–4. Strachey praises Milton for not being cynical.

on one side by taste, and on the other by good feeling. It cannot exist without the instinct which determines immediately a whole universe of social relationships, and can habitually strike the exactly appropriate balance between humility and pride. Thus the most obvious of its outward characteristics is ease,—ease, which arises from a just respect for one's companions mingled with a just respect for oneself. "Gentleman gentleman," said a Maori chief to Bishop Selwyn, "never mind what he does, but piggy gentleman very particular." [53]

And Strachey never hesitated to expose the "piggy gentleman" in the light of the ridiculous.

Likewise his own belief in freedom and toleration made him quick to expose tyranny, conventionality, and intolerance hiding behind the masks of freedom and toleration. Furthermore, Strachey scoffed at the idea that the world had become more tolerant since the time of Galileo and that "free thought and free speech came to their own once and for all in the golden years of the nineteenth century." Instead intolerance merely shifted its concern from metaphysics to ethics; in the future, he added prophetically, it might become weary of ethics and shift to aesthetics.[54] And as for politics, nothing could be more ridiculous than the naive assumption that the Liberal party of 1914 in England actually stood for liberal principles.[55]

Many modern institutions had long since ceased to serve a useful purpose. Among these was nationalism, with its instrument of diplomacy. Strachey was a complete pacifist, and the basis of his pacifism was his belief that nationalism in the modern world was contrary to the dictates of both sanity and humanity. It was served and kept alive by politicians and diplomatists, little men in whose souls humanity had shriveled up to be replaced by caution and secretiveness and in whose conduct conventionality, fervid loyalty to outworn causes, fierceness, and lack of moderation were domi-

53. "A Mirror for Gentlefolks," *Spectator*, *101* (Oct. 24, 1908), 630-1.
54. "Avons-nous changé tout cela?" *Characters and Commentaries* (New York, Harcourt, Brace, 1933), pp. 152-4.
55. "Bonga-Bonga in Whitehall," *Characters and Commentaries*, pp. 162-7.

nant.[56] One trouble with the modern world was that realistic, practical-minded political leaders, "the master spirits in the matter-of-fact business of managing mankind," were too rarely "moved by philosophical ideals towards noble aims." But the days of the diplomatist were numbered; he would go when nationalism went, and the world would not put up with nationalism much longer.[57]

Today Strachey's attack on nationalism and its accompanying evils can still be approved as farsighted and sane. We may seriously question, however, his opinions concerning ethics and Christianity, and we are probably far more inclined to do so than the Edwardians were. We can understand why Strachey's generation reacted against the moral code of their fathers and mothers as they did. It was certainly in the eyes of the younger generation an exceedingly heavy-handed moral code which made little allowance for gaiety and individual freedom. Strachey and his friends were bright creatures with color on their wings who had found flight difficult in the thick air of the Victorian age. They discovered for themselves a thinner atmosphere filled with radiance and in this sphere acted in accordance with laws which were within themselves. But one may ask whether what served for them can serve for the whole structure of society; and one may discern the fact that even they were at times perplexed at the discovery of moral anarchy in their midst.

In his attack on Christianity Strachey was, of course, active in the tradition of Gibbon and Voltaire. He had also been greatly influenced, as we have seen, by his reading of Swinburne. Christianity as it displayed itself in the world around him was certainly not of

56. After Sir Edmund Gosse in a letter to the *Times Literary Supplement* (June 27, 1918, p. 301) had protested that Strachey had been unfair in his treatment of Lord Cromer in *Eminent Victorians,* Strachey replied in a letter to the same paper (July 4, 1918, pp. 313–14) to defend his treatment of Cromer and to condemn Cromer further as one the temper of whose mind was "essentially secretive, cautious, and diplomatic."

57. "A Diplomatist: Li Hung-Chang," *Characters and Commentaries,* pp. 219–20. First published in *War and Peace,* March 1918, pp. 208–10. Strachey also indicated the diplomatists of 1918 for being "the humble pupils of journalists," the essential characteristic of whose style and thought was speciousness. "Traps and Peace Traps," *War and Peace,* June 1918, pp. 269–70.

such a nature as to command his admiration. For he found Christianity in league with artificial, insincere conventionality; with useless, antiquated institutionalism; with nationalistic politics; with hypocritical commercialism; and with creeds which perpetuated superstition and defied reason. Even in its purer forms it subscribed to a mysticism which was contrary to all common sense. Yet even the average lay student discovers in Christ many of the very qualities which Strachey admired most: love of freedom, individualism, unconventionality, love of truth, simplicity, sensitiveness to beauty, justice, moderation—yes, Matthew Arnold's "sweet reasonableness." Most important of all, His radiant, unmistakable, transcendent humanity gives the surest evidence of His divinity. But Strachey was least of all a metaphysician with a tact for reconciling the earthy with the celestial. The celestial light of metaphysics simply blinded his secular mind. The earth was his abode; on it he responded with delight when he encountered the beauty of nature and art, when he chose his path and freely wandered through a vast forest of facts and ideas, and when day by day he beheld the incessant drama of ordinary mortals playing out their little roles— delectable human beings, delectable in their admirable characteristics and delectable in their foolishness. It is probable that the essential thing which Strachey missed in the life of Christ as it has been recorded was humor. He was much more happy when in the midst of his finite fellow creatures whose natures he found infinitely varied and inexhaustibly interesting; he was content to be with them.

Hence the good biographer was one who judged his subjects, not as they might appear before the throne of God but as they appeared in the midst of the activities which made up their short lives. How well did they use their limited time? How clearly did they realize their humanity proper, and how fully did they cultivate it? With such questions Strachey prepared his bed of Procrustes for various guests, not from malice or desire to torture but from his faith in the traditional humanistic doctrine which could suggest a means toward realizing true joy, comfort, and peace.

CHAPTER 3

Critic of Elizabethan Drama

THE CRITICAL SIDE of Lytton Strachey's mind, like his style, matured early. From first to last, his views on playwrights and plays were clear, definite, and remarkably consistent. His mind possessed a basis of criticism which guided him steadily as he dealt with highly varied plays and aspects of the drama and which prevented even the mask of anonymity behind which he usually worked in his early reviews from becoming a temptation leading him into capriciousness and inconsistency.

To Strachey both the creative process and the criticism which helps to make it understood were individualistic. His critical theory had much in common with that of the English Romantics in the early nineteenth century. He had, of course, great admiration for the eighteenth century and for Boileau; sometimes he wished that "there were a Boileau once more upon the earth—a Boileau who, with his reasonableness, his common sense, and his wit, would act as a corrective to the vague and wandering spirit which seems to have seized upon so much of the poetry of the present day." [1] But Boileau, in his own school and on his own ground, was "everywhere beaten . . . by no less a master than Pope." And Boileau fell far short of the perfect critic, particularly in "that most dubious and thorny region of speculation—aesthetic theory." For Boileau had made a fundamental error. "His error lay in supposing that the beauties of simplicity and reason were alone compatible with true feeling and sublimity; he did not understand that the elaborate might be splendid and that the fantastic might be lovely; he mis-

1. "The Admirable Boileau," *Spectator, 101* (Nov. 7, 1908), 735–6.

took a precept which was useful in his own age for a universal rule." [2] Strachey's was a catholic taste. He believed that the critic should praise only that which was truly excellent but that excellence took many forms and could be found in great variety. Furthermore, excellence could be discerned only by those gifted with divination. Strachey was quite ready to commend Swinburne for eschewing analysis and relying upon intuition in his criticism of Shakespeare.[3] He agreed with Coleridge that the creative and the critical powers might often be found dwelling together in the same person. "It is often carelessly assumed that the creative and the critical faculties are either actually antagonistic to one another, or so distinct as to be mutually exclusive; but the more the facts are examined, the more certain it appears that the contrary is the case. In England the great school of Dryden and the great school of Wordsworth both drew their strength from a profound and searching criticism." [4]

The trustworthy dramatic critic always remembered that good drama was art and that art was magic. "The essence of all art is the accomplishment of the impossible. This cannot be done, we say; and it *is* done. What has happened? A magician has waved his wand." [5] Hence, in an essay on "The Age of Spenser" Strachey wrote: "The secret springs of art cannot be sounded with a foot-rule." [6] Likewise, the critic of Milton should not "look up latitudes, nor search into history"; unless he had the power to "drive by the spirit sense," all his learning would be in vain. "The truth is that only a poet is fit to be Milton's lexicographer. The most accurate

2. *Ibid.*

3. "A Poet on Poets," *Spectator, 101* (Oct. 3, 1908), 502–3.

4. "The Age of Corneille," *Spectator, 102* (Jan. 30, 1909), 182–3, a review of Arthur Tilley's *From Montaigne to Molière*. This is one of many points on which Strachey differed in opinion with Matthew Arnold. Arnold, it will be remembered, had said in "The Function of Criticism at the Present Time" that the English Romantics had strong creative impulses but lacked the power of criticism.

5. *Pope*, the Leslie Stephen Lecture at Cambridge University for 1925 (Cambridge, Cambridge University Press, 1925), p. 25.

6. *Spectator, 98* (March 23, 1907), 457–8.

net of scholarship is too coarse a grain to catch his 'winged imaginations.' " [7]

This emphasis on drama as an art rather than a science appeared in Strachey's vigorous opposition to a plan proposed by William Archer and H. Granville Barker to establish a national theater, possibly as a memorial to Shakespeare. Strachey reviewed their book, *A National Theater: Scheme and Estimates,* in the *Spectator* for December 28, 1907, and attacked the proposal again in "The Shakespeare Memorial," *Spectator,* May 23, 1908. The drama, he said, was not "a dead thing to be pinned down and classified and docketed; it is a living creature, winged and wondrous, hovering inexplicably over magical flowers, and amenable to no laws but those of fancy. Such a phenomenon, it is easy to imagine, would not stay for long in the keeping of public trustees." [8] Strachey disliked institutional authority in any form whatsoever; it was particularly objectionable to him when it claimed the prerogative of judge, with fixed rules and extrinsic criteria, in the domain of the arts.

The good critic, Strachey said in agreement with Coleridge, must first of all have "that quality of sympathy without which all criticism is a vain and empty thing. A good critic is like a good talker— he must know the difficult art of 'bringing out' an author, of realizing his strong points, and of making him show himself at his very best." [9] Ultimately, the rank of the author should be determined

7. "Milton's Words," *Spectator,* 99 (Dec. 14, 1907), 991–2, a review of Laura E. Lockwood's *Lexicon to the English Poetical Works of John Milton.*

8. "L'art Administratif," *99,* 1093–4; *100,* 820–1. Strachey also attacked Arnold's belief that the English would profit from institutional authority such as that of the French Academy and quoted Milton in opposition: "The State shall be my governors, but not my critics." See also "A Victorian Critic," *Characters and Commentaries* (New York, Harcourt, Brace, 1933), p. 175. Sidney Lee, in *Shakespeare and the Modern Stage,* a book which appeared about a year before that of Archer and Barker, had proposed the idea of a national theater as a memorial to Shakespeare; and Strachey had attacked the idea in his review in the *Spectator.* See "Mr. Sidney Lee on Shakespeare," *Spectator,* 97 (Dec. 1, 1906), 887–8.

9. "French Poetry," *Spectator,* 99 (Dec. 21, 1907), 1051–2, a review of John C. Bailey's *The Claims of French Poetry.* Strachey objected vigorously to Bailey's unsympathetic treatment of Racine.

by these strong points, not by his weak ones or by qualities which he did not possess at all.[10]

Strachey believed, furthermore, that the performance of a play was a complex matter and that a valid judgment of what was essentially the "play" was not likely to be arrived at through a simple set of rules, particularly when those rules had reference to only one aspect of the play. He felt sure, for instance, that a play should not be judged exclusively on the basis of its story, or its philosophical ideas, or its costumes. Just as futile was the kind of dramatic criticism, such as he found in A. B. Walkley's *Drama and Life*, which discussed the play entirely in terms of the physical features of the stage and theater. "Where the old-fashioned critic could only see the art or the caprice of the dramatist, Mr. Walkley can only see the four walls of the playhouse; and the history of the drama to him is little more than a history of the results which mechanical forces have brought about. Pre-eminent among these was the 'platform-stage.' " [11]

Actually, no criticism ever concerned itself less than his with the mechanical side of theatrical production. The shape of the stage, the size of the theater, the position of the curtain, the scenery, the costumes, the gestures—these things were at best merely the means to an end; and his concern was with the end itself. The real function of the dramatic critis was, to him, that of penetrating to and seizing upon the peculiar essence of the play and of displaying it in a light that would reveal its full delight and significance. "The true business of the critic is to discuss, not the story of the play, but its subject—which is an entirely different matter. He must ask himself the question: 'What is the central interest of this piece?' And though the answer is often enough a difficult and a complex one, when it is once made the way toward a correct appreciation will be opened out." [12] This principle of criticism allied itself with other strong characteristics of Strachey's mind to which it was related—to his instinct for economy and to his habit of scrupulous selection.

10. *Pope,* pp. 26–7.
11. "Mr. Walkley on the Drama," *Spectator, 99* (Nov. 16, 1907), 776–7.
12. "Three New Plays," *Spectator, 100* (June 6, 1908), 899–900.

Strachey's delight in Racine, expressed in the excellent piece of criticism which he contributed to the *New Quarterly* in June 1908, naturally suggested to him the points of contrast between the French dramatist and the Elizabethans. During the summer of 1908 he read C. E. Vaughan's *Types of Tragic Drama* and Ashley H. Thorndike's *Tragedy* and dealt with the two books in the *Spectator* for August 22, 1908, in one of his best reviews. In it we find references to Sophocles, Racine, and Shakespeare.

> It is strange to reflect that, until quite lately, the notion that there might be more than one species of literary excellence was almost unknown to criticism. The result was almost as absurd as if half the cooks in the world were to declare that all good soup must be thick, and the other half that no soup could possibly be tolerable unless it was clear.

> An English reader who turns to the tragedies of Racine from those of the great Elizabethans is like a man who comes suddenly into a little drawing room lighted up by candles, after a walk among forests and mountains illuminated by the setting sun. It is but natural that he should hastily judge his new surroundings to be tawdry and uninteresting; but let him read Professor Vaughan. . . . He shows us that, while the beauty of the sunset and the mountains is beyond dispute, the room we have entered is exquisitely furnished and admirably proportioned, and that the talk there is of the best.

Strachey asserted that the essential difference between the classical and the romantic conception of drama—between Sophocles and Shakespeare—was that the later plays were totally lacking in the quality of concentration. Every play must contain a crisis, but "in *Oedipus Rex* the crisis is the whole of the play. . . . How different is the dramatic method of the typical Elizabethan tragedy!" [13] Strachey could have mentioned *Othello* here, one of his

13. "Tragedy Old and New," *101*, 266. Strachey's comment on Ibsen here was that his work was "at its best . . . a brilliant experiment rather than a final revelation." André Maurois has written of Strachey: "He was the only English critic who ever understood Racine, and speaking generally, all French literature was familiar to him." Quoted in Cyril Clemens, *Lytton*

favorite plays, but to have done so would have spoiled the argument. Furthermore, his point was in the main well taken in its reference to Sophocles, Racine, and Shakespeare. The fusion of romanticism with classical concentration in *Othello* is simply one of Shakespeare's miracles.

Strachey's admiration for Racine clearly did not prevent him from having the Englishman's natural enthusiasm for Shakespeare. From early boyhood, when he memorized songs from Shakespeare's plays, to the last months of his life, when he was composing the unfinished essay on *Othello* and planning other essays on the great Elizabethan dramatist, he found him a perennial source of pleasure and wonder. Strachey's opinions on literature usually achieved distinction through their combination of intense delight with independence of mind, acute perceptiveness, and good sense. These qualities went into the making of his opinions on Shakespeare as he read and thought about him over a long period of years.

On June 4, 1904, he reviewed *The Praise of Shakespeare: An English Anthology,* compiled by C. E. Hughes.[14] Here, as usual, he spoke of the creative process as fundamentally mysterious. "The truth is that the genius of an artist shows itself as much in what he does not do as in what he does; every step in the mysterious process of artistic production is guided by an inspiration which it is impossible to control; and Pope, no less than Shakespeare, 'grew immortal in his own despite.' "[15] As much as he valued craftsmanship, he took the side of Shakespeare against Ben Jonson. "Had Shakespeare 'blotted' his lines as carefully as Ben Jonson wished, who knows how many precious months might have been absorbed in the process? And who would be willing to purchase a whole multitude of formal perfections, such as, let us say, the adjustment of the

---

Strachey (Webster Groves, Mo., International Mark Twain Society, 1942), Foreword. John Russell has declared, "Strachey and Maurice Baring were the first modern Englishmen to appreciate Racine, or rather to appropriate him as a constant companion" ("Lytton Strachey," *Horizon, 15* [Feb. 1947], 115). See also the *Times Literary Supplement,* Feb. 1, 1912, p. 44; and the London *Times,* May 18, 1922, p. 16.

14. "The Praise of Shakespeare," *Spectator, 92,* 881–2.
15. *Ibid.*

time-system in *Othello,* by the sacrifice of the character of Caliban
or the songs of Ariel?" Strachey added that in Shakespeare's greatest
plays "the action is still almost always simple" but that it was simple
"not from childishness but from elemental forces." He observed
that the contrast was complete "between the simplicity of his situations and the subtlety of his characters." But Hughes's anthology
was too full of praises; "orthodox eighteenth-century fault-finding"
was not adequately represented in it. It should also have included
a "judicious selection from Continental critics."

In "Shakespeare's Final Period," published in the *Independent
Review* for August 1904, but read before the Sunday Essay Society
at Cambridge almost a year before, Strachey expressed his regret
that Shakespeare, in his last plays, had turned his back upon "those
stupendous creations in character" in his great tragedies and had
written in such a way that character merely served as a miserable
prop for "the gorgeous clothing of his rhetoric." He vigorously
attacked Dowden's theory that Shakespeare's mind was serene and
tranquil in his final period and that he in some inexplicable way
passed from the writing of such a cynical comedy as *Measure for
Measure* to the composition of plays which showed that his mind
and spirit had come "to blue skies, to young ladies, and to general
forgiveness." There were dreams in these plays, but there were
also nightmares. The character of Caliban, for instance—was it
brought into being by a mind entirely sweet-tempered and quietly
philosophical? When Caliban addressed Prospero, was it not somewhat like Job addressing God? Actually, when we read these later
plays, we could not resist the conclusion that Shakespeare was getting bored—"bored with people, bored with real life, bored with
drama, bored, in fact, with everything except poetry and poetical
dreams." [16]

Strachey discussed Shakespeare's sonnets in a *Spectator* article of
February 4, 1905. He hoped very much, he said, that the mystery
of the sonnets might be solved, because the solution might bring
"a prize of extraordinary value—nothing less than a true insight

16. *3,* 405–18. "The critics who derided Strachey for scoffing at the benignity
of *The Tempest* are themselves legitimate butts for derision" (Clifford Bower-
Shore, *Lytton Strachey: An Essay* [London, Fenland Press, 1933], p. 79).

into the most secret recesses of the thoughts and feelings of perhaps
the greatest man who ever lived." He also said that the weightiest
evidence favored the belief that "W. H." was not the Earl of South-
ampton, as Sidney Lee contended, but William Herbert, Earl of
Pembroke, as H. C. Beeching maintained. And Strachey made his
own addition to Beeching's argument by quoting from Clarendon's
delightful description of Pembroke—"the most universally loved
and esteemed of any man of that age." Yet even the evidence favor-
ing Pembroke was inconclusive. The question was of secondary
importance, after all; Shakespeare's poetry was the essential thing.[17]

The completeness of Strachey's surrender to Shakespeare was
attested to in his review of J. W. Gray's *Shakespeare's Marriage,
Spectator,* July 29, 1905. "For us who have been born and bred, as
it were, under the influence of the Shakespearean star, the power
and splendor of that heavenly body come so much as a matter of
course that it is difficult to realize them. Shakespeare, like the atmosphere, enters into us so easily and naturally that we are hardly
aware of the process. It is only by holding our breath that we begin
to understand how necessary breathing is; and the best way of
bringing before our minds the true magnitude of our debt to
Shakespeare is to imagine for a moment or two that he never existed." Here Strachey also presented an interesting argument to
refute Gray's opinion that Shakespeare cared little for his reputation as a writer but merely sought to get money by catering to the
public and amusing it.

> Everyone knows that the dramatic work of the great ma-
> jority of Shakespeare's contemporaries was habitually marred
> by grossnesses which appealed directly and strongly to the bad
> taste of Elizabethan audiences. On Mr. Gray's theory, we
> surely ought to find these blemishes scattered as profusely in
> the plays of Shakespeare as in those of Fletcher or Middleton.
> But this is precisely what we do not find. Errors of taste there
> may be, but there is not a trace of that systematic vulgarization
> of thought and word which we know was the surest road in
> those days to popular success. It is difficult to resist the in-

17. "Shakespeare's Sonnets," *94,* 177–8.

ference that Shakespeare deliberately avoided that sort of applause and that sort of profit which was incompatible with the
nobler interests of art.[18]

Strachey reviewed two books on Sir Walter Scott in the *Speaker*
for October 20, 1906. One of these was a biography by Andrew
Lang, a book which Strachey found full of faults. Among them was
the extreme to which Lang carried his comparisons between Scott
and Shakespeare. "That Scott was the creator of a vast throng of
living characters is obviously true; but that these characters possessed every variety of nature, humor, and temperament is no less
obviously false . . . Scott's characters are successful in proportion
as they are simple." [19]

Sidney Lee's *Shakespeare and the Modern Stage, with Other
Essays* was the subject of Strachey's *Spectator* review on December
1, 1906. Although he found the book "full of matter, lucidly ar-
ranged and carefully substantiated," he also found that its style, in
its effort to avoid rhetoric, had gone much too far in the direction
of the commonplace, the frigid, and the dull. There were even
more serious faults. Lee had opened up the important subject of
the history of French opinion concerning Shakespeare and had
dealt with it in a very inadequate fashion. His discussion of Voltaire was particularly unsatisfactory. Strachey wrote:

> Is it quite fair . . . to say that Voltaire's "method of teaching
> Shakespeare to his countrymen" was "characteristically cyni-
> cal"? It is true that at first glance the violent invectives of
> Voltaire's old age stand out in striking contrast with the
> tributes of his earlier years; but the more the facts are ex-
> amined, the more obvious it becomes that Voltaire's attitude
> towards Shakespeare was really consistent throughout his
> life. His view was a simple one. Shakespeare was a writer of
> great force, but absolutely devoid of taste. At the beginning
> of his career, when Shakespeare was unknown in France, it
> was only natural that he should wish to impress his country-
> men with the merits of the English genius. To explain his

18. "Shakespeare's Marriage," *95*, 153–4.
19. "Not by Lockhart," *15*, 82–3.

82   LYTTON STRACHEY

subsequent change of front by imputing to him a vulgar jealousy of Shakespeare's fame is an explanation which, though it satisfied Horace Walpole, should not have satisfied Mr. Lee. Voltaire's anger was aroused, not by a fear of his own laurels, but by a genuine disgust for what seemed to him a silly craze over a foreign barbarian. The genius of the barbarian was neither here nor there; he was a barbarian, and to place him above the masters of French drama was to commit an inexcusable outrage upon literary taste.[20] And, from his own point of view, Voltaire was certainly in the right. As Mr. Lee points out, the worship which eighteenth-century Frenchmen bestowed on Shakespeare was indiscriminating in the highest degree. . . . Voltaire was more honest; he started from the same premises, and arrived at a very different conclusion: Shakespeare was a preposterous mountebank, whom it was dangerous to imitate and foolish to applaud. And the conclusion was logical; it was only the premises which were mistaken.[21]

In this review also Strachey attacked, possibly for the first time, the proposal to set up a state theater for the proper production of Shakespeare's plays. Sidney Lee favored the proposal and, Strachey said, neglected the arguments against it. He was much too ready to assume that what would be suitable for Molière and for French audiences would also be suitable for Shakespeare and for English audiences.

Mr. Lee wishes to see Shakespeare enthroned in a London playhouse just as Molière is enthroned at the Theatre Français. But the parallel suggests what is really the fundamental objection to Mr. Lee's scheme. The plays of Molière must from their very nature be acted in one way, and in one way alone; the conditions of their performance are determined not only by centuries of tradition, but by the universal agreement of French artists and critics; they are in short, "classical"

20. Strachey once wrote: "Tragedy cannot flourish without a little barbarism at its roots" ("Tragedy Old and New").
21. "Mr. Sidney Lee on Shakespeare," 97, 887–8.

plays. But the plays of Shakespeare are no less obviously romantic; they are woven upon a texture of poetry, of imagination, and of colored atmosphere which is amenable to no restriction and no law; and to reduce them to a uniformity of presentment is to run grave risks of committing "a fallacy in proportion." But it is clear that this is precisely what an official theater would tend to do. It would give us a Shakespeare more cultivated perhaps than any we have seen, but a Shakespeare in uniform. And is a Shakespeare in uniform really Shakespeare at all?

Lee's two essays on Shakespeare's philosophy were the least successful in the book. "The truth is that Mr. Lee, like all searchers after a Shakespearean philosophy, has been unable to avoid the dilemma of saying either too little or too much." Strachey quoted Arnold: "We ask and ask. Thou smilest and art still"; and Landor:

> In poetry there is but one supreme,
> Though there are many angels round his throne,
> Mighty and beauteous; but his face is hid.[22]

On June 22, 1907, Strachey reviewed T. R. Lounsbury's *The First Editors of Shakespeare*. Lounsbury's chief interest was the controversy between Pope and Theobald and their comparative merits as editors. For Theobald, Strachey had almost nothing except praise. "Theobald's edition appeared nine years after Pope's, and at once revolutionized the study of Shakespeare. His great achievement is that he introduced the methods of science into literary criticism. . . . But this was not all. He combined with the scrupulous care of a scholar the flashing insight of a genius. . . . [He was] the greatest of Shakespearean scholars." But, Strachey regretted, "The malignity of Pope was perpetuated by the carelessness of Johnson." [23]

A. S. G. Canning's *Shakespeare Studied in Six Plays* was the subject of a brief review by Strachey in the *Spectator* for October

22. *Ibid.*
23. "Shakespeare's First Editors," *Spectator*, *98* (June 22, 1907), 979–80.

5, 1907. Canning's essays, Strachey said, were conscientious but nothing more. Canning had "no conception of the subtle art with which Shakespeare had succeeded in suggesting the real mainspring of Iago's villainy—a hidden and insatiable love of evil for itself." [24] *Othello* was still in Strachey's mind when about a month later in a review of G. O. Trevelyan's edition of Macaulay's *Marginal Notes* he touched on Macaulay's reading of Shakespeare.

> He was not satisfied with praising a thing; he must declare it to be superior to every other thing in the world. . . . One would like to know what he thought of *Othello,* which, Sir George Trevelyan tells us, "Macaulay reckoned the best play extant in any language." But there are no notes upon *Othello.* "It may well be," says Sir George, "that he had ceased reading it because he knew the whole of it by heart." No doubt Macaulay's memory was equal to that feat; but may we not suppose that there was another reason for his silence? Even Macaulay, perhaps, had exhausted his vocabulary of admiration, and had simply nothing left to say.[25]

Embedded in Strachey's essay on Thomas Lovell Beddoes (*New Quarterly,* November 1907), whom Strachey praised as "the last Elizabethan," can be found an interesting observation on *Hamlet.* The tragedy of Beddoes' life, Strachey said, "like Hamlet's, was the tragedy of an overpowerful will—a will so strong as to recoil upon itself, and fall into indecision. It is easy for a weak man to be decided—there is so much to make him so; but a strong man, who can do anything, sometimes leaves everything undone." [26]

In "Shakespeariana," a review of various Elizabethan documents and some sources of Shakespeare's plays, *Spectator,* April 4, 1908, Strachey commended the editors and publishers of such works for what they were doing to throw light on the work of the great dramatist. But he added: "After all our prying, the

24. "Shakespeare and Water," *99,* 462. In the title of this review, Strachey implied that Shakespeare was Shakespeare but Canning's unconvincing criticism was water.

25. "Macaulay's Marginalia," *Spectator, 99* (Nov. 16, 1907), 743.

26. "The Last Elizabethan," *Books and Characters,* pp. 263.

qualities of his art remain as those of the magic ring in the
Arabian romances which in the twinkling of an eye made beautiful everything it touched." [27]

Strachey's "Shakespeare on the Stage," *Spectator,* April 25,
1908, was not a review; it was a fullfledged effort to write a critical
article. Strachey used as his starting point a discussion of Charles
Lamb's well-known objections to seeing Shakespeare acted. "It
is difficult not to sympathize with those fastidious people—so
great a critic as Charles Lamb was one of them—who refuse to
see Shakespeare acted. . . . Yet, when all is said and done, objections of this kind strike the hardened playgoer as somewhat
trivial and somewhat irrelevant; it is as if one were to complain
to a foxhunter that riding was intolerable because of the jolts.
Jolts or no jolts, people, as a matter of fact, continue to ride, and
whatever the susceptibilities of certain critics, the plays of Shakespeare continue to be acted." It was unfortunate, however, Strachey
said, that in modern times "the whole burden of the interpretation
of Shakespeare falls upon the actors" and that the literary critic
had deserted them. Shakespeare did not think of particular actors;
he thought of the play as a whole. Among modern actors of Shakespeare, Beerbohm Tree in particular left much to be desired;
like many other actors, he preferred what was stagy to "the image
of life itself." Strachey also strongly disliked the way in which
modern actors spoke Shakespeare's words. The point was extremely
important to him:

> Their object seems to be to buoy up the meaning of words by
> all the stage devices at their command—by exaggerated gesture
> and ceaseless movement, by forced laughter and preposterous
> sighings and undercurrents of incidental music, by an intoler-
> able slowness of enunciation, and by an intonation of the
> blank verse more barbarous than can be described. These are
> merely the refuges of weakness, like the attempts of a bad
> writer to obtain emphasis by underlinings and italic type. After
> all, Shakespeare can stand on his own merit. . . . What a
> relief it is when for a moment or two there is peace upon the

27. *100,* 536–7.

stage, and we begin to hear the words and to follow the thoughts of the highest of poets and the most profound of philosophers.[28]

A few weeks later Strachey reviewed the Malone Society reprint of the old play on King Lear. Shakespeare's *King Lear,* he commented, was, "in one sense at least, a strikingly unoriginal play." Then he added: "Indeed, the greatest works of art appear to demand, like Kings in a procession, a train of noble forerunners to prepare their way; and genius only reaches its highest manifestations when it has, so to speak, a ready-made mould to flow into." Turning to Coleridge's opinion that when Shakespeare had Gloucester's eyes plucked out on the stage he imposed on humanity something more horrible than it could bear, he disagreed. Shakespeare was justified, for Gloucester's suffering "was a contributing means toward a general artistic purpose—to make our flesh creep" and furthermore his kind of suffering provided a foil to Lear's inward suffering.[29] It should be recalled here that many years later, when Strachey was writing *Elizabeth and Essex,* he described in the most gory detail the execution of Essex and the hanging, castrating, drawing, and quartering of Dr. Lopez.

"Milton," *Spectator,* July 4, 1908, an article suggested by the celebration at Cambridge of the tercentenary of the poet's birth, drew some comparisons with Shakespeare. Milton, Strachey declared, voicing his usual opinion, was the supreme artist of our race. His imagination, however, was very different from Shakespeare's. "His imagination, within its own province, was supreme; but it was, so to speak, a material imagination, perpetually concerned with objects which, however vast and however splendid, still remained objects of sense. Between his imagination and that of Shakespeare, with its lightning flashes into the heart of man and the mystery of the universe, what a gulf is fixed!" The strikingly subjective nature of much of Milton's poetry suggested another point of contrast with Shakespeare. "If he had taken himself less seriously, perhaps he never would have written *Paradise Lost;*

28. *100,* 669–70.
29. "King Lear," *Spectator, 100* (May 23, 1908), 830–1.

. . . but who can help regretting that he took himself as seriously as he did. One wonders what Shakespeare would have said to some of the autobiographical references in Milton's prose works. But . . . we must, after all, take great men as we find them." [30] In both life and art, detachment was to Strachey one of the loftiest ideals and one of the most difficult to achieve. Here, as in so much else, Shakespeare's accomplishment was almost beyond belief. At the other extreme in Strachey's thinking was Byron, who had none of Shakespeare's detachment and none of Milton's art.

Dr. Johnson as a critic of Shakespeare was the subject of Strachey's review on August 1, 1908. The review treated a book on the subject by Strachey's old friend and teacher, Professor Walter Raleigh. Strachey the critic was at his best here—with his sense of justice, his skill in glancing at a tangled mass of facts and discovering those which were truly important, and his sure insight, which enabled him to illuminate both the student of Johnson and the student of Shakespeare. "The greatness of Johnson— apart from his mastery of English—lies entirely in the breadth and sanity of his outlook upon life. . . . But . . . life and literature are different things. Johnson was not, in essence, a critic of literature, but a critic of life; and it is this fact that accounts alike for the merits and the defects of his treatment of Shakespeare. . . . His limitation . . . becomes obvious immediately he passes from the discussion of man and things to the consideration of poetry." Again and again Johnson demonstrated an "incapacity to judge of the propriety of words—an incapacity which he seems to have shared with most of the critics of the eighteenth century. . . . Johnson did not understand Shakespeare's bold and imaginative use of words." Shakespeare's great tragic scenes moved Johnson tremendously but "through their humanity and not their poetry. It is hardly an exaggeration to say that Johnson's criticisms are such as might have been made by a foreigner of great ability and immense experience who was acquainted with Shakespeare solely in a prose translation." [31]

30. *101*, 9–10.
31. "Shakespeare on Johnson," *Spectator, 101* (Aug. 1, 1908), 164–5. Raleigh's book was *Johnson on Shakespeare.*

Several weeks later Strachey reviewed *The Shakespeare Apoc-rypha,* edited by C. F. Tucker Brooke. In general, he liked Brooke's editing, but he objected to some matters pertaining to format and to some of the editor's opinions. "The vagaries of Elizabethan printers are as a rule by no means calculated to assist towards a proper understanding of the text; they are mere stum-bling-blocks, and the unaccustomed reader soon wearies of strug-gling through the crags and boulders which in the present volume beset his path." As for Tucker Brooke's opinions, one in particular left him unconvinced—the belief that Shakespeare had written some pages in his own autograph in an extant play on Sir Thomas More. But this book impressed upon him once more the variety and the magnificence of the Elizabethan's accomplishment in the drama. "Critics—and especially German critics—have been slow to realize both the extent and the quality of the dramatic talent of that wonderful age." [32]

He repeated this opinion in his review of Swinburne's *The Age of Shakespeare* on October 3. "An Elizabethan play, whatever else it may contain, will certainly be overflowing with vitality. . . . The Elizabethan dramatists have not yet come into their king-dom." He also called Swinburne a Platonist among critics and commended his quick, intuitional method. It was refreshing at a time when "infinite analysis and universal sympathy" were the rule in criticism.[33]

On January 30, 1908, Strachey entitled his review of H. C. Beeching's *William Shakespeare, Player, Playmaker and Poet* "The Shakespeare Problem." The problem concerned nothing less than the identity of Shakespeare. Strachey praised Beeching for com-pletely refuting, in thirty-four pages, George Greenwood's con-tention, laboriously argued in a book of 500 pages, that the player Shakespeare and the poet could not have been the same person. But Strachey added:

> Full of interest as these pages are, most readers will probably
> be of opinion that so fine and scholarly a critic had done too
> much honor to a "weary, stale, flat, and unprofitable" theme.

32. "The Shakespeare Apocrypha," *Spectator, 101* (Aug. 29, 1908), 298–9.
33. "A Poet on Poets," *Spectator, 101* (Oct. 3, 1908), 502–3.

. . . It is no more incredible that a half-educated lad at Stratford should have grown up into the author of *Lear* and *Othello* than that an apothecary's assistant should have written *Hyperion,* or that an artillery subaltern should have become the ruler of Europe. The true miracle is not that Shakespeare's plays were written by Shakespeare, but that they were written at all; and that, fortunately, even Mr. Greenwood cannot dispute.

Beeching, however, emphasized "the allied graces of gentleness and manliness" as he had found them dominant in Shakespeare. To Strachey, this sounded a little too much like the benignity and serenity which Dowden had found in Shakespeare's final period. "Surely the two most obvious characteristics of Shakespeare's genius," he wrote, "have been missed—its immense complexity and its passionate force." [34]

Strachey became less and less the reviewer after 1909 as he gave more and more of his time, first to *Landmarks in French Literature,* and then to his later books. The main body of his Shakespearean criticism is to be found in the reviews and articles which he wrote before 1910. But he continued to read and reread Shakespeare through the years and to express opinions about him in his various writings after that date. In "Voltaire and England," contributed to the *Edinburgh Review* of October 1914, he returned to the subject of Voltaire's attack on Shakespeare. Voltaire was at his best, Strachey observed, in his comments on Newton and at his worst in his comments on Shakespeare. The latter "merely afford a striking example of the singular contradiction in Voltaire's nature which made him a revolutionary in intellect and kept him a high Tory in taste." He continued: "Never was such speculative audacity combined with such aesthetic timidity; it is as if he had reserved all his superstition for matters of art. From his account of Shakespeare, it is clear that he had never dared to open his eyes and frankly look at what he should see before him. . . . To the true significance of Shakespeare's genius he remained utterly blind." [35]

34. *Spectator, 102,* 185.

35. *200,* 392–411. Reprinted in *Books and Characters* (see p. 138 for the references here).

In 1918 J. A. R. Marriott published a book entitled *English History in Shakespeare* in which he attempted to prove that the evidence of the plays made it clear that Shakespeare's patriotism was unlimited and unqualified. Strachey reviewed the book for *War and Peace* in July. All the horrors of the first World War and all the evils which it had perpetrated in the name of patriotism were in his mind as he wrote. He objected both to Marriott's scholarship and to the unthinking kind of patriotism which he had assigned to Shakespeare.[36]

In "Shakespeare at Cambridge," contributed to the *Athenaeum* for June 20, 1919, Strachey praised a performance of *Henry IV, Part I* which he had seen at Cambridge shortly before. Although the play had been put on by the undergraduate Marlow Society, Strachey was very much pleased to find the acting devoid of artificiality and the emphasis where he believed that it should always be—on the words. "The actors at Cambridge were obviously amateurs in the fullest sense of the term. They had never learned to act, and therefore their acting had the charm of unself-consciousness—the charm of primitive art and the drawing and poetry of children." He spoke of his delight at hearing "the blank verse of Shakespeare spoken unaffectedly and with the intonation of civilized English" and at a demonstration of the fact that, "given a good delivery of the verse, the interest of drama and character automatically followed." The undergraduates allowed Shakespeare to do most of the work, as the good actor always should. Unfortunately, however, the student who took the part of Hotspur failed; someone had taught him how to "act." "The result was inevitable. A thick veil of all the elocutionary arts and graces—points, gestures, exaggerations, and false emphases—was thrown over the words of Shakespeare, and in the process Hotspur vanished." [37]

When Strachey's friend G. H. W. Rylands published a book called *Words and Poetry* in 1928, Strachey contributed the Introduction. Here he returned to the subject of what he considered the decadence of Shakespeare's later plays. In these, he said, the

36. "The Claims of Patriotism," *Characters and Commentaries,* p. 231.
37. *Characters and Commentaries,* pp. 237–8.

characters had grown unindividual and unreal, but the words had remained "more tremendously, more exquisitely alive than ever." Shakespeare had become the slave of words.[38]

In Strachey's unfinished essay on *Othello,* composed in 1931 a few months before his death, he contrasted this play with *Hamlet.* *Hamlet* was a vast achievement, romantic, metaphysical, complicated, at times almost a psychological treatise and at other times a novel. Shakespeare intended that *Othello,* on the other hand, should be simple. "It should avoid philosophical implications and spiritual mysteries; it should depend for its effect upon force, intensity and concentration." Shakespeare's method may have owed much to the *Oedipus Tyrannus* of Sophocles, which he could have read in a Latin translation. But Sophocles' play is primarily concerned with "a man who deliberately discovers a horror," Shakespeare's with a man who "is gradually deluded into believing a horror—a horror which is a figment." Perhaps the most interesting comment in this essay is concerned with the opinion that Iago had no motives except the love of evil for its own sake. Strachey had, as we have seen, expressed this opinion before. He knew, of course, that Coleridge and others had held it before him and that it was controversial. The question for him to deal with, therefore, was one that he had never found answered, namely, just why it was that the dramatist should create such an inhuman monster. In Cinthio's story, Shakespeare's source, Strachey reminded us, Iago had had a very real and powerful motive: he too loved Desdemona. Why did Shakespeare deliberately discard a highly convincing motive with which he had already been provided?

> The tragedy must be enormous, and unrelieved. But there is one eventuality that might, in some degree at any rate, mitigate the atrocity of the story. If Iago had been led to cause this disaster, by his love for Desdemona, in that very fact would lie some sort of comfort; the tragedy would have been brought about by a motive not only comprehensible but in a sense sympathetic; the hero's passion and the villain's would

38. *Ibid.,* p. 287.

be the same. Let it be granted, then, that the completeness of the tragedy would suffer if its origin lay in Iago's love for Desdemona; therefore let that motive be excluded from Iago's mind. The question immediately presents itself—in that case, for what reason are we to suppose that Iago acted as he did? The whole story depends upon his plot, which forms the machinery of the action; yet, if the Desdemona impulsion is eliminated, what motive for his plot can there be? Shakespeare supplied the answer to this question with one of the very greatest strokes of his genius. By an overwhelming effort of creation he summoned up out of the darkness a psychological portent that was exactly fitted to the requirements of the tragic situation with which he was dealing, and endowed it with reality. He determined that Iago should have no motive at all. He conceived of a monster, whose wickedness should lie far deeper than anything that could be explained by a motive—the very essence of whose being should express itself in the machinations of malignity. This creature might well suppose himself to have a motive; he might well explain his purposes both to himself and to his confederate; but his explanations should contradict each other; he should put forward first one motive, and then another, and then another still; so that, while he himself would be only half-aware of the falsity of his self-analysis, to the audience it would be clear; the underlying demonic impulsion would be manifest as the play developed, it would be seen to be no common affair of love and jealousy, but a tragedy conditioned by something purposeless, profound, and terrible; and, when the moment of revelation came, the horror that burst upon the hero would be as inexplicably awful as evil itself.[39]

After another sentence the essay on *Othello* breaks off. Did Strachey intend to suggest further that in this tragedy of delusion an Iago whose evil was so powerful that it recoiled upon and de-

39. *Ibid.*, pp. 289 ff. In a letter dated August 23, 1931, Strachey wrote: "I've begun a thing on Othello. It's fiendishly difficult to do, as it's all solid argument—and is perhaps rather mad; but I shall try to finish it."

luded itself was the most appropriate villain to place beside a hero who was also deluded but who, possessing both magnificent goodness and magnificent strength, could be destroyed only by such a delusion as unmitigated evil might provide? We cannot know. But the quality of this essay and of many of the observations which Strachey made upon Shakespeare causes us to realize that we suffered a real loss when death prevented him from writing the other essays on the dramatist which he had planned. The truly helpful and trustworthy critic of Shakespeare does not impose theories upon him in order to provide us with new and startling interpretations. Instead, he reads and rereads the plays in order to learn to recognize the ways of the great dramatist's mind. It may be said of Strachey that throughout his life his own mind, markedly independent as it was, grew more and more into the mind of Shakespeare and made its home in that spacious domain. It is significant that he could do so, without alienation and without servility, for it suggests that Shakespeare does not deny his critics, any more than he does the characters in his plays, the prerogatives of free individualism.

We know that Strachey also enjoyed and admired the other Elizabethans and that he believed that, in spite of all the efforts made by the elder Colman, by Hazlitt, by Lamb, by Rossetti, by Swinburne, and others to bring them into favor, they had not yet gained the esteem that they deserved.

On June 20, 1908, he reviewed Schelling's *Elizabethan Drama, 1558–1642* for the *Spectator*. He could not accept Schelling's suggestion that the "ground-note in the concert of the Elizabethan drama" lay in realism and the reproduction of contemporary life on the stage. The inner spirit of the action in an Elizabethan play, Strachey maintained, belonged, "not to the real world at all, but to a world of strange imagination and mysterious romance." He went further:

> In fact, the Elizabethans when they were most themselves turned their backs upon realism, and rushed towards the extraordinary, the disordered, and the sublime, so that if one wished to sum up their most essential qualities in a single

word, "extravagant" would probably come nearest to the
truth. Their extravagance was of course the extravagance of
greatness; it was based on strength and knowledge, and it
was controlled by the high necessities of art. An Elizabethan
tragedian worked wildly, not as a madman, but as one inspired. In his reckless disregard of convention, his supreme
determination to achieve his end by any means, however
peculiar or however absurd, he resembled the great Italian
painter who, in the access of his inspiration, seized upon the
broom with which his servant was sweeping his studio and
finished his masterpiece with that.[40]

There was much in Elizabethan drama, however, which Strachey
did not admire. Plays which revealed a great dependence on the
pastoral tradition, for instance, moved him very little, if at all.
Comus he could enjoy only for the sake of its lovely poetry. In
a review of W. W. Greg's *Pastoral Poetry and Pastoral Drama*
he made a real effort to understand the appeal which the pastoral
tradition had for the Elizabethans and their predecessors, but he
was compelled to admit that he found it virtually impossible to
respond to it with any degree of pleasure.

> For us, who can hardly conceive of any art which is not the
> expression of an individual mind, the point of view of the
> pastoral writer is peculiarly difficult to understand. His first
> duty was to be unoriginal. . . . Contemporary audiences pos-
> sessed a clue to their signification which we are without.
> They saw them set in an atmosphere of traditional beauty;
> they found in them a whole world of endearing reminiscences
> and familiar delights. The jilted shepherd, the bewitched
> shepherdess, the cruel seducer, the faithful lovers—these were
> magic symbols working long trains of memory and vision and
> thought, stretching backward and ramifying outward through
> a hundred pleasant channels, from yesterday's play and last
> year's romance to the Spanish knights of Montemayor and
> the lovely ladies of Tasso, to the dreams of Sennazzaro and
> Petrarch, to Virgil, and to the wooded uplands of Sicily.[41]

40. *100*, 975-6.
41. "The Pastoral," *Spectator, 97* (July 28, 1906), 132-3.

Euphuism, likewise, may have delighted the Elizabethans and may have been revived to some extent and with some degree of effectiveness by Dr. Johnson, but it certainly was not for people living in the twentieth century. "Euphuism, no one can doubt, is a dead thing rigged out in antiquated raiment." [42]

John Lyly himself had had some merit as a playwright, but very little in his work was still alive. In 1904 John Dover Wilson won the Harness Prize at Cambridge with a treatise on Lyly, which he soon after published. Strachey reviewed it in the *Speaker*. He called it "a thoroughly scholarly piece of work" and said that it had, further, "two negative virtues which are too rarely present in modern critical essays—it contains no irrelevance and no bad taste." Wilson, however, had laid far too great a stress upon Lyly's influence upon English literature. The future of English prose stemmed, not from *Euphues* as Wilson had contended but from Sidney's *Arcadia*. Neither did Lyly's efforts to tighten up the structure of the drama have much influence on later Elizabethans. When we think of the loose construction of most Elizabethan plays, Strachey said, Lyly's influence here was merely "of the kind that a doctor has when he kills his patient." Actually, "the essence of Lyly's drama lay not in its construction, but in its dialogue"; and to this he cheerfully sacrificed character, intrigue, and action. "Lyly was not the discoverer of a new Pacific; he was the explorer of a blind alley. . . . For what other writer is there who is at once so youthful, so happy, so ridiculous, and so infinitely dead?" Yet the youthfulness, which Wilson somehow had failed to find, was important. It did something to preserve Lyly. "It is this quality which gives charm to his lyrics, which puts something almost like life into one or two of his dramatic monologues, and which, for all the portentous mass of rococo ornament overlying it, pervades the pages of *Euphues*. Indeed, the very rigidity of his decoration is a sign of youth. He is stiff and formal as a schoolboy is stiff and formal when he goes into high collars and begins to be a gentleman." [43]

"The true Columbus of the Elizabethan age was Christopher Marlowe." In a review of the first volume of J. J. Jusserand's *A*

42. *Ibid.*
43. *13* (Dec. 9, 1905), 236.

Literary History of the English People Strachey staked out vast claims for Marlowe in both drama and prosody. "That amazing genius not only created English tragedy, and at the same time made blank verse a living reality; he also, in his *Hero and Leander,* gave to the heroic couplet a beauty and a power which it had never possessed before. In the manipulation of the couplet he is the ancestor alike of the classical school of Dryden and of the romantic school of Keats. And who, of all his progeny, has surpassed him?" [44]

The plays of Ben Jonson were meat and drink in the household in which Strachey grew up. When we think of the kinship between these plays and those of Molière and Racine, for which he had the greatest admiration, we expect to find a considerable body of his critical writing dealing with this dramatist. Here we are disappointed. Strachey recorded very few opinions concerning Jonson. Yet he certainly enjoyed and admired his plays. Shakespeare was more interesting, more moving, more provocative; but try to imagine the Elizabethan drama without the plays of Old Ben! The impression that we get from Strachey's writings is that he knew them so well and assumed that others knew them so well that discussion would be superfluous, just as a discussion of water as an item in the menu would be superfluous.

His general interest in the Elizabethan drama is attested by other bits of evidence to be found in his writings. He praised W. W. Greg's edition of Henslowe's *Diary.*[45] J. S. Farmer's edition of Massinger's *Believe As Ye List* in facsimile delighted him, for it made easily available "one of the few autograph Elizabethan plays in existence" and enabled the lover of literature "to enjoy the sight of no less a thing than the handwriting of Massinger." [46] In reviewing the third volume of the variorum edition of Beaumont and Fletcher's plays, he declared that they had "an inexhaustible capacity for arousing interest." [47] He found much in the "awful humor of Webster" and in the "morbid agonies of

44. "The Age of Spenser," *Spectator, 98* (March 23, 1907), 457-8.
45. "Elizabethans Old and New," *Spectator, 102* (March 13, 1909), 420-2.
46. *Ibid.*
47. *Ibid.*

Ford" to suggest the novels of Dostoievsky; in the presence of all three he shuddered but was filled with admiration.[48] "How constantly," he exclaimed, "amid all the complexity and the rhetoric of the Elizabethan dramatists, do we come upon passages of triumphant simplicity! And nowhere more often than in Webster." [49]

It has been a mistake to assume, as some of the critics of *Elizabeth and Essex* have done, that when Strachey ventured out of the Victorian period or the eighteenth century in his choice of a subject he was getting out of his element. Actually, the Elizabethans were his first love, as scribblings of lyrics from Shakespeare, Marlowe, Jonson, and Sidney in his earliest commonplace books show; and they were his last love, as the unfinished essay on *Othello* testifies. Preserved among Strachey's manuscripts is a work called *Essex: A Tragedy,* written in blank verse some years before the composition of *Elizabeth and Essex.* It should not surprise us that when this book on the great queen and her dashing, high-spirited, impetuous courtier was published in 1928, it was discovered that it flowed quite easily into the dramatic mold.[50]

48. "Dostoievsky."
49. "A Poet on Poets."
50. See especially G. B. Harrison, "Elizabeth and Her Court," *Spectator,* *141* (Nov. 24, 1928), 777; Francis Birrell's statement quoted in Desmond MacCarthy's "Lytton Strachey: The Art of Biography," *Sunday Times* (London), Nov. 5, 1933, p. 8; Virginia Woolf, "The Art of Biography," *Atlantic Monthly, 163* (April 1939), 506–10. For Strachey as a critic, see "Mr. Strachey's Essays," London *Times,* May 18, 1922, p. 16; J. M. Murry, "Mr. Strachey's Criticism," *Nation and Athenaeum, 31* (June 3, 1922), 346–7; Lawrence Gilman, "Mr. Strachey's Other String," *North American Review, 216* (Oct. 1922), 553–60; and Sir Max Beerbohm, *Lytton Strachey,* The Rede Lecture for 1943 at Cambridge University (New York, Knopf, 1943), p. 26.

CHAPTER 4

On Later Drama and Acting

CONCERNING British plays of the Restoration and the eighteenth century Strachey left surprisingly few comments. His essay "The Old Comedy," however, written in 1913 as a review of John Palmer's *The Comedy of Manners,* is an appreciation of Restoration comedy. In Wycherley, Vanbrugh, and Congreve, he said, we find the dominant characteristics of the English people, something Hogarthian, a "combination of solid British beef, thick British beer, stout British bodies, and . . . solid British moralizing." [1] Some years later, while expressing serious misgivings concerning the work of Sheridan, he gave Congreve the highest praise. "The work of Sheridan begins to be taken at its true value—as a clever but emasculated *rifacimento;* the supreme master of prose comedy in English is seen to be Congreve. At least, let us hope so." [2]

In English drama of the first half of the nineteenth century Strachey seems to have had, like most of us today, little interest. One kind of play belonging to this period did, however, attract his attention. To this type belonged such plays as those of Thomas Lovell Beddoes, George Darley, and Charles Wells, which in some definite manner suggested the influence of the Elizabethans. In his eloquent essay on Beddoes, "The Last Elizabethan," published in November 1907, Strachey treated him as a dramatist of great

1. *Characters and Commentaries* (New York, Harcourt, Brace, 1933), pp. 158–61. First published in the *New Statesman,* Dec. 6, 1913.
2. *Portraits in Miniature* (New York, Harcourt, Brace, 1931), p. 41. First published as a review of Montague Summers' edition of *The Works of William Congreve, Nation and Athenaeum,* 34 (Oct. 13, 1923), 56–8.

merit who had suffered from unjustifiable neglect. Edmund Gosse's edition of a small collection of Beddoes' letters, Ramsay Colles' introduction to the Routledge edition of the poems, and one other short account, "fragmentary and incorrect," of the poet's career—these had done something but not nearly enough to persuade lovers of literature to accord him the place he deserved. As far as the public knew him at all, it knew him by virtue of one or two lyrics. But his claim to distinction did not rest upon these, consummate as they were; it rested upon his "extraordinary eminence as a master of dramatic blank verse." Beddoes had been born out of his time; he actually belonged to the Elizabethan age. Some medievalism lingered in him too, as it did in the great Elizabethans. His mind was like "one of those Gothic cathedrals of which he was so fond—mysterious within, and filled with a light at once richer and less real than the light of day; on the outside firm, and towering, and immediately impressive; and embellished, both inside and out, with grinning gargoyles." [3]

Strachey drew an interesting contrast between Beddoes, Darley, and Wells. Whereas Beddoes wrote like one of the Elizabethans themselves, Darley was, at best, the clever imitator. He never quite "captured the fresh and splendid note at which he was perpetually aiming." Beddoes, "with all the spontaneity of genius, flowed naturally with Elizabethan numbers; yet his verse never loses its own individuality, and might pass easily enough as the work of some unknown dramatist of the time of Ford and Massinger. . . . The Elizabethans, as no one can help feeling, found their inspiration in the pulse and glow of actual life; while it is equally clear that Darley found his simply in the Elizabethans. His Muse was a literary lady with ink on her finger-tips, who was far more at home among the bookshops in Cheapside than on the heights of Parnassus." [4] As for Wells, in such a play as *Joseph and His Brethren* he demonstrated that he could surpass Beddoes in psychological insight and in the "rare quality of mental vision"; but Beddoes wrote better blank verse, and at times Wells's characters seemed to lose

3. *Books and Characters*, pp. 262–3. First published in the *New Quarterly*, *1*, 47–72.
4. "Elizabethanism," *Spectator, 100* (Feb. 8, 1908), 213–14.

themselves in poetry. Swinburne and Rossetti had claimed too much for Wells.[5]

Modern drama interested Strachey greatly. In the reviews and articles which Strachey wrote for the *Spectator* in the first decade of this century, he appears sharply aware that significant things were happening as new plays appeared in the London theaters. This is not to say, of course, that his appraisal of the plays which he saw then was always the same as ours today. The very first of the articles signed "Ignotus," in which he rather ambitiously put on the mantle of dramatic critic for the *Spectator*, dealt with a current play, *The Mollusc*, a comedy by H. H. Davies. His discussion of the theory of comedy in connection with it sheds important light on his own use later of the comic spirit in biography. The writer of true comedy should not be satisfied merely because he has succeeded in provoking laughter. Laughter varies greatly in its quality. "It will be no avail if the laughter which he excites—however much of it there may be—is the empty laughter of the foolish or the cruel laughter of the depraved; it must be good laughter; in other words, the basis of all true comedy is ethical. The comic writer is as much concerned with the value of persons as the artist is concerned with that of tones; in either case a misjudgment of values ruins the picture. It does not follow, however, that a comedy cannot be good unless it inculcates a particular moral lesson." [6]

5. "Elizabethans Old and New," *Spectator, 102* (March 13, 1909), 420–2.

6. "The Mollusc," *99* (Nov. 30, 1907), 867–8. An interesting editorial note, written by Strachey's cousin St. Loe Strachey, who was then editor of the *Spectator,* is attached to this, the first of the contributions signed "Ignotus." It reads as follows: "We hope to publish from time to time papers by 'Ignotus' dealing with the theater, but we desire to take this opportunity of pointing out that the critic in question expresses his personal views, and that we are not to be held editorially responsible for his judgments. As long as the opinions given make 'les honnêtes gens' laugh or think, and are honest opinions honestly expressed, as unquestionably they will be, we shall be content to leave our readers to determine for themselves whether 'Ignotus' distributes his praise and blame successfully." I do not believe that this note should be taken as evidence that the editor distrusted Lytton Strachey or was placing him on probation. Rather, I think that he was preparing his subscribers, many of whom were conservative-minded country clergymen, for the kind of thing which "Ignotus" would give them. St. Loe Strachey considered his cousin

Davies' earlier plays had been weakest when he had attempted to deal in comedy with "the deeper problems and the more serious passions of life." They had been strongest "in their studies of the ridiculous and the inane in character, and of the absurdities of social intercourse." And here Strachey held up before Davies the luminous example of Molière. "It would be difficult to discover any very profound problem or any very transcendent passion in Molière's *Femmes Savantes,* which is none the less one of the dramatic masterpieces of the world." Strachey did not believe that the happy ending of *The Mollusc* had been handled very convincingly. "Conversions, it is true, may occur in real life, but they do not make good endings to comedies." [7]

In a review headed "Three New Plays" Strachey discussed Pinero's *The Thunderbolt,* Shaw's *Getting Married,* and Maurice Baring's *The Grey Stocking.* He praised Pinero's play for the ingenuity of its construction. "What delights us and absorbs us in Mr. Pinero's play is the way in which its wheels go round." But it was not close enough to reality to be a true comedy of manners. "An attack on manners cannot be successful unless it is firmly based on actual fact. Nothing is easier than to set up cardboard images of stupidity and vice, and then to overthrow them; but nothing is more ineffectual. This, however, is what Mr. Pinero has done." Bernard Shaw, Strachey said, was the sort of bore who talked too much and told everything that he knew. *"Getting Married* might be described as a conversation carried on by a single person— the author." Baring's play was "a series of conversations carried on by a charming group of refined and intelligent men and women." The talk was always in perfect taste. But the play was clearly the

---

and Lord Cromer the two most brilliant literary critics writing for the *Spectator.* The titles and dates for the other thirteen papers signed "Ignotus" are as follows: "L'Art Administratif," Dec. 28, 1907; "Mr. Beerbohm Tree," Feb. 1, 1908; "The Sicilians," Feb. 29, 1908; "Mr. Granville Barker," March 28, 1908; "Shakespeare on the Stage," April 25, 1908; "Three New Plays," June 6, 1908; "Coquelin," June 27, 1908; "Mr. Barrie's New Play," Sept. 26, 1908; "Lady Epping's Lawsuit," Oct. 31, 1908; "Mr. Hawtrey," Nov. 28, 1908; "A Play for Children," Dec. 26, 1908; "The Follies," Feb. 13, 1909; and "Mr. Galsworthy's Plays," March 27, 1909.

7. *Ibid.*

work of an amateur; it never gripped or pleased the audience. Strachey advised Baring to learn how to combine strength with his sweetness.[8]

It may surprise us that Strachey's review of *What Every Woman Knows* bestowed little praise on either Barrie or the typical London theater audience of 1908. The success of the play on the stage was merely the result of bad judgment catering to bad taste. "Mr. Barrie in writing it seems to have made up his mind to be everything by turns and nothing long." The play delighted the audience, it had something for every taste, but it was not a work of art. It went far to prove that "the old French critics had come nearer the truth than is commonly supposed when they laid down their rigid rules as to the incompatibility of the various types of drama." Barrie's play did not produce a harmony; it was merely a succession of discordant notes. And his method of handling his characters left much to be desired. "There is no more certain test of a dramatist's command of his art than his capacity for making his characters reveal themselves; but Mr. Barrie's characters are revealed, not by themselves, but by Mr. Barrie. . . . Mr. Barrie, not alone among our dramatists, would be all the better for a lesson from Boileau." In reality, he was merely "a master of the art of theatrical bluffing . . . but it is not in the habit of audiences to reflect." [9]

In a review of October 31, 1908, Strachey returned to H. H. Davies. This time the play discussed was *Lady Epping's Lawsuit*. "There would be no fun in a farce," Strachey said, "if the audience believed in it. . . . The master of light comedy must possess the two uncommon and well-nigh incompatible gifts of the clearest common-sense and the liveliest imagination. . . . He must be familiar with the difficult and subtle art of literary balance; he must mix his opposites with delicacy, and never be so realistic as to be grave or so fantastic as to be ridiculous." Davies had demonstrated that he could accomplish this difficult feat and was "in the front rank of our living workers in this delightful field of art." Some of the characters were weak. Sometimes there was too much farce in

8. *Spectator, 100* (June 6, 1908), 899–900.
9. "Mr. Barrie's New Play," *Spectator, 101* (Sept. 26, 1908), 444–5.

the play. And it suffered greatly, of course, when it was contrasted with Molière's lighter work. But Lady Epping was an admirable piece of characterization; the points succeeded each other in gay profusion and were vivid and pleasing; and, everything considered, there was much in the play to recommend it. "Surely, no one can complain of the condition of the English stage when such work as this is being produced upon it." [10]

"Some New Plays in Verse" was the title of Strachey's *Spectator* review for December 12, 1908. There were seven of the plays, and their very names suggested their quality as poetic drama. They were T. R. Castle's *The Gentle Shepherd*, W. L. Courtney's *The Bridals of Blood*, Reginald Farrer's *Dowager of Jerusalem*, an unknown author's *King Alfred's Jewel*, Whitworth Wynne's *Undine*, L. H. Myers' *Arvat*, and Frank Baines's *The Tragical History of Leonardo Salviati*. Strachey's review could have become a riot of ridicule, but it did not. It gave faint praise to *The Gentle Shepherd*. This little idyl had the virtue of humility; it had aimed low and had managed to hit its mark. And with quiet restraint Strachey firmly dismissed the other more ambitious plays as bad. Seeking for a generalization, he asked why it was that drama in verse was unlikely to succeed in modern times. His answer to the question is worth our consideration today. The modern audience, he said, demanded drama which dealt with realities. But "no one nowadays writes poetry unless he wishes to escape from realities." Hence modern audiences found the new poetic dramas highly unsatisfactory. Furthermore, blank verse was "supreme as a means of dramatic expression"; but modern blank verse, under the influence of Tennyson, had become diluted and weak. In it "the native vigor of the rhythm" had been sacrificed to "sweetness." [11]

Two weeks later Strachey reviewed a play for children, Graham Robertson's *Pinkie and the Fairies*. Here, too, he posed a general question concerning drama. "Why is it that the theater is the most slow-moving of institutions? Why is the stage the refuge of lost causes, and the faithful mirror of modes of thought and living

10. "Lady Epping's Lawsuit," *Spectator, 101*, 673–4.
11. *101*, 998–9.

which are utterly out of date? . . . Thus Mr. Barrie proved himself a bold man when he created a stage butler who was not comic,
and when Mr. Shaw ventured to give expression in the theater to
theories which had been commonplaces of European thought for
the last thirty years he was hailed as an innovator of the most advanced type." Speaking specifically of children's plays, however,
Strachey found both Barrie's *Peter Pan* and Robertson's new play
excellent. Barrie had "proved triumphantly that a children's play
may be successful without being meretricious," and Robertson's
work had "marked another step in the same direction." Strachey
also praised Beerbohm Tree's "consummate staging" of *Pinkie and
the Fairies* and enthusiastically declared, "Miss Ellen Terry's exquisite acting makes fault-finding impossible whenever she is on
the stage." He quoted with approval, after due reference to Wordsworth, the following lines from Robertson's play:

> What lies at hand
> Why seek afar
> In distant star,
> Or far-off strand?
> Where children are
> Is Fairyland.[12]

Galsworthy's *Strife* was discussed in Strachey's column in the
Spectator for March 27, 1909. Strachey had seen it at the Haymarket as it had been produced by Granville Barker. He found the
play to be well produced and well acted. But the play itself was
defective. Although Galsworthy had obvious gifts as a dramatist,
he had failed in this play, because he had not reconciled his purpose of showing the struggle between "the prejudices and ideals of
two classes" with the purpose of also giving "a picture of conflicting
persons." He had created interest in the characters as individuals
without ever satisfying it.[13]

Strachey's opinions about acting and the production of plays
were fully as clear and definite as those concerning dramatic com-

12. "A Play for Children," *Spectator, 101* (Dec. 26, 1908), 1098–9.
13. "Mr. Galsworthy's Plays," *102,* 498–9.

position. There was no uncertain tone about his pronouncements on either, and one discerns underneath his positive manner a quiet, steady confidence that he is right. One discerns also considerable distrust of the taste manifested by London theater audiences in the early years of this century.

In a review of February 1, 1908, Strachey gave most of his attention to Beerbohm Tree, who was acting in *The Mystery of Edwin Drood* at His Majesty's Theater. The acting did not please him. The play, he said, was not a good one, and therefore Mr. Tree had to be the whole show. He succeeded only in his treatment of detail and failed altogether to produce a fine or convincing general effect. His acting was too much like a bad style of florid architecture, where the structure was obliterated and lost under the mass of irrelevant ornament. Tree was far too eager to make "points." He was like a spendthrift who produced the impression of wealth by living on his capital and who when he died turned out to have left nothing at all. Unfortunately, too, Tree gave great attention to outward appearances—to facial expression, gesture, costume, etc. —but did not speak his words well. He was fundamentally a great dumb-show actor, a master of pantomime, and nothing more. His performance fell far short of great acting in another extremely important respect: he lost his own individuality in catering to the bad taste of his audience. "The common fault of uninstructed actors is to give too little attention to their audience, to be too realistic in fact, and thus to fail in dramatic effect. Mr. Tree affords an instance of exactly the opposite error. . . . The truth is that when once an actor becomes obsessed by his audience he loses his highest functions. He loses his individuality; he becomes an echo of conventions and the slave of those whom he ought to lead. Audiences like Mr. Tree because they find themselves in him—their own emphatic, uninspired conceptions of passion and of life." [14] To Strachey, the actor no less than the biographer must maintain and be guided by his own freedom of spirit.

Strachey had not forgotten Beerbohm Tree four weeks later when he commented on the acting of the Sicilian Players, "whose

14. "Mr. Beerbohm Tree," *Spectator, 100,* 185–6.

vigorous and vivid representations of Italian peasant life are drawing full houses at the Shaftesbury Theater." Strachey regretted
that these players were like Tree in that they were primarily concerned with gesticulation.[15] Like Hamlet, Strachey would not have
the actor saw the air with his hands or tear a passion to tatters. We
may suspect also that there were times when he wished that he
could, like Dr. Johnson on one occasion, reach out and imprison
the ever-active hands and thus bring peace to his soul.

Far different were Strachey's comments in "Mr. Granville
Barker," *Spectator*, March 28, 1908. Barker was both a master of
dramatic production and an excellent actor. He was doing much
to bring intelligence and vigor to the English stage. "It is hardly too
much to say that the companies which, under Mr. Barker's leadership, drew such crowded and enthusiastic audiences to the Court
and the Savoy, accomplished something like a revolution in the
art of dramatic production in England." Barker appealed to the
intellect; his dramatic productions had "a reality and a vitality."
During his performances the stage "seemed for once no longer
stagy." Barker had had the faith and the good sense to try "the bold
experiment of treating his audience as if it were composed of
rational human beings . . . who had their wits about them." He
had realized further that "the one indispensable ingredient for a
truly natural style of acting was quickness," not, "as the old-
fashioned actor would make it [and here Beerbohm Tree certainly
came into Strachey's mind]—a collection of startlingly articulated
'points.' . . . It is the actor's business to practice not only a physical quickness in fluency of voice and subtlety of gesture, but a
quickness of mind, an alertness and adroitness of intellect, which
can pass easily from thought to thought, from emotion to emotion, which understands the art of hinting and of taking things for
granted, and knows how to be expressive by skill rather than by
force." Barker had also avoided "the fault which besets the actor
who is primarily intellectual—that of a too persistent seriousness."
And, most important of all, Barker knew how to use his voice with
full effectiveness. "He is aided by his voice, with its haunting, half-
mocking intonations, and its power of suggesting unutterable

15. "The Sicilians," *Spectator, 100* (Feb. 29, 1908), 336–7.

things. Indeed—if we might hazard the fancy—it is in his voice that Mr. Barker's spirit has its habitation." [16]

When the French actor Coquelin was playing in London in 1908, Strachey saw him a number of times. Although he observed that Coquelin got his effects "mainly through facial expressions," he was struck by the way in which the French actor was able to preserve and suggest his own individuality in the midst of a great variety of roles. "What a contrast this kind of versatility offers to some of our English actors, who, for so long as one can remember, have played along a single groove, endlessly repeating themselves with unwearied regularity. . . . Amid all these diversities M. Coquelin succeeds in preserving what is, after all, the actor's most potent spell—the sense of personality." But Strachey found Coquelin disappointing in one of the roles for which he had become famous, that of Cyrano. In general, he was weakest in parts of sentiment and romance and strongest in parts of pure comedy. But even here something was lacking. "M. Coquelin has no touch of that peculiarly English quality of sudden imaginative humor possessed, for example, in such an eminent degree, by Mr. James Welch." [17]

The best and the worst characteristics of the English tradition of acting Strachey found in Charles Henry Hawtrey. Like many other English actors, he was very much the same no matter what role he was taking. "Compared with the vast range of a Coquelin or the exquisite variety of a Bartet, Mr. Hawtrey's achievement must strike everyone as somewhat meager and somewhat monotonous." Yet one could always be sure of satisfaction in going to see Hawtrey play. One could always be sure of being served dishes that had the English flavor: they would be "simple, unassuming, unvarying, and always perfectly cooked." The very monotony of Hawtrey's roles was probably the result of an insistence by the typical English theater audience that he repeat what they had enjoyed before. His acting was impeccable. Its essence lay in "immaculate gentility"; from this arose "its central charm, its unfailing fascination." And it was the English, more than any other nation, who appreciated what was excellent in the ideal gentleman.

16. *100*, 499–500.
17. "Coquelin," *Spectator, 100* (June 27, 1908), 1029–30.

Such acting ran the risk of suggesting snobbery. Something depended upon the play. For example, the effect produced by Hawtrey in *The Men from Blankley's,* a comedy of manners which
handled its theme with utmost delicacy, was that of "a social satire
which was at once pointed and good-natured." But in a much
poorer play, Somerset Maugham's *Jack Straw,* Hawtrey acted the
role of a fine gentleman who appeared "far too conscious of his own
high breeding." In the main, however, the plays in which Hawtrey
acted mattered very little; he was always Mr. Hawtrey.

> For, after all, when Mr. Hawtrey is concerned, the play is
> emphatically not the thing. What is the thing is simply and
> solely Mr. Hawtrey. Thus to say that he is always himself is in
> reality not an impeachment of his art, but his best justifica-
> tion. For what we are interested in is his own character—
> the irresponsible, lazy, lighthearted, susceptible, and faintly
> ridiculous gentleman whom, in a curious, delightful way
> across the footlights, we have come to know so well. Mr. Haw-
> trey's art is, like all art, a method of expression; but it differs
> from that of the ordinary actor in that it is primarily con-
> cerned with expressing, not an alien character, but his own.
> Thus, from one point of view, it comes nearer to the more
> strictly creative arts, although, unlike them, it is, by its very
> nature, transitory. Its finest manifestations cannot outlive
> their author. Let us enjoy them, then, while we may.[18]

Hawtrey had carried to its utmost extreme his delightful talent
for displaying his own individuality on the stage. Henry Irving,
Strachey concluded after reading Austin Brereton's two-volume
biography of the actor, had like Beerbohm Tree done just the opposite. He had completely surrendered himself to the footlights
and fanfare of the theater, and in the midst of the glitter and the
applause his own uniqueness as a person had dissolved.

> One looks in vain for a record of intellectual effort and de-
> velopment, for expressions of noble thought or profound
> feeling, for any of those manifestations of original and unmis-

18. "Mr. Hawtrey," *Spectator, 101* (Nov. 28, 1908), 880–1.

takable genius which occur so often in the private lives of truly great men. It almost seems as if the stage had crossed the foot-lights and enveloped the whole of Irving's existence, so that the best account of it was in truth to be found in the con-temporary notices of the Press. Is this a just representation of Irving's career, or has Mr. Brereton unwittingly misrepre-sented it? It is difficult to say, but it may be noticed that a similar view—though from a different standpoint—is to be found in Mr. Bram Stoker's well-known book. And, if it be true that Irving was indeed a man who was in his very essence theatrical, we should have a clue alike to his immense success and to his undoubted artistic limitations. The more an actor lives for his art, the more popular he will be. But a great actor must have other qualifications; he must be great as a man no less than as a mime, and he must be able to look upon the stage, not only from the wings of his theater, but from the high and spacious vantage-ground of life itself.[19]

In early 1909 Strachey attended a dramatic production called *A Christmas Pantomime* put on at the Apollo Theater by a group of actors and actresses who called themselves "The Follies." The name was appropriate for them, Strachey said, for they were at-tempting to perform the same functions as those of the medieval jester. Their humor, however, lacked something in quality. For instance, puns could be admirably witty, but the puns at the Apollo were infamous. Yet Strachey enjoyed the play in the main, for it was "a rollicking burlesque of Mr. Tree's presentation of *Faust.* There could be no more pungent criticism of the melodramatic school of acting." He was also amused at "the imitation through-out the piece of the senseless and barbarous manner of declaiming verse now almost universal in our theaters." [20]

One may guess that if Lytton Strachey had been asked what within the range of his observation had been the highest point of all acting he would have replied that it had been Bernhardt in Racine. He would have conceded that in many of her other roles

19. "The Life of Henry Irving," *Spectator, 101* (Dec. 26, 1908), 1104.
20. "The Follies," *Spectator, 102* (Feb. 13, 1909), 262–3.

she had yielded too much to the taste which her age had for the spectacular, the extravagant, and the sentimental. "It is odd but certainly true that the eighteenth century would have been profoundly shocked by the actress who reigned supreme over the nineteenth." [21] It was also true that she had very little intellect. But here, Strachey said, Racine came to her rescue. "Fortunately the mightier genius of Jean Racine was of such a nature that it was able to lift hers on to its own level of the immortal and the universal. In this case there was no need on her part for an intellectual realization of the dramatist's purpose; Racine had enough intellect for both." [22] Bernhardt had a personality that adjusted itself magnificently to the demands of the great French dramatist. And she had a glorious voice through which Racine's poetry reached the ears of the audience with full power and beauty. "The words boomed and crashed with a superhuman resonance which shook the spirit of the hearer like a leaf in the wind." [23]

Strachey's comments over a period of years make it clear that he not only had a marked interest in the drama but also definite and consistent standards for appraising it. As a critic he possessed a constant impulse to ask questions, a lively curiosity, and an instinct for discrimination which served him well. He also had at his command a broad frame of reference; he had read widely. In his mind, furthermore, sober common sense worked well beside an alert, sympathetic imagination. Although more than once he failed to evaluate the plays of the day on the level which the passing of time would establish for them, all his dramatic criticism was colored by a contagious enthusiasm—enthusiasm for art and enthusiasm for man as his actions and words may delight us in the microcosm of the theater.

21. "Sarah Bernhardt," *Characters and Commentaries,* p. 257. This essay was first published in the *Nation and Athenaeum, 33* (May 5, 1923), 152–3.
22. *Ibid.,* p. 258.
23. *Ibid.,* pp. 259–60.

CHAPTER 5

*O*n *French Literature*

IT IS DOUBTFUL whether Lytton Strachey could remember a time
when he did not hear daily the clean, crisp cadence of French
speech or feel himself sharply aware of the long glories of French
literature. Not only through his study of the language and his reading of the literature, both of which began in his early childhood,
but also in his close association with his mother and his sisters
did he learn to breathe deeply in the clear, vitalizing atmosphere
of Gallic culture. We know that his mother, born a Grant of
Rothiemurchus, was the heir to an Anglo-Indian-Scottish-French
cultural tradition which for generations had been handed down
in her ancestral home in the Highlands. The French element in
this tradition was by no means the least important.[1] Throughout
her life Lady Strachey showed the highest respect for the French
people and their literature, especially for Voltaire. A frequent
guest in her household, we also know, was Mlle Marie Souvestre,
daughter of the French writer Émile Souvestre. Mlle Souvestre
was a brilliant teacher who conducted a well-known school for
girls, first at Les Ruches, Fontainebleau, and later at Allenswood,
Wimbledon, London. Four of Lytton's sisters studied under Mlle
Souvestre, Elinor and Dorothy at Les Ruches and Pernel and Marjorie at Allenswood. Dorothy herself became a teacher at Allens-

1. See the chapter on Lady Strachey in my book *The Strachey Family*
(Durham, N.C., Duke University Press, 1953), and information about the
family history of the Grants in a book by Lytton Strachey's great-aunt,
*Memoirs of a Highland Lady: The Autobiography of Elizabeth Grant of
Rothiemurchus, afterwards Mrs. Smith of Balliboys* (New York, Longmans,
Green, 1898).

wood. Mlle Souvestre, however, was more than a gifted teacher; in her the very spirit of France was embodied and alive. Her perceptiveness was quick; her intellectual grasp was clear and sure; her mind was teeming with ideas in a constant state of activity; her judgment was comprehensive, steady, and sane; and her temperament was sensitive, eager, and enthusiastic, that of a person who had the sharpest taste for life and never got enough of it. Wherever she went she was an electric stimulus.[2]

Among Lady Strachey's children there was not only much talk in French and discussion of the literature but also creative activity which showed the French influence. Throughout the 1880's and 1890's almost all the members of the household wrote verse prolifically.[3] Some of this was in English, some in French. The verse in English frequently used French patterns such as the roundel, the rondeau, and the ballade. The verse in French, also using these patterns, was intended to appeal strongly to the ear as well as to the mind. At times, fascinated by the music of the French language, the young poets attempted to see what could be done by appealing to the ear alone. Such were some of the contributions that Marjorie and Lytton made to the numerous "magazines" which they compiled, illustrated, and "idioted."

The part which Dorothy played in helping Lytton to assimilate and enjoy French culture was particularly important, both in his childhood and throughout his life. Not only had she been extremely close to Mlle Souvestre as a pupil, a teacher, and a friend, but she married a French artist, Simon Bussy. In the first half of the twentieth century her homes at Roquebrune and Nice became a center for French painters, writers, and intellectuals. She pub-

2. Mlle Souvestre and her school at Fontainebleau are presented in a somewhat fictionized form in *Olivia by Olivia,* which was published anonymously but was written by Mme Bussy (Lytton Strachey's sister Dorothy). Mrs. Franklin D. Roosevelt attended the later school, Allenswood. She tells us in her memoirs that Mlle Souvestre was both her teacher and her traveling companion on European tours. Like the Stracheys, she testifies to the remarkable qualities of mind and personality which she found in this admirable Frenchwoman.

3. Some of these poems were brought together about 1890 in *Our Rhymes.*

lished a book on Eugène Delacroix and translated books by A. Bréal, C. Mauclair, and Jean Schlumberger. André Gide was her intimate friend. She helped him to learn English and translated something like a dozen of his books.

Lytton Strachey also traveled in France from time to time throughout his life. After he became famous, he was never happier than when rummaging through Paris bookstalls in search of rare editions of Rabelais, Diderot, and Voltaire. His last diary, entitled "A Fortnight in France," records the pleasure which he experienced during a visit to the country in September 1931, just a few weeks before the beginning of his final illness.

Abundant evidence of his sustained interest in French literature is to be found not only in his admirable little book *Landmarks in French Literature* (1912) and his well-known essays on Racine and Voltaire but also in numerous other writings which he published as articles and reviews, many of them unsigned, throughout his life. His first published piece of prose was "Two Frenchmen" (1903). The essay on "Voltaire's Tragedies" was published as early as 1905.[4] The next year Strachey reviewed J. E. Farmer's *Versailles and the Court under Louis XIV*.[5] "Mademoiselle de Lespinasse" was published the same year.[6] Hereafter, a fairly continuous procession of writings on French subjects flowed from his pen. In 1907 it was "Molière" and "French Poetry"; in 1908 "The Age of Louis XIV," "Three Frenchmen in England," "Racine," "Coquelin," "The Admirable Boileau," and "Some Napoleonic Books"; in 1909 "The Age of Corneille" and "Caran D'Ache"; in 1910 "The Rousseau Affair"; in 1912 *Landmarks in French Literature;* in 1913 "Madam du Deffand"; in 1914 "Henri Beyle" and "Voltaire and England"; in 1915 "Voltaire and Frederick the Great"; in 1916 "French Poets through Boston Eyes," a decidedly unfavorable review of Amy Lowell's book *Six French Poets;* in 1918 "Rabelais"; in 1919 "Voltaire"; in 1923 "Sarah Bernhardt";

4. *Independent Review,* 5 (April 1905), 309–19.
5. "Versailles," *Speaker,* July 28, 1906, p. 387. Collected in *Characters and Commentaries.*
6. *Independent Review, 10* (Sept. 1906), 345–56. Collected in *Characters and Commentaries.*

in 1924 "The Abbé Morellet" and "Madame de Sévigné's Cousin";
and in 1931 "Madame de Lieven" and "The Président de Brosses." [7]
According to some of Strachey's friends, he was at the time of his
death giving considerable thought to a book which he hoped to
write on Voltaire.

It is certainly not true, however, that he had any kind of general
reputation as an authority on French literature when he under-
took the writing of *Landmarks* in 1910 or 1911. His publications
on the subject had been scattered through the columns of so many
journals and so much of this work appeared in the form of unsigned reviews in the *Spectator* that only the members of his own
family, some intimate friends, and a few other people knew of his
interest in this field and special knowledge of it. Strachey was conscious of his own knowledge, critical ability, and talent as a writer,
but he was also conscious of the difficulties which the nature of the
task imposed upon him. "Perhaps the best test of a man's intelligence," he wrote in his essay on Stendhal, "is his capacity for mak-

7. Published, in order listed, as follows: "Molière," *Spectator, 99* (Oct. 26,
1907), 612–13; "French Poetry," *Spectator, 99* (Dec. 21, 1907), 1051–2; "The
Age of Louis XIV," *Spectator, 100* (April 11, 1908), 577–8; "Three Frenchmen in England," *Spectator, 100* (May 30, 1908), 866–7; "Racine," *New
Quarterly, 1* (June 1908), 361–84; "Coquelin," *Spectator, 100* (June 27, 1908),
1029–30; "The Admirable Boileau," *Spectator, 101* (Nov. 7, 1908), 735–6;
"Some Napoleonic Books," *Spectator, 101* (Dec. 26, 1908), 1100–1; "The Age
of Corneille," *Spectator, 102* (Jan. 30, 1909), 182–3; "Caran D'Ache," *Spec-
tator, 102* (March 6, 1909), 371–2; "The Rousseau Affair," *New Quarterly, 3*
(May 1910), 147–57; *Landmarks in French Literature*, The Home University
Library (London, Williams and Norgate, Thornton Butterworth; New York,
Henry Holt, 1912); "Madame Du Deffand," *Edinburgh Review, 217* (Jan.
1913), 61–80; "Henri Beyle," *Edinburgh Review, 219* (Jan. 1914), 35–52;
"Voltaire and England," *Edinburgh Review, 220* (Oct. 1914), 392–411; "Vol-
taire and Frederick the Great," *Edinburgh Review, 222* (Oct. 1915), 351–73;
"French Poets through Boston Eyes," *New Statesman*, March 4, 1916, pp.
524–5; "Rabelais," *New Statesman*, Feb. 16, 1918, pp. 473–4; "Voltaire,"
Athenaeum, Aug. 1, 1919, pp. 677–8; "Sarah Bernhardt," *Nation and Athe-
naeum, 33* (May 5, 1923), 152–3; "The Abbé Morellet," *Nation* (London), *34*
(Jan. 26, 1924), 602–3; "Madame de Sévigné's Cousin," *Nation* (London), *36*
(Oct. 4, 1924), 14–15; "Madame de Lieven," *Saturday Review of Literature, 7*
(April 18, 1931), 748–9; "The Président de Brosses," *New Statesman and Na-
tion, 1* (April 11–18, 1931), 250–1, 281–2.

ing a summary." [8] When he wrote *Landmarks,* he had fortunately already formed the habit of mind which made judicious, evaluative selection as natural to him as breathing and which would manifest itself on every page of both the longer biographies and the miniatures that he was to write later.

The review of *Landmarks* in the *Times Literary Supplement* praised it as a masterly piece of compression: "Short handbooks on great subjects are among the most difficult tasks that a man of letters can undertake, and Mr. Strachey is to be congratulated on his courage and success. It is difficult to imagine how a better account of French literature could be given in two hundred and fifty small pages than he has given here. . . . Mr. Strachey has managed to combine distinction with brevity and lucidity." [9] Few of the later readers of the book have been disposed to question this judgment. The work is excellent not only in its selection of materials but also in its structure, its proportion, and its distribution of emphasis. The author consistently demonstrates his complete familiarity with the subject and his marked skill in controlling the presentation of it with firmness and steadiness. His vast admiration for what he considers central in French literature and the French mind appears again and again. But he is never for a moment uncritical. His facts are not allowed to come before the reader as mere facts; they are always facts which are being weighed and interpreted. They concern writers for whom Strachey could have had little admiration as well as those for whom he has the highest praise. He knew that in his enthusiasm for the literature he could not afford to neglect manifestations which he could not like. Hence the work is never a mere compendium of information but is a genuine guide to reading. Each author is placed in his precise relation to his age, to other writers, and to whatever else will best reveal his significance. Strachey's intention is to make each appear in his essence and thus invite us to read his books and get to know him better.

Style, too, counts for much in *Landmarks.* A few clichés stick out rather badly, and occasionally there is evidence of self-conscious

8. "Henri Beyle," *Books and Characters, French and English* (New York, Harcourt, Brace, 1922), pp. 279–80.
9. Feb. 1, 1912, p. 44.

straining after effect. But in the main Strachey's words more than do his subject justice: they honor it and clothe it with charm. As he proceeds from author to author, Strachey constantly keeps in mind his threefold purpose: to say the right thing, to say it briefly, and to say it well. The result is a book which one may dip into almost anywhere and find delightful. In the hands of Chrétien de Troyes, we are told for instance, the vague imaginations of the Celtic romances were "metamorphosed . . . into the unambiguous elegances of civilized life." As we read Du Bellay's sonnets, we may hear "the sonorous boom of proud and pompous verse." The fertility of Rabelais's spirit displays itself in a multitude of words: "His book is an orgy of words; they pour out helter-skelter, wildly, into swirling sentences and huge catalogues that, in serried columns, overflow the page. Not quite wildly, though; for, amid all the rush and bluster, there is a powerful underlying art." The "Precious" school of the second quarter of the seventeenth century valued a poet only for his "capacity for turning a somersault in verse" and a prose writer only for his skill in dragging "a complicated, ramifying simile through half-a-dozen pages at least." Pascal, Strachey says, was the creator of French prose; the style of his *Lettres Provinciales* has "the lightness and strength, the exquisite polish and delicious wit, the lambent irony and the ordered movement, which no other language spoken by man has ever quite been able to reproduce." The brilliant writers of the age of Louis XIV showed that they had learned well the lesson which Pascal had taught: "Their works became remarkable for clarity and elegance, for a graceful simplicity, an easy strength; they were cast in the fine mould of perfect manners—majestic without pretension, expressive without emphasis, simple without carelessness, and subtle without affectation." Molière had to a supreme degree the common sense characteristic of his nation; but he had much more. "He looked into the profundities of the soul, and measured those strange forces which brush aside the feeble dictates of human wisdom like gossamer, and lend, by their very lack of compromise, a dignity and almost a nobility to folly and even vice itself. Thus it is that he has invested the feeble, miserable Harpagon with a kind of sordid splendor." Racine's genius is such that he is able to perform the miracle of infusing into "the ordered ease of the Alexandrine a strange sense of brooding mystery and indefinable terror and the awful approaches of fate." Strachey is at his best in commenting on La Fontaine. He delights in humor wherever he finds it, and in La Fontaine the humor is varied and exquisite: "With equal ease, apparently, he can be playful, tender, serious, preposterous, eloquent, meditative, and absurd." Furthermore, like Strachey himself, La Fontaine knew how to enjoy nature without becoming sentimental about it: "He loved nature, but unromantically, as he loved a glass of wine and an ode of Horace, and the rest of the good things of life." Saint-Simon's *Mémoires,* with its raciness and flavor, is "like a tropical forest—luxuriant, bewildering, enormous—with the gayest humming birds among the branches, and the vilest monsters in the entangled grass." In Diderot even atheism became attractive: "His complete materialism —his disbelief in any Providence or any immortality—instead of depressing him, seems rather to have given fresh buoyancy to his spirit; if this life on earth were all, that only served, in his eyes, to redouble the intensity of its value." Voltaire was "a strange amalgam of all the most contradictory elements in human nature, and it would be difficult to name a single virtue or a single vice which he did not possess." Yet, even in attacking Christianity, he was motivated by "a passionate desire for the welfare of mankind." Voltaire's satiric style was characterized by incomparable lightness and agility: "The pointed, cutting, mocking sentences dance through his pages like light-toed, prick-eared elves." But this lightness was not to be misinterpreted as a lack of serious intention: "Voltaire's meaning is deep in proportion to the lightness of his writing . . . When he is most in earnest he grins most." Rousseau, Strachey observes, was "the only man of his age who ever wanted to be alone." "Words flowed from Victor Hugo like light from the sun"; but his intellectual scope and spiritual quality "were very far from being equal to his gifts of expression and imagination." And although Balzac was notoriously lacking in the power of self-criticism, the "whole of France" was "crammed into his pages, and electrified there into intense vitality."

Strachey's distinction as a critic of French literature, however, does not rest merely on a skill in phrasing and a sure perceptiveness in dealing with particular authors and works. In his short writings as well as in the *Landmarks,* he again and again displayed an impressive generalizing power. He realized at the same time the dangers implicit in its use as applied to something as extensive and complex as a whole national literature appearing in various forms through many centuries. Whatever the hazards and whatever degree of caution might be needed, Strachey knew, nevertheless, that the trustworthy critic must venture beyond the individual and the particular and achieve scope, comprehension, and perspective through the discovery of characteristics which the writers of a nation may share with one another. What were the characteristics of the French language, he was impelled to ask, as they were revealed in the literature of the country? Further, what characteristics of the French mind and what national traits went into the making of this literature?

Strachey believed that two strong impulses, seemingly antithetical but actually complementary, motivated most of the great works of French literature. One of these was a "positive spirit of searching and unmitigated common sense." This had given French prose its peculiar distinction, had lain at the root of the nation's remarkable critical powers, and had produced a realism of a very high quality from the time of the medieval *Fabliaux* down through Balzac to the modern novel. The other impulse was a tendency toward pure rhetoric, a love of language for the sake of itself. This Strachey found in exaggerated form in Rabelais, Bossuet, Corneille, and such nineteenth-century Romantics as Chateaubriand and Hugo. Voltaire's style, on the other hand, "so brilliant and yet so colorless, so limited and yet so infinitely sensible," was the product of its age, an age of prose and common sense. The Romantic movement, with its delight in rhetoric, was "an immense reaction against the realism which had come to such perfection in the acid prose of Voltaire." In some of the great writers of the seventeenth century, however, in Pascal, Racine, La Fontaine, and La Bruyère, the two tendencies came together and achieved a perfect balance. "In their work, the most penetrating realism is beautified and ennobled by all the resources of linguistic art, while the rhetorical instinct is preserved from pomposity and inflation by a supreme critical sense." [10]

Strachey found it illuminating to contrast the French language with the English. Many of the differences between the two could be accounted for in terms of their historic development. "The complex origin of the English tongue has enabled English writers to obtain those effects of diversity, of contrast, of imaginative strangeness, which have played such a dominating part in our literature. The genius of the French languages, descended from its simple Latin stock, has triumphed most in the contrary direction—in simplicity, in unity, in clarity, and in restraint." [11] Together with these admirable traits the style of the best French literary works possessed a closely related quality of an equally high order—what Strachey called an "exquisite precision." [12] Almost from the beginning of their national history, French writers had been conscious literary artists. The union of vigor with a highly developed sense of form, with elegance, and with precision in Pascal's admirable prose was simply a manifestation of characteristic tendencies of the French language appearing at their best.[13] The French delight in rhetoric, when accompanied by adequate restraint and literary judgment, often served to strengthen these tendencies. Even in the midst of Rabelais's profusion of words, it was to be discovered. "The final miracle of Rabelais' writing is that, in spite of its extraordinary fecundity, it yet preserves an exquisite measure, a supreme restraint. There is a beautiful quality of elegance, of cleanness, of economy, of what the French call 'netteté,' in his sentences, which justifies the paradox that he is one of the most concise of writers. His prose, in short, with all its idiosyncrasies, is characteristically French." [14] The tradition of conscious literary art, which existed in England as well as France in the fourteenth century, suffered from no such interruption in France as it did in

10. *Landmarks in French Literature* (New York, Henry Holt, 1912), pp. 201–3.
11. *Landmarks,* p. 8.
12. "Molière."
13. *Landmarks,* pp. 56–8.
14. "Rabelais," *Characters and Commentaries,* p. 210.

England during the fifteenth. In the long run, however, England did not lose too much from the interruption, for out of it emerged the Elizabethan age in all its brilliance and strength. Poetry, for instance, in France continued to flow along securely and deliberately from century to century. "Its history is a long succession of triumphs of conscious art. With us the current of poetry, starting from the same watershed, and following a similar course, suddenly and mysteriously dried up. But the misfortune was a blessing in disguise, for the stagnant waters turned into another channel and plunged into the cataract of the Elizabethan age." [15]

With all his admiration for French literature, Strachey did not argue that the long tradition of conscious literary art with its insistence upon the classical qualities of simplicity, restraint, precision, clarity, and good structure had produced a literature superior to that of his own country. He simply maintained that English writers could profit much from lessons which the French could teach. And he felt compelled to point out that some of the greatest and most characteristic French writers, notably Racine, used methods so different from those to which the British were accustomed that a cultural gap had opened between the two countries. This was to be deplored. It was bad that Voltaire could not really understand or appreciate Shakespeare, and it was bad that very few Englishmen could understand and enjoy Racine. English literature, Strachey said, was one in which rarity of style, pushed often to the verge of extravagance, reigned supreme. In it, the whole conception of the art of writing had fallen under the dominion of the emphatic, the extraordinary, and the bold. This in itself was not to be regretted. But, unfortunately, Englishmen could no longer enjoy other kinds of beauty:

> The beauties of restraint, of clarity, of refinement, and of precision we pass by unheeding; we can see nothing there but coldness and uniformity; and we go back with eagerness to the fling and the bravado that we love so well. It is as if we had become so accustomed to looking at boxers, wrestlers, and gladiators that the sight of an exquisite minuet produced

15. "Medieval Studies," *Spectator*, 97 (Nov. 17, 1906), 786–7.

no effect on us; the ordered dance strikes us as a monotony, for we are blind to the subtle delicacies of the dancers which are fraught with such significance to the practiced eye.[16]

In their effort to bridge the gap, poor translators and incompetent interpreters had been of very little help. Elizabeth Lee's book of selections from La Bruyère and Vauvenargues, which Strachey reviewed in 1903, gave slight evidence that she could qualify as either translator or interpreter. She had translated Vauvenargues into careless English and then had added insult to injury by declaring that the Frenchman "understood the art of writing, as an art, scarcely at all." Wrote Strachey: "He understood it better than Miss Lee, whose English is never good"; and he provided ample evidence against her. Since she had failed with Vauvenargues' simple style, Strachey did not expect her to succeed with the complexities of La Bruyère's brilliant language. "This would have required a special talent, a fine instinct, and a reverend mind; without these qualities it were better to leave untouched one of the great writers of the world, whose perfect French it is nothing less than sacrilege to translate into bad English." [17] Again, in a review of A. R. Waller's translation of Molière in eight volumes, Strachey expressed his disappointment. Waller's work was far from adequate: the translation was both inaccurate and flat.[18] Such books as J. C. Bailey's *The Claims of French Poetry: Nine Studies in the Greater French Poets* and St. John Lucas' *The Oxford Book of French Verse* conspicuously failed to measure up to the ideal. Both were concerned chiefly with the poetry of the Renaissance and the nineteenth century; neither extended a very warm appreciation to the productions of Louis xiv's age or the eighteenth century. Furthermore, Bailey actually contended that Racine deserved little attention. Strachey replied to him warmly: "There can surely be no doubt at all that Racine represents what is most French in French poetry, just as Shakespeare represents what is most English in English poetry. . . . Racine, more than any other French

16. "Racine," *Books and Characters,* pp. 12–14.
17. "Two Frenchmen," *Characters and Commentaries,* pp. 185–9.
18. "Molière."

poet, stands in need of an English interpreter." [19] We know that
his own essay on Racine was published a few months after he wrote
this review. W. F. Smith's *Rabelais in His Writings,* published by
the Cambridge University Press, Strachey found full of pedantry.
Smith was in "the class of those who read Rabelais for the sake of
making notes." His chapter on Rabelais's style "could, one feels,
have originated nowhere but in the University of Cambridge." [20]

Across the Atlantic, Americans were not served noticeably better
by such an interpreter and critic as Amy Lowell, who had given
lectures in Boston on six modern French poets. Strachey accorded
her little mercy in one of the most brilliantly ironical of all his
critical essays. The lectures perhaps threw more light on Boston,
he said, than on the French poets. Despite Miss Lowell's refined
enthusiasm and enlightened tolerance, a great gulf seemed to lie
between her and her subject. With lifted eyebrow, she spoke of
them as odd creatures, queer animals, or submarine fishes, rather
than living human beings. Touching on religion, she expressed
doubt whether, as Bostonians conceived the term, it was possible
to the Latin mind. Strachey thought immediately of St. Francis,
St. Theresa, Port Royal, and the French cathedrals. She had opinions about almost everything, which she voiced with complete confidence and condescension: she disapproved of that "disagreeable
mannerism of the Comédie Française" encountered when the
French poet insists on counting the mute *e* metrically, though she
should have known that Voltaire had praised the device; and she
cautioned her audience not to be surprised that Paris, as clever as
it was, nevertheless was not entirely apart from the stream of common humanity. It would be difficult to determine which Strachey
found more revolting—J. C. Bailey's complete ignorance in dealing
with such a subject as Racine or Amy Lowell's smug shallowness,
provinciality, and thinly disguised intolerance.[21]

Much more was at stake, however, than the ability of English-

19. "French Poetry."
20. "Rabelais."
21. "French Poets through Boston Eyes," *Characters and Commentaries,*
pp. 187–91. Strachey also found the fifth volume, *The Age of Louis XIV,* of
The Cambridge Modern History far from satisfactory. His comment on it
suggests his own biographical methods: "That history possesses all the essential characteristics of tragic development. . . . Nor is the superhuman element

speaking people to understand the literary manner of the French. French literature was not merely a product of certain tendencies of style and form. It was an embodiment of what was most characteristic of the French mind and embedded in it were the peculiar traits of a whole people. More than once, Strachey reminded the British of Burke's famous statement that it was a dangerous thing to indict the ideals of a whole nation. The statement applied to literature, Strachey said, as well as politics.[22]

No one knew better than he that the persistent stylistic tendencies of a literature have much more than a superficial significance. The marked impulse of French writers throughout the centuries toward clarity, toward simplicity, toward refinement, toward restraint, and toward concentration as ideals of style were closely related to corresponding qualities of mind. Simplicity was related to good judgment, which could be depended upon to select what was most important and to discard all the rest. It was also closely related, as in the plays of Racine, to a high power of mind which vitalized and intensified what had been selected. Both in their art and in their philosophy of life, the French people had realized, perhaps more clearly than had those of any other nation, that in art and life one cannot have everything and that one should therefore choose only the best in order to do as much as possible with

---

wanting—the presence of issues more stupendous than any that can be summed up in the life of a man, the death-struggle of irreconcilable ideals and forces immeasurably great. It is difficult to believe that any book constructed out of such materials as these could fail to be interesting; yet it must be confessed that the present volume has achieved this almost impossible feat. By some mysterious process it has converted the excitement and the significance of the seventeenth cntury into flatness and insipidity. The learned authors remind one of the barbarians of the Dark Ages who used the masterpieces of antique sculpture for the building of common walls. How many priceless facts have gone to the making of one of their commonplace pages? . . . This failure may doubtless be explained to a great extent by the uninspiring effects of divided authorship; but perhaps an even more potent cause is the scale upon which the history has been written. The book falls between two stools; it should have been either a great deal longer or a great deal more condensed." He adds that it should have been either like the work of Tacitus and Macaulay or like that of Montesquieu and Michelet. "The Age of Louis XIV."

22. *Landmarks,* p. 90; "French Poetry."

that. Thus they had become the people who were most fully alive.

The clarity and the consummate sense of order characteristic of the best French writers sprang from both a respect for facts and a respect for the reader. Respect for the reader presupposed that a work of literature should always be thought of as a product of a social relationship involving the effort of intelligent writer and intelligent reader to communicate with one another. Respect for facts was at the root of French scholarship, which Strachey said, with "its noble tradition of profound research and perfect lucidity" had become one of the glories of European culture.[23] It was a scholarship which, like the quality of cleanness in Rabelais's prose, came into being not merely through clear phrasing and good order but also through clear perceptions and clear thought processes. It insisted upon seeing the facts as they really were—in the light of the noonday sun and as interpreted by common sense. From respect for facts in their proper integrity arose likewise French realism, whether it was the psychological realism of Racine probing into the depths of human emotions or the realism of Balzac which brought the material things of man's environment into sharp focus and into close association with the human beings who lived in the midst of them. Sanity, we know, was always a high ideal to Strachey; to him, it did much to account for the high quality of French scholarship and French realism.

The impulse toward refinement, elegance, and restraint in French literature was likewise related to fundamental qualities of the French mind—good taste, respect for authority, and respect for civilization. Strachey himself had very little respect for institutional authority, whether it was that of a British public school or the French Academy or a national theater such as the Comédie Française.[24] Such authority was more than likely to impose dangerous artificial restrictions on human behavior and fully as danger-

23. "Voltaire and England," *Books and Characters,* p. 116. Strachey never failed to praise the liberal philosophers and the encyclopaedists of the eighteenth century. See, for instance, "The Abbé Morellet," *Portraits in Miniature* (New York, Harcourt, Brace, 1931), pp. 96–105.

24. See especially "L'Art Administratif," *Spectator, 99* (Dec. 28, 1907), 1093–4. A review of William Archer and H. Granville Barker's *A National Theater: Scheme and Estimates.*

ous restrictions on the mind of the artist. Hence it was not the Frenchman's respect for the institutions which were intended to maintain for him high standards of excellence so much as it was the Frenchman's unwavering respect for excellence itself, as it had manifested itself through a long literary tradition, that elicited his highest praise. Whatever political intrigues might at times account for some of the awards of the French Academy, the procession of French literature through the centuries offered more than adequate evidence that the young writers of the nation did not forget the lofty standards which their predecessors had kept before them. These standards were the ultimate authority of French literature.

And they were standards based upon respect for civilization. Elegance, decorum, and restraint were the good manners of literature; and the good manners of literature, when genuine, reflected the good manners of people living in society. French literature reflected the excellent manners of the French people. Theirs was a literature in which social relationships, conceived upon a high level, counted for much. Strachey found Rousseau, both the man and his teachings, intensely fascinating. Here was a complex psychological enigma, extremely interesting to look into. But to Strachey the fitting symbol of the central tendencies in French literature and culture was not to be found in Rousseau's extreme individualism and desire to seek in nature a refuge from society but rather in the Versailles of Louis XIV's time, with all its brilliance and blaze of splendor. In it, civilization was in full flower. It displayed a radiance which, despite the social, economic, and political evils of the day, was genuine. The great palace glowed with the light and warmth of a nation's life. Here all the good things of civilization were near at hand. One might catch glimpses within its walls, amidst the pomp and ceremony, of a "small, vital, passionate world which has clothed itself in ordered beauty, learnt a fine way of easy, splendid living, and come under the spell of a devotion" to its king. The appeal which Versailles made to Strachey's imagination was tremendous:

> When the morning sun was up and the horn was sounding down the long avenues, who would not wish, if only in fancy,

to join the glittering cavalcade where the young Louis led the hunt in the days of his opening glory? Later we might linger on the endless terrace, to watch the great monarch, with his red heels and his golden snuff-box and his towering periwig, come out among his courtiers, or in some elaborate grotto applaud a ballet by Molière. When night fell there would be dancing and music in the gallery blazing with a thousand looking-glasses, or masquerades and feasting in the gardens, with the torches throwing strange shadows among the trees trimmed into artificial figures, and gay lords and proud ladies conversing together under the stars.[25]

To Strachey, however, the mind of the French people as it had been reflected in their literature possessed one quality perhaps more delightful than any other. It was the ingredient which gave flavor and sparkle to a drink that was already good. Strachey gave it a precise name in his characterization of Charles de Brosses, who, he said, resembled the generous wine of Burgundy in his "combination of gay vitality with richness and strength." [26] Invigorating, intelligent laughter, the "gay vitality" of the *Fabliaux*, of Rabelais, of Molière, of La Fontaine, and of Voltaire, irrepressible and irresistible, not only provided the reader of French literature with an inexhaustible source of pleasure but also suggested much about the daily life of the French people. Strachey's own appetite for mirth was insatiable; his friends observed that if on a given day nothing amusing presented itself for his enjoyment he promptly proceeded to concoct something that would serve the purpose. Laughter was as essential to him as the air he breathed. And France was the home of good laughter. Strachey knew that not all laughter was good. He could not approve "the empty laughter of the foolish or the cruel laughter of the depraved," and he insisted that the comic writer was as much concerned with the value of per-

25. *Landmarks*, pp. 63–5. See also n. 24, above, and "Versailles," *Characters and Commentaries*, pp. 90–3. G. A. Johnston has written of Strachey, Maurois, and Ludwig: "The roots of the new biography are to be found embedded in the literature of France two hundred years ago." "The New Biography," *Atlantic Monthly, 143* (March 1929), 333 ff.

26. "The President de Brosses," *Portraits in Miniature,* p. 70.

sons as the artist was with tones.[27] But the French had taste in laughter as in other things. It appeared almost everywhere in their culture. Strachey found its essential qualities even in the caricatures of Caran D'Ache. "Those rapid, preposterous, good-humored, and somewhat scurrilous drawings," he wrote, "call up before the mind the image of one imbued through and through with some of the most marked characteristics of the French race." Here was laughter, "neither malignant nor meaningless, but eminently human." It was, at its best, elemental, as in Rabelais—"the golden and eternal laughter of the gods." [28] The greatness of Molière, likewise, lay in his union of the comic spirit with humanity.

The bright laughter, the constant flicker of vivacious wit which illuminated the minds and books of many of the best French writers, Strachey insisted, was not a quality suggesting that the people or the national literature lacked depth. Not merely was the comic spirit, as best exemplified by Molière, rooted in the utmost profundities of human nature, but the literature also gave memorable expression to the probings of the great French philosophers and theologians. It was, moreover, a literature which had produced great tragedy; it was the literature of Racine. To Strachey, Racine was a writer who, because of the imaginative grandeur of his loftiest poetry and the supreme force with which he expressed dramatic emotion concentrated within a perfect whole, deserved the right "to walk with Sophocles in the high places of eternity." [29]

As an interpreter of French literature for English-speaking people, Strachey has rendered his greatest service in his writings on Racine and Voltaire. Of the two, as he realized very clearly, Racine needed an interpreter much more. Racine had also suffered infinitely more from the misunderstanding, the lack of appreciation, and the neglect of Englishmen than either Voltaire or Molière

27. "The Mollusc," *Spectator, 99* (Nov. 30, 1907), 867–8. Strachey praises the laughter of Molière here.

28. "Caran D'Ache." It is interesting here to note Edgar Johnson's comment of Strachey himself: "Order and oddity: icy sanity and grotesque humors: these were the contrasting qualities that he held in subtle balance." *One Mighty Torrent: The Drama of Biography* (New York, Stackpole, 1937), p. 507. See also "Coquelin."

29. *Landmarks,* p. 109.

had. Molière, Strachey said, had always been popular in Great Britain; the English had always loved him.[30] But they were almost completely ignorant of the supreme master of tragedy in French literature.

The significance and success of Strachey's role as an interpreter of Racine have been attested to by more than one commentator. The writer who reviewed *Landmarks* for the *Times Literary Supplement* in 1912 observed that Strachey seemed to hold a brief for the literature of concentration as against that of expansion and that, since most Englishmen were prejudiced the other way, he was for them an extremely useful writer on French and would open their eyes to the greatness of Racine.[31]

Before Strachey wrote the essay on Racine for the *New Quarterly*, June 1908, he was aware of at least one English critic who had commented intelligently on Racine. In A. B. Walkley, whose *Drama and Life* Strachey reviewed in the *Spectator* for November 16, 1907, he had found obvious faults as dramatic critic. Even so, he was in some respects superior to Bernard Shaw: "His views, though they do not bear the impress of the vigor and originality of such a critic as Mr. Bernard Shaw, have the compensating merit of a freer play and a wider relevance." And on Racine, "for whom few English critics indeed have a good word to spare," he was "excellent." Strachey quoted with admiration Walkley's "striking" statement that the great Frenchman's tragedies show "men and women hungering for one another like wild beasts, and yet draping their desires in a style of delicate reticence as fastidious as Jane Austen's." [32] Walkley, however, although he said good things

30. "Molière."

31. Feb. 1, 1912, p. 44. For other comments, see the London *Times*, May 18, 1922, p. 16; J. Middleton Murry, *Nation and Athenaeum*, June 3, 1922, pp. 346–7; and André Maurois, Foreword to Cyril Clemens' *Lytton Strachey* (Webster Groves, Mo., International Mark Twain Society, 1942). Strachey reminded Maurois of Proust. See *Prophets and Poets*, trans. Hamish Miles (New York and London, Harper, 1935), p. 224. There are many comments on Strachey scattered throughout Maurois's publications. See also John Russell, "Lytton Strachey," *Horizon*, 15 (Feb. 1947), 115.

32. "Mr. Walkley on the Drama," *Spectator*, 99 (Nov. 16, 1907), 776–7. Shortly after publishing his essay, Strachey praised C. E. Vaughan for his

about Racine, did not say enough. Therefore, prodded by what he considered the error and inadequacy of J. C. Bailey's and St. John Lucas' books relating to French poetry, Strachey soon began writing his essay.

This essay and various passages scattered throughout *Landmarks* and a number of articles and reviews make it clear that Strachey believed his chief difficulty as an interpreter of Racine for people accustomed to tragedy as Shakespeare had handled it lay in explaining the brilliance with which the French dramatist had used the methods of classicism. In using these methods, he was not only akin to Sophocles, he was working in the central tradition of French literature. It was the tradition which aimed at concentration and demanded selection, simplicity, restraint, precision, and conformity to the rules. As contrasted with the tragedy of comprehension such as Shakespeare's *Antony and Cleopatra* it appeared greatly restricted in its movement, artificial in its regularity, and severe in its lack of ornament. Yet Racine, although not so great as Shakespeare, was a poet and dramatic genius of a very high order who had triumphed gloriously over all the difficulties which the classical method had put in his way:

> The technical restrictions he labored under were incredibly great; his vocabulary was cribbed, his versification was cabined, his whole power of dramatic movement was scrupulously confined; conventional rules of every conceivable denomination hurried out to restrain his genius, with the alacrity of Lilliputians pegging down a Gulliver; wherever he turned he was met by a hiatus or a pitfall, a blind-alley or a *mot bas*. But his triumph was not simply the conquest of these refractory creatures; it was something much more astonishing. It was the creation, in spite of them, nay, by their very aid, of a glowing, living, soaring, and enchanting work of art. To have brought about this amazing combination, to have erected, upon a structure of Alexandrines, of Unities, of Noble Personages, of stilted diction, of the whole intolerable paraphernalia of the

comments on Racine in *Types of Tragic Drama*. "Tragedy Old and New," *Spectator, 101* (Aug. 22, 1908), 266.

Classical stage, an edifice of subtle psychology, of exquisite poetry, of overwhelming passion—that is a *tour de force* whose achievement entitles Jean Racine to a place among the very few consummate artists of the world.[33]

The great danger was that English readers, to whom tragedy expressing itself through the classical medium was almost completely foreign, would fail to realize the sureness of Racine's psychology, the grandeur of his poetry, and the intensity, the force, and the depth of the passion which surged through his dramas. Unlike the romantics, who chased their ideas "through the four quarters of the universe to catch them at last upon the verge of the inane," Racine did not possess "the daring of adventure." Rather, his was the daring of intensity: "His fine surprises are seized at the very heart of his subject, and seized in a single stroke." [34] He was a writer of tremendous force, but it was the force of absolute directness. His mystery was not that which depends upon metaphysical stimulants but "the mystery of the mind of man." He was a psychological realist who showed not the accidents of character but its essentials; in his plays "the human spirit comes before us shorn of its particulars, naked and intense." In portraying his characters, he was more concerned with passion than with intellect. His chief mastery was over "the human heart—the subtleties, the profundities, the agonies, the triumphs, of love." And in conforming to the three unities he was always an artist conscious of a much higher unity which the Elizabethans frequently ignored—unity of tone.[35]

Racine interested Strachey mainly as a literary artist; Rousseau interested him mainly as a man; Voltaire interested him both as a literary artist and as a man. Moreover, he interested him fully as much as a philosopher, as one of the wisest and most provocative thinkers of all time.

This interest in Voltaire, like the interest in Racine, manifested itself early and was sustained throughout Strachey's life. One of his

33. "Voltaire's Tragedies," *Books and Characters*, p. 158.
34. "Racine," pp. 15–16.
35. *Ibid.*, and *Landmarks, passim*.

earliest published essays, as we have seen, was "Voltaire's Tragedies," published in the *Independent Review* for April 1905; and
in the years that followed he produced a succession of brilliant writings on various aspects of Voltaire's life and literary career. The
very thought of the great Frenchman seemed to quicken his mind
and was to him a constant point of reference as, in twentieth-
century England, he formulated his own active philosophy of life
and determined the standards which shaped his own career as a
man of letters. The picture of Voltaire with raised hand which
hung over his fireplace was much more than an ornament for his
study: it was a symbol and a daily reminder of the intimacy which
he felt in his relation to the French writer and of the validity and
significance of Voltaire's voice as it spoke to civilized men over
two hundred years after his death. The astonishing life which was
in Voltaire's mind had never died; to discuss him was to strike
out sparks of interest and pleasure from the most jaded readers;
and to mention his name was "to start off a whole train of delightful associations, and to raise expectations of more." [36] It was
impossible to be bored in the presence of Voltaire. When he was
alive, he carried with him everywhere "a spirit of unappeasable
excitability, which constantly drove him into the most absurd and
most discreditable predicaments, and usually ended by making the
place of his abode too hot to hold him"; but, whatever the disadvantages were that went with it, Voltaire possessed to an unusual
degree an electric energy which "seemed to convey itself into
everyone with whom he came in contact, and he could hardly walk
down the street without becoming a center of excitement." [37] He
was a very great man indeed who could touch even trivial things
and make them significant. Strachey's feeling of wonder for him
was like that which Browning once expressed for Shelley. And
just as Browning was awe-struck to meet a man who "had seen
Shelley plain," Strachey congratulated Voltaire's contemporary,
Charles de Brosses, who in a quarrel with Voltaire over the price

36. "Three Frenchmen in England." A review of J. Churton Collins' *Voltaire, Montesquieu, and Rousseau in England.*
37. *Ibid.*

of a load of wood succeeded in compelling the philosopher to pay him the 281 francs he demanded but through the transaction lost his chance to be elected to the Academy. His was a unique distinction, Strachey said; however great his loss, he would go down in history as the one man who got the better of Voltaire.[38]

Nevertheless, Strachey never himself forgot and did not fail to remind his readers that Voltaire was a strange and intricate mixture of good and bad. He was a man who devoted his life to one of the noblest causes, and yet he was "personally a very ugly customer," who was "inordinately vain, mercilessly revengeful, as mischievous as a monkey, and as cruel as a cat." [39] His nature was compounded of sense and sensibility; and throughout his life the sensibility expressed itself in many disagreeable, sinister forms.[40] Those who dealt with him soon discovered to their sorrow that he was a scoundrel. Some, however, like Frederick the Great, realized too late that he was a scoundrel of genius. Frederick naively assumed that Voltaire's spirit was that of an ordinary man or that he was a spiteful, mischievous monkey. He was not a monkey but a devil, a decidedly different thing. Frederick also made the great mistake of assuming that Voltaire had loyalty and affection for him. Voltaire was incapable of feeling either: "Nor was he personally attached to Frederick; he was personally attached to no one on earth. Certainly he had never been a man of feeling, and now that he was old and hardened by the uses of the world he had grown to be completely what in essence he always was— a fighter, without tenderness, without scruples, and without re-

38. "The Président de Brosses."

39. "Voltaire." Strachey also wrote of Voltaire in this essay: "He was a frantic, desperate fighter, to whom all means were excusable; he was a trickster, a rogue; he lied, he blasphemed, and he was extremely indecent. He was, too, quite devoid of dignity, adopting, whenever he saw fit, the wildest expedients and the most extravagant postures; there was, in fact, a strong element of farce in his character, which he had the wit to exploit for his own ends."

40. *Ibid.*, p. 240. "A vehement sensitiveness—a nervous susceptibility of amazing intensity . . . made him an artist, an egotist, a delirious enthusiast, dancing, screaming, and gesticulating to the last moment of an extreme old age." *Ibid.*, p. 241.

morse." [41] He was probably "the best-hated man in the eighteenth century." [42]

As a literary artist, likewise, Voltaire displayed many faults. His tragedies, which won great acclaim in his own day, had no merits which could be discovered in ours. Neither a poet nor a psychologist, Voltaire completely lacked the dramatic sense. The contrast between his plays and those of his great predecessor, Racine, only served to emphasize the fact:

> Voltaire, unfortunately, was neither a poet nor a psychologist; and, when he picked up the mantle of Racine, he put it, not upon a human being, but upon a tailor's block. To change the metaphor, Racine's work resembled one of those elaborate paper transparencies which delighted our grandmothers, illuminated from within so as to present a charming tinted picture with varying degrees of shadow and light. Voltaire was able to make the transparency, but he could never light the candle; and the only result of his efforts was some sticky pieces of paper, cut into curious shapes, and roughly daubed with color.[43]

As a writer of tragedies, he represented the great classical tradition in its decadence. We may only express astonishment that his audiences, watching his heroines "go mad in epigrams" and his villains "commit murder in inversions," were dazzled by "an easy display of cheap brilliance, and cheap philosophy, and cheap sentiment." [44]

That Voltaire also had serious deficiencies as a literary critic was clearly indicated by his failure to appreciate Shakespeare. To Strachey it was very curious that Voltaire seemed at times to be able to get in contact with his great predecessor and yet remained "as absolutely unaffected by him as Shakespeare himself was by

41. "Voltaire and Frederick the Great," *Books and Characters*, pp. 176, 179, 180, 181. See also "A Sidelight on Frederick the Great," *Characters and Commentaries*, pp. 193 ff.

42. "Voltaire and England," *Books and Characters*, p. 127.

43. "Voltaire's Tragedies," pp. 158, 160.

44. *Ibid.*, pp. 162, 163.

Voltaire." [45] It was practically impossible for Voltaire to admire anything outside the confines of the classical tradition in which he himself worked. Yet Strachey believed that the changes which appeared to take place in Voltaire's attitude toward Shakespeare as it veered from enthusiastic praise in his earlier years immediately after his return from England to emphatic denunciation and even disgust in his old age had been subject to serious misrepresentation and erroneous interpretation. The facts did not indicate that he was inconsistent or that in his later years he became increasingly jealous of Shakespeare as he discovered the growing admiration which the French public displayed for the English dramatist. Strachey's own interpretation was stated most clearly and convincingly in an early review, that of Sidney Lee's *Shakespeare and the Modern Stage* (1906):

> It is true that at first sight the violent invectives of Voltaire's old age stand out in striking contrast with the tributes of his earlier years; but the more the facts are examined, the more obvious it becomes that Voltaire's attitude towards Shakespeare was really consistent throughout his life. His view was a simple one. Shakespeare was a writer of great force, but absolutely devoid of taste. At the beginning of his career, when Shakespeare was unknown in France, it was only natural that he should wish to impress his countrymen with the merits of the English genius. To explain his subsequent change of front by imputing to him a vulgar jealousy of Shakespeare's fame [might have seemed reasonable to Horace Walpole but should not satisfy the modern scholar]. . . . Voltaire's anger was aroused, not by a fear for his own laurels, but by a genuine disgust for what seemed to him a silly craze over a foreign barbarian. The genius of the barbarian was neither here nor there; he was a barbarian, and to place him above the masters of French drama was to commit an inexcusable outrage upon literary taste. And, from his own point of view, Voltaire was certainly in the right. As Mr. Lee points out, the worship which eighteenth-century Frenchmen bestowed on Shake-

45. *Ibid.*, p. 161.

speare was indiscriminating in the highest degree. They went into ecstacies over *Othello,* while they converted the speeches of Iago into stilted Alexandrines, and transformed the last act of the play into "a dazzling scene of domestic bliss." Their adaptations showed clearly enough that they recognized, no less than Voltaire, that their idol had feet of clay; they believed, just as he believed, that no tragedy which disregarded the "unities" and contained the word "handkerchief" could be a great work of art. They accordingly concocted a Shakespeare of their own,—a Shakespeare who had read Aristotle, wore a full-bottomed wig, and never spoke of a handkerchief as anything but a *gage d'amour.* Voltaire was far more honest; he started from the same premises, and arrived at a very different conclusion: Shakespeare was a preposterous mountebank, whom it was dangerous to imitate and foolish to applaud. And the conclusion was logical; it was only the premises that were mistaken.[46]

Strachey obviously did not intend to condone Voltaire's serious error in literary judgment. Many years after writing this review he asserted that to the true significance of Shakespeare's genius Voltaire remained utterly blind. Even the paragraphs on Shakespeare in the *Lettres Philosophiques* showed Voltaire at his worst: "Never was such speculative audacity combined with such aesthetic timidity; it is as if he had reserved all his superstition for matters of art. From his account of Shakespeare, it is clear that he never dared to open his eyes and frankly look at what he should see before him." [47] If Voltaire had been nothing more than a critic, poet, and dramatist, Strachey might have concluded that the faults and limitations of his work in the three fields, together with his faults and limitations as a person, made him an inviting subject for satire and nothing more.

But there was a supremely great Voltaire, a Voltaire whose im-

46. "Mr. Sidney Lee on Shakespeare," *Spectator,* 97 (Dec. 1, 1906), 887–8.
47. "Voltaire and England," p. 138. I find Charles Vouga's treatment of the subject somewhat unfair to Strachey in "Mr. Strachey and the French Mind," *Bookman,* 57 (March 1923), 44–6.

mortality was not open to question. This was the Voltaire whose essential qualities were to be found in the *Lettres Philosophiques,* the dialogues, the *Dictionnaire Philosophique, Candide,* and the immense corpus of personal letters which accumulated during his long life. In these works Voltaire's best style came into play. Even this was not quite the perfect style, because it lacked breadth and color. But such shortcomings frequently seemed to become, through Voltaire's wizardry, positive merits. The narrowness of style became sharpness, not like "the sweeping blade of Pascal" but like "a rapier—all point." [48] The lack of color often appeared as pure, transparent brightness, intense, vivid, brilliant. It was also, however, a style in which the tradition that had begun with Pascal, the tradition which was based on the assumption that the supreme qualities of style were clarity, simplicity, and wit, was brought to its culmination. Voltaire's style was like a pirouette "executed with all the grace, all the ease, all the latent strength of a consummate dancer." [49]

It was Strachey's opinion that Voltaire's style reached its highest level in *Candide.* But the same admirable qualities were to be found in the style of all of Voltaire's best works. A literary form which interested Strachey particularly was the dialogue. Voltaire had brought it to perfection. It was a form which "suited him exactly, with its opportunities for the rapid exposition of contrary doctrines, for the humorous stultification of opponents, and for witty repartee." [50] Strachey's own dialogues are modeled on Voltaire's. Most of these remain in manuscript, but a representative specimen, "A dialogue between Moses, Diogenes, and Mr. Loke," appeared, nestling comfortably and fittingly between two essays on Voltaire, in *Books and Characters.*[51]

48. *Landmarks,* p. 181. Leonard Bacon has observed that what Strachey said about Voltaire's style applies also to his own, "like a rapier all point." "An Eminent Post-Victorian," *Yale Review,* N.S. *30* (Winter 1941), 311.

49. *Landmarks,* p. 181.

50. *Ibid.,* p. 173.

51. Strachey's dialogues are brilliant and deserve early publication. Among them are those with the following titles: "Julius Caesar and Lord Salisbury," "Sennacherib and Rupert Brooke," "Cleopatra and Mrs. Humphrey Ward," "Catullus and Lord Tennyson," "Boccaccio and General Lee," "King Herod

Voltaire's style, with its wonderful mingling of gaiety, irony, and common sense, was put at the service of the high cause for which Strachey himself cared most. His was a frivolity of manner only; in his purpose he was entirely serious. There was no limit to his courage or to his faith in the doctrines which he labored to make prevail. His efforts were vigorous, ingenious, and unrelenting: "With what a reckless audacity, what a fierce uncompromising passion he charged and fought and charged again!" [52] And the precise nature of the cause for which he fought was never for a moment in doubt; it was the cause of truth, of freedom and tolerance, and of humanity. The enemies were ignorance and superstition, tyranny and narrowness, and all the formidable and sinister forces which through history had threatened to crush the human spirit and to prevent men from achieving maximum well-being during their lives on earth.

Thus Voltaire was to Strachey a champion of humanism; he was the redoubtable Erasmus of the eighteenth century. He was one of the three men who had become intellectual masters of Europe. What Bernard of Clairvaux had been to the Middle Ages and what Erasmus had been to the Renaissance Voltaire had been to his age. He was the center and chief spirit of the movement which produced the French Revolution. The observations which he brought back from England to France made him a pioneer of modern cultural internationalism. It was he who made France aware of Newton, and he steadfastly labored to persuade his countrymen to let the new science take the place of the older mistaken science of Descartes and of mere superstition. His persistent attack on Christianity arose from his detestation of all the tyrannies which the Church had imposed on human beings and from his firm belief that throughout history its priesthood had stubbornly and blindly sought to prevent the spread of truth and tolerance.

---

and the Reverend Mr. Malthus," "Gibbon, Johnson, and Adam Smith," "Salter and Cleopatra," and "Headmaster and Parent." Mr. Aldous Huxley wrote in a review of *Books and Characters:* "Mr. Strachey is the eighteenth century grown-up; he is Voltaire at two hundred and thirty." *On the Margin* (London, Chatto and Windus, 1923), p. 142.

52. "Voltaire and England," p. 141.

Strachey himself was, we know, in the most radical sense a rebel against what he considered to be the colossal iniquities of the old order. The cause in which he believed was precisely that for which Voltaire had battled so valiantly.

And Strachey was confident that the cause of Voltaire was invincible. Erasmus had been a tragic figure. He had lived to see the barbarism of the Middle Ages rise up against his teaching and, except in England, overwhelm it:

> By a curious irony, the Renaissance contained within itself the seeds of its ruin. The very enlightenment which seemed to be leading the way to the unlimited progress of the race involved Europe in the internecine struggles of nationalism and religion. England alone, by a series of accidents, of which the complexion of Anne Boleyn, a storm in the channel, and the character of Charles I were the most important, escaped disaster. There the spirit of Reason found for itself a not too precarious home; and by the beginning of the eighteenth century a civilization had been evolved which, in essentials, was not very far distant from the great ideals of the Renaissance. In the meantime the rest of Europe had relapsed into medievalism.[53]

The essential work of Voltaire was to revive in Europe the humanistic spirit of the Renaissance which he had discovered with admiration alive and productive in England. But the irony of history manifested itself once more as a new and formidable enemy of this spirit appeared in Voltaire's day. The Industrial Revolution began to spawn its problems and evils. "By a strange chance, no sooner was medievalism dead than industrialism was born. The mechanical ingenuity of a young man in Glasgow plunged the world into a whole series of enormous and utterly unexpected difficulties, which are still clamoring to be solved. Thus the progress which the Renaissance had envisioned, and which had seemed assured at the end of the eighteenth century, was once more side-

53. "Voltaire," p. 239.

tracked." [54] Strachey wrote the essay on Voltaire from which the last two passages have been quoted in 1919, after he had lived through all the horrors of the first World War. Yet he added significantly in this essay, "The work of Voltaire was not undone," and asserted his conviction that nothing less than some overwhelming catastrophe could obliterate the great teachings of the French philosopher from the minds of men. Nothing was more characteristic of Strachey, Keynes, and other members of the Bloomsbury group than the unwavering faith which they maintained in their humanistic creed, the courage and skill with which they sought to make it prevail, and the confidence which they had in ultimate victory. Keynes continued the battle in full vigor and with undiminished hope down through the second World War and until his death in 1946. If Strachey had lived, he would have been active, in his own way, close beside his friend throughout it all. Thus we may understand how Voltaire—not to mention some of the other great writers of France who had an intimate intellectual kinship with Voltaire—was much more to him than an important name in literary history. At stake was a way of life which largely through Voltaire's astonishing force and brilliance had become a part of the central tradition of the French people. It had much in common with the highest ideals of all Western peoples. To Strachey, therefore, Voltaire was a living presence, a source of strength, and an inspiring leader in the only war worth fighting.

54. *Ibid.,* p. 240. It is a great pity that Strachey did not live to write his life of Voltaire. The subject was fitted to his hand. He had exactly the qualifications required: an adequate style, a live and intelligent interest in the complexities of Voltaire's personality, critical balance in the examination of Voltaire's literary productions, a sympathetic understanding of Voltaire's greatest doctrines, and a sure and extensive knowledge of the history, culture, and literature which made up Voltaire's background. I believe that this would have been Strachey's greatest work.

CHAPTER 6

*O*n *the Eighteenth Century*

LYTTON STRACHEY loved the past, but he was not a Miniver Cheevy or a Henry Adams. He never for a moment felt that he was born too late. His temperament had much in common with that of Thackeray: he found the eighteenth century full of charm; he was critical of his own age, but he thoroughly enjoyed living in it. Like Thackeray, too, as Clive Bell has pointed out, Strachey not merely knew the past, he realized it: "To him the Athens of Socrates and the Paris of the Encyclopaedists are as real as the Oxford of Newman or the London of Lord Morley."[1] His was an ever-probing, discriminating, evaluating mind; and he was just as critical of the past as he was of his own day. Like other wise men, Strachey went to the past not to escape from life but to increase it. He has been spoken of as a Voltaire over two hundred years old; or as a Voltaire, Rousseau, and Chateaubriand rolled into one for the edification and amusement of the twentieth century.[2] But he did not borrow servilely from them or from their age, and he fully appreciated the vantage point from which to study them that the intervening years gave.

Some ages, however, were better than others. The eighteenth century, particularly the second half of it, was one of the best. "There can be no doubt," Strachey wrote, "that the latter half of the eighteenth century attained to a height of civilization unknown

1. "Lytton Strachey," *New Statesman*, 21 (Aug. 4, 1923), 496–7.
2. *Ibid.;* Edwin Muir, "Lytton Strachey," *Nation and Athenaeum*, 37 (April 25, 1925), 102–4; D. S. (Prince) Mirsky, "Mr. Lytton Strachey," *London Mercury*, 8 (June 1923), 175–84.

in Europe since the days of Hadrian." [3] Even more emphatically he once declared: "In the troubled sea of History two epochs seem to stand out like enchanted islands of delight and of repose—the Age of the Antonines and the eighteenth century." [4] No other age in English history, before or since, had had higher respect for literature. And what test of the height of civilization achieved by a nation in any period could be more valid than the degree of respect manifested toward literature? [5]

Although the Romantics and the Victorians were probably justified in rebelling against the eighteenth century, which they found "intolerably rigid, formal and self-satisfied, devoid, to an extraordinary degree, of sympathy, adventure, and imagination," thoughtful people in the twentieth century, rebelling in turn against their immediate predecessors, had begun to realize that for the purposes of "a historical vision" the eighteenth century was precisely what was wanted. [6] Strachey believed that he and his generation might

3. "Horace Walpole," *Characters and Commentaries* (New York, Harcourt, Brace, 1933), p. 85. In this as in many other ways, Strachey's mother had much to do with forming his mind and taste. Extant is a letter from her to him, dated February 14, 1899, in which she bestows the highest praise on the eighteenth century, on Gibbon and Voltaire particularly.

4. "English Letter Writers," *Characters and Commentaries,* p. 11.

5. "Pope," *Characters and Commentaries,* p. 7.

6. "The Eighteenth Century," *Characters and Commentaries,* pp. 280–1. One cannot fail to perceive the sympathy with which Strachey treats Lord Melbourne in *Queen Victoria*—"a child of the eighteenth century whose lot was cast in a new, difficult age" and "an autumn rose" (New York, Harcourt, Brace, 1921, p. 88); or Mary Berry, a typical eighteenth-century lady with whom Horace Walpole in old age had been in love, who lived on until 1852, deploring her "sadly insignificant existence" (*Portraits in Miniature* [New York, Harcourt, Brace, 1931], pp. 106–17). On the other hand, Sir Edmund Gosse found in Lord Cromer, unfavorably treated in Strachey's "General Gordon," a man who by taste and temperament seemed to belong to the eighteenth century. *Some Diversions of a Man of Letters* (New York, Scribner's, 1919), pp. 204–7. Gosse also believed that there was an eighteenth-century side to Queen Victoria's own character which Strachey did not bring out sufficiently. "But perhaps he might have dwelt a little on Victoria's attitude to State as contrasted with private religion. In the latter direction she was purely eighteenth century; she suspected zeal, and was repelled by enthusiasm." *More Books on the Table* (London, Heinemann, 1923), pp. 3–10.

very well use a little eighteenth-century cynicism and skepticism
to clear away the fog which the religious atmosphere of the Victorians had cast over everything.[7] Likewise, the early twentieth-
century drift toward formlessness and intellectual obscurity might
profit greatly from a few lessons from Boileau, with "his reasonableness, his common sense, and his wit." [8] Such a dramatist as J. M.
Barrie, who in *What Every Woman Knows* attempted to be "everything by turns and nothing long," very much needed the lessons.[9]
So did many of the poets. The William Butler Yeats of 1908, to
Strachey a perfect example of the extreme romantic, wrote poetry
so wildly imaginative that it could properly be defined as "romance in process of decomposition." Dr. Johnson, Strachey said,
would have reserved for Yeats his "most annihilating common-
sense." [10] Poets should always remember what Pope and Milton
had clearly realized, namely, that a hard core of reason is a good
thing for verse. And poets who sought to outdo Wordsworth in
their susceptibility to nature compelled one to seek relief in
eighteenth-century matter-of-factness. In August 1908 Strachey
wrote as follows from Skye to his friend J. M. Keynes: "We're nine
miles from Portree, the nearest center of civilization (and beauty),
and we're surrounded by deserts of green vagueness, multitudes
of imbecile mountains and eternal rain." [11] By itself, however, this
passage is hardly representative of Strachey's attitude toward nature. He was far from being blind to the loveliness of landscapes.
But he found little to admire in a treatment of nature which reflected Wordsworth's enthusiasm without Wordsworth's sanity—
a treatment which was all intense feeling and lush description. Unusually susceptible as he was to the charm of places, like many
writers of the eighteenth century he found them delightful mainly
because of their associations with human beings and human
affairs.[12]

7. "A Statesman: Lord Morley," *Characters and Commentaries*, pp. 215–16.
8. "The Admirable Boileau," *Spectator, 101* (Nov. 7, 1908), 735–6.
9. "Mr. Barrie's New Play," *Spectator, 101* (Sept. 26, 1908), 444–5.
10. "Mr. Yeats's Poetry," *Spectator, 101* (Oct. 17, 1908), 588–9.
11. R. F. Harrod, *The Life of John Maynard Keynes* (New York, Harcourt,
Brace, 1951), p. 106.
12. However, Strachey could comment favorably on what Rousseau re-

Likewise, Strachey had little patience with those romantics who would dismiss the great body of eighteenth-century poetry with contempt because it lacked music, mystery, and imaginative expansiveness. He believed that there were many kinds of poetry and that it was ridiculous to be governed entirely by the taste of any particular school. On the positive side, moreover, readers of poetry in the twentieth century might find much in the solid sense of eighteenth-century writers that would give balance and health to their minds.

> We are still under the spell of "The Ancient Mariner"; and poetry to us means, primarily, something which suggests, by means of words, mysteries and infinitudes. Thus, music and imagination seem to us the most essential qualities of poetry, because they are the most potent means by which suggestions may be invoked. But the eighteenth century knew none of these things. To Lord Chesterfield and Pope, to Prior and to Horace Walpole, there was nothing at all strange about the world; it was charming, it was disgusting, it was ridiculous, and it was just what one might have expected. In such a world, why should poetry, more than anything else, be mysterious? No! Let it be sensible; that was enough.[13]

Most of Strachey's own poems written after his Cambridge period are in rhyming couplets and reflect eighteenth-century taste.

Both the skepticism and the selfishness of the eighteenth century had been misunderstood. With all its reputation for skepticism, the age was actually one in which beliefs were "rigid, intense, and imperturbable." It was the romantics who had lost their faith: "They rose against the old dispensation with all the zeal of rebels and heretics." [14] As for the selfishness, the eighteenth century frankly recognized in it one of the fundamental urges of human nature. Nevertheless, so great was the value that the age

ceived from Nature. See "Three Frenchmen in England" (a review of J. Churton Collins' *Voltaire, Montesquieu, and Rousseau in England*), *Spectator, 100* (May 30, 1908), 866–7.

13. "The Lives of the Poets," *Books and Characters* (New York, Harcourt, Brace, 1922), pp. 78–9.

14. "Pope," pp. 9–10.

attached to social relationships and the graces by which they might
be realized at their best that selfishness in the eighteenth century
rarely degenerated into what was unpleasantly personal and petty:

> Thus while in one sense the ideal of such a society was an
> eminently selfish one, it is none the less true that there have
> been very few societies indeed in which the ordinary forms of
> personal selfishness have played so small a part. The selfish-
> ness of the eighteenth century was a communal selfishness.
> Each individual was expected to practice, and did in fact prac-
> tice to a consummate degree, those difficult arts which make
> the wheels of human intercourse run smoothly—the arts of
> taste and temper, of frankness and sympathy, of delicate com-
> pliment and exquisite self-abnegation—with the result that
> a condition of living was produced which, in all its superficial
> and obvious qualities, was one of unparalleled amenity.[15]

Thus the wisdom of the eighteenth century lay not in attempting
to deny or suppress selfishness altogether but in using the social
arts to keep it under the surface.

The classicism of the eighteenth century naturally appealed to
Strachey very powerfully. With his strong conviction that history
and literature should always be considered as arts, he found much
to admire in an age which insisted on selection, restraint, clearness, decorum, and proportion. He liked the statement which he
found in W. P. Ker's *Essays on Medieval Literature* that the period
of Pope and that of Chaucer had much in common because in them
more than in most ages writers were consciously artistic, remarkably secure in their command of their resources.[16] It was no wonder
that the classic writer and the romantic writer often found it difficult to understand one another. The contrast between their methods was very sharp. The romantic used the method of accumulation to achieve the effect of variety; the classic used selection to
achieve a powerful simplicity:

> The object of all art is to make suggestions. The romantic
> artist attains that end by using a multitude of different

15. "Madame Du Deffand," *Books and Characters*, pp. 89–90.
16. "Medieval Studies," *Spectator, 97* (Nov. 17, 1906), 786–7.

stimuli, by calling up image after image, recollection after recollection, until the reader's mind is filled and held by a vivid and palpable evocation; the classic works by the contrary method of a fine economy, and, ignoring everything but what is essential, trusts, by means of the exact propriety of his presentation, to produce the required effect.[17]

An excellent example of classicism could be found in Gibbon, who aimed not at comprehension but at illumination and who "drove a straight, firm road through the vast unexplored forest of Roman history." Hence Gibbon realized clearly that from beginning to end his fundamental problem was one of exclusion.[18] Even in the nineteenth century Stendhal showed that the classical method could be used to great advantage. His was the method "of selection, of omission, of unification, with the object of creating a central impression of supreme reality." [19] Strachey's own impulses were often those of a romantic. In his reading he found almost equal delight in the masterpieces of romanticism and those of classicism. But in a country and age in which such supreme works of classicism as the dramas of Racine were neglected and unappreciated, he was prompted to spend much time and effort in explaining the method and extolling the merits of classicism. And his own methods were largely those of classicism.[20]

Strachey believed also that each method had its characteristic dangers. The dangers of romanticism were irrelevancy, redundancy, vagueness, obscurity, and a loss of power through diffusion. The

17. "Madame Du Deffand," p. 102.

18. "Gibbon," *Portraits in Miniature*, p. 159.

19. "Henri Beyle," *Books and Characters*, p. 279. Strachey also wrote of Stendhal: "We find a succession of colorless, unemphatic sentences; we find cold reasoning and exact narrative; we find polite irony and dry wit. The spirit of the eighteenth century is everywhere." Pp. 276–7.

20. Although the review of *Landmarks in French Literature* in the *Times Literary Supplement* (Feb. 1, 1912, p. 44) was in the main favorable and commended Strachey for opening the eyes of some to the greatness of Racine, it suggested that at times Strachey may have carried his preference for classicism too far and that one should not slight *Les Miserables* in order to praise *Manon Lescaut* the better: "To have read Hugo's tremendous achievement and not to have been overcome by its torrential prodigality of power is to convey the suggestion that one prefers a hothouse to the winds of heaven."

great danger of classicism was that it might exclude too much.
Boileau's rigid system of aesthetics was inadequate because it ignored the fact that beauty was, perhaps "more often than not—
complex, obscure, fantastic, and strange." [21] Classicism in the
drama, for instance, when carried to its utmost extreme, produced
plays like those of Voltaire, "the most consummate of artists,
dancing in a vacuum on the tight-rope of his own wit." [22] Furthermore, the biographer who attempted to limit himself entirely to
the classical method would certainly be seriously handicapped.
The method which served Hume and metaphysics very well might
prove to be woefully lacking in a treatment of the complexities of
human nature. While working on *Elizabeth and Essex,* Strachey
observed: "A generalized, colorless, unimaginative view of things
is admirable when one is considering the law of causality, but one
needs something else if one has to describe Queen Elizabeth." [23]

But the eighteenth century at times displayed other shortcomings, some of them much worse than those suggested by the limitations of classicism. In its manifestations of these the first half of
the century in particular seemed at times to be a "still half-
barbarous age." Lady Mary Wortley Montagu, with all her cleverness, had some of the worst faults of her time: "She was, like her
age, cold and hard; she was infinitely unromantic; she was often
cynical, and sometimes gross." [24] Strachey could tolerate indecency
and cynicism. There were times when he even advocated them as
antidotes for prudery and shallow optimism. He was well aware too
of the importance of reining in the romantic impulses. But the
coldness and the hardness—the lack of fundamental humanity—
were faults which he could not condone. When he encountered
it, as he did in the double cruelty from which Voltaire suffered

21. *Landmarks in French Literature,* The Home University Library (New
York, Henry Holt, 1912), p. 76.
22. "Molière," *Spectator, 99* (Oct. 26, 1907), 612–13. It is interesting to
compare Strachey's comments on some Chinese lyrics, after reading them in
Professor Giles's translation: "The spirit is the classical spirit—that in which
the beauties of originality and daring and surprise are made an easy sacrifice
upon the altar of perfection." "An Anthology," *Characters and Commentaries,* p. 139.
23. "Hume," *Portraits in Miniature,* p. 145. First published Jan. 7, 1928.
24. "Lady Mary Wortley Montagu," *Characters and Commentaries,* p. 116.

when Rohan had him whipped in public and when French aris-
tocrats for weeks afterward laughed at him because of his misfortune, he could only shudder and try to keep his eyes shut. He did
not mince words in denouncing it: the convention which made
misfortune the proper object of ridicule was "callous and stupid." [25]

Not merely in this inhuman convention but also in the great
lengths to which the eighteenth century was inclined to carry most
of its conventions, both good and bad, did Strachey discover a
weakness. He had, for instance, great respect for the conventions
of good manners and great admiration for the kind of society that
the eighteenth century had demonstrated they made possible. But
Chesterfield's systematic thoroughness threatened to reduce the
whole subject to an absurdity. Strachey observed: "All the important things in manners are either so easy that it is not worth while
teaching them, or so difficult that they can never be taught." [26]
And wherever one turned in the eighteenth century—in books,
on the stage, in life—there were conventions, big and little, good
and bad. Fanny Burney gathered up many of them in her novels:
"Conventional feelings, conventional phrases, conventional situations, conventional oddities, conventional loves,—these were the
necessary ingredients of their perfect novel; and all these Miss
Burney was able, with supreme correctness, to supply." [27] Certainly
the most ridiculous conventions of all were those reflected in the
sentimental dialogue often to be found in the novels and plays of
the time. Strachey was greatly amused at one of Miss Burney's
passages:

> "And then consider how thy full coffers may hereafter make
> reparation for the empty catalogue of thy virtues."
> "Anan!" cries Mr. Briggs, in reply to these noble senti-
> ments; and that—whatever it may mean—is perhaps the best
> rejoinder.[28]

25. "Voltaire and England," *Books and Characters,* p. 118.
26. "English Letter Writers," p. 28.
27. "The Wrong Turning," *Characters and Commentaries,* p. 78. First published as a review of Austin Dobson's *Fanny Burney.*
28. *Ibid.,* p. 79.

Not only in his comments on Miss Burney but also in his consideration of others representative of the period, Strachey demonstrated that the general enthusiasm which he had for the eighteenth century was not uncritical. Whether he dealt with Thomson or Swift or Hogarth or Theobald or Pope or Walpole or Johnson, he was habitually careful to sift and to assay. He found much in them that gave him intense delight and brought forth the warmest expressions of praise; but on more than one occasion he treated them with downright severity—even Pope, for whom his admiration was tremendous.

James Thomson to him was certainly not a great poet. Strachey reviewed the volume on him which G. C. Macaulay had contributed to Macmillan's "English Men of Letters" series and concluded that Thomson scarcely deserved to have a whole book written about him. All that needed to be said upon the subject of Thomson, according to Strachey, could be said in a magazine article of a dozen pages. Neither in his life nor in his poetry did he deserve more space. There was nothing of particular interest about his life; it passed, "without incident and without romance, in easy independence among congenial friends and patrons." The only one of Thomson's poems which Strachey could admire was "The Castle of Indolence." This, he conceded, possessed a beauty of "a rare and charming kind." As an imitation of Spenser, it was "graceful, easy, and, above all, light"; and throughout it had "an atmosphere of charming languor and beautiful repose." Here, for once, Thomson "wears his fancy dress with the distinction and gaiety of a man of breeding." But "The Seasons" could claim no such praise. To the average reader of modern times the poem was "an intolerably tedious piece of work." Absent from it was the most striking characteristic of Wordsworth's treatment of nature —its intense subjectivity. Thomson's vague generalizations used to describe nature were not to be compared with Wordsworth's descriptions in terms of the particular and the concrete. Thomson was not a landscape painter but a rhetorician. He had extremely annoying habits, such as that of "employing the definite article so as to produce the most indefinite effects." He was far more interested in words than in things. In "The Seasons" he was "a solemn dwarf strutting in a giant's robe"; and, unfortunately, his empty generalizations and academic pomposity "exactly fell in with the weak side" of eighteenth-century taste. But Strachey adds significantly: "Perhaps the present age would have reason to be thankful if its own errors in taste were no worse than those." [29]

Jonathan Swift was another matter entirely. Strachey voiced no complaint about the scope of the project when he gave his attention to Temple Scott's edition of Swift's prose in twelve volumes.[30] Rather, he commended Scott for doing "no small service to English letters." "Swift was something more than a great writer, he was a great man; and the interest attaching to his name has always depended as much upon his character as upon his works." It was a great pity, Strachey felt, that although a number of portraits of Swift were produced in his day, he was never painted by a master: "Thus, though his features are familiar to everyone—the high forehead, the arched nose, the arrogant lips, the eyes 'quite azure as the heavens,' and the black terrific eyebrows above them—yet they live for us on no supreme canvas, and we are fain to do our best with our imagination to clothe with the force and fire of genius the dull presentments we possess." Strachey's instinct for psychological probing naturally made the controversial question of Swift's relations with Stella and Vanessa an intensely fascinating subject for him. Whether or not Swift actually married Stella was for him a matter that remained "in the region of doubtful speculation." He was not sorry, for the real question did not lie here:

> Whatever the answer, we shall be no nearer the central mystery of Swift's life. What was the nature of his feelings towards the two women whose fates were so strangely twisted around his own? What were the compelling forces, what were the crucial acts, of that tragedy? We shall never know more than we know at present, and that is so little that the most careful biographers are able to come to totally contrary conclusions upon the most important points at issue. Thus Sir Leslie Stephen inclined to believe that Swift was in love with Vanessa

29. "The Poetry of Thomson," *Spectator, 100* (March 14, 1908), 421–2.
30. "Jonathan Swift," *Spectator, 102* (Feb. 27, 1909), 341–2.

and not with Stella, while Dr. Bernard is of opinion that he was in love with Stella and was never anything more than Vanessa's intimate friend.

Strachey agreed with those who considered Swift one of the great masters of English prose. He found his parallel among painters in Velázquez, in whom restraint, economy of effort, and sobriety of tone produced effects which were brilliant and unforgettable. It was useless to look beneath the ease and simplicity of either one in an effort to discover the secret of his art:

> We ask in vain by what magic those quiet and commonplace ingredients have been converted into the visible image of life and force. Swift's is the least emphatic of styles, and the most powerful. His mind, infinitely unpoetical, turned naturally towards the detailed, the dry, and the material, discarding all the dazzling allurements of fancy, and seeking its inspiration, often enough, in the dirt. It relied for its effects upon its own strength, and upon that alone. The only ornament in his writing is the rhythm, so that, compared to the decorative and imaginative prose of such a writer as Sir Thomas Browne, it resembles the naked body of an athlete beside some Prince in gorgeous raiment. Who can say which is the more beautiful? Who can balance the subtle vigor of nudity against the splendor of glowing color and elaborate form?

If Swift lost nothing through comparison with Velázquez and contrast with Sir Thomas Browne, it might be even more illuminating to compare him with a great eighteenth-century writer of prose with whom he had much in common—Voltaire. Strachey found in both Voltaire and Swift "the same clarity and sobriety, the same unerring precision of statement, the same preoccupation with the concrete and the real." Nevertheless, to go from *Candide* to the "Modest Proposal" was to discover a highly significant difference: "Both are masterpieces of irony; both are intensely serious; but the Frenchman attains his end by means of a ghastly gaiety, while Swift employs a more deadly weapon still, an impassive and unrelaxing gravity which never fluctuates, which shrinks from nothing,

which advances rigidly and logically to the most preposterous conclusions, and leaves us at last in an agony, as if the curtain had
gone down on a tragic scene." There could be no style more true
and more transparent than Swift's. Strachey liked the analogy which
compared it to "a sheet of plate-glass through which every object
appears in the form and color of absolute reality." [31] Even Voltaire's style seemed artificial beside it, and Sir Thomas Browne's
was in another manner altogether: "Compared with the sober
daylight of Swift's style, that of a writer like Voltaire seems to resemble the brilliancy of drawing room candles, and that of a
writer like Sir Thomas Browne the flare of a midnight torch." [32]

To turn from Swift to Hogarth was to be struck by other important points of contrast. It was not merely that the one used the
pen and the other the brush. The really important point of difference was that "Swift's was a prose genius through and through,"
while Hogarth's genius was "fundamentally poetical." [33] Yet Hogarth's was the poetry of realism. "He is pre-occupied with life,
with the real gestures, the real vivacities, the real atmosphere of
living human beings." [34] In his works one found the very essence
of spontaneity. In contrast to Reynolds, with his elaborate craft
and carefully prepared effects, Hogarth was a great improviser in
whose best moments "conception and execution came almost simul-
taneously." *Southwark Fair* provided a delightful example of this
technique: "The group of actors tumbling helter-skelter from a
falling stage—so astonishingly instinct with movement and vitality
—was painted with an inspired and running brush." Strachey did
not presume to be a critic of painting or one who fully understood
and appreciated it. It may be doubted, nevertheless, whether he

31. "English Letter Writers," p. 19. Strachey uses the same figure in comparing Stendhal's style with legal language: "A statement of law can have no
place for irrelevant beauties, or the vagueness of personal feeling; by its very
nature, it must resemble a sheet of plate glass through which every object
may be seen with absolute distinctness, in its true shape." "Henri Beyle," p.
277.

32. "English Letter Writers," p. 19.

33. "Jonathan Swift."

34. "The Old Masters at Burlington House," *Spectator, 100* (Jan. 11,
1908), 61–2.

ever experienced many moments happier than those which he spent among the pictures in Burlington House one day near the beginning of 1908. For he came upon a room almost entirely devoted to Hogarth. And the pictures there revealed a Hogarth who was not always a satirist but who could with "exquisite tenderness" and impeccable skill set forth the most delicate sentiments and the most joyous situations. The *Happy Marriage* he already knew, and now he lingered in delightful study of such pictures as the *Music-Piece* and the *Green Room at Drury Lane*. The last picture appealed especially to his imagination and seemed to sweep him back into the heart of many of the best things of the eighteenth century:

> There, in that comfortable chamber, one might listen a whole morning, or a whole eternity, to Barry rehearsing Romeo in his beautiful brown coat, while one turned one's eyes from Lavinia Fenton in her sky-blue silk to Miss Pritchard in her wonderful pale-plum-colored hoop, or smiled over Quin's queer gestures or Fielding's silhouetted nose. There, in those airy forms, those simple, exquisite colors, one might find, one feels, all the good things of civilization,—tranquillity, and easy talk, and familiar friendship, and smiles, and the happiness of love.[35]

When the full charm of the eighteenth century came thus upon him, it seemed to him that he was in the presence of what was an almost perfect symbol of the good life.

Few of those who love eighteenth-century life and culture would be disposed to quarrel with anything that Strachey has said about Hogarth. Pope, however, has proved to be another matter. Since the appearance of Strachey's essay "Pope," the Leslie Stephen Lecture at Cambridge for 1925, first published in June of that year, Strachey has been attacked bitterly more than once. The point at issue has been what Strachey said about Pope the man and the basis of Pope's personal satire. He found in Pope some of the

35. *Ibid.* Another side of Hogarth, a down-to-earth kind of realism indigenous to England, is described by Strachey as a "combination of solid British beef, thick British beer, stout British bodies, and . . . stolid British moralizing." "The Old Comedy," *Characters and Commentaries*, pp. 158–61.

cruelty and some of the malignancy which occasionally, he believed, appeared in a very sinister form in the eighteenth century.
He told his audience at Cambridge:

> To us, after two centuries, the agonies suffered by the victims
> of Pope's naughtiness are a matter of indifference; the fate
> of Pope's own soul leaves us cold. We sit at our ease, reading
> those *Satires* and *Epistles,* in which the verses, when they were
> written, resembled nothing so much as spoonfuls of boiling
> oil, ladled out by a fiendish monkey at an upstairs window
> upon such of the passersby whom the wretch had a grudge
> against—and we are delighted. We would not have it other-
> wise: whatever is, is right.[36]

Noteworthy among the replies made to Strachey are those of Sir
Edmund Gosse and Professor George Sherburn. Gosse sprang to
the rescue of Pope almost immediately. Although he could "cor-
dially approve" of Strachey's remarks about the technique of Pope's
poems, he was horrified to hear that when Strachey spoke of Pope
as being a fiendish monkey his Cambridge audience broke out in
laughter. "If it had been my privilege to be present," Gosse said,
"I must have buried my face in my hands." It was a matter of
temperament, Gosse continued, whether to like Pope or not; certainly there were some in the twentieth century who were not left
cold by the question of the fate of Pope's soul but who kept a warm
place in their hearts for Pope. Strachey's idea of a monkey fling-
ing boiling oil at everybody, without responsibility and without
selection, might be amusing, but it was completely unjust. If
Strachey had been there, he would not have been scalded. The
people who got the oil deserved it. Furthermore, if a monkey
inspired the "Third Epistle," it was "a pity that we have not all
got tails." [37] Strachey made one other very serious mistake, Gosse
declared; he forgot that Pope's leading characteristic was "loyalty
to the dignity of literature." [38]

36. *Characters and Commentaries,* p. 261.

37. "Pope and Mr. Lytton Strachey," *Leaves and Fruit* (London, Heinemann, 1927), pp. 103–7. This volume is dedicated "To Lytton Strachey with
Affectionate Admiration."

38. "Cibber's Apology," *Leaves and Fruit,* p. 128.

Professor Sherburn, in the introduction to his excellent edition, *Selections from Alexander Pope* (1929),[39] said that Pope wrote couplets which could not have come from a mere peevish invalid and that he possessed traits that do not coexist with rage and venom. The religious, social, and political abnormality of the time warped Pope into a satirist. Not innate malignancy but the operation of such influences, in the twentieth as well as the eighteenth century, accounted for the attitude of the satirist. Here Strachey and his fellow satirists of the twentieth century exaggerated and misjudged the difference between Pope and themselves. "A satirist who hunts living game," Sherburn suggested further, with cutting reference to Strachey's choice of biographical subjects, "is not necessarily less sportsmanlike than one who attacks the dead." None of Pope's intimates considered him a fiendish monkey, and if the Dunces did, why take their word for it?

Superficially, the quarrel here seems to be between partisans of Pope who have a strong personal liking for him and an enemy of Pope who has an intensely personal dislike for him, or, as Gosse suggested, between those who by temperament either like or dislike Pope. But such a conclusion is much too simple and, moreover, is not really fair to any of the parties concerned, including Pope.

Strachey undoubtedly found much in Pope the man that he could not admire. Years before giving the lecture at Cambridge he had, in reviewing George Paston's two-volumes, *Mr. Pope: His Life and Times* (1909), commented on the poet's "singular and vexed career." He had concluded then that the complicated devices and deceptions which Pope used in relation to his correspondence were alone sufficient to indicate the perverted temper of the man. The language which Strachey had used in connection with Pope in this review was fully as definite and emphatic, and almost as picturesque, as that which he used later at Cambridge: "It is clear enough that this crooked habit of mind was simply one manifestation of that deformed and sickly state of being which

39. (New York, Thomas Nelson and Sons), pp. xxxv–viii. Professor Sherburn speaks of Strachey here as "the man who brilliantly ruined the art of biography."

had dwarfed and twisted his body, and made one 'long disease' of his whole life. . . . If you looked at him, he would spit poison, and he would wind himself into an endless meshwork of intrigues and suspicions if you did not." Thus it is not a bright new idea which Strachey voiced at Cambridge in an effort to produce a striking effect but the lifelong opinion of one who returned to the consideration of Pope again and again and who was aware of much in both the poet and his age to which he could give the highest praise. The critic's habit of discrimination was strongly fixed upon him, and even in dealing with a writer whom he admired as much as he did Pope he could hardly avoid separating the good from the bad. All his life, for instance, he thought of Voltaire as one of his great heroes among men of letters; yet he did not hesitate to point out his faults. To him, it would have seemed absurd to hold that Pope and Voltaire, or Bacon and Shelley, merely because they often wrote well, were altogether admirable. On the other hand, even in the early review he had been careful to point out that Pope had had "a power of affection as unmistakable as his power of hate." [40]

An extremely important point missed by both of Strachey's critics is that in the passage to which they took such vigorous exception the attack is made fully as much against the twentieth century and its failure to evaluate the various kinds of satire before enjoying them as it is against Pope. The twentieth century, Strachey says, does not seem to care whether Pope was a good or bad man, whether he was motivated by reason or by grudges so long as he wrote brilliant satire. Strachey does care. Technique and brilliance of thrust are not enough for him. He could never have agreed with Sherburn that the satirist simply responded to the forces of his age. Such an assumption would to him have seemed as unsound as naturalism in fiction or as any form of determinism whatsoever. Character was primary with him; good satire sprang from good motives. The evidence of personal malice and malignancy in Pope was too glaring to be ignored. Not merely the people who deserved the dunce cap which Pope put on their heads would agree with Strachey that Pope was a fiendish monkey; Theobald

40. "Alexander Pope," *Spectator, 103* (Nov. 20, 1909), 847–8.

and Addison had felt the burning oil. It would have been ridiculous to ask them whether Pope harbored grudges.

Sherburn has insinuated that Strachey's attacks on the dead were unsportsmanlike. Possibly they were *unsportsmanlike* (we seem to live in an age in which the word cannot be escaped even as it may be used to designate a high norm in scholarship and literary criticism), since the dead cannot reply. But certainly Sherburn does not mean that we should never find fault with the dead or that such faults as we may discover in them should never be made the subject of ridicule. And, though it may be unsportsmanlike, it is certainly better manners to ridicule the dead than the living. It is also more in accord with the quiet processes by which great art comes into being. Strachey's was a peaceful, steady temperament, aiming at justice even where he missed it; and he could hardly have agreed that art—even satire—is the product of a method analogous to that by which an athletic contest is conducted. Furthermore, the historic instinct was highly developed in him. He liked the perspective and the possibility of selection which only time can give. As for Gosse's emphasis on Pope's loyalty to "the dignity of literature," Strachey would probably yield on that point, if he ever had really forgotten such an important fact about Pope. But he would probably object to the pompous connotation of the word "dignity" in this context and express regret that Gosse was not the only twentieth-century critic who had grown fond of the cliché.

Strachey's conclusions about the serious shortcomings of Pope as an editor of Shakespeare had little in them that could be challenged. Theobald's edition, which appeared nine years after Pope's, was infinitely superior.[41]

For Pope's poetry Strachey had very great admiration. It was nonsense for Matthew Arnold to dismiss Pope or anyone else from the ranks of the great poets because "high seriousness" was lacking or to speak of Pope as a master of prose rather than a master of verse. The often-repeated charge against Pope of "cold correctness" could have been made only by those who had no understand-

41. "Shakespeare's First Editors," *Spectator*, *98* (June 22, 1907), 979–80. A review of T. R. Lounsbury's *The First Editors of Shakespeare*. Cf. Chapter III, above.

ing of his kind of poetry. "It is always easy to deny poetic inspiration to a writer whose most striking qualities are those of refinement, proportion, and clarity." Boileau had suffered from the
same charge. But Pope was superior to Boileau and had everywhere beaten the Frenchman on his own ground. To turn from
Pope to Boileau is "to turn from the heat and movement of life
itself to what, for all its brilliance, remains merely talk about life,
—the after-dinner talk of an accomplished wit." [42]

Pope's worst fault on the side of technique, according to Strachey,
was unevenness. His work was spasmodic and fragmentary. He was
a writer of purple patches, "a genius, that is to say, who worked
according to the caprice of inspiration, by fits and starts." But Pope
cleverly concealed this fact by the "elaborate and amazing art
with which he constructed transitions, smoothed down excres-
cences, and gave to the whole surface of his writing a uniform
texture of brilliance and grace." [43]

Yet Pope should be judged not by what he lacked but by what
he had. If poets were judged by what they did not have, where
would one end? "One might point out that Wordsworth had no
sense of humor, that Shelley did not understand human beings,
that Keats could not read Greek, and that Matthew Arnold did not
wear a wig." [44] Far from being cold, Pope was a "master of moving beauty and concentrated passion." [45] Blank verse, Strachey said,
was the best medium for the expression of passion. Ostensibly,
rhyming couplets were hardly suited at all for the purpose. And yet
Pope had expressed passion through his couplets with astonishing
success:

> How is it possible that verse so regular, so ordered, so scru-
> pulously exact, so "smooth," as the eighteenth-century phrase
> went, should be the language of passion? Everyone knows that

42. "Pope," pp. 11–14; "French Poetry," *Spectator, 99* (Dec. 21, 1907),
1051–2. The second is a review of J. C. Bailey's *The Claims of French Poetry*
and of St. John Lucas' *The Oxford Book of French Verse*. See also "The Admirable Boileau."
43. "Alexander Pope."
44. "Pope," pp. 26–7.
45. "French Poetry."

passion is a rough, disordered, fitful thing, chafing at artificial
rules, and bending the stiff conventions of verse-making to
its own vigorous and unexpected purposes; the true vehicle
for passion is the varied blank verse of the Elizabethans, not
the even couplet of Pope. . . . He succeeded in expressing
passion, not by means of his medium, but in spite of it.[46]

The secret of his success lay in his art: "The essence of all art
is the accomplishment of the impossible." We know that art was
always, to Strachey, a kind of magic. And Pope was a magician in
his mastery of the couplet.[47] He had profited greatly from the lessons which Waller had taught: Waller "saw that regularity implied balance, that balance implied antithesis; he saw that balance
also implied simplicity, that simplicity implied clarity, and that
clarity implied exactitude. The result was a poetical instrument
contrary in every particular to Blank Verse—a form which, instead
of being varied, unsymmetrical, fluid, complex, profound, and indefinite, was regular, balanced, antithetical, simple, clear, and exact." [48] Such verse was certain to be artificial; but Strachey said
that there was only one kind of verse that was not artificial, namely,
bad verse.[49] Pope had demonstrated brilliantly, furthermore, that
couplets, despite the rigidity of their requirements, were capable
of producing effects of great variety: "But an exact, regular, and
ordered treatment of the heroic couplet no more implies mechanical monotony than the rigid form of a fugue. Within the limits of
the convention there is an infinite scope for subtle and dexterous
handling, for those fine shades and delicate gradations of sound and
expression of which the secret is only known to the true artist; and
it is precisely here that Pope is supreme." [50]

A good poet often gains much from the enthusiasm of those who
have almost unlimited admiration for him. If they are intelligent,
they may intensify the delight which others experience in reading

46. "Alexander Pope."
47. "Pope," p. 25. Compare Strachey's similar remarks on the drama.
48. *Ibid.,* p. 19.
49. *Ibid.,* p. 20.
50. "Alexander Pope."

his works. But he may gain even more from the critic whose treatment of him is characterized by judicious balance. Hence, we need not fear that the reputation of Pope or the pleasure which readers in the future may find in him will suffer greatly from the comments of Lytton Strachey.

Horace Walpole had a strong attraction for Strachey both because he displayed highly interesting individual traits as a writer and because in his work the letter was admirably exemplified as a literary form. When the first four volumes of Mrs. Paget Toynbee's edition of Walpole's letters appeared in 1903, Strachey greatly enjoyed reading them in their new format, which he found entirely appropriate: "It is pleasant to think that henceforward it will be possible to read with ease the most readable of books, and that the lightest of writers is no longer too heavy to carry." [51] But Strachey discovered to his dismay that Mrs. Toynbee had bowdlerized the letters. He protested vigorously against the omissions: "The *jeune fille* is certainly not an adequate reason, and, even if she were, the *jeune fille* does not read Walpole. Whoever does read him must feel that these constant omissions are so many blots upon perfection, and distressing relics of an age of barbarous prudery." [52] He protested even more vigorously many years later when Paget Toynbee in an additional two volumes of the letters dropped a number of passages "on the score of propriety." Strachey's objections were expressed in a review in the *Athenaeum;* [53] Toynbee defended himself in the columns of the *Athenaeum;* [54] and Strachey returned to the attack with even greater force: "It is too late to be prudish: Catullus, Rabelais, and a hundred others stare us in the face; the horse is gone, and no locking of the stable door will bring him back again." [55]

51. "Horace Walpole," p. 82.
52. *Ibid.,* p. 83.
53. "Walpole's Letters," *Athenaeum,* Aug. 15, 1919, pp. 744–5.
54. Aug. 29, 1919, p. 823.
55. *Athenaeum,* Sept. 5, 1919, p. 853. In "The Eighteenth Century," first published in the *Nation and Athenaeum* (May 29, 1926) as a review of a supplementary volume of Walpole's letters edited by Paget Toynbee, Strachey again complains because of Toynbee's expurgations. "Apparently we should

The ideal letter, Strachey once said, was a happy cross between the prose essay and small talk.[56] Its essential qualities were "lightness of touch, ease of expression, brilliance which is never forced, and amiability which is never exaggerated and never forgotten." [57] Wordsworth could never have been a great letter writer: "He could not spin charming sentences out of airy nothings." [58] Carlyle, likewise, was "too self-conscious, too conscientious, too anxious to deliver up the very depths of his soul" to write excellent letters.[59] His wife's letters, especially her later ones with their amazing sparkle and vivacity, were much better.[60] Possibly the essential element in the letter writer's make-up was a certain strain of femininity.[61] And he must by all means be an egotist; the fundamental purpose of the letter was to express the personality of the writer: "Only those who are extremely interested in themselves possess the overwhelming pertinacity of the born correspondent. No good letter was ever written to convey information, or to please its re-

blush too much were we to read the whole of Walpole's letters; those privileges have been reserved to Dr. Toynbee alone." He voiced the same complaint in reviewing C. B. Tinker's edition of Boswell's letters: "When will this silly and barbarous prudery come to an end?" "James Boswell," *Nation* (London) *36* (Jan. 31, 1925), 609–10. He seems to have found no such blemishes in Walpole's *Reminiscences,* edited by Paget Toynbee, which he reviewed in "Mary Berry," *Nation* (London), *36* (March 21, 1925), 856–8. But when Gilbert Murray objected to the obscenity of modern literature, Strachey replied to him in vigorous words: "Has he really forgotten all about Aristophanes, Catullus, Rabelais, and Swift? . . . It is therefore useless to attempt to discredit the novelists of the eighteenth and twentieth centuries by eulogizing those of the nineteenth century." "Obscenity in Literature," a letter to the editor, *Nation and Athenaeum,* March 30, 1929, p. 908.

56. "Wordsworth's Letters," *Spectator, 100* (March 21, 1908), 460–1. A review of William Knight's *Letters of the Wordsworth Family from 1785 to 1855,* in three volumes.

57. "Some New Carlyle Letters," *Spectator, 102* (April 10, 1909), 577–8. A review of *The Love Letters of Thomas Carlyle and Jane Welsh,* ed. Alexander Carlyle, two vols.

58. "Wordsworth's Letters."

59. "Some New Carlyle Letters."

60. *Ibid.*

61. "Walpole's Letters."

cipient; it may achieve both those results incidentally." [62] Further-more, even the best letter gained something from being part of a sequence; it received light and color from other letters to which it was related. "Good letters are like pearls: they are admirable in themselves, but their value is infinitely enhanced when there is a string of them." [63]

Walpole's letters met all the requirements. Letters of earlier times had had more profundity and more grandeur. They had been more serious and more instructive. But the new type of letter was far more entertaining, and in Walpole this type was to be found at its best. In it there was ample compensation for what had been lost, for it had the charm which could come only through lightness of touch, clarity, and play of personal feeling. Walpole's mind and temperament were compounded of precisely those elements which make possible the perfect letter writer: "The distinguishing mark of his writing is a curious mixture of the careless and the elaborate. He is able to spin the most fanciful similes, to heap image upon image and embroidery upon embroidery, and yet to preserve an almost colloquial tone." [64] His resourcefulness was apparently without any limit. His writing was like lace: "The material is of very little consequence, the embroidery is all that counts; and it shares with lace the happy faculty of coming out sometimes in yards and yards." Moreover, in Walpole quantity and quality went along together. In his letters one could always count on finding "a per-petual procession of sparkling imagery." Strachey found it interest-ing to contrast Byron's "exuberance of vitality" with Walpole's "prolific ease": "The former is all vigor and hurry, all chops and changes, all multitudinous romance; he is salt and breezy and racy as the sea. Walpole flows like a delightful river through his end-less pages, between shady lawns and luxurious villas, dimpling all

62. *Ibid.* This was written in 1919; in "Some New Carlyle Letters" (1909) Strachey had written that the "first business" of a letter writer was "that of putting his correspondent into a good temper," a thing which Carlyle could not always remember.
63. "Walpole's Letters."
64. "English Letter Writers," pp. 8, 37.

the way." [65] Strachey delighted to the utmost in the charm of Walpole, as he did in that of Pope. In both instances the charm was something peculiar to the eighteenth century. Pope, like Bach, without for one moment departing from the uniformity which the age loved, displayed striking effects of variety, feeling, beauty, and color. Walpole exploited the aesthetic possibilities of the serene and the unruffled and demonstrated that intense joy is just as likely to be found dwelling with these as with strenuous activity. Hence there was much in him and in his age which Strachey found to be the proper ally of his own spirit.

Samuel Johnson was to Strachey an embodiment, in large proportions and magnificent strength, of the good sense which the eighteenth century exalted to the height of an ideal. But far more important were the depth and capaciousness of Johnson's humanity. In Hamlet's very sense of the word, he was a man. And he was a man who knew men. He knew what they were, and he knew how to deal with them. Furthermore, he shared in the high respect which his age had for literature.

Strachey had enthusiastic praise for both Boswell and Johnson as biographers. Johnson's *Lives of the Poets* was to him a perennial source of delight.[66] There one found a rare knowledge and sound appraisal of men on almost every page. And Strachey could not join Hazlitt and others in complaining about Johnson's style. Since, to him, there was no one perfect prose style to the exclusion of all others, he found in the vast range of literature plenty of room for variety and individual differences. Hence his admiration for Swift did not mean that he could not like Sir Thomas Browne or Bacon or Lincoln or Johnson. Taste in style, he knew, varied from age to age. Consequently he defended what Johnson did for English prose: "With the *Christian Morals* to guide him, Dr. Johnson set about the transformation of the prose of his time. He decorated, he pruned, he balanced; he hung garlands, he draped robes; and he

65. "Horace Walpole," pp. 83–4.
66. "The Lives of the Poets," *Books and Characters*, p. 73. Clifford Bower-Shore in *Lytton Strachey: An Essay* (London, Fenland Press, 1933, pp. 43–7) points out a number of similarities between Johnson and Strachey as biographers.

ended by converting the Doric order of Swift into the Corinthian order of Gibbon." [67] Johnson was in his own manner one of the masters of English prose.

As a critic, however, he had his limitations. Although Strachey declared that much of Johnson's greatness lay in "the breadth and sanity of his outlook upon life," he also pointed out that life and literature were different things. Johnson was not, in essence, a critic of literature but a critic of life. This fact accounted for the merits and defects of his treatment of Shakespeare. His limitations became obvious as soon as he passed from the discussion of men and things to the consideration of poetry. He could not understand Shakespeare's bold and imaginative use of words. He demonstrated an "incapacity to judge of the propriety of words,—an incapacity which he seems to have shared with most of the critics of the eighteenth century." He thus could not approve of those who did not use words as he used them. Shakespeare's great tragic scenes moved him tremendously but "through their humanity and not their poetry." [68]

All in all, however, Johnson was to Strachey as to Carlyle another hero among men of letters. Like his age, he was not perfect. But Johnson no more than Pope should be judged by what he lacked. When one judged him for what he had, and was, he towered up impressively—one of the giants of literature. The magnificent dimensions of Boswell's biography were entirely appropriate to his grandeur and to the wide scope and high quality of eighteenth-century culture. Later generations were indeed fortunate to be able to read such a book, to gain an intimate knowledge of such a man, and to find trustworthy guidance in the civilization of such an age. It is not surprising that Strachey said that his Boswell, once he had opened it in early life, had never again been shut.

67. "Sir Thomas Brown," *Books and Characters,* p. 36.
68. "Shakespeare on Johnson," *Spectator, 101* (Aug. 1, 1908), 164–5. A review of Walter Raleigh's *Johnson on Shakespeare.*

CHAPTER 7

On the Victorian Age

WHEN Queen Victoria died on January 22, 1901, Lytton Strachey was almost twenty-one years old. His father, who had been born in 1817, was still living. His mother, who had been born in 1840, was also living and would not die until 1928. Alive too were a number of uncles and aunts and brothers and sisters who had been born throughout the various decades of the long nineteenth century. The world which Strachey knew in 1901 contained, in addition, many of his parents' old friends and friends of the family belonging to his own generation who had already spent a considerable part of their lives during the reign of Queen Victoria. Raymond Mortimer has written truthfully that the weapons which Strachey and Virginia Woolf turned on the Victorians were forged in Victorian homes.[1] He could have added that those who wielded the weapons were themselves, in considerable part, the product of the age which they were attacking. Rebellious children of that age, they never quite succeeded in emancipating themselves from it. It had been bred in their bones, and they loved it even while they fought with vigor against it.

The symbol of Victorianism to Strachey was his memory of a house at 69 Lancaster Gate just north of Kensington Gardens— the house where his family had begun to live when he was just four years old and where they continued to live until he was almost thirty. The old house represented all that was repulsive and all that was fascinating about the period from which he was to choose the subjects of some of his most successful studies. Particularly sus-

1. "Mrs. Woolf and Mr. Strachey," *Bookman* (New York), 68 (Feb. 1929), 625 ff.

ceptible as he was to the influence of places, he remembered this abode of his childhood and youth as something gigantic and formidable which cast a potent spell over his emotions and imagination. Long years after he had left it he was still aware of it, haunting his mind, forbidding, horrible, but irresistible. In 1922 he wrote an autobiographical essay in which he analyzed his thoughts concerning it. From this essay we can discover much concerning his attitude toward the Victorian age. After speaking of himself as a "confirmed dreamer" and saying that he has often dreamed that he was back at Lancaster Gate, he added significantly that, although he would be disgusted if the family should actually return there, the dream always caused a feeling of intimate satisfaction to come over him.

"Apart from my pleasure at it, no doubt it is hardly surprising that Lancaster Gate should haunt me. For it was a portentous place, and I spent in it the first twenty-five years of my conscious life. . . . One might say that Lancaster Gate was, in essence, the crowning symbol of the large family system." Strachey goes on to describe the large drawing room, built to hold not only the immediate family—Sir Richard and Lady Strachey with their ten sons and daughters—but all the other branches of the family on Sunday afternoons. The gathering often included two highly eccentric uncles: Uncle William, a gentleman in spats, who had been well known at Holland House in the middle of the century and who, having once visited Calcutta, henceforth kept his watch set by Calcutta time, a habit which was somewhat disconcerting to his friends in England; and Uncle George, "bent double with age and eccentricity, hideously sniffling, and pouring out his opinions on architecture to anyone who ventured within his reach."

The Strachey family had seen better days, especially in the second half of the eighteenth century when the first Sir Henry Strachey, the secretary and intimate friend of Lord Clive, was able to entertain important members of the Government not only at his house on Hill Street but also at country houses in Surrey and Somerset. Even in the early years of the nineteenth century, Strachey's grandparents, the Edward Stracheys, were moderately wealthy and were important benefactors and friends of the struggling young Carlyle. But now the good days of the Stracheys and of many other Englishmen had ended:

> What had happened was that a great tradition—the aristocratic tradition of the eighteenth century—had reached a very advanced stage of decomposition. My father and my mother belonged by birth to the old English world of countryhouse gentlefolk—a world of wealth and breeding, a world in which such things as footmen, silver and wine were the necessary appurtenances of civilized life.[2] But their own world was different: it was the middle-class professional world of the Victorians, in which the old forms still lingered, but debased and enfeebled, in which Morris wallpapers had taken the place of Adam paneling, in which the swarming retinue had been reduced to a boy in livery, in which the spoons and forks were bought at the Army and Navy Stores. And then, introducing yet another element into this mixture, there was the peculiar disintegrating force of the Strachey character. The solid bourgeois qualities were interpenetrated by intellectualism and eccentricity.
>
> Yet the total effect, materialized and enormously extended, was of tremendous solidity. Lancaster Gate towered up above us and around us, an imperturbable mass—the framework, almost the very essence, so it seemed, of our being. Was it itself perhaps one vast filth-packet and we the mere *disjecta membra* of vanished generations, which Providence was too busy or too idle to clear away? So in hours of depression, we might have unconsciously theorized: but nevertheless, in reality, it was not so. Lancaster Gate vanished into nothingness, and we survived. To me, that that regime would inevitably, some day, come to an end was a dreadful thought—one not to be dwelt upon—like death; what would, what *could* happen, when we went away from Lancaster Gate?
>
> Circumstances—a diminished income—brought about at

---

2. A strong Whig tradition dominated the political thought of most members of the Strachey family from the time of the Glorious Revolution of 1688 down to Lytton Strachey's own day. And a Whig, to Lytton Strachey, was not a fierce rebel but a highly respectable and dignified gentleman.

length the unspeakable catastrophe; but I see now that, whatever had happened, however rich we might have continued,
Lancaster Gate was in fact doomed. The disintegration would
have grown too strong for it at last.[3]

Strachey's mixed feelings concerning the Victorian period are
reflected throughout his writings. It appealed to both his instincts
and his curiosity, for not only had it claimed his earliest and most
impressionable years but it was an era of striking immensity, complexity, variety and inconsistency. It was a paradox in history, full
of contradictions, decadent grandeur, absurdity, and interest. In
the essay on "Carlyle" published in 1928, Strachey described it
as "a most peculiar age: an age of barbarism and prudery, of nobility and cheapness, of satisfaction and desperation; an age in
which everything was discovered and nothing was known; an age
in which all the outlines were tremendous and all the details sordid; . . . when one sat for hours with one's feet in dirty straw
dragged along the streets by horses, when an antimacassar was on
every chair, and the baths were minute tin circles, and the beds
were full of bugs and disasters." [4]

In an essay on Matthew Arnold published in 1914, four years
before *Eminent Victorians,* Strachey likewise wrote of the Victorian period as something complex and grotesque possessing a
strange hypnotic power which his emotions and imagination could
not resist. The spell of Lancaster Gate was still heavy upon him
when he wrote this passage—as it always would be. Here too, as in
speaking of his old home, he was afraid of what had fascinated

3. Quoted from the manuscript.
4. *Portraits in Miniature,* pp. 189–90. In this essay Strachey also referred
to the friendship between his grandfather, Edward Strachey (1774–1832), "an
Anglo-Indian of cultivation and intelligence," and Carlyle. The manuscripts
provide evidence that Strachey associated his grandmother, Julia Kirkpatrick
Strachey, with Evangelical religious faith, for which he had very little respect.
She was a friend of Arthur Young and other members of the Clapham Sect
and attended their gatherings. Carlyle mentions Mr. and Mrs. Strachey many
times in his *Reminiscences* and letters. The Stracheys have always insisted
that the original of Blumine in *Sartor Resartus* was Mrs. Strachey's cousin,
Catherine Aurora ("Kitty") Kirkpatrick, and that Mrs. Strachey herself was
the Duenna Governess. This was Mrs. Strachey's own opinion.

him, and made a vigorous effort to be just in commenting on a thing which, in the main, filled him with revulsion:

> To the cold and youthful observer there is a strange fascination about the Age of Victoria. It has the odd attractiveness of something which is at once very near and very far off; it is like one of those queer fishes that one sees behind glass at an aquarium, before whose grotesque proportions and somber menacing agilities one hardly knows whether to laugh or to shudder; when once it has caught one's eye, one cannot tear oneself away. Probably its reputation will always be worse than it deserves. Reputations, in the case of ages no less than of individuals, depend, in the long run, upon the judgments of artists, and artists will never be fair to the Victorian Age. To them its incoherence, its pretentiousness, and its incurable lack of detachment will always outweigh its genuine qualities of solidity and force. They will laugh and they will shudder, and the world will follow suit. The Age of Victoria was, somehow or other, unaesthetic to its marrow-bones; and so we may be sure it will never loom through history with the glamor that hangs about the Age of Pericles or the brilliance that sparkles round the eighteenth century. But if men of science and men of action were not inarticulate, we should hear a different story.[5]

5. *Characters and Commentaries* (New York, Harcourt, Brace, 1933), p. 174. In a letter of November 8, 1912, Strachey wrote: "Is it prejudice, do you think, that makes us hate the Victorians, or is it the truth of the case? They seem to me a set of mouthing, bungling hypocrites; but perhaps really there is a baroque charm about them which will be discovered by our great-great-grandchildren, as we have discovered the charm of Donne, who seemed intolerable to the 18th century. Only I don't believe it. Thackeray and G. Meredith will go the way of Calprenède and Scudèry; they'll be curious relics in 50 years. I should like to live for another 200 years (to be moderate). The literature of the future will, I clearly see, be amazing. *At last,* it'll tell the truth, & be indecent, & amusing, & romantic, and even (after about 100 years) be written well. Quelle joie! To live in those days, when books will pour out from the press with all the filth of Petronius, all the frenzy of Dostoievsky, all the romance of Arabian Nights, and all the exquisiteness of Voltaire! But it won't only be the books that are charming then.—The people!"

In attempting to understand and appraise the Victorian period, Strachey himself wrote as an artist and was clearly conscious of the fact. It was the artist in him that shuddered when he was confronted by the Victorian age. But there was another side to Strachey —a very important one—which responded with wonder and admiration when he beheld the solidity and force of the period, with its amazing men of action and its brilliant scientists. Queen Victoria might be stupid and almost completely devoid of the sense of beauty; but her energy was tremendous, her force of character subdued almost all that came before it; and she was, all in all, too substantial to be treated with complete frivolity. As for the men of action, Strachey remembered with pride various stories about members of his own family who had served in India and explored Tibet in the first half of the nineteenth century. His own father, brilliant and versatile, had had a truly remarkable career in India, where he had had a horse shot under him in battle, had dug canals and built bridges, had constructed railways and served as the president of the largest and most prosperous one in that part of the world, and had set up the forestry division of the government there. Furthermore, his father was a distinguished scientist, the friend of Galton and Huxley and a Fellow of the Royal Society, who had gained recognition for his discoveries in many fields. From first to last, Strachey had great respect for scientists.

It is true that Strachey often seems to be very severe in dealing with men and women of action—with Essex, with Arnold of Rugby, with Gladstone, with Disraeli, with Florence Nightingale, with General Gordon. But it was not the man of action as such that he objected to. One of the best of his uncollected essays is entitled "The Prose Style of Men of Action" in which he pointed out the elemental force to be found in the words of Cromwell, Clive, Hastings, and Lincoln, all men of action whom he admired.[6] But two types of men of action he did not admire: those who were deluded and those who were too fervid and zealous in pursuing even a good cause. Essex was to him a rather foolish though gifted nobleman deluded by visions of outworn, medieval chivalric grandeur.

6. *Spectator*, *100* (Jan. 25, 1908), 141–2. Possibly written in collaboration with the editor.

Arnold of Rugby, with his hustle and bustle, dramatized all the misconceptions concerning the objectives and the government of British public schools which Strachey disliked most and from which he had suffered as a boy. Gladstone, like the age to which he belonged, was compact of numerous contradictions and, like a skillful juggler, had acquired the habit of balancing them upon the tip end of his nose with astonishing ease.[7] Disraeli, brilliant politician that he was, had an extremely superficial philosophy of life and became the dupe of "the glittering outside of things." Florence Nightingale took herself and her commendable work so seriously that she drove herself and her most loyal friends to destruction. And General Gordon, with his Bible, his bottle of brandy, and his sword, was a mystic who often got lost in the cobwebs of his own mind.[8]

Strachey's purpose was not to condemn the Victorian age as a whole but to subject it to a sifting process by which the good and the bad might be separated. He knew, of course, that it is natural for one age to react against the age which had immediately preceded it; and he knew that he was participating in just such a reaction against the Victorians.[9] Certainly he saw his own role in the reaction

7. See Strachey's subtle and brilliant analysis of Gladstone in *Eminent Victorians* (London, Chatto and Windus, 1926), pp. 264–9. His suspicion toward Asquith during the first World War was fully as strong as that toward Gladstone.

8. For Strachey on Disraeli see *Queen Victoria* and, especially, "Dizzy," *Characters and Commentaries*, pp. 252–4. On March 4, 1898, the eighteen-year-old Strachey wrote in his diary: "Dizzy was personally quite the most interesting man of the last generation." In early 1919 Strachey's mother attempted to persuade him not to write a biography of Queen Victoria but to write one of Disraeli instead. For Strachey on Gordon, see not only *Eminent Victorians* but also "A Diplomatist: Li Hung-Chang," *Characters and Commentaries*, 219–20.

9. Edmund Wilson has written that Strachey's chief role was "to blast once for all the pretensions to moral superiority of the Victorian Age" and that he found that age "an insult to the human spirit" but that after *Eminent Victorians* his ferocity steadily abated. "Lytton Strachey," *New Republic*, Sept. 21, 1932, pp. 146–8. The *Times Literary Supplement* for May 16, 1918, called *Eminent Victorians* "an extraordinarily witty book" which surviving Victorians would read with "mixed feelings" but also spoke of it as "a very sincere and scholarly attempt to understand" the preceding generation. P.

against the Victorians in clear perspective; and he aimed at detachment in dealing with them as in dealing with various other subjects.

But the weaknesses of the Victorians were, nonetheless, real weaknesses; and the evils were real evils. It was unintelligent to proceed, in the name of fairness, with false assumptions. In Strachey's mind there was no doubt about what those weaknesses and evils were. Some of them were extremely serious and had already borne terrifying consequences in the history of the early twentieth century:

> The Victorian Age, great in so many directions, was not great in criticism, in humor, in the realistic apprehension of life. It was an age of self-complacency and self-contradiction. Even its atheists (Lord Morley was one of them) were religious. The religious atmosphere fills his book, and blurs every outline.[10] We are shown Mr. Gladstone through a haze of reverence, and Emerson, and Marcus Aurelius. We begin to long for a little of the cynicism of, precisely, the Age of Diderot, Rousseau, and Voltaire. Perhaps—who knows?—if Lord Morley and his contemporaries had been less completely devoid of those unamiable and unedifying qualities, the history of the world would have been more fortunate. The heartless, irreverent, indecent eighteenth century produced the French Revolution. The Age of Victoria produced—what? [11]

The essay from which this passage is quoted was first published in February, 1918.

To say that any age, however great it may be otherwise, has failed "in criticism, in humor, and in the realistic apprehension of life" is certainly to make a major indictment against it. An age

---

230. Clifford Bower-Shore stated the truth precisely in his very fine critical essay, *Lytton Strachey* (London, Fenland Press, 1933), when he wrote (p. 52): "Strachey was not responsible for the reaction against the Victorian Age, although his work did, to a certain extent, foster that reaction. The pioneer revolutionists were Ruskin, Swinburne, Wilde, Butler, Shaw, and Wells."

10. The book was Morley's *Recollections*.

11. "A Statesman: Lord Morley," *Characters and Commentaries*, pp. 215-16. First published in *War and Peace*, Feb. 1918.

which has vigor but which lacks humor is like a powerful machine without a balance wheel. To Strachey, the Victorian age was just such a machine, throwing its force clumsily and haphazardly in this direction and that. But did the Victorians really lack humor? Strachey made no real effort to prove his indictment. Yet certainly for us much of Victorian humor has dated. Almost anyone today who turns the pages of a volume of *Punch* carrying a date in the 1850's would be very likely to agree with Strachey. Much of Dickens and some of Thackeray strikes us as rather quaint and antique humor at best. Strachey himself found Dickens extremely tedious at times. Of course, *Punch* and Dickens and Thackeray represent only a part of the vast and sprawling body of Victorian humor. The age was generous in its output of humor as it was in almost everything else. But it was not the quantity or even the variety of Victorian humor with which Strachey was concerned. He was concerned with its quality. He did not believe it to be great. The humorists whom he admired most—Aristophanes, Chaucer, Rabelais, Shakespeare, Cervantes, Molière, Swift, and Fielding—had one striking characteristic in common: They wrote as adults for adults. They carried laughter with them into the very midst of the facts and problems of a world which only adults could know. Now Victorian humor as Strachey thought of it, not only the humor of Dickens and Thackeray but that of George Eliot and Lewis Carroll and Edward Lear, also had a striking characteristic running through most of it. Victorian humor seemed to find its ultimate form and its immortality when it succeeded in making little children laugh. Austin Dobson's was admittedly a different kind of humor, but Austin Dobson's home was really in the eighteenth century although he lived in the nineteenth. This tendency of humor to withdraw from the adult world and to take sanctuary in the nursery was what alarmed Strachey most. Gilbert and Sullivan, with their pin-prick satire, did in a sense ridicule the foibles and shortcomings of the Briton and his institutions; but they did so in a delightful fairyland of their own creation which they skillfully used their art to insulate against the rude, noisy, bustling Victorian world in which adults were compelled to struggle. Dickens' world seemed real; but it too was actually, as G. K. Chesterton observed,

a kind of fairyland. Hence, in Strachey's mind the Victorians' failure in humor was closely related to their failure in criticism and
in the realistic apprehension of life.

Two of the chief Victorian critics exemplified these shortcomings. Ruskin was one of them. At the age of eighteen Strachey read
some of Ruskin and then laid him aside with great disappointment.
Although he found Ruskin clear, the lack of humor and a sense
of proportion were too much for him.[12] There is little evidence to
show that he ever returned to Ruskin again. To Matthew Arnold
he gave much more attention. In Strachey's mind Arnold played
the role of a rather formidable adversary who must be destroyed,
whatever the cost might be.

Arnold the poet was not too bad. Strachey in some of his early
reviews did not hesitate to quote with approval some of the passages
from Arnold's poems.[13] But Arnold had also claimed for himself
a major role as a Victorian critic of literature and society. Unfortunately his influence had been great. Strachey believed that "the
essential and fatal weakness of the Victorian Age" was "its in-
capability of criticism" and that in Arnold this weakness displayed
itself in an extreme form. Arnold was such a poor critic that he did
not represent even Victorian criticism adequately. "Surely, before
it is too late, a club should be started—an Old Victorian Club—
the business of whose members would be to protect the reputation
of their Age and give it a fair chance with the public. Perhaps such
a club exists already—in some quiet corner of Pimlico; but if so,
it has sadly neglected one of its most pressing duties—the hushing
up of Matthew Arnold." [14]

What was wrong with Arnold's criticism? Strachey's answer to
this question indicates that his own strongest affinity as a critic
was not, as one might suspect, with Boileau and the critics of the

12. It will be recalled that Strachey made an entry in his diary as early
as March 11, 1898, in which he tells of reading *Sesame and Lilies* and finding
it an unsatisfactory book.

13. See "The Praise of Shakespeare," *Spectator, 92* (June 4, 1904), 882;
"Mr. Sidney Lee on Shakespeare," *Spectator, 97* (Dec. 1, 1906), 887–8.

14. "A Victorian Critic," *Characters and Commentaries,* p. 175. First published in the *New Statesman,* Aug. 1, 1914.

Enlightenment but with Coleridge and the Romantic critics. For
Strachey, like the Romantics, began with the individual writer or
artist, with his purpose, and with his prerogative of freedom. Hence
he condemned Arnold's authoritarianism which insisted on sub-
jecting all new works of art to certain extrinsic tests or "touch-
stones," selected specimens of the "best." In the essay on Racine
Strachey denounced this method in no uncertain terms. It was, he
said, a "method which attempts to define the essential elements
of poetry in general, and then proceeds to ask of any particular
poem whether it possesses these elements, and to judge it accordingly." Then he added with emphasis: "How often this method
has been employed, and how often it has proved disastrously falla-
cious. For, after all, art is not a superior kind of chemistry, amenable to the rules of scientific induction. Its component parts cannot
be classified and tested, and there is a spark within it that defies
foreknowledge." The only trustworthy way to determine the value
of a poet was to seek out the best that he had done. "There is only
one way to judge a poet, as Wordsworth, with that paradoxical sobriety so characteristic of him, has pointed out—and that is, by
loving him." [15] To begin with the consideration of what a poet
lacked might soon lead to absurdity.[16]

But to look for the best did not mean that the critic should become so sympathetic that he lost all power of discrimination. Dowden, another Victorian critic, had done just that in his biography
of Shelley. Strachey felt some hesitation before he could make up
his mind which was worse—Dowden's or Arnold's treatment of
Shelley:

> It is unfortunate that the critics and biographers of poets
> should be for the most part highly respectable old gentlemen;
> for poets themselves are apt to be young, and are not apt to
> be highly respectable. Sometimes the respectable old gentle-
> men are frankly put out; but sometimes they try to be sym-
> pathetic—with results at least equally unfortunate. In Shelley's

15. *Books and Characters* (New York, Harcourt, Brace, 1922), p. 12.
16. "Pope," the Leslie Stephen Lecture for 1925 (Cambridge, Cambridge
University Press, 1925), pp. 26–7.

case it is difficult to decide whether the distressed self-right-
eousness of Matthew Arnold's famous essay or the solemn
adoration of Professor Dowden's standard biography gives a
false impression. Certainly the sympathetic treatment is the
more insidious. The bias of Matthew Arnold's attack is obvious; but the process by which, through two fat volumes,
Shelley's fire and air have been transmuted into Professor
Dowden's cotton-wool and rose-water is a subtler revenge of
the world's upon the most radiant of its enemies.[17]

Although Arnold was not soft, he was firm about what careful
scrutiny revealed to be the wrong things. Poetry, he had said, must
be a criticism of life. Conduct, he had declared with a suspicious
neatness, was three-fourths of life. And the great poet must have
"high seriousness." Strachey found in Arnold a critic who, with
all his brilliance and persuasiveness, could not separate aesthetic
from moral values. Thus Arnold was the child of his age and manifested its chief weakness. But he also sinned against good sense in
his use of a mincing hocus-pocus by which he was able to call Pope
a classic of prose rather than a classic of poetry.[18] As for Arnold's
doctrine of high seriousness, Strachey recognized in it—a doctrine which led Arnold to deny Chaucer a place among the great
poets—a fatal lack of true sense of humor and appreciation of it
which had distressed him in his reading of other Victorian writers.[19]
The high-toned humanism of Arnold had too little humanity in
it to satisfy Strachey, for he believed that human life could enjoy
full scope for its multiform manifestations and functions only
when it was free, free to live and free to laugh. In Strachey's position there was a danger that individualism would be carried to
the point of intellectual and social anarchy; it was to combat just
such an anarchy that Arnold had wrought out his doctrines of
criticism and culture. Yet Strachey's strictures upon Arnold have

17. "An Adolescent," *Characters and Commentaries*, p. 201.
18. Even Gosse praised Strachey for boldly asserting that Pope's poetic
criticism of life was, "simply and solely, the heroic couplet." "Pope and Mr.
Lytton Strachey," *Leaves and Fruit* (London, Heinemann, 1927), p. 107.
19. "Pope," pp. 11–14.

significance for us because of two truths which they emphasize: first, that the critic who seeks to establish universal standards must take great pains to avoid any principle which results in narrowness; and, second, that works of art have a significance within themselves apart from the significance which they possess in their relationship to other works of art, just as individual human beings have a significance apart from that which they possess as members of society.[20]

But Strachey knew, as we have seen, that Matthew Arnold was not merely a critic; he was also a poet, with a well-developed sense of beauty. There had appeared in him, particularly in his younger days, something of the rebel and the romantic. Arnold was not altogether bad, even in Strachey's eyes, but Arnold's father was. As a matter of fact, all that was worst in Arnold himself could be traced back to the father. The emphasis upon ethics and conformity, the suffusing of religion through all things, the distrust of humor unless it was on the level of a child's mind, a faith in institutions, and the assumption that extrinsic measurements could be devised by which intrinsic substances could be appraised with entire validity—these were primary errors which had misled father and son. Behind the Arnolds stood Oxford and Aristotle, and Strachey had little faith in either.[21] Toward Oxford he manifested the pride and prejudice of a Cambridge man. As for Aristotle, it should be remembered that Strachey with all his love of order, perspicacity, and the definite regarded both art and life as complex and mysterious. Life was a wondrous thing, never completely understandable, and art was magic. Aristotle, with his generaliza-

20. One of Strachey's unpublished satirical dialogues takes place between Cleopatra and Mrs. Humphrey Ward, Matthew Arnold's niece. Guy Boas says that one of the subjects for biography which Strachey was considering at the time of his death was Matthew Arnold. He adds that Strachey was also considering Browning, General Booth, and Benjamin Jowett as possible subjects. *Lytton Strachey,* English Association Pamphlet N. 93, Nov. 1935.

21. Readers of Stanley's *Arnold* will recall that Dr. Thomas Arnold, himself an Oxford man, seriously considered sending Matthew to Cambridge but finally decided that he must go to Oxford, because Aristotle was not neglected there. Matthew Arnold in "The Study of Poetry," it will be remembered, gave Aristotle credit for the phrase "high seriousness."

tions, classifications, and simplifications, could never arrive at
the heart of the mystery. Dr. Arnold was not merely an Aristotelian;
he was also a fervid Christian who desired to make adherence to
Christian principles in conduct a qualification of citizenship.
Strachey had no faith whatsoever in Christianity or Christian institutions. Moreover, Dr. Arnold was usually esteemed to be the
father of the British public-school system as it existed in most of
the nineteenth century and part of the twentieth. Strachey could
see nothing but stupidity and evil in the British public schools as
he knew them.[22] All in all, everything that Arnold of Rugby stood
for was palpably absurd. And yet he had been one of the most
influential teachers of the Victorians: he had done much to determine the tone and temper of their age.[23]

22. Another of Strachey's satirical dialogues is entitled "Headmaster and
Parent." In it a very stupid headmaster makes a completely unconvincing
defense of his educational objectives and methods. For evidence that there
were other Cambridge men who agreed with Strachey about the public schools
of their day, see E. M. Forster's *G. Lowes Dickinson* and Lionel Trilling's
E. M. Forster.

23. Strachey's intimate friend J. M. Keynes in "My Early Beliefs," an important memoir written in Sept. 1938 (over six years after Strachey's death),
virtually admits that he and the other members of the Cambridge-Bloomsbury
group carried their revolt against conventions and against conformity to
institutions too far. He says that they based their thinking and conduct on the
much too optimistic assumption that man as an individual may be entirely
rational. "We were not aware that civilization was a thin and precarious
crust erected by the personality and the will of a very few, and only maintained by rules and conventions skillfully put across and guilefully preserved.
. . . We carried the individualism of our individuals too far." But Keynes
also has much to say in favor of his group. He believes that they were particularly fortunate in escaping from the Benthamite tradition. "But I do now
regard that as the worm which has been gnawing at the insides of modern
civilization and is responsible for its present moral decay. We used to regard
the Christians as the enemy, because they appeared as the representatives of
tradition, convention and hocus-pocus. In truth it was the Benthamite cal-
culus, based on an over-valuation of the economic criterion, which was de-
stroying the quality of the popular Ideal. Moreover, it was this escape from
Bentham, joined with the unsurpassable individualism of our philosophy,
which has served to protect the whole lot of us from the final *reductio ad
absurdum* of Benthamism known as Marxism." *Two Memoirs* (London, Rupert Hart-Davis, 1949), pp. 96–7, 98–101. Although Strachey often saw eye to

To Strachey, it was an age which displayed a fundamental weakness in the ease with which it allowed itself to become the dupe of Dr. Arnold and other religious fanatics. Cardinal Manning, too, with his fierce egoism, his unlimited ambition, his skill in pulling the strings of ecclesiastical politics, his ruthlessness, and his rigid allegiance to orthodox Catholic dogma, found it to be an age in which he could make his way with very little difficulty. "What had happened? Had a dominating character imposed itself upon a hostile environment? Or was the Nineteenth Century, after all, not so hostile? Was there something in it, scientific and progressive as it was, which went out to welcome the representative of ancient tradition and uncompromising faith? Had it, perhaps, a place in its heart for such as Manning—a soft place, one might almost say?" [24] It was an age which boasted of its liberalism and tolerance, but it was not tolerant, certainly not in the realm of ethics; and it was most likely to favor energetic persons such as Manning, Dr. Arnold, Disraeli, and Gladstone, who combined suppleness and agility of method with a firm and consistent appeal to the middle-class prejudices which were characteristic of the time.[25]

For the middle class was supreme in the nineteenth century. The virtues and the weaknesses of the age were both those of this class. "The last vestige of the eighteenth century had disappeared; cynicism and subtlety were shrivelled into powder; and duty, industry, morality, and domesticity triumphed over them. Even the very chairs and tables had assumed, with singular responsiveness, the forms of prim solidity." [26] In the main, it was an age of decadence, and the decadence was particularly marked in the area of manners. The genuine manners of landed Whigs and of other

---

eye with Keynes, we can only guess whether he would have agreed with him if he had been alive in 1938. Arnold of Rugby, we should remember, had great admiration for Coleridge, the chief early nineteenth-century critic of Benthamism.

24. *Eminent Victorians*, pp. 1–2.

25. See "*Comus* at Cambridge," *Spectator*, *101* (July 18, 1908), 94–5; and "Avons-nous changé tout cela?" *Characters and Commentaries*, p. 152.

26. *Queen Victoria* (New York, Harcourt, Brace, 1921), p. 195.

eighteenth-century people who wore their manners easily and were born to them now gave way to the cheap ostentation and self-conscious behavior of tea merchants and factory owners. Strachey was never one who considered manners merely superficial, and the loss here was to him a great one. In "Madame de Lieven," as in "Lancaster Gate," he spoke with some feeling of this decline of manners: "for a generation it was just possible to be an aristocrat on manners alone. Then, at last, about 1830, manners themselves crumbled, undermined by the insidious permeation of a new— a middle-class—behavior; and all was over. Madame de Lieven was one of the supreme examples of the final period. Her manners were of the genuinely terrific kind." [27] In Victorian manners, as in most things characteristically Victorian, there was contradiction. It displayed itslf in the welcome which Victorian England gave to Sarah Bernhardt. "It is odd but certainly true that the eighteenth century would have been profoundly shocked by the actress who reigned over the nineteenth. . . . Every age has its own way of dealing with these matters; and the nineteenth century made up for the high tone of its literature and the decorum of its behavior by the luscious intensity of its theatrical displays." [28]

Strachey's opinions concerning Victorian writers show that as a critic he was remarkably consistent in adhering to the principle that authors and their works should be judged as individual persons and things. He was not guilty of condemning them wholesale because they were Victorian but was careful in dealing with them as in dealing with the age to discriminate and to form his judgments on the basis of intrinsic qualities. A brief examination of what he said about a few Victorians whose opinions, talents, and works varied widely will illustrate his practice here.

His opinion concerning Swinburne was about what one might expect. We know that while he was at Cambridge he gave much time to reading his poems. He liked Swinburne's love of freedom, his individualism, his paganism, his glorification of man, and his critical attitude toward the older Victorians. He wrote poems such

27. "Madame de Lieven," *Portraits in Miniature,* pp. 118–19.
28. "Sarah Bernhardt," *Characters and Commentaries,* p. 257.

as the "Hymn to the Flesh" in imitation of Swinburne.[29] He responded with intense pleasure to the vigorous rhythms of Swinburne's verse and gave him credit for exerting a strong influence
on such poets as Kipling. "It is difficult to believe that the *Barrack-
Room Ballads* would ever have been written if Mr. Swinburne had
never lived." [30] He was delighted with the Elizabethan strain in
Swinburne's poetry. Swinburne's prose commentary, *The Age of
Shakespeare,* he praised highly; and he defended his method as a
literary critic. Swinburne, he said, was a Platonist rather than an
Aristotelian. "His criticism makes no use of the careful and patient
methods of comparison and analysis, but works rapidly and boldly
by the light of intuition. . . . This kind of criticism is not to be
despised, though it happens to be out of fashion. These are the days
of infinite analysis and universal sympathy." [31] Yet Swinburne,
Strachey knew, was quite capable of being swept off his feet by enthusiasm. After Swinburne and Rossetti had "discovered" a play
by Charles Wells entitled *Joseph and His Brethren,* first published
without attracting much attention in 1824, and after Swinburne
had helped to get it republished with an introduction in which he
had praised Wells's efforts to recapture the Elizabethan manner
and had even drawn some comparisons with Shakespeare, Strachey
rebuked Swinburne for his extravagance: "What genius is there in
the whole of literature which does not seem a trifle flat and a trifle
empty when it is compared with Shakespeare's?" [32]

Strachey's attitude toward Tennyson suggests the influence of
Swinburne. When Strachey was at Cambridge he wrote a parody
of Tennyson's "Frater Ave Atque Vale." [33] One of his satirical
dialogues written in imitation of Voltaire takes place between
Tennyson and Catullus.[34] In it the Roman poet scolds the Victorian
laureate for misrepresenting him. Strachey regretted, also, that

29. Dated in the manuscript April 25, 1902. This poem has not been published; but another Swinburnian poem "Ningamus Serta Rosarum" was published in the *Cambridge Review,* 22 (June 5, 1901), Supplement, xiii.
30. "Provincial Letters," *Spectator, 98* (April 13, 1907), 574–5.
31. "A Poet on Poets," *Spectator, 101* (Oct. 3, 1908), 502–3.
32. "Elizabethans Old and New," *Spectator, 102* (March 13, 1909), 420–2.
33. Unpublished. The date on the manuscript is September 1902.
34. These dialogues, of which there are about a dozen, are not dated in

Tennysonian blank verse had had an influence for the worse on modern plays in verse. Although he believed that blank verse was "supreme as a means of dramatic expression," he was convinced that modern blank verse, under the influence of Tennyson, was that "in which the native vigor of the rhythm is sacrificed to sweetness."[35] But Strachey took delight in melody wherever he found it, whether in Mozart, Swinburne, or Tennyson. He was particularly impressed by the trueness of Tennyson's ear.[36] Moreover, despite Tennyson's preoccupation with moral and religious ideas, the poet and the biographer had far more in common than appears at first glance. Both thought of writing as art and kept before them constantly an ideal of excellence in craftsmanship. Both produced work which, in the main, suggests the ivory smoothness of classicism; but in the lives as well as the work of both there was a shaggy quality—vigorous, untamed, unpredictable. Such a buried pool of rough energy was to them a problem and also a secret source of strength when it could be made to subject itself to the discipline of classicism.

To rebel against the Victorians was not, in Strachey's eyes, necessarily to reflect credit on oneself. Carlyle, hurling thunderbolt after thunderbolt as a Victorian among Victorians, was certainly wordy; but so also was Bernard Shaw.[37] And W. E. Henley, a critic

---

the manuscript, but their crisp, economical style suggests the period from 1912 to 1932.

35. "Some New Plays in Verse," *Spectator, 101* (Dec. 12, 1908), 998–9. Strachey's mother, who had shared her enthusiasm for Jonson, Donne, and Milton with her son, had met Tennyson several times. He had once read one of his poems to her. She liked to hear poetry read with emphasis on meaning rather than on sound, and she did not like Tennyson's chant. She was the friend of Browning and very much preferred him as a poet. See Jane Maria Lady Strachey, "Some Recollections of a Long Life," *Nation and Athenaeum, 34* (Jan. 5, 1924), 514–5; (Feb. 23, 1924), 730–1; *35* (July 12, 1924), 473–4; (Aug. 30, 1924), 664–5.

36. "Music and Men," *Spectator, 101* (Dec. 19, 1908), 1059–60.

37. "Some New Carlyle Letters," *Spectator, 102* (April 10, 1909), 577–8; "Carlyle," *Portraits in Miniature*, pp. 178–90; "Three New Plays," *Spectator, 100* (June 6, 1908), 899–900. One of the plays reviewed in the last article was Shaw's *Getting Married*. Strachey wrote: *"Le secret d'ennuyer c'est de tout dire;* and Mr. Shaw insists upon saying everything."

and poet who had promised to lead literature out of the Victorian wilderness, had displayed very serious faults. When four volumes of Henley's collected works appeared in 1908, Strachey reviewed them for the *Spectator*. He found Henley's pages "crowded not only with words which are in themselves unusual, but with curious and unexpected verbal combinations"; and his opinion was that the "far-fetched words and queer constructions not only catch our attention, they worry it." Henley belonged to the romantic school but was not a master of its method:

> He could imitate the boldness and the singularity of the great romantics—their extravagance of tone, their strange and varied vocabulary—but he lacked the crowning art which with them lifts what would otherwise be merely an odd assemblage of heterogeneous details into the region of imperishable beauty. Great poetry, whatever else it may be, is always harmonious; and this truth is nowhere more apparent than in those writers who, like the major Elizabethans, succeed in blending together the most diverse elements into a single whole, so that their poetry resembles a varied landscape flooded with evening light.

Henley lacked "the supreme and passionate sense of beauty" which makes such an achievement possible. Henley's criticisms were "full of fire and variety"; they were the work of "a broad and masculine mind." Yet in them emphasis became an affectation. "They produce the effect of a man who is forever shouting and slapping his thigh and poking one in the ribs." In truth, Henley was hardly a writer: he was a talker. For a writer there was no more dangerous fallacy than the belief that what is admirable in conversation is no less admirable in print. The prose of conversation was a very different thing from the prose of writing. All in all, one found in Henley's prose "a rapid throwing out of happy things rather than a mature utterance of wise ones." Henley was at his best when he was not aiming high—when he was deliberately light.[38]

38. "The Works of W. E. Henley," *Spectator*, *101* (Aug. 8, 1908), 196–7. An excellent piece of criticism.

The Victorian writers whom Strachey felt the least hesitation about praising were those who, despite the formidable forces of their age, managed somehow to be themselves and to express their particular talents, however different they might be from those of other writers. Emily Brontë had done just that in *Wuthering Heights*. Strachey valued highly the sanity, the breadth, and the relaxed manner which he believed were characteristic of the central tradition of the English novel—of Fielding, of Thackeray, and of Dickens; but he also delighted in the novel of concentrated imaginative power and intense passion. In *Wuthering Heights* he found such a novel, somewhat lonely among other English novels; and he paid Emily Brontë the high tribute of comparing her work with Dostoievsky's, in which extravagance and frenzy seethe through the pages with almost unbelievable force and with a genius suggesting that which created unearthly beauty in the midst of a thunderstorm and the ravings of madmen in *King Lear*.[39]

Strachey also found an individualism which possessed integrity in T. E. Brown's dialect verse. Brown had humor, the humor of simple folk who lived upon the Isle of Man, humor with a local habitation and a name. But Brown also had other admirable qualities. "He belongs to the same school as Chaucer and Browning— the school of vast and varied observation, of humorous and intimate sympathy, and of abounding force." [40] Likewise, Strachey joined his cousin St. Loe Strachey, editor of the *Spectator,* and Thomas Hardy in great admiration for William Barnes and his poems in the Dorset dialect. Barnes used a method, Strachey said, which depended upon a combination of inward simplicity of spirit with an outward elaboration of form, like that of Theocritus and unlike that of Burns:

39. "Dostoievsky," *Spectator, 109* (Sept. 28, 1912), 451–2. Strachey read Dostoievsky's novels in Constance Garnett's translations as they appeared in 1912 and 1914. He had in general great admiration for the Russian and was particularly impressed by his psychological insight. It should be noted that he read the novels in the years just before the composition of *Eminent Victorians* (1918). Dostoievsky was an important influence on Strachey. See also "A Russian Humorist," *Characters and Commentaries,* pp. 168 ff. First published in the *Spectator, 112* (April 11, 1914), 610–11.

40. "The Poetry of T. E. Brown," *Spectator, 100* (June 13, 1908), 938–9.

Through the refinement, the subtlety, the elaboration of his expression, we become acquainted with a tranquil and tender mind. We breathe the atmosphere of the open country, we come face to face with sober goodness and innocent affections and unostentatious mirth. No poet brings us closer to the beauty of an English landscape—the fields and the hills and the hedges, the friendly trees and the changing skies, the old houses with the stone windows, the tripping figure along the lane. His colors are all of the purest—blues, greens, whites —dyed with that soft brilliance, which has never been seen out of England, and which, once seen, can never be forgotten.[41]

Prizing humor as highly as he did, Strachey gleaned the Victorian fields in search for it. And he found it in one of the minor poets in whom some readers have found only sentimentalism. He found humor, as the Victorians themselves had found it, in Thomas Hood, the poet whom most of us know only because he wrote "The Song of the Shirt" and "The Bridge of Sighs." Strachey was delighted with Hood's punning "Epitaph on a Candle" and other similar verses.[42] He loved the Elizabethans and Charles Lamb too well to despise the pun. "Good puns," he declared, "may be extremely witty—those of Hood are, of course, the classic examples, in which the play of words exhibits, with marvellous neatness, some queer intellectual crux." [43]

But Strachey did not really rediscover the humor in Tom Hood. He did not have to. Tom Hood's puns were an important part of the atmosphere of Lancaster Gate. There was much in that atmosphere, as Strachey himself has told us, which weighed down upon him like an incubus and which he had to throw off in order to enjoy freedom of spirit; yet surviving at Lancaster Gate

41. "The Poetry of William Barnes," *Spectator, 102* (Jan. 16, 1909), 95–6.
42. "Light Verse," *Spectator, 102* (Feb. 20, 1909), 304–5.
43. "The Follies," *Spectator, 102* (Feb. 13, 1909), 262–3. Strachey also quotes Thomas Love Peacock—another Victorian humorist—with admiration here. Peacock had worked in the India House beside Edward Strachey, the biographer's grandfather, and they were intimate friends. Both loved humor and more than once derided their colleague James Mill, who, it seemed to them, was unable to laugh.

was a robust and vigorous tradition of laughter which helped to protect it from what Virginia Woolf in *Orlando* has called the "damp" of the nineteenth century. A Strachey in the Elizabethan period had laughed with his friends Ben Jonson, John Donne, and perhaps Shakespeare. A Strachey in the third quarter of the seventeenth century had laughed over Cervantes and quaint German tales with his friend John Locke. Carlyle tells us that his friend and patron Edward Strachey, Lytton Strachey's grandfather, was a man of great sense and mirth who constantly quoted Chaucer. And in the drawing room at Lancaster Gate on Sunday afternoons in the late nineteenth century one might occasionally find, in addition to Strachey's eccentric Uncle William and Uncle George, another uncle of a very different sort—Uncle Edward. Sir Edward Strachey (1812–1901) was truly an eminent Victorian. A versatile man of letters who contributed to the *Quarterly Review, Fraser's Magazine,* the *Spectator, Notes and Queries,* and the *Atlantic Monthly,* he was one whose conversation, like that of his father, was spiced with quotations from Chaucer and other great humorists. One of his articles contributed to the *Quarterly Review* was entitled "Nonsense As a Fine Art." Here he analyzed and discussed nonsense as it had appeared in "The Nun's Priest's Tale," Cervantes, the Icelandic "Lay of Thrym," the writings of Erasmus and of Luther, Shakespeare, Charles Lamb, and Thomas Love Peacock, as well as in many other places. "One of the last official fools of the English court was Archie Armstrong," wrote Sir Edward, "[who] died on the First of April (1646)." The Victorian successors of Armstrong, he said, were the elder Matthews, Albert Smith, Corney Grain, and Tom Hood.[44]

Thus we may in part understand how Strachey could love the Victorian age even while he was struggling to emancipate himself from it. He was well aware that in "that great ocean of material" there was, certainly for him, an undertow and that the tide of reaction against Victorianism in which he participated was not altogether a movement in one direction. He was the better critic of the age for not being content to judge it by what seemed to be happening on the surface of that vast sea.

44. *167* (Oct. 1888), 335–65.

CHAPTER 8

Conception of Biography

"HUMAN BEINGS are too important to be treated as mere symptoms of the past. They have a value which is independent of any temporal processes—which is eternal, and must be felt for its own sake." These two sentences, embedded in the well-known preface to *Eminent Victorians,* must always be the starting point and a constant point of reference in any discussion of Strachey's conception of biography. The basis of all good biography must be, he firmly held, the humanistic respect for men—men in their separateness as distinct from lower creatures and in their separateness apart from economical, political, ethical, and religious theories; men in their separateness as distinct from one another, men as individuals, various, living, free. It has been well said that Strachey wrote with "a glowing conviction that character is the one thing that counts in life" and with a realization that individual human beings, however simple they may appear, are enigmatical, complex, and compact of contending elements.[1] Each person carries his secret within him, and the biographer is one who has the gift for discerning what it is.[2] Hence individual human beings are not

1. Arthur Waugh, "Mr. Lytton Strachey," a letter to the *Spectator, 148* (Jan. 30, 1932), 146. John Russell's comment on Strachey in the following passage is excellent: "Other writers have used portraits to give pause to their narratives; but with Strachey the narrative is all portrait, and if we look into the eyes of his Voltaire or, more surprisingly, of his Prince Consort, we seem to see, reflected in their pupils, the gaze of their bland inquisitor. All the other facts of history are dimmed and thrust backward by this intense and continuous scrutiny of individuals." "Lytton Strachey," *Horizon, 15* (Feb. 1947), 93.

2. Strachey's Aphorism 32 reads: "The worst and best parts of us are the secrets we never reveal."

only highly important; they are also highly interesting. The puzzle
which the biographer has to solve in dealing with ordinary people
is fascinating enough; but when the subject is a great man the
biographer works with his problem in an atmosphere of intense
excitement, for about all great men there is something wondrous
and incredible.[3]

To lose interest in human beings and the sense of their importance was to Strachey a sure sign of literary decadence, not
merely in the biographer but in the novelist and dramatist as well.
Fanny Burney could have become a much greater novelist if she
had not turned away from an honest treatment of characters in
order to give her attention to various other matters which had en-
gaged her interest.[4] And it was a great pity that Shakespeare's later
plays, full of glorious poetry as they were, revealed this same kind
of decadence. In them, the dramatist turned his back on "the stupendous creations in character" in his great tragedies and con-
tented himself with a method in which character served merely as
a "miserable prop" for the "gorgeous clothing of his rhetoric." [5]
He allowed words, which had been his servants, to dominate him
completely. "Shakespeare, certainly, knew what he was doing;
and yet, in the end, those little creatures were too much for him.
. . . In Shakespeare's later works character has grown unindividual and unreal; drama has become conventional or operatic;
the words remain more tremendously, more exquisitely alive than
ever—the excuse and the explanation of the rest. The little creatures had absolutely fascinated their master; he had become their
slave." [6] On the other hand, when the reader discovered the real
thing—individual human character—there could be no doubt in
his mind about its relative importance: "What makes Sterne im-

3. The last clause is quoted almost verbatim from Strachey's Aphorism 63.
4. "The Wrong Turning," *Independent Review*, 2 (Feb. 1904), 169–73. In
the same article Strachey objected to Burke's praise of the unreal characters
in Fanny Burney's later novels: ". . . by 'characters' Burke meant just what
he should not have meant—descriptions, that is to say, of persons who might
exist."
5. "Shakespeare's Final Period," *Independent Rev.*, 3 (Aug. 1904), 405 ff.
6. Strachey's introd. to G. H. W. Ryland's *Words and Poetry*, rptd. in
Characters and Commentaries (New York, Harcourt, Brace, 1933), p. 287.

mortal is not his sentiment, nor his indecency, nor his asterisks, but his Mr. Shandy and his Uncle Toby." [7]

Only art could show a Mr. Shandy, an Uncle Toby, a Hamlet, or an Iago active and alive on the printed page or in the theater. Only art could make "created" or imaginary characters live before us. Moreover, and the fact had been too often overlooked, only art could make real people who had once lived, who had had their place in time, awaken and become alive again for us to see. Only art could show us what they had really been in their very essence. History, therefore, was art. And biography was art—"the most delicate and humane of all the branches of the art of writing." [8] What Strachey has said about history can be applied with equal force to his conception of biography. "It is obvious that History is not a science: it is obvious that History is not the accumulation of facts, but the relation of them. Only the pedantry of incomplete academic persons could have given birth to such a monstrous supposition." [9] The biographer must so exercise his art that he will convince the reader that he understands the motives of his characters and "the actual conditions of their lives." "No study of a man can be successful unless it is vital; a portrait-painter who cannot make his subject live has very little reason for putting brush to canvas." [10]

7. "The Wrong Turning." Strachey believed that Carlyle had many faults as a writer but that when he drew his "inimitable portrait-sketches" he was at his best: "Some New Carlyle Letters," *Spectator, 102* (April 10, 1909), 577 ff.

8. Preface to *Eminent Victorians.*

9. "Gibbon," *Portraits in Miniature* (New York, Harcourt, Brace, 1931), p. 158.

10. "The Italian Renaissance," *Spectator, 101* (Nov. 21, 1908), 838 ff. "It was Mr. Strachey's distinction in reinstating biography as an art to draw attention to the formlessness of literature generally. He did this in common with writers very unlike him, for whom he could have had little sympathy: with such writers as Mr. Joyce and Mr. Eliot." Edwin Muir, "Lytton Strachey," *Nation and Athenaeum, 37* (April 25, 1925), 102. "If Strachey was to influence biographical art dangerously, at least his influence was deliberate, and not a chance bomb thrown on the highway by a lunatic. He knew perfectly well what he was about, and announced his intentions as clearly in his Preface as Milton in his Foreword to *Paradise Lost.*" Guy Boas, *Lytton*

There were plenty of examples in English of how *not* to practice the art of biography. Some of these were older works; others were new ones which Strachey came to grips with as a reviewer for the *Spectator* and other journals in the years from 1903 onward. Such works convinced him that England was very much in need of a great biographical tradition like that of the French. "The art of biography seems to have fallen on evil times in England. We have had, it is true, a few masterpieces, but we have never had, like the French, a great biographical tradition." [11] The seventeenth-century Samuel Butler's characters, for instance, "after the manner of Theophrastus," were "curiously unreal to us, and this effect is heightened by his method of vituperative caricature. . . . And, in addition, their very wealth of matter proves a stumbling block. The mind is overburdened by the serried succession of ideas, the immense accumulation of images." [12]

Edmund Gosse's biography of Sir Thomas Browne had the very great merit of an entertaining style but suffered from two major faults: failure to adhere to a proper principle of selection and lack of a clearly defined point of view. Browne's works were not the kind which, if they were to be understood, required the biography of the author as a commentary. Browne was very much unlike Byron in this respect. "The Glasgow merchant who read through *Don Juan* and asked at the end whether the author was a married man was surely in need of some enlightenment." [13] But

---

Strachey, English Association Pamphlet No. 93, Nov. 1935, p. 10. When the University of Edinburgh awarded Strachey the Order of Merit in literature, July 20, 1926, the citation read in part: "Mr. Strachey has blazed a trail through the thicket of this crowded epoch for which every future explorer passing that way will have reason to thank him. He is eminently worthy of our Order of Merit in the department of letters, if only for restoring to the delectable but almost forgotten art of biography its proper style, proportion, and attitude."

11. Preface to *Eminent Victorians*.

12. "The Author of *Hudibras*," *Spectator, 102* (Feb. 6, 1909), 224 ff. (a review of A. R. Waller's *Samuel Butler: Characters and Passages from the Notebooks*).

13. "A New Book on Sir Thomas Browne," *Speaker*, Feb. 3, 1906, p. 441.

for writers like Browne "it is sufficient to know that they have lived." [14] Gosse's book, therefore, "would have gained if it had told us a little more about Sir Thomas's style and a little less about his sons." And, unfortunately, "Mr. Gosse is apparently so anxious to be impartial, to look at things from every point of view," that it is at times difficult to discover his own point of view.[15]

Strachey found G. C. Macaulay's *James Thomson* much longer than the subject justified. Even if the length were deserved, Macaulay's style, which consisted of "copious paraphrase interspersed with copious quotation," was certainly not a happy one.[16]

Strachey's review of Andrew Lang's *Sir Walter Scott,* published in the *Speaker,* October 20, 1906, was almost savage. Not anyone's reputation, he said, could be enhanced by Lang's book. Lang seemed to have brought "neither care, nor diligence, nor attention" to his work. His style was slovenly, "shapeless and invertebrate stuff." And the whole book was filled with "a mass of affectation which would have made Scott's gorge rise." [17]

George Paston's biography, *Lady Mary Wortley Montagu and Her Times,* had some of the same faults—and others. Strachey de-

14. *Ibid.* Compare this passage from Strachey's review of Mary E. Coleridge's poems: "The greatest poetry is always impersonal. . . . The biographies of great poets are of interest merely from the historical and psychological point of view; so far as poetry is concerned they are, so to speak, works of supererogation; we could do very well without them. The voice of Homer will ring for ever in the ears of the world, though it be a voice and nothing more. . . . But there is another kind of poetry, which . . . depends less on pure artistic achievement than on the power of personal revelation. . . . It is on this select and quiet shelf of the Muses that the late Miss Mary Coleridge's little volume of poems will find a place." "The Late Miss Coleridge's Poems," *Spectator, 100* (Jan. 4, 1908), 19.

15. "A New Book on Sir Thomas Browne."

16. "The Poetry of Thomson," *Spectator, 100* (March 14, 1908), 421–2.

17. "Not by Lockhart," *Speaker,* Oct. 20, 1906, pp. 82–3. Strachey's letters show that he read Lockhart's *Scott* with great pleasure in the spring of 1906. He also reviewed G. L. G. Norgate's abridgment to Lockhart's *Scott* in this article and was able to commend it as "simply what it pretends to be, a condensation of Lockhart's life. It is straightforward, ordinary, and (like all condensations) dull. But it is neither careless, nor affected, nor pretentious; it is an honest piece of work."

plored "its slipshod writing, its uninstructed outlook, its utter lack
of taste and purpose." It was a "bulky" book, "unwieldy and pretentious." It was "a fair specimen of the kind of biographical work
which seems to give so much satisfaction to large numbers of our
reading public. Decidedly, 'they order the matter better in France,'
where such a production could never have appeared." [18]

Such a work as H. Noel Williams' *The Women Bonapartes,* in
two volumes, was simply dull.[19] And Austin Brereton's *The Life of
Henry Irving,* also in "two large volumes," with its superficiality,
its unreality, its failure to evaluate its materials, its eulogistic tone,
and its complete lack of psychological insight, could provide an
excellent object lesson in how biography should not be written.

> The interest of these two large volumes lies almost en-
> tirely in their record of outward facts; and the result is that,
> to the ordinary reader, they can hardly fail to be disappoint-
> ing. Mr. Brereton has made no serious attempt to draw a pic-
> ture of the man. He has been content to fill out his work with
> an immense number of quotations from contemporary Press
> notices—quotations which, curious though they may be as
> documents in the history of taste, throw only a confused light
> upon Irving's artistic methods, and produce an atmosphere
> of superficiality which strikes the reader as altogether out
> of place in a biography intended to be definitive. Indeed, the
> total impression made by the book is not only singularly super-
> ficial but singularly unreal. As one turns over Mr. Brereton's
> pages, one finds oneself transported into a strange world of

18. "Lady Mary Wortley Montagu," *Albany Review, 1* (Sept. 1907), 708 ff.
When Strachey reviewed George Paston's *Mr. Pope: His Life and Times* over
two years later, he objected to its rambling structure but, despite its two
volumes, praised its "easy, unaffected style." "Alexander Pope," *Spectator, 103*
(Nov. 20, 1909), 847–8.

19. "Some Napoleonic Books," *Spectator, 101* (Dec. 26, 1908), 1100–1. In
the same review Strachey gave Joseph Turquan's *The Sisters of Napoleon*
credit for being amusing. As for his opinion concerning the Bonapartes themselves, he wrote: ". . . the fundamental characteristic of the Bonaparte
family was meanness. . . . Really, it is difficult to decide which was the more
remarkable thing about Napoleon—his generalship or his lack of humor."

limelight, attitudes, splendor, and endless applause,—a world all scarlet carpets and waving palms and lovely ladies, where after-dinner speeches are the only form of utterance, and nothing is drunk except champagne. The very headlines of the chapters from a kind of triumphant procession—"Tribute of the Press," "Chicago Conquered," "A Great Reception," "Compliments Galore," "A Brilliant Audience," "A Memorable Season," "An Honor from Germany," "Appears at Archbishop's House"—the mind grows bewildered by the catalogue. "The supper was a very elaborate affair," etc. But, if we are to believe Mr. Brereton, the supper always was very elaborate, the guests always the most distinguished, and every moment proud. One looks in vain for a record of intellectual effort and development, for expressions of noble thought or profound feeling, for any of those manifestations of original and unmistakable genius which occur so often in the private lives of truly great men. It almost seems as if the stage had crossed the footlights and enveloped the whole of Irving's existence, so that the best account of it was in truth to be found in the contemporary notices of the Press.[20]

In the preface to *Eminent Victorians* Strachey gave a clear and concise summary of the faults which he had found in many English biographies:

We have had no Fontenelles and Condorcets, with their incomparable *éloges,* compressing into a few shining pages the manifold existences of men. With us, the most delicate and humane of all the branches of the art of writing has been relegated to the journeymen of letters; we do not reflect that it is perhaps as difficult to write a good life as to live one. Those two fat volumes, with which it is our custom to commemorate the dead—who does not know them, with their ill-digested masses of material, their slipshod style, their tone of tedious panegyric, their lamentable lack of selection, of detachment, of design? They are as familiar as the *cortège* of the under-

20. "The Life of Henry Irving," *Spectator, 101* (Dec. 26, 1908), 1104.

taker, and wear the same air of slow, funereal barbarism. . . . To preserve, for instance, a becoming brevity—a brevity which excludes everything that is redundant and nothing that is significant—that, surely, is the first duty of the biographer. The second, no less surely, is to maintain his own freedom of spirit. It is not his business to be complimentary; it is his business to lay bare the facts of the case, as he understands them. That is what I have aimed at in this book—to lay bare the facts of some cases, as I understand them, dispassionately, impartially, and without ulterior intentions.

Modern English biographers could learn much, Strachey believed, not only from Fontenelle and Condorcet but from other writers, French, English, and even Russian, and from some writers who were not biographers. The study which Strachey made of Racine, reflected in the brilliant essay published in the *New Quarterly* for June 1908, was of incalculable value in preparing him to be a biographer. In Racine's plays he found three of the qualities which he admired most in biography: an unfailing sense of reality, selection made in accordance with true judgment, and psychological insight of a very high order. Racine's art might be declared "the sublime essence of reality, save that, after all, reality has no degrees." It was as a psychologist that Racine had achieved his most remarkable triumphs; his concern had been primarily with "the mystery of the mind of man." It provided him with a principle of selection. "Every art is based upon a selection, and the art of Racine selected the things of the spirit for the material of its work. . . . When Racine is most himself, when he is seizing upon a state of mind and depicting it with all its twistings and vibrations, he writes with a directness which is indeed naked, and his sentences, refined to the utmost point of significance, flash out like swords, stroke upon stroke, swift, certain, irresistible." [21]

Saint-Simon was likewise one from whom Strachey was willing to learn much. In him a concentrated psychological insight and a rare

21. *1*, 361–84. Here given the title "The Poetry of Racine" but reprinted with alterations as "Racine" in *Books and Characters* (New York, Harcourt, Brace, 1922).

vitalizing power were associated with great skill in selection. "It is upon the inward creature that he expends his most lavish care— upon the soul that sits behind the eyelids, upon the purpose and the passion that linger in a gesture or betray themselves in a word. The joy that he takes in such description soon infects the reader. . . . Nor in spite of the virulence of his method, do his portraits ever sink to the level of caricatures. His most malevolent exaggerations are yet so realistic that they carry conviction. . . . he never forgot, in the extremity of his ferocity, to commit the last insult, and to breathe into their nostrils the fatal breath of life." [22] There is certainly much here to suggest Strachey's own biographical method. Strachey had great admiration for Clarendon, "who had the advantage of drawing from the life," as a prose portrait painter but, even so, maintained that "his fine and sympathetic studies" fell far below "the fiery presentments of Saint-Simon" and "the brilliant profiles of La Bruyère." [23]

Among English biographers not only Clarendon but also John Aubrey deserved praise. Brief biography was not the only kind, as Boswell had clearly demonstrated, but Aubrey had shown early what could be done through the art of brevity. "He was accurate, he had an unfailing eye for what was interesting, and he possessed —it was almost inevitable in those days—a natural gift of style. . . . A biography should either be as long as Boswell's or as short as Aubrey's. The method of enormous and elaborate accretion which produced the *Life of Johnson* is excellent, no doubt; but, failing that, let us have no half-measures; let us have the pure essentials—a vivid image, on a page or two, without explanations, transitions, commentaries, or padding. This is what Aubrey gives us." [24]

22. *Landmarks in French Literature,* Home Univ. Library (New York, Henry Holt; London, Thornton Butterworth, 1912), pp. 150–1.

23. "The Author of *Hudibras.*" In *Landmarks in French Literature* Strachey wrote that La Bruyère's character studies were "caricatures rather than portraits—records of the idiosyncrasies of humanity rather than of humanity itself" (p. 125). D. S. (Prince) Mirsky goes too far when he says that Saint-Simon, dealing with history and biography as a complex thing, is "the only author to whom Mr. Strachey is essentially indebted." "Mr. Lytton Strachey," *London Mercury, 8* (June 1923), 175 ff.

24. "John Aubrey," *Portraits in Miniature,* pp. 28–9 (first published in

As for Boswell himself and as for Johnson the biographer, from the beginning to the end of his life Strachey found them both irresistible. No greater mistake could be made than to assume that Strachey rebelled against the Boswellian conception of biography or against Boswell's methods. It was not Boswell that he objected to; it was the Boswellian technique after it had fallen into the less skillful hands of those who had perverted it—into the hands of those who wrote the wearisome "two fat volumes" in the nineteenth and early twentieth centuries. But Boswell—and Johnson —were a perennial delight. "No one needs an excuse for re-opening the *Lives of the Poets;* the book is too delightful. It is not, of course, as delightful as Boswell; but who reopens Boswell? Boswell is in another category; because, as every one knows, when he has once been opened he can never be shut." [25] In *The Life of Johnson* there was to be found something which no mere compilation of facts possessed, "Boswellian artistry . . . that power of selection and evocation which clothes its object with something of the palpable reality of life." [26]

Strachey also admired Lockhart's *Life of Scott* and Carlyle's portraits from life.[27] Possibly he was impressed by the detachment and the slight suggestion of irony in Froude's treatment of the Carlyles.

the *Nation and Athenaeum, 33,* Sept. 15, 1923, 741-2). Cf. Strachey's much earlier comment on William Barry's *Newman:* "The author of this readable monograph writes in fetters and is quite aware of the fact." He "writes eloquently, occasionally rather too eloquently. But, on the whole, the book is a sound performance in every sense, and hits the happy medium between scrappiness and oppressive amplitude." "Cardinal Newman," *Spectator, 93* (Oct. 1, 1904), Suppl., 457.

25. "The Lives of the Poets," *Independent Review, 10* (July 1906), 108 ff. In the same article Strachey wrote: "It is sufficient for us to recognize that he [Johnson] is a mountain, and to pay all the reverence that is due."

26. "A Sidelight on Frederick the Great," *New Statesman* (Jan. 27, 1917), pp. 397 ff. In the diary which Strachey, at the age of eighteen, kept for a while during 1898, when he was attending Liverpool College, he wrote that Boswell's *Johnson* was "the best biography ever written" and expressed his indignation over the poor format of a copy which he had recently examined. See also "James Boswell," *Nation* (London), *36* (Jan. 31, 1925), 609–10, a review of C. B. Tinker's *Letters of James Boswell.*

27. See notes 7 and 17 and Harold Nicolson, *The Development of English Biography* (London, Hogarth Press, 1933), pp. 117, 143, 153.

He certainly disapproved of Alexander Carlyle's angry references to Froude and stood ready to defend Froude's right to exercise his freedom of spirit.[28] Edmund Gosse's unsigned "The Character of Queen Victoria," published in the *Quarterly Review* in April 1901, only two or three months after the queen's death, had not only skillful selection and good style but also remarkable objectivity in the light of its date. The footnotes of Strachey's *Queen Victoria* significantly contain a number of references to this article. Gosse's *Father and Son* (1907) also had qualities which Strachey admired: judicious selection, a definite point of view, and an excellent style. Like Strachey, Gosse kept before his eyes the best French models of biography. Strachey knew Gosse in later years and did not greatly respect him. He believed that Gosse was too often careless in his handling of facts. It is possible, however, that Strachey owed more to Gosse than he himself realized.[29]

It is certain that he admired greatly and owed much to the great Russian novelist Dostoievsky. About 1909 he began reading Dostoievsky in French translations; he also read Constance Garnett's

28. *Ibid.,* p. 143, and "Some New Carlyle Letters."

29. Nicolson, *Development of English Biography*. For Gosse's identification of himself as the author of the article on Queen Victoria in the *Quarterly Review* for April 1901, see his *More Books upon the Table* (London, Heinemann, 1923), pp. 3–10, where he speaks with some gratification of Strachey's borrowings from the article. E. F. Benson has written that Gosse in *Father and Son* was really the first to revolt against the Victorian method of biography. "It was Gosse who broke through that tradition of pious unreality. . . . Strachey undoubtedly followed Gosse, though without sacrificing one whit of his own originality" ("Strachey and Gosse," London *Sunday Times*, Sept. 4, 1932, p. 4). Strachey's antipathy for Gosse was partly personal and partly a feeling that Gosse's scholarship could not be trusted. In a letter of July 30, 1907, he wrote to one of his sisters: "I am writing an article on Beddoes for the Quarterly. . . . Of course the wretched Gosse has managed to trail his slug's mind over the poor man, and has left a slimy track. I shudder to think what Beddoes would have said if he'd foreseen who his editor was to be." Concerning Gosse's *Father and Son* he wrote in January 1908: "Modern books don't seem to come to much. Mr. Gosse's, though, was amusing—did you see it? . . . I'm sure you'd like *it,* though not *him*—he comes out of it rather worse than usual." On one occasion something by Gosse was published with his name misspelled "Goose." Henceforth to Strachey he was always "Goose Gosse."

translations of *The Brothers Karamazov, The Idiot,* and *The Possessed* when they were published in 1912 and 1914 and reviewed them in the *Spectator*. Strachey's taste was never exclusively classical, and his enthusiasm was almost unbounded for Dostoievsky's rich, Gothic complexity, his genius for filling his pages with concentrated, burning human passion, and his psychological profundity. He was amazed at "the wonderful intensity and the subtlety of Dostoievsky's psychological insight" and declared, "Here, no doubt, lies the central essence of his genius." [30]

There was at least one early twentieth-century biography in two large volumes to which Strachey gave high praise. It was Logan Pearsall Smith's *The Life and Letters of Sir Henry Wotton*, which he reviewed in the *Spectator* for November 23, 1907. Here was a copious work abounding in good things. In it were to be found fresh and significant materials which Smith by diligent research had unearthed "among the manuscript collections of our great country houses." Smith's and Izaak Walton's lives of Wotton supplemented one another neatly. Smith gave the facts; Walton "preserved all the fragrance of the subject and very few of the facts." But Smith's work was no mere compilation of facts; his pages, "in spite of the weight of learning at the back of them, are eminently readable, for they are full of stirring narrative and vivid description, and they are informed throughout with a sympathy and a distinction such as it is a rare pleasure to find." The review, one of Strachey's best, provides clear evidence that Smith's biography made

30. "Dostoievsky," *Spectator, 109* (Sept. 28, 1912), 451–2. It is interesting to note here Freud's opinion that *The Brothers Karamazov* was the greatest novel ever written. See also "A Russian Humorist," *Spectator, 112* (April 11, 1914), 610–11, where Strachey maintained that Dostoievsky had not only psychological insight but humor: "And so it happens that, by virtue of that magic power, his wildest fancies have something real and human in them, and his moments of greatest intensity are not melodramatic but tragic." There is little evidence that Strachey was influenced directly by George Eliot, but his mother knew and admired her as a person and was enthusiastic about her novels; Strachey surely must have read them. He and his brothers and sisters grew up reading Henry James, and preserved among his MSS is a short piece entitled "The Fruit of the Tree" (dated June 1901) which he wrote in imitation of James.

Wotton live for Strachey, for in it Strachey sketches Wotton's life and character with an economy, a sharpness, and an eye for the picturesque detail which suggest his later profiles.[31]

The survey which we have made above of Strachey's pronouncements concerning various faulty and admirable biographies leaves little doubt as to what characteristics he believed the good biography should have. It should be based on the facts. It should be art, with judicious selection, good structure, and good style. It should make its subject live again before the eyes of the reader. It should be written from a definite point of view. It must be the product of a free mind, bound only by considerations of impartiality and justice. And, as to length, it must be either long or short; it must either use the Boswellian art which produced a life-size portrait or it must use the art of brevity, the art of the profile. The two arts must be kept separate; to try to find the halfway ground between the two was to court disaster.

To what extent did Strachey realize his ideal in his own biographies? With regard to part of the answer his readers have been in agreement. They have agreed that both the longer and the shorter works have been highly readable, with excellent style, proportion, and structure. They have agreed that the author has consistently dominated his materials, maintained his own point of view, and exercised his own freedom of mind and spirit. They have agreed too that Strachey possessed a rare gift for breathing life into his subjects.

When one pauses for a moment to consider just how Strachey succeeded in making his subject live again, one cannot avoid noting his strong preference for the dramatic method and the consistency and skill with which he used it. It should be noted that throughout his life he was writing not only biographies but also

31. "Sir Henry Wotton," *Spectator, 99* (Nov. 23, 1907), 821–2. Strachey also spoke here of the pleasure which he had received from reading Walton's *Reliquiae Wottonianae.* It must have pleased Strachey to find that one of the documents which Smith had unearthed was a letter from John Donne to Wotton, then British ambassador at Venice, recommending to him his friend William Strachey, the biographer's ancestor and the author of one of the best early histories of the Virginia colony.

poems and plays, most of which are still preserved in manuscript. He took delight in writing dramatic criticism, in seeing plays, in acting in them. Virginia Woolf has gone so far as to say that his biographies are the product of a frustrated dramatist.[32] Possibly so, but if so his unusual interest in the drama and the marked degree to which the dramatic instinct was developed in him served him well as a biographer. For in Strachey's conception of biography the subject is not merely written about. Rather, the main character and all those persons significantly related to him are quick once more and act out again the various roles which life had formerly assigned to them. But although they are alive and active, they are now confined within the framework of art—art which excludes all the irrelevancies, discerns and emphasizes whatever is truly significant, and controls the behavior of all those on the stage. Edwin Muir has discussed well the skill with which Strachey transferred the dramatic method to the purposes of literary biography:

> He went out in search not of great figures and noble characters, but of human nature, and he always found it. Having found it, he set it out in his own terms. All his characters passed through his eighteenth-century workshop, and emerged in the ironically appropriate costumes he had devised for them. They emerged, if not in their own shape, then in some shape which revealed it. For the time being their author's puppets, they played over again the game which they had played far more intensely, sometimes in tears and agony, in the actual world. Mr. Strachey held the strings which moved this puppet play, and they were constantly being manipulated, but very rarely did we catch sight of them. The figures seemed to be going through the ballet of their own lives, a ballet simplified and stylized to the last detail; and it was only in the conventionalization of the costumes and attitudes that one recognized the choreographer.[33]

But Strachey's characters, stylized though they may be, are not mere puppets in a dumbshow; they talk. And the words which they

32. "The Art of Biography," *Atlantic Monthly*, *163* (April 1939), 506 ff.
33. "Lytton Strachey," *Nation and Athenaeum*, pp. 103-4.

utter are, in the main, the very words which they once said or wrote. As important as their actions are, it is through their words that we get to know them best. Strachey believed that people in actual life may be reasonably successful in concealing their real nature as long as they do not talk. But let them once open their mouths, and soon we know them for what they are—know far more than they wished to reveal and usually far more than they realized that they have revealed.[34] It is thus with the characters in Strachey's biographies. Their own words, skillfully selected and put in quotation marks, betray them and become a mocking echo of what they really were.

The question remains as to whether Strachey in making his characters live again and in compelling them to re-enact their lives on a stage of his own devising was able to deal with them in accordance with his own ideal of justice and in accordance with the accepted biographical facts. The prerogative of selection which was necessary to him as a literary artist was one certain to throw temptations in the way of anyone who exercised it. Did he succeed in resisting the temptations? Those who have attacked him during his lifetime and later say that he did not.

One such critic was Sir Edmund Gosse. Although it is true that, roughly classified, Gosse and Strachey both belong to the school of biography which reacted against the Victorians, Gosse found *Eminent Victorians* in general and its portrait of Lord Cromer in particular too much for him. Only a few weeks after Strachey's book appeared, he wrote a letter of protest to the *Times Literary Supplement*. In it he conceded that the book had been received "publicly and privately with a chorus of praise" and that the author possessed "wit and vigor." But he regretted that Strachey had used his gifts in "a pyrotechnical display of satire. He reduces the demigods

---

34. Note Strachey's Aphorism 22: "We meet people about whom we cannot make up our minds; their features, their manners, and their dress might equally be those of a vulgar or a cultivated person, and, observe as we may, we can find no detail of their appearance which is not as indeterminate as the rest; we search, we balance, we hesitate, we rack our imaginations, we are on the point of giving up in despair; when they speak, and we know at once that they are impossible."

of our youth to the Gog and Magog of Bartholmy Fair. It is very amusing, and gratifying to those who grudge the dead their prestige. But even what is sparkling should be just. The late Lord Cromer is the object (among others) of Mr. Strachey's sardonic humor, and as Mr. Strachey is being accepted as an oracle, Lord Cromer's friends can but expostulate." Strachey's representation of Cromer was "a caricature, and not a good-natured one . . . our friend is hardly to be recognized." Furthermore, Strachey was unfair to indicate that Cromer was ignorant of the East in his efforts to administer colonial affairs, for actually there was nothing in which Cromer took more interest than in the East. Gosse admitted that Strachey wrote "with extreme ability and in a most attractive style" but warned, "It is therefore all the more important to check his statements before they are crystallized into history." [35]

In his prompt reply to this letter Strachey did not retreat one inch. Gosse, he said, had written as a friend of Cromer. He himself had made "a detached examination of Lord Cromer's published writings and public acts." Although Cromer may have talked with his friends intimately and confidentially, the evidence showed that "the temper" of his mind did not suggest trustworthiness. As for the East (and here Strachey must have been conscious of his own

35. June 27, 1918, p. 301. Gosse had written an article entitled "Lord Cromer As a Man of Letters," published in the *Fortnightly Review* for March 1917 (collected in *Some Diversions of a Man of Letters* two years later). Ironically, much of what he said about Cromer can be applied to Strachey himself. Witness the following excerpts: "He would have been at home in the fourth quarter of the eighteenth century, before the French Revolution." "I have always found him amusingly impervious to ideas of a visionary or mystical order." "He himself hated mere eulogy, which he said had ruined most of the biographies of the world. . . . 'I don't want Mr. ———,' he would say, 'to tell me what I can learn for myself by turning up the file of the *Morning Post*. I want him to tell me what I can't find out elsewhere. And he need not be so very much afraid of hinting that his hero had faults, for if he had not had defects we should never have heard of his qualities. We are none of us perfect, and we don't want a priggish biographer to pretend that we are." Cromer was an intimate friend of St. Loe Strachey, editor of the *Spectator* and first cousin of Lytton Strachey. For Gosse's condemnation of Hallam Tennyson's life of his father as one of the worst "two-fat-volume" Victorian biographies, see *Some Diversions of a Man of Letters*, pp. 320–1.

father and of generations of his family who in unbroken succession back to the time of Lord Clive had distinguished themselves in India), possibly Cromer had manifested an interest in Eastern administrative questions. "But Eastern administrative questions are not the East." In ending, he returned with additional emphasis to the importance of the principle of detachment in biography. "My description of Lord Cromer is not a full-length portrait; it is an incidental sketch of the Sir Evelyn Baring of 1884. Nobody could regret more than I do that it should seem to Mr. Gosse, and others of his friends, to be a bad likeness, but the fact in itself does not appear to be a sufficient reason for thinking that it is. Unfortunately, in this world, it is not always a man's friends who know him best." [36]

If Sir Edmund Gosse objected to Strachey's Lord Cromer, Mrs. Rosalind Nash in an article published in the *Nineteenth Century* for February 1928 objected fully as much to his Florence Nightingale. Like Gosse, she insisted that her objection rested upon a basis of fact. She was, she said, very well acquainted with Sir Edward Cook's biography of Florence Nightingale, was herself conversant with Miss Nightingale's papers which Sir Edward had used in the life, and had also known Miss Nightingale, her parents, and other

36. "The Character of Lord Cromer," a letter to the editor, *TLS*, July 4, 1918, pp. 313–14. Consider in this connection Strachey's Aphorism 31: "Is it not true that a man's tables and chairs know more about him than his most intimate friends? When he is left alone, who can guess what words escape him? What gestures he gives vent to? What strange expressions come into his face? His looking-glass, perhaps, could tell us most. When he does, those unfathomable depths are abolished, that multitude of secrets is extinguished, that whole vast universe of mysteries too mysterious to be revealed; and what do the friends about the bed know of all these things? It is the bed itself that knows." May we assume, then, that Strachey believed personal intimacy such as Johnson had with Savage, Boswell with Johnson, and Froude with Carlyle to be of little value to the biographer? Possibly so, since the ideal of detachment meant much to him. Certainly he chose his own subjects from the dead whom he could have never known. Yet much of the "private information" referred to in the notes to *Queen Victoria*, probably his best work, came from Lady Lytton, whom he visited frequently when he was writing this biography. For a friendly, conciliatory letter from Gosse to Strachey, dated May 21, 1922, see Evan Charteris, *The Life and Letters of Sir Edmund Gosse* (New York and London, Harper, 1931), pp. 464–5.

---

relatives, "I think I may say well, from my childhood in the 'sixties and 'seventies until their death." Then Mrs. Nash proceeded to give a fairly long list of errors which she had found in Strachey's work. We may note a few of them. The dog was not Florence's dog but the shepherd's, not a pet but a valuable working dog. Florence did not apply elaborate splints to it but ordinary hot-water fomentations. Further, "It is difficult to think of dainty Parthe 'tearing up dolls.' " Mr. Nightingale did not suggest that a husband might be advisable; the mother was the matchmaker. The room in which Florence Nightingale died was not gloomy; it was full of light. And as for Strachey's main point, not demoniac fury but calm persuasiveness characterized Florence Nightingale. "Sir Edward Cooke's *Life* disposed of the mythical figure, and left in its place a very human personality. But the *Life* was not for the many, and Mr. Strachey could not resist the temptation to go a step further. What fun, he seems to have said to himself, to turn the saint into a fiend! . . . Is the result biography?" [37]

Queen Victoria seems to have proved itself generally satisfactory to those who have insisted that biography should be entirely faithful to the facts. *Books and Characters,* as we have seen, with its studies of Racine and Beddoes, did much to give Strachey a reputation for directing attention to deserving writers who had been neglected and for rescuing important facts that had been forgotten.

---

37. "Florence Nightingale according to Mr. Strachey," *Nineteenth Century,* *103* (Feb. 1928), 258–65. Compare what Strachey wrote to his mother about Florence Nightingale on January 15, 1914: "She was a capable woman, but rather disagreeable in various ways—a complete egotist, and also full of very tiresome religiosity; and I don't think really intelligent. In spite of spending all her life in medical concerns, she never seems to have got a scientific grasp of things." Concerning two of Strachey's victims to whom I happen to have given some study I must say a word of defense. Dr. Arnold had a vigor and breadth of intellect and a human warmth which are entirely lacking in Strachey's caricature. And Julius Charles Hare, introduced as a minor character in "Cardinal Manning," was not a fanatical Low Churchman, as Strachey represented him as being, but a scholarly Broad Church latitudinarian, thoroughly steeped in Plato and in British, French, and German liberal theology, a disciple of Coleridge, and the friend of F. D. Maurice and John Sterling.

But with the publication of *Elizabeth and Essex* in 1928, there were new indictments of Strachey's scholarship. The most important of these was made by G. B. Harrison, an acknowledged authority in the field of Elizabethan history and literature. Harrison admired Strachey's portrait of the queen herself; she "lives most vitally," he said. Strachey's Bacon, too, was praiseworthy—"dissected with especial skill." Essex he found much less convincing. Essex, he observed, was a man of action; and Strachey did not understand him. Furthermore, Strachey failed to give the stories which he could have given to explain the great popularity of Essex. Neither did he show one very important side of Essex. "Essex was over-sensitive to laughter; and he often made himself ridiculous." Whereas Strachey indicated that Essex destroyed Lopez from a motive of patriotism, actually he destroyed him out of revenge: Lopez had once made the queen and others laugh at him. Harrison questioned such suppressions and manipulations as "privileges denied to the pedestrian scholar." The bibliograpny at the end of the book, he added, was "disturbing to the creeping critic—the pedant—who reads such things; for it omits at least five of the most important sources for the life of Essex." [38]

38. "Elizabeth and Her Court," *Spectator, 141* (Nov. 24, 1928), 777. Cf. E. G. Clark, "Mr. Strachey's Biographical Method," *Catholic World, 129* (May 1929), 129–35; Christopher Hollis, "Elizabeth and Mr. Strachey," *Dublin Review, 186* (Jan. 1930), 21–30; Edmund Wilson, "Lytton Strachey," *New Republic, 72* (Sept. 21, 1932), 146–8. Max Beerbohm wrote in 1943 that *Elizabeth and Essex* was "a finely constructed work, but seems to me to be essentially guess-work." *Lytton Strachey,* Rede Lecture for 1943 at Cambridge University (New York, Alfred A. Knopf, 1943), p. 20. For an accusation that Strachey was guilty of both carelessness and deliberate falsification in his "Cardinal Manning," see F. A. Simpson, "Methods of History," *Spectator, 172* (Jan. 7, 1944), 7–8. A similar attack, but with other points added to the indictment, is made by James Pope-Hennessy in "Strachey's Way," *Spectator, 182* (Feb. 25, 1949), 264. On the other hand, Desmond MacCarthy has written: "I believe that as time goes on *Elizabeth and Essex* will be rated much higher." "Lytton Strachey: The Art of Biography," *Sunday Times* (London), Nov. 5, 1933, p. 8. In 1947 a distinguished British historian told me that he had found *Elizabeth and Essex* to be essentially true, that he admired it very much, and that "Dr. Arnold" was the only one of Strachey's characterizations which seemed to him seriously distorted and unfair.

Even André Maurois, who admired Strachey greatly and owed much to him, found him "in some instances a shade nastier than is really fair" and said that we sometimes get tired of "the plucking of dead lions by the beard." [39] Leonard Bacon has declared that Strachey was temperamentally unfitted to practice the art of the historian. "Unless truth was piquant or dramatic, unless a fact could be forced, by fair means or foul, into the strait jacket of his ironic preconception, or made to lend color to one of his superb imaginative paintings, he was fully capable of ignoring it, in favor of something more poignant and more legendary." [40] Edgar Johnson has likewise said that Strachey's "most reprehensible fault as a responsible biographer" was that he did not hesitate to manipulate either facts or documents to secure a more striking effect." According to Johnson, Douglas Southall Freeman in 1936 described Strachey as "one of the most pernicious influences in modern biography." [41]

39. "The Modern Biographer," *Yale Review*, N.S., *17* (Jan. 1928), 231 ff. Maurois also wrote here that Strachey was "a very deep psychologist" and was "the father and master of modern biography." A little later he wrote: "A biographer, such as Mr. Strachey, who has the power to diffuse through his record of facts the poetic idea of Destiny, of the passage of Time, of the fragility of human fortune, brings us in fact a secret comfort. . . . There is no such thing as progress in literature. Tennyson is not greater than Homer, Proust is not greater than Montaigne, Strachey is not greater than Boswell. They are different." *Aspects of Biography*, trans. S. C. Roberts (New York, D. Appleton, 1929), pp. 142, 203.

40. "An Eminent Post-Victorian," *Yale Review*, N.S., *30* (Winter 1941), 321–2. Bacon has also taken exception to Strachey's Cromer and suspects "some personal animosity" (p. 318).

41. *One Mighty Torrent: The Drama of Biography* (New York, Stackpole, 1937), pp. 511, 520. But Johnson praised Strachey for insisting that the biographer must have a clear and definite point of view. "No portrayal of character can be purely objective, because our conception of a personality is the intersection between it and ourselves. Strachey's great achievement was that he forced this fact into the open. The author's point of view became explicit instead of being a muzzy, unacknowledged projection of his personality" (pp. 522–3). Among others who have attacked Strachey are James Truslow Adams and Hugh Kingsmill. Adams wrote: "Among the psychological school of biographers the unquestioned leader and by far the most influential practitioner is Lytton Strachey. His influence has been little short of disas-

On the other hand, Strachey's command over facts and respect
for them have greatly impressed some of the commentators on him.
Claude W. Fuess has described Strachey as "a scholar of remarkable industry, who examined sources with assiduity and discre-
tion." [42] F. L. Lucas praised his "restraint and intellectual honesty"
and spoke of him as one who "wrote fastidiously and little, but read
enormously." [43] Some of Strachey's friends who knew him best say
that he seemed to be reading constantly and that he almost always
had a book in his hand.[44] Undoubtedly, also, the long thesis which
Strachey wrote at Cambridge between 1903 and 1905—a thesis dealing with extremely complicated and difficult questions concerning
the charges against Warren Hastings—gave him valuable training
in the techniques of historic research and a respect for the integrity
of historic facts. It is noteworthy, furthermore, that throughout
his life he battled for the principle of the uncorrupted text. It mattered not whether an editor's motive was to bowdlerize or to im-
prove by alteration, he had done what in Strachey's eyes was un-
pardonable if he had tampered with the text. When he himself
in his last years edited the Greville *Memoirs*, most of the notes to
which he completed before his death, he resisted every temptation
to say spicy things in the footnotes. The spice, he seems to have
assumed quite rightly, should all be Greville's. When he was reviewing an edition of Blake's poems as early as May 1906, he was
unsparing in his condemnation of the editors, who, he said, had

---

trous." "New Modes in Biography," *Current History, 31* (Nov. 1929), 258.
Kingsmill was vehement in his dislike for Strachey. He first parodied Strachey's
style in "Joseph, from *Eminent Egyptians*," *English Review, 54* (April 1932),
399–404, and then attempted to turn the tables on a biographer who had
taken great liberties with Victorian subjects by having him annihilated in an
imaginary passage by Carlyle: "Our Wart-School of Modern Portraiture I
name Biographer Strachey and his apes, blasphemously scribbling for pence
their *Acta Stultorum*, or Deeds of the Fools. As tho there were no other
veracity about a Hero but his warts! As tho brave Oliver's monition to Court
Painter Lely has been: 'Meddle not with my face! Paint my warts only'!"
"Some Modern Light-Bringers Extinguished by Thomas Carlyle," *English
Review, 56* (Jan. 1933), 25–6.

42. "Lytton Strachey," *SRL, 8* (Feb. 6, 1932), 501.

43. "Lytton Strachey: An Artist in History," *Observer* (London), Jan. 24,
1932, p. 5.

44. Private information.

praised Blake's meter and then emended it. "This is Procrustes," Strachey wrote, "admiring the exquisite proportions of his victim." Blake's poems should have been left just as he wrote them; "Add a comma to the text of Blake, and you put all heaven in a rage." [45] It cannot be maintained that Strachey admired scholarship but did not know what modern scholarship really was. One would be hard pressed to find a more clear and satisfactory statement of the nature of modern scholarship than Strachey gave in a passage dealing with the historian Mandell Creighton:

> Born when the world was becoming extremely scientific, he belonged to the post-Carlyle-and-Macaulay generation—the school of Oxford and Cambridge inquirers, who sought to reconstruct the past solidly and patiently, with nothing but facts to assist them—pure facts, untwisted by political or metaphysical bias and uncoloured by romance. In this attempt Creighton succeeded admirably. He was industrious, exact, clear-headed, and possessed of a command over words that was quite sufficient for his purposes. . . . In his work a perfectly grey light prevails everywhere; there is not a single lapse into psychological profundity; every trace of local colour, every suggestion of personal passion, has been studiously removed. In many ways all this is a great comfort. One is not worried by moral lectures or purple patches, and the field is kept clear for what Creighton really excelled in—the lucid exposition of complicated political transactions, and the intricate movements of thought with which they were accompanied. The biscuit is certainly exceedingly dry; but at any rate there are no weevils in it.[46]

In the same spirit, shortly after the death of Sir Sidney Lee, Strachey commended his labors as editor of *The Dictionary of National Biography,* "one of the most useful books in existence, and the motto of which was: 'No flowers, by request.' " [47]

45. "The Poetry of Blake," *Books and Characters,* pp. 222–3. First published in the *Independent Review,* May 1906.

46. "Creighton," *Portraits in Miniature,* pp. 204–6. First published as "Mandell Creighton," N. Y. *Herald Tribune Books,* May 26, 1929, p. 6.

47. "A Frock-Coat Portrait of a Great King," *Daily Mail,* Oct. 11, 1927, p. 10. A review of Lee's *King Edward VII, 11.*

But the achievement of a Creighton or of a Sir Sidney Lee was far from adequate when tested in the terms of Strachey's ideal of history and biography. To him, true history and true biography must be art. And to be art they must deal with facts as they were interpreted and at times even transmuted by the imagination. Imaginative refraction, with its readjustment of line and its addition of color, was far different from mere willful distortion of fact. Strachey had far more in common with Macaulay than has perhaps been generally realized. He was greatly superior to Macaulay in intellectual subtlety and psychological insight; and although both used rhetoric, Strachey was much more successful than Macaulay in controlling rhetoric so that it would not become ostentatious. But, like Macaulay, he made errors of fact; he was very sure of his own mind and had very positive opinions; he disliked misty generalizations and philosophical obscurity; he read widely and constantly; and he studied and wrote history primarily for the sake of its appeal to the imagination. To both, history and biography were drama with a story which marched, proudly and vigorously, and in which all the details were vivid, alive, significant. Macaulay spoke of the work of the historian being comparable not to that of the ant but to that of the bee. To Strachey also, history and biography were not the mere gathering of facts but, far better, a sweet distillation of their very essence.[48] It is significant that both held Thucydides in high admiration—Thucydides with his lucid order, his conciseness, his vividness, and his sure sense of the significant.

Actually, three years before he published his first book, Strachey stated the principle which would guide him in relating his scholarship to his art. He did so in his comments on Guglielmo Ferrero's *The Greatness and Decline of Rome,* which he reviewed for the *Spectator,* January 2, 1909:

> When Livy said that he would have made Pompey win the
> battle of Pharsalia if the turn of the sentence had required

---

48. It is important to note his manner of reading here. His friend Desmond MacCarthy said that he was not "a born scholar" and that "though he read immensely, lazily, attentively, he was not learned." "Lytton Strachey," *Sunday Times* (London), Jan. 24, 1932, p. 8. An excellent obituary.

it, he was not talking utter nonsense, but simply expressing an important truth in a highly paradoxical way,—that the first duty of a great historian is to be an artist. The function of art in history is something much more profound than mere decoration; to regard it, as some writers persist in regarding it, as if it were the jam put around the pill of fact by cunning historians is to fall into grievous error; a truer analogy would be to compare it to the process of fermentation which converts a raw mass of grape-juice into a subtle and splendid wine. Uninterpreted truth is as useless as buried gold; and art is the great interpreter. It alone can unify a vast multitude of facts into a significant whole, clarifying, accentuating, suppressing, and lighting up the dark places with the torch of the imagination. More than that, it can throw over the historian's materials the glamour of a personal revelation, and display before the reader great issues and catastrophes as they appear, not to his own short sight, but to the penetrating vision of the most soaring of human spirits. That is the crowning glory of the greatest history— that of Thucydides, for instance, or Tacitus, or Gibbon; it brings us into communion with an immense intelligence, and it achieves this result through the power of art. Indeed, every history worthy of the name is, in its own way, as personal as poetry, and its value ultimately depends upon the force and the quality of the character behind it.[49]

But, remembering the strong objections of those who have insisted that some of Strachey's portraits do violence to the facts, one may still ask whether his conception of the art of biography is actually tenable and, from the point of view of the literary artist, practicable. The question is whether even the most gifted literary artist can have his cake and eat it too: can have his facts and still retain his personal point of view and his prerogative of exercising his own freedom of imagination and spirit. We know that he can in the drama and in the historical novel, for we remember Jonson's *Sejanus* and Thackeray's *Henry Esmond*. But

49. "A New History of Rome," *Spectator, 102* (Jan. 2, 1909), 20–1.

we also remember Shakespeare's *Julius Caesar* and *Henry IV* and
the novels of Scott, in which the dramatist and the novelist deal
with facts very freely. May the biographer take the same liberties
with facts as Shakespeare and Scott took? It is seriously to be
doubted, for in history and biography facts are particularly stubborn, and rightly so. In them, facts are not subordinate to the
purposes of art, as they may be in *Julius Caesar* and *Kenilworth,*
but must be kept constantly in view as the solid substance of which
art is the shaping and interpreting power. History and biography
are the arts which master them but which preserve them in their
proper integrity. It follows that they are extremely difficult arts.
Strachey's main point was that to be mastered by the facts was
not to write biography. He would certainly agree, on the other
hand, that the biographer who has achieved art at the expense of
the facts has failed to solve his problem. Did Strachey always
succeed in solving it? Certainly not always, but the frequency
with which he did succeed is remarkable when we consider the
difficulty of his art in general and of some of his subjects in particular. He did succeed with his Manning and his Gordon, with
almost all the portraits, both major and minor, in *Queen Victoria,* with such complex and difficult subjects as Cecil, Bacon,
and the queen in *Elizabeth and Essex,* and with scores of other subjects which he has given us in delightful profiles. And where he
has failed, he has simply failed, as I think he has with his "Dr.
Arnold" and possibly with some of the other portraits which
have been objected to. To admit as much is to admit not that
his conception of biography was invalid but that he was not
infallible as a literary artist. The real distinction of Lytton Strachey as a biographer is that he succeeded as often as he did and
that his literary gifts were usually found working in close association with unusual learning.

One further point must be insisted upon. He wrote even his
biographical failures as an artist, not as a reporter; and his works
must be judged as portraits, not as photographs. A good photograph is a convincingly realistic copy; a good portrait has verisimilitude. A photograph which is not a likeness is altogether
worthless; but a portrait may have a value independent of its

subject. How much does it matter how faithfully Rembrandt represented his subjects or how closely Browning's portrait of the Lost Leader resembles Wordsworth? Strachey, however, aimed at verisimilitude and usually achieved it. Where he did not, he usually produced brilliant caricatures, as I think he did in his treatment of Dr. Arnold, Florence Nightingale, and Lord Cromer. And although Strachey aimed at portraiture rather than caricature, even unintentional caricature if it is the work of an artist may be worth something. Not only does the good caricature seize upon and emphasize through exaggeration the traits which the artist finds interesting and important, but it also has the great virtue of creating an interest in its subect and of arousing curiosity which may lead to investigation. Strachey's "Dr. Arnold" is both brilliant caricature and an invitation to read Stanley's biography of the headmaster of Rugby. A highly intelligent friend of mine has made what I believe to be precisely the right approach to Strachey's "Florence Nightingale." She first read Strachey's treatment and found it delightful. She then read very carefully the sketch of Florence Nightingale in *The Dictionary of National Biography* and was greatly impressed by the difference between the impression that it made and that made by Strachey's work. Then she returned to Strachey and read him again—with even more pleasure than before.

CHAPTER 9

Longer Biographical Works

STRACHEY did not write any biographies which in length are comparable to Boswell's *Johnson*, Lockhart's *Scott*, Sandburg's *Lincoln,* and Freeman's *Lee* and *Washington*. His words of praise for Boswell and Lockhart tell us that he realized very clearly that such lives, wrought on a grand scale with impressive amplitude, scope, and fullness, could be works of art. He was also undoubtedly aware of the difference between long biographies which were artistic and "the two fat volumes" which were not. Possibly, if he had assayed such a colossal subject as Voltaire, he would have felt compelled to utilize Boswellian scope. Yet he would have found the change radical and difficult, for all his instincts and habits made for selection and compression. As it is, what he has left us is short biographies and shorter ones. The methods used in all these relate closely to the purpose of exploiting effectively the technique of brevity. In this respect, *Queen Victoria* is to Boswell's *Johnson* as Hardy's *The Mayor of Casterbridge* is to *Tom Jones*. Furthermore, Strachey's works such as *Queen Victoria* and *Elizabeth and Essex* were not intended to be an artistic compromise between his shorter works, the miniatures, and Boswell. More than once he warned biographers against trying to mix methods and thus enjoy the values of both fullness and brevity. Such efforts, he was convinced, would always lead to disaster. Much depended upon the subject. The technique of brevity skillfully applied to Queen Victoria or to Queen Elizabeth would naturally result in a much longer work than that produced by the same technique applied to Lady Hester Stanhope.

The first of Strachey's longer biographies, *Eminent Victorians,* was published in England by Chatto and Windus on May 9, 1918. Frank Swinnerton, then an editor at Chatto's, has told us how the book came to be published. Swinnerton's associate, Geoffrey Whitworth, who was an Oxford man, a lover of drama and the arts, and a friend of many of the young intelligentsia, had asked Roger Fry to write a book on post-impressionism. Fry, in refusing, said that a friend of his, Clive Bell, was writing such a book and that he would ask him to submit it to Chatto. This book, *Art,* which Chatto published, became an instant success. Bell told Swinnerton and Whitworth about the manuscript of *Eminent Victorians* and at the same time suggested to his friend Strachey that the manuscript be submitted to Chatto. In due time the editors received the manuscript and, Swinnerton says, read it in the winter of 1917–18 with great excitement: "In those days, outside Cambridge literary circles, Strachey was known only as the author of a good little primer on French literature. . . . Whitworth and I were as excited before publication as the world was after it." [1]

We know that the world was excited after it. People read the book and were delighted. But some of them were not quite easy about the pleasure which they derived from the book. An imp of laughter danced through all its pages, and this imp quite frequently had its sport at the expense of what to many old Victorians and even to many other people in 1918 seemed high and holy.

The reviewer in the *Times Literary Supplement* fell in with Strachey's spirit by heading his article "Megatheria" (ponderous, clumsy sloths or ant-eaters). He praised the book as extraordinarily witty and its author as "urbane, impartial, detached, and full of observation and curiosity." He was also impressed by the author's sincerity and scholarship. Strachey's use of minutiae in exploring depths of character was, he believed, a new thing in the art of biographical portraiture. On the other hand, he observed that surviving Victorians would certainly read it with mixed feelings;

1. *The Georgian Scene* (New York, Farrar and Rinehart, 1934), pp. 360–8; *Autobiography* (New York, Doubleday, Doran, 1936), p. 126. Swinnerton believes that Sainte-Beuve, with his brief and illuminating portraits, was the primary inspiration of Strachey's life.

and he himself found one fault in it. It was too amusing. "The Victorian Age was something more than a joke." [2]

Probably the most influential praise of the book was that given by the Earl of Oxford and Asquith in his Romanes Lecture, "Some Aspects of the Victorian Age," delivered in the Sheldonian Theater at Oxford on June 8, 1918. Asquith pointed out to his audience that the Victorian age had had some great merits which should not be forgotten. At the same time, he was almost completely unrestrained in expressing his admiration for Strachey's portraits:

> In a recently published volume—the most trenchant and brilliant series of biographical studies which I have read for a long time—Mr. Lytton Strachey, under the modest title *Eminent Victorians,* has put on his canvas four figures (as unlike one another as any four people could be). . . . They are in less danger than ever of being forgotten, now that they have been re-created for the English readers of the future (not in a spirit of blind hero-worship) by Mr. Strachey's subtle and suggestive art.[3]

Some of those who read the book, however, were outraged. An article on Strachey in *Current Opinion,* October 1918, carried the ominous title "Is There a Menace of Literary Prussianism?" and accused Strachey of the kind of brutality in his treatment of biographical subjects which most of the British and the Americans then associated with German methods of dealing with an enemy during a war.[4]

2. May 16, 1918, p. 230.

3. (Oxford, Clarendon Press, 1918), pp. 6–12. In this lecture Asquith speaks of Sir George Trevelyan's *Macaulay* as the greatest of Victorian biographies.

4. *65,* 253. For some further comments on *Eminent Victorians,* see Sir Edmund Gosse, "The Character of Lord Cromer," a letter to the editor, *Times Literary Supplement,* June 27, 1918, p. 301; and Gosse's "The Agony of the Victorian Age," in *Some Diversions of a Man of Letters* (New York, Scribner's, 1919), pp. 313–37; Stephen Gwynn, "Lytton Strachey," *Fortnightly Review, 137* (March 1932), 387–8; Hugh Kingsmill, "Joseph, from *Eminent Egyptians,*" *English Review, 54* (April 1932), 399–404; and Kingsmill's "Some Modern Light-Bringers Extinguished by Thomas Carlyle," *English Review,*

These early comments on Strachey's book, when taken together, pretty well set the pattern of criticism which it has received up to now. Later critics have varied greatly in their pronouncements on *Eminent Victorians*. As we listen to them, we hear that the book contains brilliant portraits, has psychological soundness, subtlety, and depth, and breathes life once more into its Victorian subjects; or that it is motivated by malice, spite, and cruelty, turns its subjects into puppets to be jerked about the stage to suit a mischievous, capricious author, has a superficial cleverness, superficial psychology, and superficial sense of moral values, provides comedy by violating what is sacred in order to please those who have a depraved, perhaps sadistic, sense of humor, falls far short of truth by excluding all that is not ridiculous in its subjects, and uses a cheaply sensational style which reflects the author's determination to achieve his effects whatever the cost may be. Yet through the years since 1918 all has by no means been controversy among those who have sought to appraise and interpret this book. Literary history and literary criticism during these years has in the main assumed that the work was important, both intrinsically as a literary masterpiece of permanent value and historically as the beginning of a "new school" of biography. The future of this kind of biography will, by its very nature and requirements, prove to be full of hazards; the faults of Strachey's imitators in the past have been great, and his imitators in the future are not likely to be more successful. His method, to be used effectively, must fall into the hands of a writer who is more than an imitator, a writer who possesses both literary talent and freedom of mind and spirit. Only such a writer can meet the double requirement of exploiting

---

56 (Jan. 1933), 25–6; Louis Kronenberger, "Lytton Strachey," *Bookman* (N.Y.), *71* (July 1930), 375–80; Raymond Mortimer, "Mrs. Woolf and Mr. Strachey," *Bookman* (N.Y.), *68* (Feb. 1929), 625–9; J. W. Krutch, "Lytton Strachey," *Nation* (N.Y.), *134* (Feb. 17, 1932), 199–200; Edmund Wilson, "Lytton Strachey," *New Republic, 72* (Sept. 21, 1932), 146–8; James Pope-Hennessy, "Strachey's Way," *Spectator, 182* (Feb. 25, 1949), 264; and Virginia Woolf, "The Art of Biography," *Atlantic Monthly, 163* (April 1939), 506–10. There are many other comments too numerous to list.

to the fullest the method which has been handed down to him and at the same time stamping his own uniqueness upon every sentence that he writes.

This is precisely what Strachey did when he wrote *Eminent Victorians,* and it was his brilliant success in doing so that made the book a classic. He was too well schooled in the thought of the Enlightenment to consider himself original in the ultraromantic sense of the word. He knew very well that he was working in a tradition the essence of which was common sense, realism, critical laughter, and painstaking literary art. It was the tradition of Chaucer, of Erasmus, of Rabelais, of Fielding, and of Voltaire. Many people in 1918, living like their parents and grandparents in what was certainly "the best of possible worlds" (whatever the meaning of the first World War might be), were naturally shocked when suddenly the awful laughter was heard again and unrelenting eyes which saw and judged everything seemed to be fixed upon the manifold doings of human beings across the face of the land. What had really happened was that civilized man had once more wakened from a half-dreaming state. His eyes were now wide open; all the faculties of his judgment were alert; his sense of the ridiculous was keyed to highest pitch; he was aware of danger, of something which seriously menaced the values and the kind of life in which he believed; he was courageous and undaunted; he was articulate.

To suggest a comparison between *Eminent Victorians* and such works as *The Canterbury Tales* and *Tom Jones* is to invite the accusation of overstatement. The risk, however, must be run. Actually, the only way to study Strachey in his proper context is to make such a comparison. For the spirit in which he wrote was precisely that which motivated Chaucer and Fielding; all three were realists; all three based their judgments on criteria suggesting humanism; all three exploited the comic spirit to the fullest; and all three sought to use the resources of literary art to delight their age and to preserve it for posterity. The fact that Strachey wrote about the age of his mother and father rather than what was, strictly speaking, his own age is of superficial importance only, because the two ages overlapped and were very closely bound together. The practical difference was that Strachey had to depend more than Chaucer and Fielding on techniques of research and had to adjust the lens of his camera slightly to make allowance for distance; but having done so, he achieved the sharp focus, the effect of the contemporaneous, and the intimacy with subject which we associate with his great predecessors. And the "old Victorians" were there to read his book—many of them with laughter and delight—when it was published.

The question arises whether Strachey's laughter in *Eminent Victorians* is, like that of Chaucer and Fielding, good laughter. Is it really impish, irresponsible, licentious, undiscriminating, and malicious, motivated by a desire to shock or to "exploit the uses of irreverence"; or does it maintain constant reference to an acceptable and trustworthy sense of what deserves ridicule? Strachey's ideal, we know, was good laughter. That he measured up perfectly to this ideal would be too much to expect. His point of view and therefore his sense of the ridiculous could not be entirely separate from the peculiarities of his personal experience and from antipathies which were not entirely the product of detached thinking. He was a Cambridge man, and he laughed at Oxford accordingly; he had suffered greatly from the public schools which he had attended, and accordingly the father of such schools, Arnold of Rugby, became a preposterous impostor and clown; he had followed Gibbon and Voltaire in finding Christianity not merely irrational but evil, and accordingly he laughed with complete abandon at what seemed to him the *reductio ad absurdum* of Christian ecclesiasticism, the Roman Catholic Church. To some extent Strachey's readers, like the readers of Chaucer, Erasmus, Rabelais, Fielding, and Voltaire once more, must decide for themselves whether the right things are being laughed at.

But we must also determine whether Strachey's humor is in general frivolous and irresponsible. Let us look at some of the objects of ridicule in *Eminent Victorians* and ask whether Chaucer did not laugh at similar things. Strachey laughs at ecclesiastics who are the victims of their own vanity, worldliness, and ambition; at ecclesiastics who with a great show of piety justify their own egocentric behavior in terms of the conventional language of the church; and at ecclesiastics who are completely credulous in believing all the humbug which had come into being under the shelter of the church. He laughs at orators who make speech an affectation, who waste words, and who do not mean what they say. He laughs at casuistry that proceeds so far, as in the case of Gladstone, that the very soul of the person who has used it becomes minced into little pieces. He laughs at prigs, at persons who in the name of a noble cause feverishly work themselves and other people to death, at extremely conscientious but stupid government officials who cannot move because of the high respect which they have for red tape, at egotistical, superstitious-minded generals who in seeking glory for themselves constantly refer to themselves as instruments of destiny, at false humility, at professional athleticism, at frenzied expression of religious emotion, at starchy formalism in social relations, at various kinds of self-delusion, various kinds of egotism, and various kinds of intolerance.

It is important to note here some things at which Strachey does not laugh. He does not laugh at the life of reason dwelling in the independent mind or at the contributions to knowledge and to comfortable living which Victorian science had made. He does not laugh at utilitarian improvements in sanitation, transportation, engineering, or government. He does not laugh at or minimize the nature of Florence Nightingale's achievement in founding modern nursing. He does not laugh at General Gordon's unquestionable bravery or his skill as a military tactician. He does not laugh at Lord Hartington's solid, substantial humanity or at the trust which the British people placed in him as they recognized in him an embodiment of the best traits of their race. He does not laugh at Wilton, Sidney Herbert's ancient and lovely country house under whose elms Sir Philip Sidney had once walked, a house which was the symbol of a refined and gracious way of life and a culture which had proved itself in the lives of people for many generations. He does not laugh at Sidney Herbert himself, a tragic figure whose spirit had its true home only at Wilton but whose very nobility has made him a victim of Florence Nightingale and the ever-active demon which did not tolerate rest. And Strachey does not laugh at the art of great literary prose through which Newman made the story of his religious faith immortal in the *Apologia pro Vita Sua.*

The sure and constant sense of values which underlie the four parts of the book provide for it a single "point of view" and thus do much to bring the parts into unity. Unity, however, is also achieved in other ways. All four subjects, for instance, are studied against the same background, the Victorian age. Behind them we see the same queen, the same wars, the same Industrial Revolution, the same reform movements, the same church controversies, the same Imperialism, the same prime ministers, and the same waves of feeling surging through the masses of the British people. At times, moreover, unity is suggested by the appearance of characters in more than one part: Clough appears in both the "Nightingale" and the "Arnold"; Manning plays the main role in his part and then reappears in the "Nightingale." And unity also pervades the book through the potency of Strachey's style—sensitive, precise, sharp, flexible, lucid, and alive.

Strachey's prose style—his skill in exploiting the vast resources of the English language—does much to make *Eminent Victorians* a work of art. The art of the book, however, reaches far beyond what style and unity by themselves can give. If they were not to degenerate into monotony and rigidity, something must be added to them. Strachey certainly had this important fact in mind when he made pencil jottings, perhaps somewhat playfully, after the titles of the parts in his own copy of *Eminent Victorians.* After "Cardinal Manning" he wrote "Allegro Vivace," after "Florence Nightingale" "Andante," after "Dr. Arnold" "Scherzo," and after "The End of General Gordon" "Rondo." Thus the same theme and tone were to persist throughout, but there were to be variations; and the form and tempo of the work as it progressed were to adjust themselves to the purpose of balancing stability with change. The comic theme was to be dominant, but complication and the interweaving of other themes were to produce enrichment.

Strachey's primary purpose was the same as Chaucer's, to study character in its various individual manifestations. Chaucer, we know, often worked from living models whom he touched up a bit and then, more often than not, gave new names to, as artists are wont to do. Strachey also touched up the subjects which he had drawn from life, but then, with terrifying audacity, inscribed their very names beneath the portraits. Here he was to some extent following in the footsteps of Saint-Simon and Carlyle. But his characters, like Chaucer's, are stripped to their barest essentials and yet somehow presented in vivid detail. In both, the interest is primarily psychological. And in both the general technique is the same: analysis of character is reduced to the minimum, and the subjects reveal themselves through dramatic dialogue and narrative. Conflict is the essence of dramatic narrative, and in Strachey as in Chaucer the stories unfold as a series of struggles between persons. Manning enters combat with Newman and with others who get in the way of his ambition. Florence Nightingale fights many battles, and is a very formidable antagonist indeed. Dr. Arnold is in general opposed to the enemies of liberalism, of educational reform, and of the Christian religion. And Gordon not only fights the Chinese and the fanatical Moslem followers of the Mahdi in Egypt but also finds it necessary to have tilts with Gladstone, Lord Cromer, and others. There is less dramatic struggle in "Dr. Arnold" than in the other three pieces, and this is one reason why it is the least successful of the four.

Balance and contrast count for much in Strachey's method. Not merely Chaucer's impeccable technique but also Boswellian artistry with its constant interweaving of lights and shadows must have influenced Strachey's art here. In all three the contrast is of two kinds: contrast within the subject, as the good is weighed against the bad, and contrast of the subject with other people who are used as foils. In "Dr. Arnold," unfortunately, there is very little contrast of either kind. Strachey can discover almost nothing in the headmaster of Rugby to admire and does not really develop his struggle with his opponents. Dr. Arnold appears alone on the stage, an extremely ridiculous puppet full of zeal and energy. He seems considerably worried about the battle, but with all his bustle and strenuosity we never get to see him pitted in battle with a strong personal adversary. He is never even allowed to stand still beside anyone, as we know he did stand by his friend Wordsworth, in order that the reader might realize a sense of similarity, dissimilarity, or scale. The drama is all farce, and the portraiture is all caricature. The real Arnold contained possibilities for artistic portraiture which Strachey failed to develop.

"Cardinal Manning" is far superior to the "Arnold." In it there is plenty of dramatic struggle. Furthermore, Strachey provides in it opportunity after opportunity for comparing and contrasting Manning with Newman and many other persons in his story. But the portrait of Manning is not altogether convincing and lacks depth because no contrast within the subject is suggested. As in the "Arnold," the subject contains no shadows and depths to provide relief for all the fiery brilliance of the comedy.

In "Florence Nightingale" and "General Gordon" we have masterpieces of the first rank in which both kinds of balance are fully and skillfully exploited. The comic spirit still guides the hand that holds the brush; but as stroke follows stroke in rapid succession one gradually becomes aware of profundities on the canvas which have nothing to do with comedy—of Rembrandt shadows, of heroism and self-sacrifice, of noble suffering, of infinite yearning, of the unfathomable mysteries of the human soul. As victims of delusion both subjects remain ridiculous to the end; but they are not merely ridiculous, they are also tragic.

It would be a great mistake to overlook the importance of the minor characters in *Eminent Victorians* and the astonishing skill with which many of them are set forth. They are often important not merely for the light which they throw upon the principal actors but also for what they are within themselves. Strachey's mastery of the art of brevity serves him well in dealing with them. At least thirty or forty of them appear, endowed with life and individuality, in this short book. Some are scarcely true to their originals. It was not just to Julius Hare, liberal theologian and scholar that he was, to represent him as a Low Churchman. It was not just to Cromer to squeeze the last ounce of humanity out of his nature and make him as hard and cold as steel. Strachey's Arthur Hugh Clough, completely lost in a wilderness of question marks, naively content to spend his time tying up parcels in brown paper for Florence Nightingale, is pure caricature. But most of the minor characters reveal themselves when the moment comes as bearing with them their proper attributes and as displaying traits which are recognizably those which history has repeatedly told us were theirs.

Some of the minor portraits are done with impressive fullness. It is much more than a glimpse that we get of Gladstone, Newman, Sidney Herbert, Lord Panmure, Lord Hartington, and Lord Cromer. Others are sketched in with deft, vivid, memorable strokes as Strachey employs the art which was to serve him well in his later miniatures. It is not merely as names or figures in the background or as comparatively insignificant agents in the plot that we remember Hurrell Froude, W. G. Ward, A. H. Clough, Monsignor Talbot, the Mahdi, J. A. Froude, Dr. Pusey, Charles Kingsley, Cardinal Wiseman, Pope Pius IX, Mark Pattison, Mrs. Nightingale, Dr. Andrew Smith, General Simpson, Benjamin Hawes, Aunt Mai, Dr. Sutherland, Li Hung Chang, Arthur Rimbaud, and Major Kitchener. Many of these characters we recognize as old friends and feel little if any indignation as Strachey maneuvers them in his comedy so that, more often than not, only their amusing side appears. Those to whom knowledge matters know what the other sides are and thus are able to enjoy the comedy more fully because they possess this knowledge.

Possibly the most brilliant minor portrait is that of Lord Hartington. The sure and painstaking skill with which Strachey drew him for us was not the result of capricious impulse which had no bearing upon the central purpose of the book. In terms of values Lord Hartington, appearing as he does near the end of the work, is a key figure not merely for "General Gordon" but for the whole piece. If one were compelled to find the hero of such a work, he would be it. His closest rival would be Sidney Herbert. Sidney Herbert, however, had admirable culture without the manly strength needed to complement it. Hartington has more strength than he ever needs or shows and more culture than he is conscious of or would ever be willing to admit having. He is the proper foil of nearly all the dupes in the comic piece. He is as rough and as real and as solid and as active and as hard to handle and hard to fool as Squire Western. He is impartial in all his dealings without making pious reference to high principles. Common sense is the basis of all his thinking and prevents him from ever being

deceived by anything. He has faults. He is dull. He is slow, tragically slow, or he could have saved Gordon. But he also has a conscience. There is nothing anywhere in Strachey's writing better
than his account of Hartington's conscience. It is a perfect conscience, constantly in use and as sure as day; but Strachey tells
us that Hartington scarcely knew that he had it and that, if he
had been aware of it, he would probably have apologized for it.
How good and substantial Hartington appears, honest, sensible,
easygoing fellow that he is, as we place him beside Manning with
his overweening personal ambition and pious religious prattle,
or beside Florence Nightingale working herself and other people
to death and corresponding with Professor Jowett on the subtleties of Platonic mysticism, or beside Dr. Arnold with his endless
chapel sermons and his sixth-form bullies and his priggish disciples and his incessant activity, or beside Gordon with his mind
full of wild and whirling dreams of glory in battle and of vistas
in eternity, or beside Lord Cromer with his chilly sagacity and
prudence and machine-like exactitude, or beside Gladstone with
his pompous references to the great doctrines of Christianity, on
one hand, and his sawdust casuistry, his dilly-dallying, and his
delays, on the other. When we contrast Hartington with all these,
humanity seems to break out from him at all points. He loves
life, he loves horse races, he loves country fairs, he detests nonsense, and he is simply what he is, without boast and without
apology. No wonder the British people trusted him! Let us examine a part of Strachey's portrait of Hartington and as we do so
ask ourselves whether this kind of writing would not have pleased
Chaucer:

> Gordon, silent in Khartoum, had almost dropped out of
> remembrance. And yet, help did come after all. And it came
> from an unexpected quarter. Lord Hartington had been for
> some time convinced that he was responsible for Gordon's
> appointment; and his conscience was beginning to grow un-
> comfortable.
> Lord Hartington's conscience was of a piece with the rest
> of him. It was not, like Mr. Gladstone's, a salamander-con-
> science—an intangible, dangerous creature, that loved to live

in the fire; nor was it, like Gordon's, a restless conscience; nor, like Sir Evelyn Baring's, a diplomatic conscience; it was a commonplace affair. Lord Hartington himself would have been disgusted by any mention of it. If he had been obliged, he would have alluded to it distantly; he would have muttered that it was a bore not to do the proper thing. He was usually bored—for one reason or another; but this particular form of boredom he found more intense than all the rest. He would take endless pains to avoid it. Of course, the whole thing was a nuisance—an obvious nuisance; and everyone else must feel just as he did about it. And yet people seemed to have got it into their heads that he had some kind of special faculty in such matters—that there was some peculiar value in his judgment on a question of right and wrong. He did not understand why it was; but whenever there was a dispute about cards in a club, it was brought to *him* to settle. It was most odd. But it was true. In public affairs, no less than in private, Lord Hartington's decisions carried an extraordinary weight. The feeling of his idle friends in high society was shared by the great mass of the English people; here was a man they could trust. For indeed he was built upon a pattern which was very dear to his countrymen. It was not simply that he was honest: it was that his honesty was an English honesty—an honesty which naturally belonged to one who, so it seemed to them, was the living image of what an Englishman should be. In Lord Hartington they saw, embodied and glorified, the very qualities which were nearest to their hearts—impartiality, solidity, common sense—the qualities by which they themselves longed to be distinguished, and by which, in their happier moments, they believed they were. If ever they began to have misgivings, there, at any rate, was the example of Lord Hartington to encourage them and guide them—Lord Hartington, who was never self-seeking, who was never excited, and who had no imagination at all. Everything they knew about him fitted into the picture, adding to their admiration and respect. His fondness for field sports gave them a feeling of security; and certainly there could be no nonsense about a man who confessed to two ambitions—to become Prime Minister and to win the Derby—and who put the second above the first. They loved him for his casualness—for his inexactness—for refusing to make life a cut-and-dried business—for ramming an official dispatch of high importance into his coat-pocket, and finding it there, still unopened, at Newmarket, several days later. They loved him for his hatred of fine sentiments; they were delighted when they heard that at some function, on a florid speaker's avowing that "this was the proudest moment of his life," Lord Hartington had growled in an undertone "the proudest moment of *my* life was when my pig won the prize at the Skipton fair." Above all, they loved him for being dull. It was the greatest comfort—with Lord Hartington they could always be absolutely certain that he would never, in any circumstances, be either brilliant or subtle, or surprising, or impassioned, or profound. As they sat, listening to his speeches, in which considerations of stolid plainness succeeded one another with complete flatness, they felt, involved and supported by the colossal tedium, that their confidence was finally assured. They looked up, and took their fill of the sturdy obvious presence. The inheritor of a splendid dukedom might almost have passed for a farm hand. Almost, but not quite. For an air, that was difficult to explain, of preponderating authority lurked in the solid figure; and the lordly breeding of the House of Cavendish was visible in the large, long, bearded, unimpressionable face.

One other characteristic—the necessary consequence, or indeed, it might almost be said, the essential expression, of all the rest—completes the portrait: Lord Hartington was slow. He was slow in movement, slow in apprehension, slow in thought and the communication of thought, slow to decide, and slow to act. More than once this disposition exercised a profound effect upon his career.

Many good books may be likened to a river which, gradually gaining strength and momentum as it winds along its course, strikes, just before it reaches its destination, upon a tremendous boulder. The gigantic obstacle over which the waters must dash serves to test the force of the stream, to diffuse its water with air and sunshine and thus show its quality, and to subdue the fury of the stream and prepare it for rest after its long journey. *Eminent Victorians* is such a book, and Lord Hartington is the boulder upon which its rapid, merry waters dash.

Eminent Victorians prepared the public for the appearance of *Queen Victoria* three years later; and Lord Hartington prepared Lytton Strachey for the formidable task of dealing justly and adequately with the queen.

Queen Victoria, in parts only, began to appear in the *New Republic* on March 30, 1921. The last of this series of parts was published on June 8, but in the meantime, in April, Chatto and Windus brought out the complete work as a book. It was met immediately by a chorus of praise. The *Times Literary Supplement,* on April 7, struck several notes which were echoed many times by other commentators in the years that followed. Strachey had demonstrated that biography should represent even a queen, not as a plaster saint but as a flesh and blood human being: "He has found Victoria the woman more captivating with all her flaws than any statue of faultless marble. The result is a book which we place high above *Eminent Victorians."* Victoria's "other than earthly glamour" Strachey had "caught the gleam of"; it had fallen on his page "in rays of wistful beauty." And Strachey's portrait of Prince Albert was "perhaps the most original thing in the book." [5] There were some dissenting words in other reviews, but in the main they agreed with the *Supplement.*

5. P. 224. See also the London *Times* of the same date, p. 13. Through Strachey's letters we can, to some extent, follow his progress in composing *Queen Victoria.* January 4, 1919: "I am beginning a serious study of Queen Victoria; but it is difficult to say as yet whether anything will come of it." December 9, 1919: "Queen Victoria, poor lady, totters on, step by step. As she's still in her youth, what will she be like in age, at this rate? I can only hope that she may proceed in inverse fashion—growing speedier and speedier as she gets older, and finally fairly bundling into the grave." May 19, 1920: "Victoria proceeds at a fine rate." July 26, 1920: "Victoria drops a lengthening chain, damn her. It is not easy to be sprightly with such a Majesty." October 20, 1920: "I *hope* to have finished **Vic by Christmas.**" November 11,

Even Sir Edmund Gosse, who had been very unhappy about Strachey's treatment of Lord Cromer in *Eminent Victorians,* capitulated. He had, of course, some reservations about the new book. Strachey was slightly unjust in his treatment of the queen's language habits and religion. Nevertheless, *Queen Victoria* was "a riper, a more finely balanced, a more reasonable" study than its predecessors. Gosse too expressed great admiration for Strachey's portrait of Albert. But the picture of the queen filled him with amazement. Gosse was perhaps the first to observe that Strachey had fallen in love with the queen. As he remembered his own brief, scholarly, but cautious study of the same subject published in the *Quarterly Review* in April 1901, only a few months after the queen's death, he marveled at the changes in the public mind which made Strachey's daring success possible.

> What would have been the fate of Mr. Lytton Strachey if he had published his monograph in April, 1901, I shudder to imagine! He would have been pursued to the reading-room of the British Museum and there scraped to death with oyster-shells. He would have been told that he was not merely rude but criminal, not merely "cruel" but infamous. And yet from one end of his book to the other there is not a touch, or hardly a touch, of unkindness. . . . But he has emancipated himself from the last strands of that web of legend which had woven itself around her memory. He is the earliest of her biographers to insist that even a cat, and still more a careful student of the whimsicalities of life, may look steadily at a Queen.[6]

André Maurois has written that on a visit to Cambridge in 1928 the distinguished historian G. M. Trevelyan observed to him: "The most important event in the history of English biography in the twentieth century is not the portrait of Queen Victoria by Strachey; it is the conquest of Strachey by Queen Victoria."

1920: "It seems to me still rather doubtful whether I shall kill Victoria, or Victoria me."

6. "Queen Victoria," *More Books on the Table* (London, Heinemann, 1923), pp. 3–10.

Maurois's comment on Trevelyan's remark is highly significant both as an explanation of Strachey's attitude toward the queen and as a key for interpreting the biography. Maurois points out the common ground on which the queen, Lord Hartington, and Lytton Strachey all stood: "But the conquest [of Strachey by the queen] was easy. It counted for something that Strachey sprang from one of the great Whig families. He could depict with true understanding those solid, silent characters, seemingly proof against all enthusiasms, whose sound sense ensures the permanence of England and saves her from all freakish dangers." [7]

Probably the most informed praise, however, which *Queen Victoria* received in the years immediately following its publication came from Harold Nicolson in his *The Development of English Biography* (1927). Nicolson was greatly impressed both by Strachey's craftsmanship and by the validity of his point of view:

> The mass of his material was overwhelming. He was faced with eighty-one solid years. . . . To compress all this within some three hundred pages; to mould this vast material into a synthetic form; to convey not merely unity of impression but a convincing sense of scientific reality; to maintain throughout an attitude of detachment; to preserve the exquisite poise and balance of sustained and gentle irony and to secure these objects with no apparent effort; to produce a book in which there is no trace of artificiality or strain—this, in all certainty, is an achievement which required the highest gifts of intellect and imagination. Mr. Strachey, inevitably, has his point of view; and it is his point of view which dictates his method. Already in *Eminent Victorians* (1918) he had attacked the complacent credulity of the nineteenth century. . . .
>
> [But] behind it all lay something far more serious and important—a fervent belief, for instance, in intellectual honesty;

7. *I Remember, I Remember* (New York and London, Harper, 1942), p. 194; *Aspects of Biography,* trans. S. C. Roberts (New York, D. Appleton, 1929), pp. 24–5; and *Prophets and Poets,* trans. Hamish Miles (New York and London, Harper, 1935), pp. 240–1.

an almost revivalist dislike of the second-hand, the complacent, or the conventional; a derisive contempt for emotional opinions; a calm conviction that thought and reason are in fact the most important elements in human nature; a respect, ultimately, for man's unconquerable mind.[8]

Careful examination of *Queen Victoria* discovers abundant evidence that the enthusiastic praise bestowed upon it has not been undeserved. It is not difficult to determine why many reputable critics have ranked it above *Eminent Victorians*. Both works are primarily studies in character in which rich and variegated human nature has been skillfully compressed and displayed by art. In both realism counts for much: psychological realism, the realism of historic facts provided by research, and the realism of extrinsic detail, sharp, specific, vivid, in narration and description. In both the comic spirit, unfailingly quick and alert, animates the revelation of character. In both a fixed and definite point of view is clearly and consistently maintained, a point of view determined by Strachey's sense of values, the historic perspective provided by the time in which he was writing, and by his own temperament and freedom of spirit. In both, considerations which have to do with unity, structure, proportion, and emphasis are never forgotten. In both there is remarkable use of selection, restraint, and economy. And in both Strachey makes extensive use of dra-

8. (London, Hogarth Press, 1933), pp. 148–50. See also the comments on *Queen Victoria* made by Gwynn, Mortimer, Krutch, and Virginia Woolf (n. 4, above) and also by Clifford Bower-Shore, *Lytton Strachey: An Essay* (London, Fenland Press, 1933), pp. 55, 98, and *passim;* A. B. W[alkley], "Flamboyancy: Sidelights from Mr. Strachey," London *Times,* May 18, 1921, p. 6; F. L. Lucas, "Lytton Strachey: An Artist in History," *Observer,* Jan. 24, 1932, p. 5; New York *Times,* Jan. 22, 1932, p. 18; Ben Ray Redman, *Saturday Review of Literature,* Oct. 29, 1949, p. 21; Sir Max Beerbohm, *Lytton Strachey,* the Rede Lecture for 1943 (Cambridge, Cambridge University Press, 1933), p. 10 and *passim;* and Edith Plowden, letter to the London *Times,* Jan. 28, 1932, p. 6. H. L. Mencken wrote that Strachey had progressed from the "vaudeville" of *Eminent Victorians* to the "more solid and coherent drama" of *Queen Victoria.* "Spiritual Autopsies," *Literary Review,* April 8, 1922, p. 562.

matic methods to strengthen and enliven his exposition and narration.

On the other hand, although the reader feels that both books are impressive works of art, *Eminent Victorians* with all its flash and brilliance somewhat noticeably forces its materials and bends humanity to serve the purpose of art, while *Queen Victoria* bends its art, which is remarkably adequate and effective, to serve its subject with all its complexity, profundity, and grandeur. Strachey's statement on a preliminary flyleaf that authority for every important statement of fact in *Queen Victoria* would be found in the footnotes was not an idle one. He had not neglected research when he wrote *Eminent Victorians;* but the scholarship which went into the making of his later book was more thorough, more careful in its verification of facts, and more vigilant in sustaining a respect for them in their proper integrity throughout the whole process of composition. Fundamentally, Strachey's respect of scholarship was almost as strong as his delight in creating art: in *Queen Victoria* the two sides of his mind achieve balance and synthesis. Hence this work much more nearly approximates what Nicolson calls "pure biography"—writing in which all materials and all devices are subordinated throughout to illuminating the character of the subject with absolute truthfulness—than any other work which Strachey wrote.

Eminent Victorians was, as we have seen, in a sense a comic sonata, with changes of tempo and tone and color in the parts but full of music which was vivacious, sportive, bright, and gay. In it the dominant tone was that of mirth; and all other things, including deep undertones of seriousness, were keyed to that. *Queen Victoria* likewise possesses abundant humor. Here again, as in Chaucer, Hogarth, Fielding, and we may add Meredith, the comic spirit and the spirit of veracity are boon companions. All write with the conviction that the artist needs to keep his sense of the ridiculous near at hand both in exploring human nature and in telling the truth about it. Strachey does not therefore dismiss the comic spirit, as Henry v dismisses Falstaff, before undertaking more serious business. How persistent and varied the humor of *Queen Victoria* is! The constant play of irony, with many nuances and changes; the slapstick and the bathos as when in the high drama of the Coronation scene old Lord Rolle trips on his own mantle and falls down the steps of the throne, and Victoria goes to her rooms after the splendid ceremony and gives her dog Dash a bath; and the humor which reveals the shortcomings of Victoria's own sense of humor and sense of balance in the picture of the queen earnestly making a thorough study of the question whether sailors in the Royal Navy should wear beards—these titters, and chuckles, and sometimes open outbursts of hilarious laughter are in Strachey's brilliant technique so many glimpses and flashes of illumination to show us that a great queen can be revealed with all her human shortcomings and absurdities and still not lose her personal charm, her mysterious royal potency, or her grandeur. Nevertheless, the comic spirit is more carefully controlled in *Queen Victoria* than in *Eminent Victorians;* still playful and agile, it is watched and kept subordinate; it, like all other things in the book, functions as Her Majesty's humble servant.

Similarly, problems relating to unity, structure, proportion, and emphasis are all solved in terms of the central purpose, that of throwing adequate and trustworthy light on the character and life of a single person. Here Strachey found the unity ready in his single subject and could there use his art merely as the instrument by which it was revealed and strengthened. In dealing with questions of structure, proportion, and emphasis, he received further guidance from his artistic sense and his sense of values. To reveal the queen as she really was, the artist had to decide what was important about her and her life; then he had to decide how things could best be presented in order to suggest their relative importance. Since his concern here as in his other works was chiefly with the inner intangibles of mind and character, he showed us outward experiences, acts, and words in order to give us hints about what was going on within. For this reason he gives almost three-fourths of his space to the queen's life up to the death of Prince Albert in 1861, although nearly half of her years remained. The early period covered her formative years when what was important about her could be seen growing and developing; and this was the period when, as Strachey is careful to tell us she herself believed, she had been happiest, most active, and most fully alive. It was the period when the intense vitality of the spirit within her was most likely to give outward indications of the true substance of her nature with all its simplicities and with all its enigmas.

Strachey characteristically makes a full use of dramatic methods in *Queen Victoria*. The plot is composed of materials which have been carefully selected not only for their value in illuminating character but also for the dramatic effectiveness. The action is as carefully controlled and shaped as that of a well-constructed play; and the story unfolds neatly by clearly marked stages in scene after scene, from that of the nursery at Kensington on to the Coronation and then on and on until finally many of the scenes are reviewed in reverse order as they flash vividly through the mind of the dying queen. Strachey is alert and ingenious in his use of incidents which are both interesting in themselves and effective as dramatic preparation, such as the prophecies preceding the death of the Duke of Kent and the ascension of Victoria and such as Victoria's dismal forebodings of death shortly before her mother and the Prince Consort died in 1861. Moreover, in *Queen Victoria* as in *Eminent Victorians* the primary method is that of dramatic self-revelation; and the reader judges the queen and the other characters not so much by what he is told about them as by what he sees them do and hears them say as he watches scene after scene and encounters quotation after quotation. The characters are all alive and play their various roles against a living background of events, movements, and places with which each character interacts in accordance with his nature and through which the reader is carried into the very heart of the Victorian age with all its optimism, its worries, its controversies and complexities, and its multifarious activities. The background against which Strachey allows us to study the queen is one in which the student of history recognizes Robert Owen and his socialistic experiments at New Lanarch, the great Reform Bill of 1832 and much subsequent legislation motivated by the purpose of reform, the Chartist movement, the Oxford movement, the Broad Church movement, the Metaphysical Society, the great discoveries of Victorian scientists, Russia and the Crimean War, the American Civil War, the Great Exhibition, the Irish question, Prussia, Bismarck, and the unification of Germany, cultural trends such as the Gothic revival in architecture and the popularity of Tennyson's poetry, places such as Balmoral, Osborne, and Windsor which became closely integrated with the queen's life, British imperialism in India and Africa, and the powerful, changeable waves of mass feeling which beat against the steadfast throne throughout the long years.

The interaction between Victoria and these waves of public opinion is not the least significant of the numerous dramatic antagonisms which enliven the story. The queen's relation to her subjects is not simple. Their feelings are predominantly middle class, and so are hers; she shares their prejudices, their common sense, and their instinctive preference for what is solid and tangible. The strength of the Throne and of the nation lies in the common understanding and common traits which bind the queen close to her people. But she is also an individual woman with impulses, prejudices, peculiarities, even eccentricities that are all her own. Hence there are times, such as that immediately following the death of Albert when, living in retirement as the Widow of Windsor, she finds in her subjects the most formidable adversary of her own will.

Yet this was but one of the battles which she fights and, in the main, wins. Her conviction that she must exercise independence and even dominancy for her own good and for that of her people brings her into conflict with her own mother, with Uncle Leopold, with Lehzen, with Peele, Russell, Palmerston, and Gladstone, and even, early in her marriage, with Albert.

Often her opponents serve as foils to her character. Uncle Leopold's weakness and his indirect methods emphasize her fundamental strength and effective directness. Gladstone's oratorical manner and pompous piety emphasize the simplicity, the sincerity, and the common sense with which the queen speaks and the unaffected, down-to-earth quality of her unquestionable goodness. Albert's German traits call attention to her English traits; his intellectual strength suggests her deficiencies of mind; his

overweening strenuousness and zeal serve to show the virtue of
her more easygoing, less methodical, more enduring way of meeting
life. Other characters throw various kinds of light upon her. The
wicked uncles of her childhood provide contrast for her innocence and goodness. Her early fondness for Lord Melbourne,
an "autumn rose" really belonging to the preceding age, informs
us that Victoria had her eighteenth-century side, a side which she
never quite lost. When Strachey places her beside the Empress
Eugénie, with her flashing beauty, her flounces, and her finery,
we understand not merely that Victoria is plain but that she is
superior by merit of her simple charm, her solid strength, and
her depth of character.

Much has been written about Strachey's remarkable success in
painting the portrait of Prince Albert. It is beyond any question
a brilliant piece of work dealing with a subject which, ostensibly
at least, brought with it many difficulties. The Victorians themselves had not found it an easy one. Tennyson had found it a
decidedly ticklish subject even to touch upon; and Sir Théodore
Martin, as Strachey tells us, had toiled with considerable ability
and indefatigable industry for fourteen years on a biography of
the prince without greatly pleasing the queen or anyone else.
Strachey's picture succeeds mainly because it has balance. This
is not a balance of technique only. Strachey delights in this kind
of balance and uses it with great skill in his portrait of the prince
as he allows us to look deeper and deeper into the soul of a human being through a succession of lights and shadows and as he
sharply delineates his subject against the background of its most
effective foils—the queen herself, her ministers, and her people.
But the balance which strikes us most in this portrait springs from
attitudes which were deeply rooted in Strachey's own nature and
sense of values. We know that he never liked people who were
too zealous and strenuous, who took themselves and their objectives too seriously, who lacked humor, who could not relax
and allow their natural, healthy humanity to penetrate the hard
crust of formalism and rise spontaneously to the surface, or who
were too systematic, thorough, and businesslike in their manner
of dealing with the routine work of each day. It was therefore

natural for him to make sport of the stiff, dignified, earnest
Albert who must always make a memorandum of everything, however significant or however trivial. There was much about the
prince and his way of living which appeared to Strachey simply
ridiculous. On the other hand, it was always easy for Strachey
to sympathize with misunderstood persons and his natural impulse
was to try to explain them. Prince Albert had suffered terribly
from loneliness in his lifetime; Stockmar perhaps understood him,
but he needed a companionship which Stockmar could not give
and which, tragically, the queen and the British people with whom
his life was cast failed to give. It was easy, likewise, for Strachey
to sympathize with the sufferings of a nonathletic person who
found himself in the midst of people full of a rough vigor; and
of a sensitive, refined, highly intelligent student of music, the
fine arts, philosophy, and literature who had found that he must
live with practical-minded, materialistic Philistines and their
Philistine queen.

The portrait of Albert, however, fully drawn and impressive
as it is, remains properly subordinate to the grand figure in the
piece, that of the queen herself. And in this comparatively short
biography, how impressive are the proportions of this portrait,
how rich and varied are the materials which go into its making,
how ingenious are the devices of technique by which it is set
forth in sharp line and clear color, how skillfully is the narrative
managed throughout to bathe the portrait with many kinds of
light and thus to show us all the subject has to offer on its surface
and in its depths! From beginning to end the picture of the
queen is animated by what seems to be the enormous vitality
which she once actually possessed and glows with the radiance
and warmth of her invincible humanity. She is stupid about many
things; she could never be an intellectual or understand an intellectual; she is sentimental and is much given to gushing in her
talk and her letters; with her projecting upper teeth and receding
chin, she looks stubborn and is stubborn; she has almost no imagination, and her sense of humor is limited to that which makes
farces enjoyable; she has stamped upon her all the stodginess, the
slowness, and the lack of interest in philosophical ideas which

characterize the middle class; she is money-minded, close in her financial dealings, and in old age grotesquely acquisitive. Her taste in books, architecture, painting, and the other arts reflects the most glaring aesthetic shortcomings of her age. She is quite capable of making important decisions upon the impulse of whim and quite susceptible to the blandishments and the glitter of a superficial political adventurer like Disraeli.

But this is by no means all to be found in Strachey's portrait of Victoria. With her faults are to be found great virtues, and with her simplicities a complexity which challenges the mind. Strachey's fundamental image in representing her, that of the smooth, round pebble that may be held and examined in one's hand, undergoes important changes and reveals much that is not on the surface as the queen's life unfolds dramatically before our eyes. How full of life she is and how intensely she lives! As a young girl and a young wife she dances on and on into the night without a thought of fatigue; and even in the old queen the love and power of life are there, sometimes smoldering like fire within a volcano and sometimes breaking out with tremendous force to become united with the activities and the enthusiasms of her people. How natural and unassuming are the poise and dignity which are hers from the first day of her reign to the last! How impressive are her honesty and sincerity as they prove themselves effective in the midst of schemes and political maneuvers based upon the assumption that no point can ever be gained in life except through tricks and deceptions! And how very good she is! She is not merely formally and conventionally good but naturally good through and through, overwhelmingly good like some of the patriarchs of the Old Testament because she loved righteousness from the beginning of her days and could not with any pleasure walk in any other path. Strachey could protest with great effectiveness against systems of ethics and against prattle about morality; but he became humble and was almost reduced to reverent silence in the presence of Queen Victoria's unquestionably real and largely unconscious goodness. Yet his Victoria is also intensely human. Just as her love of life is without limit, her very thought of death is filled with unspeakable dread and terror. Her happiness during her married life with Albert can be matched only by the depths of her suffering in the dark years following his death. Her own subjects bring her additional sorrow and even rebuke when she attempts to shed the role of a queen and, simply as a grief-stricken woman, give herself over to private sorrow. But these same subjects discover her greatest traits, rely upon them, and in a sense share in them. They trust her as they trust Lord Hartington, and for similar reasons. They find that her humanity is substantially the same as theirs, solid, palpable, genuine, unfailing. She has the instincts by which the British people live and endure. She is slow, but she can be counted on to do the right thing. She has no subtlety and no marked power of intellectual perception, but she is nevertheless no fool. She has what her people like better than subtlety and intellectual power—common sense and a native sagacity. Her love for her people and for the nation over which she rules is never to be questioned; her people know that she belongs to them and therefore respond without murmur or even hesitancy to the magic potency of her authority. Thus her impressive greatness lies in an exquisite blending of her queenliness with her vast and profound humanity.

When *Elizabeth and Essex, a Tragic History* appeared in 1928, it received much less than the almost universal praise which had been accorded *Queen Victoria*. To be sure, G. B. Harrison recognized it immediately as "tragical-historical drama" set forth in a style of great vividness and brilliance. He expressed admiration for the tremendous vitality of Strachey's Queen Elizabeth, for the skill and justice with which Strachey analyzed the character of Francis Bacon, and for the appropriateness of the manner in which the narrative ends, with Cecil, one who did much to determine the later history of England, dominating the stage. Harrison objected, however, to what he considered Strachey's "suppressions" and "manipulations" of facts and found the representation of Essex's character incomplete and unconvincing.[9]

9. "Elizabeth and Her Court," *Spectator, 141* (Nov. 24, 1928), 777. Harrison says that Strachey should have given the stories which explain Essex's tremendous popularity. He also says that Essex, despite the fact that he often made himself ridiculous, was extremely sensitive to laughter and that he destroyed Lopez, not out of patriotism as Strachey suggested but out of revenge because Lopez had made the queen and others laugh at him.

Christopher Hollis made a vigorous attack on the book in the *Dublin Review*.[10] E. G. Clark, in the *Catholic World,* protested against the uncritical nature of the praise which *Elizabeth and Essex,* together with the "whole school" of biography to which it belonged, had received. Such works, Clark said, were often guilty of indelicacy and bad taste. Under "the green light of Mr. Strachey's morbid prose," he declared, Queen Elizabeth had been distorted beyond recognition. Clark added that those who had developed a taste for the "spicy modernity" of Strachey's style needed to read Stebbing, Martin Hume, James Spedding, and J. R. Green.[11] Clifford Bower-Shore, who, generally speaking, admired Strachey's writings, criticized the style of *Elizabeth and Essex* as "a semi-flamboyant, resonant style which suited the period but revealed him as a romantic to the detriment of his original genius." Furthermore, Bower-Shore, like Harrison, believed that there were serious faults in the scholarship which went into the making of the book; and he asserted that the work was "essentially a work of imagination, not of investigation." [12] A number of other commentators, including Sir Max Beerbohm,[13] have joined him in speaking of this book as one based to an alarming extent on guesswork. George Dangerfield has gone so far as to call the book a failure—"an exquisite failure." [14]

Nevertheless, *Elizabeth and Essex* has had readers not altogether given to uncritical judgments who have surrendered to it almost entirely. One of these, Desmond MacCarthy, predicted in 1933 that it would enjoy a much higher reputation in the future than it had in the past.[15] G. F. Bowerman found it a work of pure delight from beginning to end: "Strachey's latest book, *Elizabeth and Essex, a Tragic History,* is but newly published, and as I write this paper I am glowing with the pure joy of its reading. It is an ex-

10. "Elizabeth and Mr. Strachey," *186* (Jan. 1930), 21–33.

11. "Mr. Strachey's Biographical Method," *129* (May 1929), 129–35.

12. Bower-Shore, *Lytton Strachey,* pp. 62, 65.

13. Beerbohm, *Lytton Strachey,* p. 20.

14. "Lytton Strachey," *Saturday Review of Literature, 18* (July 23, 1938), 17.

15. "Lytton Strachey: The Art of Biography," *Sunday Times,* Nov. 5, 1933, p. 8. MacCarthy also records the fact that Francis Birrell had pointed out the striking dramatic qualities of the book.

traordinarily brilliant piece of work. It is not only fine as literary craftsmanship, but it has commended itself to the historians, who thus far have been able to pick very few flaws in it." [16]

Although Bowerman's language, especially his last statement, appears extravagant when studied beside the various strictures which have been made on the book, the respectable bibliography which Strachey places at the end does not tell us the whole story concerning his knowledge of the Elizabethans. To realize what went into the making of this work, we must remind ourselves of the countless hours which from childhood Strachey spent in delightful reading of the prose writers, the poets, and the dramatists of the great Age of Elizabeth, and we must recall the dozens of books relating to the period which he read and reviewed for the *Spectator* and other journals during the early years of his literary career. His great respect for modern scientific methods in the discovery and verification of historic facts, furthermore, did not permit him in this work or in his other biographical writings to content himself with what might be called essential truth as distinguished from what can be accepted as indisputable historic facts. It is highly unlikely that such errors as he committed were intentional. Probably there are some; the most careful scholars slip at times in dealing with the Elizabethan period—and with some other periods.

But one cannot do justice to Strachey's book by treating it merely as history. *Elizabeth and Essex* was intended to be a work of art and therefore can be read with full understanding only in the light of the author's precise purpose. The subtitle, *A Tragic History,* and Strachey's method on every page and in every sentence leave no doubt about what that purpose is. The primary purpose is not to be that of informing and explaining through the use of historic data; rather, it is to be that of one of the greatest forms of literary art—tragedy—in order to arouse the intellect, vitalize and intensify the imagination, and stir the emotions deeply. The effect aimed at is nothing less than a catharsis. The important fact to grasp in

16. "The New Biography," *Wilson Bulletin, 4* (Dec. 1929), 154. See also Esther Murphy, "The Elizabethan Enigma," *Bookman* (N.Y.), *68* (Jan. 1929), 596–8.

reading *Elizabeth and Essex* is that in it drama has become the first consideration. All other things, whether they are the illumination of history or the setting forth of character through skillful biographical portraiture, although they may remain important, have become subordinate. Drama has taken everything into solution. The writer is now using all the means at his command for the purpose of stirring his reader to the very depths and of producing in him a purging through pity and fear.

Thus we are struck by the distance separating *Eminent Victorians* and *Elizabeth and Essex*. Whereas in the former dramatic and biographical method are bent to the purpose of creating mirth with tragic undertones, in the latter even while the point of view remains very much the same the mirth now flickers only occasionally in the manner of comic relief; history and biography, though still important and still preserved in their proper integrity, are made to serve a higher purpose, and the tone and theme of high tragedy are sounded again and again as the sorrowful story of mighty opposites unfolds in moving grandeur.

It is dramatic narrative "ranging sadly over the vicissitudes of mortal beings." Its tragic theme is that of uncertainty: uncertainty in the efforts of human beings to understand themselves, other people, the world around them, and its workings; and uncertainty in their efforts to master and control this ambiguous reality as they try to direct events and shape their own lives. The theme is appropriate to its Elizabethan subject. Readers of Renaissance literature have encountered it in *Hamlet, Don Quixote,* and elsewhere. Queen Elizabeth herself, with her confusing behavior and policies and her baroque attire, all of which seem to work together to hide rather than to reveal her real intentions and her real nature, is a fitting symbol of the theme. The nature of the theme may be in large degree responsible for the opinion of some critics that *Elizabeth and Essex* is the product of guesswork. Actually the use of historic and biographical materials for the purposes of art is not more sure or conscientious in any of Strachey's other works. The guesswork is not in his scholarship or craftsmanship but is a basic part of the philosophical problem which is the foundation upon which the action of the play rests. The Elizabethan age, Strachey tells us repeatedly, was one of perplexing contradictions, an age in which the indefinite, the ambiguous, the indeterminate, the dissembling, the labyrinthine, the fantastic, the unstable, the inconstant, and the fluctuating seemed to surround people on all sides; and the people were like their age.

The theme is not merely appropriate to a work dealing with an Elizabethan subject but has universal importance. Readers of Strachey's book in the middle of the twentieth century do not have to rely altogether on scholars who have attempted to write a clearcut biography of Shakespeare or Marlowe or on critics who have attempted to elucidate *Hamlet* and *Don Quixote* for confirmation of the validity of Strachey's theme as applied to the purposes of tragedy or to any honest, intelligent effort to understand human nature and the mysterious universe which is its abode. Strachey's approach to reality should not require much explanation in an age like ours in which there is so much that is indisputably real and yet unreal—real and significant in its practical relation to our own lives but too complicated or too confused or too tremendous or too abstract for us to conceive of or manage. Thus among the things which we cannot afford to ignore in our world, we find much that seems almost equally conceivable and inconceivable: the atomic bomb, infinitely complicated and sprawling financial systems with which our insurance policies and mortgage payments are interlocked, groups of nations which are united but not united, and diplomatic conferences which in their outward appearances and announced results are fully as ambiguous, deceptive, and confusing to onlookers and probably to participants as was the baroque manner and dress of Queen Elizabeth. It should not be too difficult to show to readers of Freud that Queen Elizabeth, partly because of a sexual abnormality with which she was born and partly because her nature was in general so thoroughly mixed up, found it impossible to understand herself, to predict what her impulses might lead her to do next, or to explain even to herself all her decisions and acts adequately after they were in the past. It is significant that this book, in which uncertainty counts for so much in determining the tragic course of the story, is the only one in which Strachey reflects the influence of Freud's brilliant probings into the enigmas of the human mind.

Strachey's drama in many respects shows the influence of Shake-

speare's conception of tragedy and its craftsmanship. For one
thing, his action finds its life and potency in intensified conflict,
whether it is the outside conflict of scheme clashing with counter-
scheme as powerful rivals struggle to win the queen's favor; or as
far more terrible, the two mighty principals, the Earl of Essex
and the queen herself, who are both lovers and violent antagonists,
fight for dominancy; or the inner struggle—the debate of the mind
with itself—which goes on in Elizabeth, Essex, Cecil, and Bacon.
The action gathers its force as it moves to a double catastrophe,
first with the execution of Essex and then with the death of Elizabeth. Violence and blood are no more out of place here in the
vivid accounts of uprisings, wars, and gory executions than in the
sensational means which the Elizabethan stage used to produce its
effects of terror. And as in the best Elizabethan plays interest in
characters counts for much through similarity and dissimilarity,
in Strachey's book the reader is permitted to watch not merely the
principals but such varied persons as King Philip, John Donne,
Dr. Lopez, the Cecils, Sir Walter Raleigh, Sir John Harington,
and others play out their respective roles. All the minor characters
are sharply delineated individuals and, while they are clearly recognizable in terms of their place in history, are now alive once more.

The principal characters, like those of Elizabethan drama, are
wrought out in large proportions. They are also complex and defy
those who would fathom them to the very depths. Of these, Bacon,
despite his philosophical profundity, is most easily understood. Yet
even he is a strange mixture of apparently incongruous elements.
He has wisdom and strength of intellect; he is an artist, both in his
refined taste and in his admirable command of language. On the
other hand, in his eye one can often see with a shudder a "cold
viper-gaze," and his wisdom in practical affairs is often that of the
serpent; he is extravagant in his appetites; he is far too much the
slave of worldly ambition; he is capable of Machiavellian intrigues
of the most hideous kind; he lacks imaginative and psychological
insight; and, most serious of all, he lacks humanity. In the story of
Elizabeth and Essex he plays the role of a powerful villain; but his
story is tragic also, and one cannot read Strachey's book without
sensing something of the horror and pathos of his later catastrophe

in which the wise, the noble, and the mighty plunges to degradation and disgrace.

Strachey's Essex is compounded of elements some of which suggest Hotspur. He is a late embodiment of chivalry and has inherited the benign mantle of the gentle Sir Philip Sidney. He is bold, open-minded, and sincere. It would be impossible for him to dissemble in any of his dealings. His emotions are too powerful to be controlled. He has great charm of personality and is romantic in his quest for adventure and glory. He delights in military activity and is courageous, but he is not a skillful tactician. He lacks judgment and a level head. He is impetuous and rash. In a crisis, he is not cool and steadfast, but instead his mind flies off wildly to extremes. He lacks balance. He cannot examine life quietly and realistically. His motives are not always clear, to others or to himself. And even in his chivalry he is an anachronism, seeking glory through manners and means no longer effective.

When we turn to Elizabeth, we are even more greatly impressed by the seemingly ill-assorted elements of which she is composed; and we are not surprised that Essex and others who know her well find her bewildering. Her protean mind, emotions, and policies; her hedging; her dilly-dallying; her delaying; her half-measures; her vanity; her three thousand dresses; her strong passion for handsome young men and her unfortunate sexual incapacities; her learning and humanism; her sure and deadly use of the English language; her unwavering devotion to her country; her courage; and her absolute power of dominance—all these things and much else go into her make-up. She can appear strong, and she can appear weak; she can be wise, and she can be foolish; she can be ablaze with all the glitter of her attire, and she can be a drab and ugly old woman; she can be soft and fond and sentimental, and she can be hard and cruel and entirely without mercy. Her very tragedy is a combination of opposites: that which she loves she must destroy.

We know that in Shakespeare tragedy derives partly from flaws in the characters and partly from outward circumstances over which they have no control. While we admire the characters for their virtues and their qualities of magnificence, we recognize their faults and can understand the relation between these faults and their suffering. We have utmost pity for them because we know of their admirable qualities and see them suffer far more than their faults suggest that they deserve. In Strachey's *Elizabeth and Essex* the same formula is used to call forth maximum pity from the reader. Perhaps it is more successful in its application to Elizabeth than to Essex. Essex has been so foolhardy and rash that Elizabeth is compelled by the highest motives and by considerations of utmost importance from which she cannot escape to condemn him to death. The reader may be tempted to conclude that Essex got just about what he deserved. Possibly Strachey could have achieved a more powerful catharsis if he could have brought himself to use his historical materials more freely. Even so, however, we pity Essex. We remember that it is, after all his faults are known, a very changeable, complex, deceptive world which he has attempted to brave in his bold, open, honest, courageous way. The Ireland which brought disaster down upon him, the mysterious, enchanted Celtic land which came and went, was there and was not there, assumed substantial form one moment and then a moment later evaporated into thin air, became for the unfortunate Earl a precise symbol of the entire world.

We must conclude by observing one extremely important way in which *Elizabeth and Essex* is not influenced by Shakespearean drama. It does not have the loose, sprawling, comprehensive structure of the typical Elizabethan play. Strachey follows instead the classical tradition and gives to his action the tight unity, the concentration, and the careful shaping which he associated with the tragedies of Sophocles and Racine. His style perhaps makes slight borrowings of romantic color and embellishment from the language of the Elizabethans; but in the main it, too, successfully aims at qualities suggesting classical simplicity, smoothness, and purity. It is quite a feat to have set forth such a turbulent story in such language and to have compressed that restless, ever-changing, ever-expanding world into the intense stillness of that compact mold.

CHAPTER 10

Miniature Portraits

STRACHEY's brief studies in character and the admirable "psychographs" of the American Gabriel Bradford belong roughly to the same period of literature and have been often compared. Naturally, there has been some speculation concerning a possible influence of the one on the other and talk about whose work appeared first.[1] The similarities in the work of the two biographers are obvious at a glance. Both aimed at economy and brevity; both depended on psychological insight in their efforts to discover what was essential in their subjects; and both believed that biography should be literary art of a very high quality. There was some correspondence between the two in late 1921, when each

1. See especially H. L. Mencken's "Spiritual Autopsies," *Literary Review*, April 8, 1922, p. 562, where he says: "This Bradford is the man who invented the formula of Lytton Strachey's *Queen Victoria*. It throws a green, evil light upon the state of critical science in America that not a single reviewer noted the fact during the late vogue of the Strachey book. I do not except myself. I noted it in the end, but not until my review of *Queen Victoria* had been printed." Mencken adds that the new method gets rid of what clutters the style of biographies and skillfully probes into its subject's intimate, private habits of mind, that such a method has obvious perils, but that it is effective when mellowed by Strachey's "gentle irony" or by Bradford's "New England common sense." He does not suggest that Strachey was influenced by Bradford but simply states that Bradford was first in the field. It should be noted, however, that some of the best and most characteristic among Strachey's miniatures were published quite early: "Horace Walpole," *Independent Review* (May 1904); "Mademoiselle de Lespinasse," *Independent Review* (Sept. 1906); "The First Earl of Lytton," *Independent Review* (March 1907); "Lady Mary Wortley Montagu," *Albany Review* (Sept. 1907); and "The Swan of Lichfield," *Spectator* (Dec. 7, 1907).

received and read with admiration some of the works of the other. But both emerged from this reading with the conviction that the dissimilarity of their work was more marked and significant than the sameness. Strachey seems to have found the subject boring and soon broke off the correspondence. Bradford, at first filled with despair by the brilliant literary art of *Eminent Victorians* and *Queen Victoria,* soon was able to reassure himself in the light of what he took to be distinctive in his own work. In later years he grew exceedingly weary of the comparisons which were frequently made between him and the English biographer.[2]

Actually, there is no evidence of influence one way or the other. The mind of each had become firmly set in its individual mold before either knew of the work of the other. Both were independent-minded and self-sufficient to a remarkable degree. The superficial sameness which has so often suggested a comparison of their works is to be explained partly in terms of the value which their age placed on psychological studies, partly in terms of a similar reading diet containing much French and eighteenth-century literature, and partly in terms of the fact that both men suffered chronically from poor health and were compelled to husband their strength with great care and through the art of brevity make the slightest expenditure of energy produce results of maximum value. Though their tastes were at points similar, temperamentally they had little in common. Strachey's mind was more free, and he could never have brought himself to limit his theory or practice of biography to a formula such as that suggested by the word *psychograph,* even though he may have been aware that Bradford worked

2. See *The Journal of Gamaliel Bradford (1883–1932),* ed. Van Wyck Brooks (Boston and New York, Houghton Mifflin, 1933), pp. 188–9, 329–30, 478–9, 508; *The Letters of Gamaliel Bradford (1918–1931),* ed. Van Wyck Brooks (Boston and New York, Houghton Mifflin, 1934), pp. 99–100, 105, 289, 303. Bradford was at times extremely humble in his self-appraisal and in his admiration for Strachey. In a letter dated 1927 he wrote: "After all, what makes biography, like any other literary form, really worthy to endure, is style, and the question that agonizes me is, whether my work has style, the high literary quality that essentially and finally counts. This I suppose is the quality that Strachey has and, alas, I fear my work mainly has it not. Without it all the rest is merely dust and ashes." *Letters,* p. 289.

without servility and with astonishing versatility. Probably the very name Bradford caused him to shudder, suggesting as it did whole generations of sober-minded, long-faced New England Puritans. All in all, it is just as well that Strachey and Bradford each remained in his own workshop without any visiting back and forth.

Strachey's masters as he wrote his brief studies were the same as those to whom his mind made constant reference as he composed his longer works. They were Thucydides, Tacitus, Walton, Aubrey, Clarendon, La Bruyère, Saint-Simon, Sainte-Beuve, Boswell, and Carlyle. He gained a little from this one and a little from that, but the ultimate synthesis and the final impress which his works displayed were his own.

The technique which produced Strachey's shorter studies is very much the same as that which produced the portraits of minor characters in the longer works. It was, however, a technique which had become a sharp tool in his hands long before he wrote *Eminent Victorians*. He uses the word "profile" as early as February 6, 1909, when in a review of A. R. Waller's edition of Samuel Butler's *Characters and Passages from the Notebooks* he praises the "brilliant profiles of La Bruyère." [3] But the word occurs rarely in his writings. Furthermore, it is hardly adequate to denote the exact nature of his shorter biographical pieces. His own name for them is that used as the title of one of his books: *Portraits in Miniature*. The word "portrait" carries with it a connotation of color, warmth, and depth which the word profile lacks. It was their metallic style and lack of color that caused Strachey to rank Macaulay's character sketches far below the highest. They were, he said, steel engravings, not living portraits.[4] When he found the same lack of color in Greville's sketches, he thought of the great contrast with Saint-Simon's vivid, burning pen portraits.[5]

When we consider the full range of Strachey's miniature portraits, from his earliest work to his latest, what we are most struck

3. "The Author of *Hudibras*," *Spectator*, *102* (Feb. 6, 1909), p. 224.
4. "Macaulay."
5. "Charles Greville," in *Biographical Essays* (London, Chatto and Windus, 1948), p. 244.

by is their variety—variety of subjects and variety of treatment.
The subjects are all individuals, some living in this period of
history, some in that, some in France, and some in England, each
preserved in his proper essence and breathing his own atmosphere.
Strachey's technique in each instance adjusts itself to suit the
peculiar needs of the subject; and as a result the portraits vary
as much as the subjects do. This is not to say, however, that they
share no common qualities with which they have been endowed
by the artist who created them. They are all, in the first place,
studies in brevity. The process by which they come into being is
that of leaving out and then drawing out. And what is kept is
not merely useful for the purpose of making the portrait but is
usually interesting in itself. The drawing out emphasizes and, if
possible, sharpens the point of the interest; it touches up and
tones down; and it must without fail breathe life into the whole
subject. What Strachey likes to keep for use in his portraits is
worth noting. He not only enjoys dealing with character in infinite variety, with plenty of room for the enigmatic, the eccentric,
the silly, the praiseworthy, and the tragic, and with plenty of opportunity for psychological probing; but he also relishes all sorts
of lost or neglected facts; all sorts of curious, odd, or picturesque
details; all sorts of anecdotes as long as they have a point; queer
quirks of fate as they so often determine the course of human
lives; and, especially, humor, which was to Strachey a substance
like free gold lying in his path whenever he chanced upon it. A
humorous anecdote not particularly relevant to the subject or
purpose was the thing that tested Strachey's power of excision
most strongly. He kept it if he could.

The miniatures are written from the same point of view as
that to be found in the longer works. In them the subjects are
never merely presented; they are placed upon the most delicately
adjusted scales and weighed. If they deserve to be mocked, they
are mocked; if they deserve pity, they receive it; if they merit
praise, it is bestowed upon them. The tone, the depth, and the sub-
stantiality of the portraits vary greatly as Strachey proceeds from
subject to subject. In some we are almost dazzled by bright colors
displayed in brilliant light; in others shadow deepens against

shadow on and on into infinite gloom like a succession of mountain ranges receding into the distance.

The style of the miniatures likewise varies somewhat with the subject. In practically all of them, however, considerations of brevity have led Strachey to use with utmost skill a style that is rapid, economical, spontaneous, alert, sensitive, incisive, deft, and alive. It is a racing style mysteriously pregnant with intense illumination, and it awakens as it runs through the immense forest of historic and biographical facts. Much has been said concerning Strachey's unusual power in whetting the reader's appetite for further reading about his subjects. When we read him it is certainly true that the more we know the more we want to read, and the more we read the more we want to know. He brings all the excitement of a highly romantic temperament to bear on the business of scholarly investigation and on the clearest and most intelligent presentation of its findings. In all the miniatures the style is electrified by this kind of excitement and by the ardent spirit of intellectual adventure which goes with it. Although Strachey's point of view is always clear, definite, and steadfast, his style is almost never dogmatic in tone. Rather, possibly its most significant characteristic is that of inquisitiveness, a vivid revealing which is also a seeking. Some writers through an unfortunate combination of brilliance and error spoil subjects for later investigators for several generations, but the curiosity reflected in Strachey's style produces the opposite effect. His torch not only floods with light the room immediately in front of the reader but also reaches into the distance and shows other delightful doors waiting to be opened.

When we attempt to classify the miniatures according to subject, we find that some of them are too complex to be classified neatly and that some fall into more than one class. Nevertheless, these portraits in their full range of variety suggest certain classifications with considerable definiteness. When we study them, furthermore, we find that they gain something from being considered within established classifications. One group of studies, for instance, deals with silly creatures, with people who are almost completely deluded. These are interesting and amusing because of their very emptiness and because they turn life into a farce. Another group deals with people who, though they are not empty and silly, are fascinatingly eccentric or odd. Still another deals with admirable people, prominently displayed in full light. Boldness rather than complication usually counts in these portraits. A fourth group is made up of character studies in which background, whether it is historic atmosphere and incident, manners, relation to an institution, achievement in literature and the arts, or something else, is almost as significant and interesting as the persons themselves. A fifth class is that in which dramatic narrative and anecdote count for much and character is revealed almost entirely through story. And still another class—a very important one—might be termed the dark studies or studies in depth. These deal with people who are in many ways completely opposite to the shallow, silly, deluded creatures treated in the first group. The subjects here are complex, tragic, and somewhat magnificent. There is much of shadow in their composition; they are in part enigmatic, and it is not easy to fathom their souls to the depths. Although not altogether admirable, they are richly substantial; and when they suffer, as they do, from the ironical quirks of fate they move us to pity and terror. Further classifications may be found, and even then some of the portraits may defy classification; but an examination of representative examples of each of the six groups listed above may do much to show the remarkable range and variety of subject and workmanship in Strachey's miniatures.

An early example of the treatment of a silly, shallow, affected person is to be found in one of the uncollected *Spectator* reviews entitled "The Swan of Lichfield" (December 7, 1907).[6] It is, like so much of Strachey's best work, a by-product of his reading. The book which he reviewed was E. V. Lucas' *A Swan and Her Friends;* and the silly swan that sits for a portrait in Strachey's review is Miss Anna Seward, who lived in the town where Dr. Johnson was born and who is mentioned "somewhat dimly" in Boswell, in Fanny Burney's diary, and in Horace Walpole's letters—in the last, always with a laugh. Strachey speaks of her as belonging to

6. *99,* 929–30.

"that class of persons who are interesting by virtue of their very fatuity, who deserve notice simply as colossal figures of fun." "There was never anything so entertaining or so dull!" he exclaims of her, borrowing an expression from Horace Walpole. Her combination of faults make her a delightful spectacle to behold: her endless complacence, her infinite affectations, her poses and her pretensions, her unfathomable ignorance, and her inconceivable lack of taste. She belongs to a sentimental circle of writers in which "mutual adoration was the rule"; and she "was always in an ecstasy either of feeling or of flattery." She greatly admires fine writing and knew what it really was—"for the best of reasons, she practiced it herself." Strachey provides quotations from the lady that leave us in no doubt. When Coleridge and Wordsworth appear on the literary horizon, Miss Seward is shocked to see them well received. Strachey's portrait of her is almost entirely composed of mockery and the laughter which farce and caricature provoke. Yet it is not so altogether; there are slight undertones which are to the lady's credit. She corresponds with Sir Walter Scott, and Strachey notes significantly: "Scott seems to have had a genuine liking for her; and that perhaps speaks more in her favor than anything else. It would be impossible to think altogether ill of anyone who was a friend of Scott's. Doubtless Miss Seward's works were the worst part of her." The justice of this final touch throws the comedy into relief, endows the subject with a saving though slight depth of humanity, and rescues the portrait from its tendency to become a farcical sketch and nothing more. And, for those who know, the reference to Lichfield and to important literary people and movements bring associations which tinkle like a delightful bell all through the piece.

To this classification such studies as "Lady Hester Stanhope" (1919) and "Dizzy" (1920) may also be assigned. As a matter of fact, "Lady Hester" may be examined with almost equal profit either as a portrait of a silly creature or as that of an eccentric. Either way, however, the subject is represented as being so fantastic as to be ridiculous, and humor is the net result. Lady Hester is the tag-end of a great family—the Pitts—and she has the Pitt nose, in former generations the symbol of great strength and justifiable pride. In her it is "a nose of wild ambitions, of pride grown fantastical, a nose that scorned the earth, shooting off, one fancies, toward some eternally eccentric heaven." Strachey relates everything in his subject's extravagant behavior to this nose and has her die with it tilted upward toward the skies. Her affected Orientalism, her travels in the Near East and assumption of power there, the attire of a Turkish gentleman which she put on, her lavish expenditures and taste for the grandiose, her refusal to return to her native country and behave like an Englishwoman —all these things and numerous others suggested to her by her completely irrational and capricious imagination are in Strachey's portrait the means by which "the solid glory of Chatham had been transmuted into the fantasy of an Arabian night." She becomes as ignorant and superstitious as the masses of people around her who fear and love her. In her last days, spent in a run-down palace, Strachey tells us, "Three dozen hungry cats ranged through the rooms, filling the courts with frightful noises," and some of those around her did not know whether to cry or laugh. Nothing could be farther removed from the common sense and the slow, substantial, practical, down-to-earth human traits which Strachey always admired and which he believed were central in the English character than Lady Hester is to him. The touch of beauty as, shortly before her death, she revisits her beloved rose garden just outside her palace does not redeem her. She is completely deluded and ridiculous—an extreme example of what a woman ought not to be—and for Strachey merits nothing except mockery and laughter.

Disraeli's portrait is also that of a silly creature, a man this time, "the absurd Jew-boy, who set out to conquer the world" and who reached his destination. The brilliant miniature "Dizzy" (1920) is, perhaps with the exception of "Voltaire," the most closely packed of all Strachey's short studies. A thoughtful reading of its three and one-half pages is to be strongly recommended to those who assume that Strachey had no sense of values. Disraeli is to Strachey a conspicuous example of what egotism, vanity, and ambition may make of a man who has some talent for action and for dealing with men, some artistic sensitivity, and considerable fondness for the theatrical. He often carries his point; and he earns the respect of Bismarck and, more important, the approbation of Queen Victoria. But Strachey asks whether all his achievements testify to greatness and is compelled to answer that they do not. Disraeli has been duped by the glittering outside of things. He has greedily devoured happiness like a grub on a leaf until in old age nothing is left. He has never really become an adult but is boyish and immature to the very end. He is, all told, a piece of painted pasteboard. From the outside he is a gorgeous sphinx; but on the inside all is hollow and without depth. Strachey says that a moralist like Thackeray would describe him in old age as "a silly, septuagenarian child, keeping itself quiet with a rattle of unrealities" and as a "vain-glorious creature, racked by gout and asthma, dyed and corseted, with the curl on his miserable forehead kept in place all night by a bandana handkerchief, clutching at power, prostrating himself before royalty, tottering to congresses, wheezing out his last gasps, with indefatigable snobbery, at fashionable dinner tables." Strachey had thought much about Disraeli before he composed this miniature and at times had considered writing a full-length biography of him. Thus he was prepared to provide in this brief study with its magnificent compression a portrait which may serve admirably as a specific antidote for thousands of shallow success stories.

It may be interesting to note in passing that in *Eminent Victorians* both Dr. Arnold and Cardinal Manning clearly belong to the classification of vain, egotistical, silly creatures.

When we turn to our second classification, the studies in eccentricity, we discover that in Strachey's work oddity and peculiarity are not always faults and that the persons who possess them are not necessarily absurd. They may be laughable without being ridiculous. Their very idiosyncrasies may make them more picturesque and thus richer and more delightful subjects for portraits. Strachey obviously enjoyed working with subjects of this kind; his portraits of Shelley and his father, Greville, Harington, Muggleton, Dr. North, Rousseau, and others may be placed in this classification.

His delight in the eccentric seems to have been almost instinctive and appears in some of his earliest work. One finds more than a suggestion of it in his earliest *Spectator* review (January 9, 1904), that of A. W. Ward's *The Electress Sophia and the Hanoverian Succession*. The following passage from the review deals with the grotesque coarseness characterizing the sense of humor reflected in Sophia's letters and those of her niece:

> Her correspondents were as varied as her lovers. Among them was that remarkable lady, Elizabeth Charlotte, Duchess of Orléans, who did her best to enliven her exile in the French Court by writing scurrilous letters to her aunt at Hanover. Dr. Ward has not thought fit to present more than a superficial view of *Madame's* extraordinary character, and it would be difficult to give any adequate illustration of the colossal coarseness of her German wit. . . . Her Teutonic brutality sticks at nothing. . . . That the Electress shared her niece's peculiar vein is evident from that *correspondance fort étrange,* as a French editor calls it, which passed between the two Princesses upon a subject calculated to make a modern reader hold his nose. But these jests of a healthy barbarism—jests that Smollett would have delighted in—are as different from the civilized nastiness of the Regency as an honest guffaw is from an insinuating leer.[7]

Strachey does not condemn what he finds here or find it absurd. Rather, he simply enjoys it because it is queer, fascinating, and amusing.

A similar fascination is reflected in Strachey's treatment of Caliban in another early piece of writing, "Shakespeare's Final Period" (May 1904). "The 'freckled whelp hag-born' moves us mysteriously to pity and to terror, eluding us for ever in fearful allegories, and strange coils of disgusted laughter and phantasmagorical tears." In a *Spectator* review of October 24, 1908, Strachey makes much of Edward FitzGerald's eccentricities, such as that reflected by the fact that he always wore a silk hat and a fur boa when he and his friend "Posh" happily went to sea.[8]

7. *92,* 55–6.
8. *101,* 635.

Among the collected miniatures, "Muggleton" is noteworthy because it shows to what extreme lengths Strachey was at times willing to go in tolerating eccentricity, in this instance even that of religious fanaticism, purely for the sake of its very oddity and picturesqueness. Possibly the most charming of the miniatures in this group, however, is "Sir John Harington." In it the style is playful and indulgent throughout, quite appropriately, for Harington, a courtier, wit, inventor, scholar, and poet in the bright days of Queen Elizabeth, was such a funny, harmless fellow. Suddenly inspired, he invented the water-closet. Then with similar inspiration he wrote a book which could serve as the companion piece to it and gave this work a title which contained a horrible pun, *The Metamorphosis of Ajax.* The queen was amused, installed one of the new inventions in Richmond Palace, and hung a copy of the *Ajax* on the wall by it. But Harington, nothing if not sprightly and energetic, could also be fancy. He could translate poetry from the Italian, especially when it contained passages of questionable decency; and he shocked the ladies of the court by producing an English version of the twenty-eighth book of Ariosto's *Orlando Furioso.* He was fond of scribbling scurrilous epigrams, which he sent to his mother-in-law, old Lady Rogers. Strachey tells us that she roared with laughter when she read them but that, when she died, she failed to leave him the legacy which he had expected. The fact that he could not refrain from a "scurvy jest" got him in trouble more than once. And the "curious lantern" which he constructed for King James of Scotland did not bring him the reward that he had hoped for. All was by no means comedy in his life. There were times when his chief solace was his dog Bungay, which, Harington declared, on one occasion took a pheasant from a dish at the Spanish Ambassador's table and then, after a sign from its master, returned it to the very same dish. In his last years Harington was racked by various diseases and at the age of fifty-one passed into oblivion. Strachey says that he has pretty well remained there. The miniature itself comes to the rescue by salvaging within the subject odd facts and curious details which are too interesting not to be known and enjoyed.

To the third class of portraits, those of admirable people, we may assign such writings as "A Statesman: Lord Morley" (1918), "The Abbé Morellet" (1924), "Gibbon" (1928), and "Hume" (1928). These and many of Strachey's other characterizations could not have possibly been written by a muck-raker. To discriminate, as Strachey constantly does, is not to show a bent toward fault-finding. Strachey was a positive writer, not a negative one. But he did test his subjects, and he dealt very seriously with the question: What is worthy of admiration? As Leonard Bacon has said, Strachey's praise was on a gold basis.

An important early example of Strachey's miniatures treating admirable persons is to be found in the sketch of Sir Henry Wotton which is a part of his review in the *Spectator* (November 23, 1907) of Logan Pearsall Smith's biography treating that subject. Strachey rapidly but vividly runs over the events of Wotton's life—his youthful career, which "was adventurous enough to go straight into historical romance," and the long period later when he was British ambassador at Venice. He finds much that gives him pleasure all along the way, even in Wotton's dispatches with their somewhat heavy elaboration of style. But Strachey's conclusion is what is most important:

> After all, however, Isaak Walton was a doubtless right, and the true background for Sir Henry Wotton is not the bustle and glamor of Italian diplomacy, but the quietude of the cloisters of Eton. How pleasantly one can imagine the kind old Provost ending his life there in happiness, with his tabacco and his *viol de gamba* and his fishing-rod, and the occasional company of "a religious book or friend"! His best letters were written at this period of his life, and they show us the very qualities of gentle humor and refined simplicity which shine out so clearly from the features of the charming portrait in the Provost's Lodge at Eton. Mr. Pearsall Smith compares Wotton to Cowley and Marvell and Gray and other poets of the kind, but the old Ambassador hardly falls within the category of poets. Primarily he was not a man of letters, but a man of the world, though he wrote poems and wrote

them well, like the rest of his generation. He belongs to the same class to which (with so different a temperament) his collateral descendant, Lord Chesterfield, also belonged—the class of literary politicians. But though Chesterfield himself might have envied the wit which went to the making of Wotten's famous definition of an Ambassador—"an honest man sent to lie abroad for the good of his country"—Wotton's cast of mind had none of the high rigidity of the eighteenth-century Earl's. Perhaps his predominant characteristic was that of cheerfulness. His letters are nearly always gay, and one feels—one does not always feel it with good letter-writers —that he himself was more charming than his letters. He took life lightly and calmly; he had the secret of contentment of which illness and debt and loss of friends did not deprive him; he could linger over the current of his existence as happily as he lingered over the quiet Thames with Isaak Walton beside him. He was indeed his own model in his "Character of a Happy Life":

> This man is freed from servile hands,
>   Of hope to rise, or fear to fall:
> Lord of himself, though not of lands:
>   And having nothing, yet hath all.[9]

Strachey's portrait of Lord Morley represents him as suffering somewhat from a dark cloud of Victorian solemnity which hung over him; nevertheless, in the main he is admirable. He is a true statesman rather than a diplomatist, for he constantly refers problems to great principles. His dealings with Lord Minto and with complex questions relating to India are characterized by the allaying of hatreds, the avoidance of extreme measures, and the eluding of numerous difficulties and of great dangers. He is effective by merit of gentle persuasions, tactful acquiescences, and subtle suggestions of compliment. Yet in his letters to Minto one occasionally catches "a glimpse of underlying steel." He is a

9. *99*, 821–2.

realist, with "an acute perception of the facts with which he had
to deal." Moderation, perspicuity and hardheadedness, tact, and
philosophical integrity are always to Strachey high qualities.

Hume's style is colorless and somewhat too formal and stiff;
but there is much in the man and the historian to praise: detachment, "reason, in all her strength and all her purity," the excitement of an intense and eager intelligence, clarity, elegance, irony,
touches of the colloquial, and the genial charm and happy temperament of a philosopher, who faces death "with ease, with
gaiety, and with the simplicity of perfect taste." He writes with
economy, particularly in his autobiography, which Strachey admires as "a model of pointed brevity." [10] Gibbon is a great artist
and a happy man. In his life Strachey finds "an epitome of the
blessings of the eighteenth century . . . the rich fruit ripening
slowly on the sun-warmed wall, and coming inevitably to its
delicious perfection." [11] And "The Abbé Morellet" is a study
of intelligence and friendship, the study of an encyclopaedist who
was a charming person and who lived a delightful life as the
friend of Diderot, d'Alembert, Mademoiselle de Lespinasse, and
Madame Helvetius.[12]

A fourth class of miniatures is that in which the background and
all that is associated with the subject become particularly interesting and important. Associations are significant and pleasant
to note in all of Strachey's biographical studies, but in this class
they appear almost as important as the subject themselves, at

10. See also the comments on Hume in "Gibbon."

11. For Strachey on Gibbon, see not only "Gibbon" but also "The Age
of Louis IV," *Spectator, 100* (April 11, 1908), 577–8; "A New History of
Rome," *Spectator, 102* (Jan. 2, 1909), 20–1; and "Walpole's Letters." The
subject of one of Strachey's unpublished dialogues is "Gibbon, Johnson, and
Adam Smith." Joseph Wood Krutch has written that we go to Strachey for
the same literary delight that we seek in Gibbon. "Lytton Strachey," *Nation,
134* (Feb. 17, 1932), 199–200.

12. It is of interest that the author of *Queen Victoria* gives us another
portrait of what he considers an admirable subject in "A Frock-Coat Portrait of a
Great King," a portrait of Edward VII, whose loose behavior as Prince of
Wales had worried his mother. *Daily Mail,* Oct. 11, 1927, p. 10.

times even more important or interesting. The subjects never lose their importance, but their background makes them appear far more important than they could ever be without it; and there are some instances in which the subjects seem to be studied more for the sake of their background than for what they are.

In "Horace Walpole," for example, the background of late eighteenth-century refinement and the art of letter writing mean so much to the portrait that it is difficult to imagine what this miniature would be without it. Likewise, in what could be profitably examined as a companion picture, "Mary Berry," the indispensable background includes Horace Walpole himself in old age, a vignette of late eighteenth-century life, and a contrasting sketch of the first half of the nineteenth century with Thackeray and others in it. "Li Hung-Chang" interests us mainly because modern international diplomacy, modern China, and General Gordon provide a provocative background. If James Boswell had never written his biography of Johnson or flourished in the second half of the eighteenth century, Strachey's sketch of him would be of little interest to us. In "Madame de Lieven" the emphasis is upon manners, the genuinely aristocratic manners which Lieven acquired in the eighteenth century contrasted with the crude manners of the middle class with which she has to deal in the nineteenth. High society and people of high quality—salons in London and Paris, Metternich, Guizot, and Lady Holland—compose a background here of color, life, and movement. In one of the best of the uncollected *Spectator* reviews, "Canning and His Friends," the period of the regency is delightfully reflected. After observing the contrast between George Canning's reputation with his contemporaries, who believed him to be motivated almost entirely by odious egotism and crafty ambition, and the picture which Canning's letters give of him—sympathetic, warm-hearted, and affectionate—Strachey concentrates his attention on a study of British life and manners in the first quarter of the nineteenth century. He notes that almost everyone seems to have been joking in those days, and the jokes have a family likeness in that they are all high spirited. Gone is the fastidious refinement of Horace

Walpole's world; a somewhat rough, playful, masculine vigor and freedom have taken its place. The contrast with our modern world is also striking:

> It was an age which seems almost as remote from that which immediately preceded it as it does from our own. . . . The difference is complete between the boisterous, open-air jocularity of these fine fellows of the Regency and the subtlety, the delicacy, the exquisite ingenuity of the eighteenth-century wit. As we turn over these pages we seem to step back into a strange bright world of good-natured giants, all incredibly healthy, vigorous, happy-go-lucky, and amused. Curricles dash past with jests, and laughter, Dukes hob-nob with boxers, Foreign Ministers fight duels on Putney Heath. . . . In London, the great doors are opened to one by the "old crimson footman," and dinner is served precisely at half-past six. Pigtails are still worn, but they are going out of fashion, and they vanished altogether—it was the end of an epoch—in the year after Canning's death.[13]

Some of the biographical studies in which background is particularly important take the form of a highly successful blending of portraiture with literary criticism. Such a blending one finds in "Macaulay," "Froude," "Creighton," and "Sarah Bernhardt." Behind the historian Macaulay, with his platitudes, his poor aesthetic judgment, and his great skill as a story teller, we see an age in which some of the aristocracy of traditional Whiggism becomes combined with the intellectual coarseness, the ingenuous optimism, and the materialism of Victorian Philistines. Macaulay's colorless, metallic style seems appropriate to a period in which machines are doing so much to give comfort and power to the middle class.[14] "Froude" is the portrait of a biographer and his-

13. *102* (March 27, 1909), 499–500. A review of Captain Josceline Bagot's *George Canning and His Friends.*

14. For Strachey on Macaulay, see also "Horace Walpole"; "Macaulay's Marginalia," *Spectator,* *99* (Nov. 16, 1907), 743; "Warren Hastings," *Spectator,* *104* (March 12, 1910), 429–30; and "Congreve, Collier, Macaulay, and Mr. Summers."

torian who suffered much from his early experiences in school and from the influence of a father whose philosophy of life was far too austere and solemn. Froude appears as somewhat warped and narrowed by the kind of formative influences which made him what he was. Although he was a true scholar and possessed a style capable of depicting history with color and irony, he was greatly limited by the ethical conceptions and the Protestant bias characteristic of his time. Thus he was a historian writing for the Victorian age; and, lacking the comprehensive point of view of Gibbon and Tacitus and the "mysterious wisdom of Thucydides," did not succeed in writing for all ages.[15] In the background of "Creighton," the study of another Victorian writer of history, we see the long succession of great scholars which, to its eternal glory, the Church of England has produced; and we see the important new school of scholars using scientific methods which result in accuracy and dryness. We also see in Creighton himself the successful administrator and man of affairs to considerable extent characteristic of his age as he wins his way through the use of common sense and compromise. The portrait "Sarah Bernhardt" belongs to this class because, even though the divine Sarah with her golden voice and astonishing talent is certainly a person in her own right, she is primarily a creature of the theater. At her worst she appears as the central figure in a nineteenth-century theatrical display, with all its "luscious intensity" and bravura; and at her best she is lifted gloriously by Racine's great art.

Almost all the miniatures contain some narrative. Strachey does not miss many chances to use incident and anecdote to vitalize his portraits and to give them vividness and color. Furthermore, he obviously enjoys for the sake of themselves anecdotes which have point, spice, and humor. Many of these are to be found

15. For Strachey on Froude, see also "Some New Carlyle Letters," *Spectator*, *102* (April 10, 1909), 577–8. At the time of Strachey's death an editorial in the New York *Times* observed that Strachey had been "too much of a philosopher to reveal the 'naked' truth, as Froude did, or thought he did, about Carlyle. Mr. Strachey dedicated himself to an amply clothed and highly civilized truth." Jan. 22, 1932, p. 18.

scattered through his writings. One which certainly delighted him is in "John Aubrey," a sentence quoted from Aubrey's *Miscellanies:* "*Anno* 1670, not far from *Cirencester,* was an Apparition; Being demanded, whether a good Spirit or bad? Returned no answer, but disappeared with a curious Perfume and most melodious Twang." Narrative counts for much in "The Life, Illness, and Death of Dr. North" and in "Lady Hester Stanhope." "The Président de Brosses" is not merely a pen portrait but is also a character story in which Voltaire plays an important role. And "The Sad Story of Dr. Colbatch" is excellent narrative throughout, with plenty of scheming, action, and dramatic conflict. It seems almost too good to be true that the whole story comes straight from history, that the setting is actually Trinity College, and that the extremely formidable antagonist is none other than the great eighteenth-century scholar and master of Trinity, Richard Bentley.

The sixth class of portraits among Strachey's miniatures may be designated as studies in depth. Nearly all the portraits have some depth, but in these depth leads into depth and shadow fades into shadow on and on without end. The portraits here are dark studies in which the subjects, with all their complexity and profundity, can never be completely exposed or fully understood. The light which plays upon them is brilliant and penetrating; all that it reveals is delightfully interesting; but the succession of shadows beyond its reach appeals fully as much to the imagination as do the details which can be seen. In their richness and their power to suggest the somber mystery of human personality they inevitably suggest the work of Rembrandt. In them the subjects may be in part laughable and in part pitiable; but in the main they are to be wondered at. Examples of portraits belonging to this class are "Lady Mary Wortley Montagu," "Carlyle," "Mademoiselle de Lespinasse," and "Madame du Deffand."

Lady Mary's life is one of tragedy made noble by unmitigated honesty in the facing of facts, by intellectual eminence, and by courageous fortitude. Lady Mary is cold, hard, often cynical, and sometimes gross. She is altogether incapable of sympathetic feeling or imaginative perceptions. But in her brilliant letters she proves herself to be both a wit and a moralist. She is clever and high spirited and has a taste for serious reading very unusual among eighteenth-century women. When she falls in love with Edward Wortley, her intellectual equal, the depth of her emotion is proportionate to the capacity of her intellect. Wortley also loves her, but the path of the lovers is not smooth. Each is too complex for love to be with them a simple matter, and the most formidable of all difficulties for lovers, those relating to temperament, provide obstacles, "They were not ordinary lovers; they were intellectual gladiators." She is of a strongly independent nature, and the more her feelings deepen in intensity, the more she is determined not to be carried away by them. Not long before the marriage finally takes place, Wortley writes to her: "If we should once get into a coach, let us not say one word till we come before the parson, lest we should engage in fresh disputes." The marriage is a complete failure, proceeding through gradual estrangement to indifference. Lady Mary, "disillusioned, reckless, and brilliant," plunges into fashionable society, first in London and later in Italy. She grows old and unattractive. Horace Walpole sees her in Florence and describes her as an "old, foul, tawdry, painted, plastered person." To Strachey, though Walpole suggests the truth about her old age, it is only the superficial truth. Strachey writes: "As she grew older, her emotions became even more arbitrary and sterile, her intellect more penetrating and severe. Her dream of perfect love, which Wortley had shattered, haunted her like a ghost." Nevertheless, she does not "palliate her situation" but faces her wretched failure "without flinching and without pretence." It is this attitude toward life and the strength of character which lies behind it that "lifts her melancholy history out of the sordid into the sublime." Her story suggests the mysterious power which sometimes appears and makes human beings indomitable in their suffering as, year after year, they face and bear the worst that life may bring.

"Carlyle" is a study of colossal genius which is largely wasted. In the subject here Strachey finds great exuberance of vitality and the rare gifts of an artist. But unfortunately these are not controlled and directed so that they produce the work of a high order of which Carlyle was capable. The energy frequently takes the form of spasm, violence, and irritability. Carlyle's art suffers from his belief

that he is primarily a prophet and a moralist, when actually his
highest gifts are those which serve him when he observes human
beings—his contemporaries and those encountered in history—
and produce his admirable pen portraits. He inherits the narrowness of a Scottish peasant and considers French literature trash.
He succumbs to a superman mania and loses precious years in
working on a life of Frederick the Great. He has no inward harmony. With all his genius, he has not begun to discover how to be
happy; and the contrast is complete between him and Gibbon, who
could be joyful, even gay, while at work. Carlyle mismanages matters so badly that he often succeeds merely in making himself and
his brilliant wife miserable. Strachey's Carlyle is a tragic picture
of a great man who never really finds himself or gets himself in
hand.[16]

"Mademoiselle de Lespinasse" is remarkably sure as a work of
art considering its early date of composition (1906). The sorrowful
keynote, the strange mixture of burning, intense passion and cruel
irony which determines the course of life of a gifted woman, is
announced early in the piece and is never once forgotten. Lespinasse is one of the most brilliant of all letter writers, and she is
also brilliant as a figure in society and a conversationalist. She has
everything needed for success in social relations: "She had tact,
refinement, wit, and penetration; she was animated and she was
sympathetic; she could interest and she could charm." She is
"the crowning wonder, the final delight," in the circles of excellent
talkers which she dominates. "To watch the moving expressions
of her face was to watch the conversation itself, transmuted to a
living thing by the glow of an intense intelligence. 'There is a
flame within her!' was the common exclamation of her friends. Nor
were they mistaken; she burnt with an inward fire. It was a steady
flame, giving out a genial warmth, a happy brilliance." But tragedy
stalks her throughout life. First there is the sudden and violent
termination of her friendship with Madame du Deffand, another
gifted Frenchwoman much older than herself. This, Strachey says,

16. For Strachey on Carlyle, see also the praise of Carlyle's portrait of
Coleridge in his life of Sterling, "Coleridge's *Biographia Literaria*," *Spectator*,
100 (March 7, 1908), 376–7; and "Some New Carlyle Letters," above.

was inevitable: "The two women were much too alike for a tolerable partnership; they were both too clever, too strong, and too fond of their own will." But tragedy has its way in her life chiefly through passion and "all its fearful accompaniments." Her moving story is that of a woman whose feelings are exceptionally intense, strong, and deep, helplessly finding herself entangled in a web which includes three men. First, there is the noted philosopher, her kinsman, d'Alembert, who discovers and falls in love with her early and, when she does not return his love with equal fervor, patiently waits in hope that some day she will. Then there is clever, handsome Mora, "a young Spaniard of rank and fortune," with whom she falls wildly in love and who fully returns her love. Mora, however, begins to show serious symptoms of consumption. In the meantime, she meets the Comte de Guibert, an accomplished man of the world, and, "with a flash of intuition, recognized his qualities as precisely those of which she stood most in need." She goes through anguish as her heart is torn between the ill Mora and the irresistible Guibert. Mora dies, however, and more and more realizing that there is no steadfastness and strength in Guibert's feeling for her, she attempts to emancipate herself from him—without success. "She was a wild animal struggling in a net, involving herself, with every twist and every convulsion, more and more inextricably in the toils." She finally collapses completely, shattered in body and mind. Too late, Guibert hurries to her; she refuses to see him. The faithful d'Alembert watches beside her bed until she dies. When after her death the letters which she has saved and cherished in her heart are examined, it is discovered that not the name of Guibert or of d'Alembert but that of Mora appears in them like a wail again and again. Guibert is overwhelmed with remorse; d'Alembert is crushed with disappointment. She has been a pearl the value of which could not be told, and she has been lost. Strachey ends the piece with the mournful loveliness of the melodious Italian words *doloroso passo*.

"Mademoiselle de Lespinasse" is a study in depth in which the portrait is skillfully embedded in and illuminated through story. Thus in a sense it belongs to two of the classifications which we have dealt with. "Madame du Deffand," a study in depth of even

more tremendous shadows and of greater complexity, in its techni-
cal resourcefulness and richness of texture shows a kinship with a
number of them. The portrait has a wealth of associations with
eighteenth-century culture, letter writing, conversation, and with
important persons such as Lespinasse, Horace Walpole, and Voltaire. Deffand's letters reflect eighteenth-century common sense
and eighteenth-century precision. Her behavior and everything
else about her reflect the supreme refinement and manners of the
eighteenth century. But she is also an eccentric, serving tremendous
dinners at which the brilliant conversation lasts far into the night
and after which she loathes to go to bed. She suffers from a taste
which is so sophisticated and refined that, intellectual that she is,
most books and almost everything else in life are to her unspeaka-
bly boring. She has her vanities and her shortcomings. She does not
like young people and does not know what to say to them when they
appear. Story, set forth in curious detail, counts for much in her
portrait. She is admirable also, admirable in the brilliance of her
conversation, the strength and exactness of the style in which she
writes her letters, the absolute integrity of her mind and the consistency with which she examines all things in the light of common
sense, the psychological insight which enables her to tear the masks
off those who deceive others, and the depth and strength of her
passion for Horace Walpole. And her story is tragic. She really
belongs to the first half of the eighteenth century and yet is compelled to spend many years of her life in the second, in an age
dominated by the *Philosophes* whom she detests. Her suffering is
great when her friendship with Mademoiselle de Lespinasse comes
to an end and many of those who have frequented her salon depart
with Lespinasse. At the age of fifty-seven she becomes totally blind.
She is extremely lonely in her old age, and her strong love for the
much younger Horace Walpole is reciprocated only to a very slight
degree. As she gradually approaches death, her self-repression,
boredom, and bitterness grow more and more complete. Neither
her character nor the complications of her life have been altogether
understandable. Into her tangled web many dark threads have been
woven. Strachey comments near the end of her story: "When one
reflects upon her extraordinary tragedy, when one attempts to

gauge the significance of her character and of her life, it is difficult to know whether to pity most, to admire, or to fear." Pathos, grandeur, terror—such are the powerful elements which enter into the composition of this admirable miniature.

CHAPTER 11

Some Comments on Poets and Poetry

STRACHEY left no systematic body of criticism dealing with the theory of poetry and no thorough and detailed treatment of the work of any poet. Most of his opinions concerning poetry and poets have to be gathered from articles and reviews written from time to time through a period of many years. Doubtless some of his opinions changed as time went on. It is probable, moreover, that some of them would have been modified if he had dealt with them against the context of a detailed, systematic treatment of the subjects to which they relate. Nevertheless, these opinions are worth examining, both for their own intrinsic worth and for the light which they reflect on the development of Strachey's judgment and taste. We have already encountered his opinions concerning Racine, Marlowe, Shakespeare, Thomson, Pope, Tennyson, Swinburne, Henley, Barnes, Brown, and Yeats in the chapters on French literature, the drama, the eighteenth century, and the Victorians. Our purpose here will be to bring together his ideas about the nature and purpose of poetry and his various comments on Chaucer, Donne, Milton, Wordsworth, and Hardy.

In considering Strachey as a critic of poets and poetry, we should remind ourselves of the fact that he himself wrote poems from the time of early childhood until his death. It was thus characteristic of him to try to understand, interpret, and evaluate poets and poems from the inside with the aid of an imaginative sympathy and insight which only a fellow practitioner could possess.

He attacked those critics who seemed to forget that poetry was art and who proceeded with great assurance to lay down definitions of the nature and functions of poetry. Such generalizations, he said, would be more satisfactory if it were not for the poets: "One can never make sure of that inconvenient and unreliable race." [1] It would be easy, he also said, to construct a complete and perfect code of the laws of poetry if there were no poets. But it was not the business of poets or of other great writers to obey formulas or be guided by generalizations concerning what the critics thought poetry should be. One of their functions, as Wordsworth had shown, was "to destroy cut-and-dried precedents, and to give the lie to *a priori* theorizings upon the art of literature." [2] Hence it was that Strachey had little respect for Arnold's touchstone test for determining the quality of poetry or for his requirement that great poetry should possess high seriousness.[3] Likewise he could not accept John Churton Collins' assertions that good poetry was essentially didactic in the highest sense of the word and that poetry and pessimism should never be combined. Poems were rather to be thought of and valued as individual things: "We love poems, as we love the fields and the trees and the rivers of England, and as we love our friends, not for the pleasure which they may bring us, nor even for the good which they may do us, but for themselves." [4] If poetry was not primarily a means of instruction or a source of a certain kind of refined pleasure, was there any general dictum broad and valid enough to be applied to it? Strachey believed that there was. He believed that there was a profound and fundamental sense in which poetry might be spoken of that carried with it "notions of high sublimity and passionate force." It was to be found in Wordsworth's conception of poetry:

1. "Mr. Hardy's New Poems," *Characters and Commentaries* (New York, Harcourt, Brace, 1933), p. 181. Cf. "The Age of Spenser," *Spectator, 98* (March 23, 1907), 457–8; "L'Art Administratif," *Spectator, 99* (Dec. 28, 1907), 1093–4.

2. "The Grandiloquence of Wordsworth," *Spectator, 100* (May 9, 1908), 746–7.

3. "A Victorian Critic," *Characters and Commentaries*, p. 178; "Pope," The Leslie Stephen Lecture at Cambridge University for 1925 (Cambridge, Cambridge University Press, 1925), pp. 11–14.

4. "The Value of Poetry," *Spectator, 97* (July 21, 1906), 93–5.

When we praise a poem for its "inspiration," we are praising it for some other quality than that of its power "to communicate delight"; we imply that its value lies in the noble intensity with which it suggests to us what is most beautiful and wise and good. This was the conception of poetry which Wordsworth had in his mind when he said that "to be incapable of a feeling for poetry, in my sense of the word, is to be without love of human nature and reverence for God." Such a dictum as that is perfectly applicable to the world's greatest poems. A man who was left unmoved by the most inspired passages of Shakespeare and Dante would, we feel, be in the parlous state which Wordsworth speaks of.[5]

Great poetry, then, should have a "noble intensity"; it should possess the power to move us and to appeal to and strengthen what is highest in our humanity. There is much in this conception of poetry to suggest Shelley as well as Wordsworth.

Strachey wrote this in a review of 1908 entitled "Modern Poetry" dealing with Walter Jerrold's *The Book of Living Poets*. When he turned his attention to the modern poets represented in Jerrold's book and sought to determine the extent to which their work measured up to his conception of good poetry, he found them, with only one or two exceptions, sadly lacking. They could please; some of them were excellent craftsmen; but they did not possess the inward fire. They did not have originality. They were still working in the romantic tradition of Wordsworth and Coleridge, but in them romanticism had lost its freshness and force. To some extent the true flame of romanticism still flickered in Swinburne's work. Austin Dobson and A. E. Housman managed to be original by deliberately narrowing their fields and being content to reign supreme over tiny kingdoms. But who would emancipate poetry from the worn-out tradition of romanticism? "In many respects the poets of today occupy a position analogous to that of the writers who preceded Wordsworth at the close of the eighteenth century. Like Hayley and Pye and Erasmus Darwin, they are the heirs of an effete tradition;

5. "Modern Poetry," *Spectator, 100* (April 18, 1908), 622–3.

but where shall we find the new great poet who shall free us from the bondage of Wordsworth, just as Wordsworth himself freed his contemporaries from the bondage of Pope?" [6]

Another major shortcoming of this verse was its failure to be realistic. Although it might deal occasionally with love, in general it did not make sufficient reference "to any of those matters with which we are most habitually and most deeply concerned." It preferred to remain in an imaginary world of pure enchantment and beauty:

> We are told a great deal about sunsets, and magic, and dryads, and roses in the moonlight; but how little of our daily interests and pursuits, of the problems that perplex us, and the recreations that delight us, and the human beings among whom we live!

> "Here, in the fairy wood, between sea and sea,
>   I have heard the song of a fairy bird in a tree,
>   And the peace that is not in the world has flown to me."

> So writes Mr. Arthur Symons, and his lines are a summary of the attitude of the modern poet towards the functions of his art. So long as the poet remains lost in a fairy wood, and is content to spend his time listening to fairy birds, his art will continue to be a mere object of amusement, without any vital hold upon the deeper issues of life.

Even Kipling, "the only contemporary writer of verse whose genius is uncontestable," was in a sense unrealistic. He had "boldly discarded the conventional unrealities of romanticism" and had made use of "an astonishing power of vivid and vernacular expression" in the illustration of the thoughts and feelings of private soldiers and mechanics. But to most of his readers his art was exotic, "almost as unfamiliar and romantic as the 'fairy wood' of Mr. Arthur Symons." [7]

6. *Ibid.*

7. *Ibid.* Hence we discover why Strachey could not admire the poetry of Yeats in this period. See "Mr. Yeats's Poetry," *Spectator, 101* (Oct. 17, 1908), 588–9. Hence also his unwillingness to accept Keats's identification of truth

It was precisely the realism which he discovered in Thomas
Hardy's poems which caused Strachey to welcome *Satires of Cir-
cumstance* when he reviewed the poems in 1914. Here at last
was a poet who brought "the realism and sobriety of prose"
into the service of his poetry. Strachey found relief in the "utter
lack of romanticism" and the "common, undecorated presentment of things" which he found in these poems. Hardy lacked
the correctness, the skill, and the assurance of many of the poets
in Jerrold's book; but he had the indispensable qualities which
they did not have: "What a relief such uncertainties and inexpres-
sivenesses are after the delicate exactitude of our more polished
poets! And how mysterious and potent are the forces of inspiration
and sincerity!" Here was the very pessimism which Churton Collins
had said poetry should not have. Here was irony based upon a
close observation of men and their daily activities, of their hopes,
their disappointments, and their failure: "Mortality, and the
cruelties of time, and the ironic irrevocability of things—these
are the themes upon which Mr. Hardy has chosen to weave his
grave and moving variations. If there is joy in these pages, it is joy
that is long since dead; and if there are smiles, they are sardonical.
The sentimentalist will find very little comfort among them." [8] Strachey believed that the essence of Hardy's genius lay in this ironic
realism rather than in the romantic passion of his early novels,

---

with beauty. This unwillingness is reflected in an almost terrifying incident
involving Rupert Brooke which J. M. Keynes gives in a letter to Duncan
Grant (Jan. 19, 1909): "On Sunday at breakfast, Sheppard delivered an
indictment on poor Rupert for admiring Mr. Wells and thinking truth beauty,
beauty truth. Norton and Lytton took up the attack and even James and
Gerald (who was there) stabbed him in the back. Finally, Lytton, enraged
at Rupert's defences, thoroughly lost his temper and delivered a violent
personal attack." R. F. Harrod, *The Life of John Maynard Keynes* (New York,
Harcourt, Brace, 1951), p. 147. Strachey also objected to the way in which
poetry was read in this day and declared, "These are the days of quick reading and hasty assimilation"; then he touched on Spenser: "A page or two of
his writings will no more contain the true significance of his work than a
bucket of sea-water the strength and glory of the sea." "The Poetry of T. E.
Brown," *Spectator, 100* (June 13, 1908), 938–9.

8. "Mr. Hardy's New Poems." First published in the *New Statesman*, Dec.
19, 1914.

his sympathetic studies of peasant life, or the varied wealth of his description of Wessex landscape, excellent though these were. Moreover, he could not accept the statement of Harold Child, whose book on Hardy he reviewed, that *The Dynasts* was "incomparably the greatest work that Hardy has ever produced, one of the greatest works in literature." Strachey conceded that *The Dynasts* had grandeur of scheme, brilliant incidental beauties, wide historical grasp, descriptive power, and even a pervading humanity. But, to him, it was an example of ambition that had overleapt itself. "In art, if not in life, it is better to aim low and to succeed than to aim high and to fail." It could not be compared with other works of large scope such as *War and Peace, Antony and Cleopatra,* or *Prometheus Unbound.* Hardy's essential genius was not in it. "There is more of that mysterious quality in thirty pages of *Life's Little Ironies* than in all the nine hundred of *The Dynasts.*" [9]

Realism was to be had in great abundance in Chaucer. But on Chaucer Strachey has not left us detailed comments. It is with Chaucer as it is with two other great writers whom Strachey certainly admired, Ben Jonson and Fielding. He seems to have known and loved them so well that he simply took them for granted. Furthermore, they did not need to be rescued from neglect, as Racine and Beddoes did. Yet Strachey wrote much about Shakespeare, and he had certainly not been neglected. He knew and loved Shakespeare even more than he did Chaucer. Why did he not take Shakespeare for granted also? The answer is, of course, that he could not, just as most of us cannot. Shakespeare more than any other writer creates a feeling of delightful intimacy between himself and each intelligent reader which gives the reader the impression that the poet has whispered in his ear secrets which no other has yet possessed. All true lovers of Shakespeare feel that they must some day do a book on him. Chaucer has much of this same power, but not so much as Shakespeare.

9. "A Short Guide to Thomas Hardy," *New Statesman,* March 11, 1916, pp. 551–2. In general Strachey liked Hardy's poetry much better than his novels, which he actually found rather boring. See Virginia Woolf, *A Writer's Diary* (London, Hogarth Press, 1954), p. 122.

Strachey could read him, enjoy him, and admire him without talking very much about him.

Nevertheless, we may glean some comments on Chaucer from Strachey's writings. We know that he spoke of Chaucer's "divine amenity." [10] We know too that he deeply lamented, as a good biographer naturally would, the fact that Chaucer's letters, along with those of Marlowe and Shakespeare, had vanished.[11] He recognized in Chaucer enduring qualities which would make him, "in spite of his archaisms, beloved as long as the human race exists." [12] He was filled with admiration for Chaucer's conscious art, which suggested that of classicism. Chaucer was the chief representative of the tradition "of accomplishment, of graceful ease, of formal beauty" which had culminated at the end of the fourteenth century in England.[13] We know also that Strachey spoke of Chaucer's "vast and varied observation, . . . humorous and intimate sympathy, and . . . abounding force." [14] Thus he found in Chaucer some of the qualities which he valued most in poetry: realism, psychological insight, humor, and power to move. He has suggested an interesting comparison between the realism of medieval writers such as Chaucer and Froissart and that to be found in the fiction of Balzac and Flaubert. The medieval writer's attitude toward details was "wonderfully innocent"; unlike realistic writers of more recent times, he delighted in details for the sake of themselves:

> The story which he was supposed to be telling was often very little more than the framework for a series of minute and elaborate inventories. With the great realists of our own age—with Balzac, for instance, or with Flaubert—the case is very different; for, though their wealth of detail is at least as great, their use of it is not a prodigal extravagance,

10. "Carlyle," *Portraits in Miniature* (New York, Harcourt, Brace, 1931), p. 179.
11. "English Letter Writers," *Characters and Commentaries*, p. 3.
12. "Medieval Studies," *Spectator*, 97 (Nov. 17, 1906), 786–7. A review of W. P. Ker's *Essays on Medieval Literature*.
13. *Ibid.*
14. "The Poetry of T. E. Brown."

but a careful and deliberate investment. Balzac's description of the *Pension Vauquer* would (if it had been a palace instead of a boarding house) have delighted a medieval chronicler; but he would have stopped short at the description; he never would have dreamed of converting such a marvelous mass of detail into nothing more than the background for the tragedy of Père Goriot. The medieval love of detail for its own sake was, in fact, curiously childlike; and this simplicity of mind appears no less in the delightful naiveté of medieval psychology.

Strachey added significantly, however, that the innocence of medieval writers did not indicate that they lacked emotional and spiritual maturity: "In truth, the childishness of the Middle Ages was only an intellectual childishness; it did not touch the heart. 'Amor che a nullo amato amar perdona,'—that is not the voice of a child; it is the voice of man, who has learnt something that no child can ever know." [15]

Realism was also a quality of John Donne's poetry. In this and in his intellectuality he was the heir of Chaucer. But a great gap in literary tradition had intervened. Strachey reviewed H. J. C. Grierson's edition of Donne's poems in January 1913 and rejoiced that the poet's work could now be read in a trustworthy text. His review reflects a great interest in the history of Donne's reputation and influence. Although Chaucer had gone before him, Donne found it necessary to rebel against such Elizabethans as Spenser and his imitators.[16] Dryden, in his turn, after taking the realism and intellectuality which he found in Donne and developing it further, proceeded to discard much of what remained in Donne's poems:

> Dryden, we know, was in his youth an enthusiastic disciple of Donne, and his early work shows the signs of his admiration plainly enough. There is nothing surprising in this.

15. "Medieval Studies."
16. For further comments on Spenser, certainly not one of Strachey's favorite poets, see "The Age of Spenser," above, and "The Poetry of Thomson," *Spectator, 100* (March 14, 1908), 421-2.

Apart from Chaucer, Donne was the first English writer to grasp to the full the importance of the realistic and intellectual elements in poetry. It was he who, by leading a revolt against the sugared and sensuous style of Spenser, opened the way to that great movement in our literature which culminated in the Satires of Pope. And it was through Dryden that the way lay. Dryden's eminently rationalistic and mundane mind recognized in Donne the master who could teach him how to use verse both as an instrument of argumentative exposition and as a brilliant mirror of actual life. Having learnt this, he went a step further, discarded what was *baroque* and unessential in Donne's manner, and introduced once for all the modern spirit into poetry. Thus, in a sense, he superseded Donne, but the magnificent original conception of the great Elizabethan lies at the root of Dryden's finest work, and of that of his numerous spiritual progeny.[17]

But it was not merely the realism and intellectuality that Strachey enjoyed in Donne. He delighted in the complexity of Donne's genius. Examined superficially, his poems were indeed strange mixtures of heterogeneous elements. The ingenious ribaldry of Butler's *Hudibras* and the mystical frenzies of Crashaw's *Hymn to Saint Teresa* both owed something to him. His love poems were probably the most extraordinary in the world: "Loaded with complicated reasonings, learned allusions to obscure writers, abstruse references to philosophical systems, it seems almost impossible that they should be anything but frigid and absurd." But they were neither. Dr. Johnson was wrong when he failed to see more in these poems than a preposterous collection of "conceits." And when Dryden objected that Donne affected metaphysics and perplexed "the minds of the fair sex with nice speculations of philosophy when he should engage their hearts," Strachey said that

17. "The Poetry of John Donne," *Spectator, 110* (Jan. 18, 1913), 102–3. Strachey and other members of his family had been reading Donne for many years, but it should be noted that the date of this review, for which he reread the poems and gathered his thoughts concerning them, comes not long before he began writing *Eminent Victorians*.

he displayed "the blindness of a reformer." The point was that Donne was another artist, another magician in the use of words. "The criticism seems perfectly just until we turn to the poems themselves, and find that Donne really has achieved the impossible." Through their burning intensity and passionate force Donne's poems triumphed over oddity and complexity. In spite of the poet's "bizarre and highly strung individuality," his poems were deeply moving. Among Strachey's favorites were the two "Anniversaries," commemorating the death of Elizabeth Drury at the age of fifteen. It was a great mistake for Grierson to apologize for anything in these two poems, because in them Donne expressed with eloquence and poignancy the awe which he felt as he contemplated mysterious, miraculous humanity. His hyperboles were not an affectation; he actually meant more than he said. "He saw in Elizabeth Drury, not only the type, but the actual presence, of all that is most marvelous in the spirit of man." Strachey generally disliked, we know, disorder and mysticism. But even these were acceptable to him, whether in Donne's poetry or in Dostoievsky's novels, when genius was behind them with its power to move us deeply.[18]

It was a greater poetic power, associated with much greater artistry, which caused Strachey to have almost unlimited admiration for Milton, in spite of what he considered serious shortcomings. Milton, however, was not merely a great poet and literary artist, he was a great man. Strachey found him highly interesting, both as a writer and as a person. Although he made no lengthy study of him, he referred to him often in his writings and published a number of short articles and reviews on the poet. Particularly significant are four contributions made to the *Spectator* in 1908, when Great Britain was celebrating the tercentenary year of Milton's birth.

In the early summer of that year Strachey visited Cambridge

18. *Ibid.* For further comments on Dryden, see "The Age of Corneille," *Spectator, 102* (Jan. 30, 1909), 182–3. Strachey seems to have planned an article on Dryden about the time that he reviewed Grierson's edition of Donne's poems. His mother wrote him on December 4, 1913: "I am very sorry you had to drop Dryden for the Quarterly."

and examined the portraits, prints, and manuscripts relating to
Milton in the memorial exhibition at Christ's College. He was
struck especially by one portrait which, though its authenticity
was supposed to be merely traditional, seemed to him to be the
most sympathetic of the pictures—a charming presentment of
Milton as a young man. As he studied this portrait, he was impressed by "the beautiful oval face," "the arched nose," "the long
hair," and "a curious delicacy, an aristocratic refinement" about
the features which reminded him of Milton's own words about
himself when he spoke of his "honest haughtiness and self-esteem."
Strachey also found the countenance in the portrait to be "full
of the exclusiveness and of the preciosity of a youthful artist who
has just begun to recognize his own high worth." There was "a
dreamy sensuousness in the eyes and in the full lips" that suggested the author of the minor poems. It also suggested Milton's
definition of poetry as being "simple, sensuous, and passionate"
and a strain of what might almost be called paganism which ran
through even the later work and complemented its Puritanism.
Milton's was a sensuousness, however, over which art always
triumphed.[19] Although Milton truthfully told Dryden that Spenser
was his original—Spenser, described by Strachey as "the sweetest,
softest, and most enervating of all English poets"—and although
in his early works he was completely obsessed by his love of beauty,
the "rigidity of his moral nature prevented his artistic faculties
from losing themselves in their own sweetness, while they on their
side endowed the most exalted of his conceptions with color,
warmth, and form." [20]

But there were other characteristics which one associated with
pictures of the older Milton. Strachey asked, "Who does not
know the grave, majestic countenance with the Roman features
and the great eyes?" [21] Here was a person of tremendous force
of character: "The high determination with which at the beginning of his career he set out to accomplish a task of superhuman difficulty, and the triumphant success which crowned the

19. "Milton," *Spectator, 101* (July 4, 1908), 9–10.
20. "John Milton," *Spectator, 101* (Dec. 5, 1908), 933–4.
21. *Ibid.*

guiding resolution of his life,—these are things for which it is difficult to find a parallel, and which, when one reflects upon them, seem more thrilling than the strangest romance." [22] Milton's character was not feminine; on the contrary, it was extremely masculine. This masculinity was apparent both in his attitude toward women and in his public life. He was unusually susceptible to women's beauty and grace and yet easily provoked to go to the opposite extreme of anger and disdain. He was torn between his sensibility and his masculine egoism. If he had been more feminine and more sympathetic, he would have been more dispassionate. In his public life his masculinity took a practical turn: "He was a dreamer; but he carried his dreams into the market-place, and did his best to put them into action." [23]

Strachey, like others, was impressed by Milton's aloof egoism. There was none of Shakespeare's intimacy in his character or in his writings. One could imagine oneself the friend of Shakespeare, "infinitely the greater man"; but "The soul of Milton was unapproachable." Milton's egoism, however, was lofty, not petty; it was not that of vanity but that of pride.[24] Strachey quoted with approval the comment of "that fine critic," Coleridge: "It is a sense of intense egotism that gives me the greatest pleasure in reading Milton's works. The egotism of such a man is a revelation of spirit." [25]

Two great faults, however, were related to Milton's egoism: his lack of humor and his lack of sympathy. He was therefore, Strachey believed, seriously handicapped in his dealings with people and in his writings conspicuously lacking in the power of dramatic insight:

> His domestic severity, his want of humor, his harsh and uncompromising habit of mind,—these things were inevitable in a personality which could neither understand nor imagine the thoughts and feelings of other people. The same qual-

22. "Milton."
23. "John Milton."
24. *Ibid.*
25. "Milton."

ity may be noticed in his poetry. Milton is the least dramatic of great poets, and the least tender. It is only at the height of his sublimity—in his treatment of Satan and Samson—that he is truly pathetic; it is only then that his sympathy seems to be really aroused. He is gay in his earliest poems, but nowhere else. In his middle and later life he had lost the sense of joyousness, of that convivial light-heartedness which springs from the happiness of others; he gave himself up altogether to the difficult, the sublime, and the severe. Thus he represents in the highest degree the strength and the weakness of Puritanism,—its grandeur and its narrowness, its noble sincerity and its coldness of heart.[26]

Related, likewise, were the complacent moralizings which Strachey found extremely objectionable in *Comus*. Underlying the poetry of this masque was "an air of solemn sententiousness and self-approval." There was something unhealthy about the attitude behind such a play, "something not far removed from the kind of hot-house morality which runs riot in the novels of Richardson." Furthermore, in this play talk about morality tended to take the place of action. "Priggishness upon the stage," Strachey declared emphatically, "is inexcusable, unless it is put there expressly to be laughed at." [27]

Whatever Milton's faults might have been, he was still a Titan among the poets. His was an imagination of almost infinite scope, and he was "the supreme artist of our race." "He has none of the intellectual subtlety of Donne, none of the psychological intensity of Pope, none of the spiritual tenderness of Wordsworth; his merits depend almost entirely upon a faculty of lofty and grandiose vision coupled with an almost complete mastery of the resources of verbal sound." [28] While Byron was the most notorious example of an English poet without a style, Milton clearly stood at the head of the opposite school.[29] His verse was all the outcome of

26. "John Milton."
27. *"Comus* at Cambridge," *Spectator, 101* (July 18, 1908), 94–5.
28. "Milton."
29. "Andrew Marvell," *Spectator, 96* (April 14, 1906), 582–3. A review of Augustine Birrell's *Andrew Marvell*. Strachey used the same contrast here in

"patient care and infinite craft." [30] He was the most deliberate of all English poets. Strachey was again struck by the contrast with Shakespeare: "His greatest and most characteristic effects are the result of subtle workmanship, of learned preparation, of conscious and elaborate art. The spontaneity and catholicity which make the works of Shakespeare hardly distinguishable from those of Nature herself were qualities totally alien to Milton's temper of mind. He was the least natural writer who ever lived." [31] Shakespeare worked as no conscientious artist would work, hastily and unevenly; Milton fastidiously took pains with every line and every phrase. The contrast was striking when one went from the "exquisite unforced" lyrics of the Elizabethans to those of *Comus* with their consummate art. After Milton English poetry could not again be the "half-unconscious thing it had been before." [32]

The contrast between Milton and the Elizabethans was also apparent in his choice of words. He was much more careful to select than they had been:

---

dealing with Marvell and Cowley. "No one can doubt that Cowley is one of those poets whose claim to distinction rests upon their matter; his elegy on the death of Harvey is a striking instance of literary excellence without literary style, just as 'Lycidas' is a proof that style alone may confer immortality. After reading the former poem, it is difficult to remember the expression, and it is impossible to forget the feelings expressed; after reading the latter, the expression seems to have absorbed into itself the whole value of the work, so that there is nothing else upon which the mind can dwell. . . . Marvell belongs as clearly to the Miltonic type as Cowley does not. His poems possess the crowning quality of style,—their meaning has become an integral and inseparable part of the words by which it is expressed." Concerning Byron, it is interesting to note one of the aphorisms which Strachey wrote at Cambridge: "It is the highest proof of the genius of Byron that he convinced the world he was a poet." Everything considered, Strachey's low opinion of Byron is as remarkable as Byron's high opinion of Pope. See also "The Value of Poetry."

30. "Milton."

31. "Milton's Words," *Spectator*, 99 (Dec. 14, 1907), 991-2. A review of Laura E. Lockwood's *Lexicon to the English Poetical Works of John Milton*.

32. "Milton." It is not too easy to determine which type of lyric Strachey really preferred. He also wrote in 1908: "The ideal lyric never dots its *i's;* it is content to hint and to half-reveal." "The Poetry of T. E. Brown."

Apart from the preponderance of its Latin words, his vocabulary is perhaps chiefly remarkable for its exclusions. Milton was the heir of the Elizabethans; without that marvelous heritage, his work as we know it could never have existed; and yet no sooner had he come into his fortune than he threw half of it into the sea. His diction, compared with that of the Elizabethans, is curiously devoid of vivid color, of variety, of contrast,—in short, of those very qualities of superabundant wealth which was the chief glory of "the giant age before the flood." But superabundance was not what Milton wanted; he wanted perfection; he wanted the grand style, the vast sublimity, the superhuman splendor which meet one so triumphantly on every page of *Paradise Lost*.[33]

But what the diction lacked in variety the "beautiful, infinitely varied sentences" and the elaborate rhythms made up for. For this reason Milton's verse was, "with the exception of that of Shakespeare's latest manner," the most difficult in English literature to recite well; it required "all the expressiveness and all the modulation at the actor's command."[34] Variety was the very essence of Milton's blank verse, which Strachey spoke of as "the combination formed by rhythmical variety playing over an underlying norm."[35]

Strachey's own prose shows that he was not only impressed but also influenced by the brilliant skill with which Milton exploited the principle of variety. He was also delighted by Milton's verbal music and in turn influenced by it. In reading Milton he was "overwhelmed by a flowing river of enchanting sound."[36] Re-

33. "Milton's Words." See also "The Poetry of William Barnes," *Spectator, 102* (Jan. 16, 1909), 95–6.

34. *"Comus* at Cambridge."

35. "Pope," pp. 16–17. It is interesting to compare Strachey's statement about rhyme: the central argument for it is in its "power of creating a beautiful atmosphere, in which what is expressed may be caught away from the associations of common life and harmoniously enshrined." "Racine," *Books and Characters* (New York, Harcourt, Brace, 1922), p. 27. Nearly all of his own verse rhymes.

36. "Milton."

flected in the lovely sounds of Milton's words was the delight he took in music itself: "Milton can never touch upon music but an added intensity comes into his words,—his writing seems to vibrate with the echoes of the art which he loved so well, an art which, in its aloofness, its elaboration, and its splendor resembles so closely his own." [37] Milton, no less than Sir Thomas Browne, helped to determine Strachey's literary taste and exemplified a high ideal of excellence in art to which Strachey made repeated and salutary reference.

Strachey believed that Milton's grandiloquence was at times echoed in Wordsworth, after May 1802, when Dorothy read him Milton's sonnets aloud, and that henceforth he showed that he realized fully the virtues of ornate diction in poetry. But Wordsworth was "never an echo—even of the greatest—for long." [38] Strachey admired Wordsworth even though he could not approve of the taste for metaphysical stimulants and for infinitudes which his poetry had done much to form.[39]

Wordsworth's was a character of impressive sobriety and simplicity, qualities which were reflected not only in his poetry but also in his letters:

> His character was a singularly homogeneous one; and the same mood of solemn elevation which gave birth to his greatest poetry clung to him through all the trivialities of epistolary intercourse, and makes his letters—especially the later ones—move heavily and slowly, with an air of being more important than they are. Verbal felicities are rare in them, considering they were written by a consummate artist in words; though here and there they do occur.[40]

37. "John Milton."
38. "The Grandiloquence of Wordsworth." A review of *The Poems of William Wordsworth*, ed. Nowell Charles Smith.
39. "Racine," pp. 19–20; "The Lives of the Poets," *Books and Characters*, pp. 78–9.
40. "Wordsworth's Letters," *Spectator, 100* (March 21, 1908), 460–1. A review of *Letters of the Wordsworth Family from 1795 to 1855*, 3 vols., ed. William Knight.

Although Strachey could not rank Wordsworth's letters among the best, in the "barest and coldest of them" he found "an underlying sense of grandeur." Strachey followed Coleridge in explaining the essential qualities of Wordsworth's mind in terms of a reconciliation of opposites—of egotism, introspection, and love of freedom with fundamental sanity and instinctive caution:

> Though from some points of view he was as modern as his great predecessor Rousseau, from others he was as old-fashioned as the Patriarchs. He was at once the first of the Romantics and the last of the Romans. "Rydal is covered with ice, clear as polished steel," he tells Coleridge in one of the newly discovered letters. "I have procured a pair of skates, and tomorrow mean to give my body to the wind; not, however, without reasonable caution." The proviso is typical of the whole cast of his mind. He was perpetually setting out to give his thought to the wind of the spirit which bloweth where it listeth, and at the same time to do so with "reasonable caution." In his best years he succeeded in achieving the impossible feat; and it is in this bold and triumphant reconcilement of opposites that the heart of his greatness lies.[41]

This principle of reconciliation accounted for the success of his diction. He was one of the greatest of innovators; "He was the first poet who fully recognized and deliberately practiced the beauties of extreme simplicity; and this achievement constitutes his most obvious title to fame." Coleridge, in the main an excellent critic of Wordsworth, attempted to estimate his theory of diction by old standards and gave his friend advice which resulted in alterations for the worse.[42] On the other hand, the lesson from Milton which Wordsworth learned was of incalculable value to him. He learned how to combine the strength of pure simplicity with a love of splendor and elaboration. He became aware, Strachey said, "of the remarkable and beautiful effects of contrast which

41. *Ibid.*
42. "Coleridge's Biographia Literaria," *Spectator, 100* (March 7, 1908), 376–7. A review of J. Shawcross' edition.

can be produced by the close juxtaposition of Anglo-Saxon words with those of Latin origin," as in "incommunicable sleep" and "earth's diurnal course." [43]

As we examine Strachey's comments on these poets, we cannot escape the conclusion that English poetry was much more than a source of pleasure to him. It was a source of nurture. It would be much too simple to assume that, mixed in proper proportions, Hardy's realism and irony, Chaucer's humor and psychological insight, Donne's subtle intellectuality, Milton's careful artistry with its varied sentence patterns, rhythms, and sounds, and Wordsworth's combination of imaginative power with sanity, of freedom with caution, and of the simple with the ornate would produce a biographer like Lytton Strachey. But we may safely assume that they helped to produce him and that his reading of these poets was no insignificant part of the preparation for writing *Eminent Victorians.* Furthermore, his comments on them tell us where his affinities lay and thus help to explain both the methods and the sense of values which went into the making of his biographies. It was not merely through the eyes of Voltaire that he studied the Victorians; he had read the English poets thoughtfully and sympathetically, and they were by his side as he wrote.

43. "The Grandiloquence of Wordsworth." For other comments on Wordsworth, see "The Poetry of Thomson" and "The Age of Corneille."

CHAPTER 12

Some Comments on Style

IT WOULD BE IMPOSSIBLE to determine just how early Strachey began to show an interest in style and to find delight in it. What may be an instinctive love of style is clearly reflected in a parody, "The Decline and Fall of Little Red Riding Hood," in a style which imitates Gibbon, written at Leamington in his seventeenth year. In young Strachey's tale, the mother warns her daughter against the wild beasts of the forest and bids her to beware of "the fierce savagery of the lion, the fatal embraces of the bear, and the crafty malignity of the wolf." Red Riding Hood trembles with fear as she suddenly beholds "the crafty eye, the sinister jowl, and the gaunt form of a wolf, aged alike in years and in deceit." But the wolf offers her flowers "with a punctilious deference almost amounting to a chivalrous politeness." Soon he is able to put into effect his evil plan, "as harmless in appearance as it was diabolical in reality." He races to the grandmother's and arrives there long before the young girl. He enters into battle with the old lady, from which he emerges victorious:

> At last, having traversed twice as quickly as Red Riding Hood a road twice as short as that which she had taken, he arrived in triumph at the house of the redoubtable though comatose octogenarian. History does not reveal the details of the interview. It can only be gathered that it was a short and stormy one. It is known for certain, however, that the wolf obtained at the same moment a victory and a meal, and that when Little Red Riding Hood entered her grandmother's

abode, the arch deceiver, occupying the bed, and arrayed in the nightgown of his unfortunate victim, was prepared to receive the child with a smile of outward welcome and of inward derision.

Strachey handles the climax as follows, after the girl has exclaimed, "What big teeth you have!":

"The better," answered the wolf, seeing the culmination of his plan coincide with the humor of the situation, "the better to eat you with, my dear!" Suiting the action to the word, he leapt out of bed and with incredible savageness threw himself upon his victim. Then he divested himself of his borrowed raiment and slipped quietly out of the cottage.

Throughout the story Strachey attempts to exploit to the utmost a style intended to suggest mock-history. Strachey's comment on his parody, expressed in a letter to his mother dated February 15, 1897, is both interesting and significant: "I'm afraid the great wolf of a style has almost devoured the little lamb of a story!"

His early interest in style is also reflected in some of the aphorisms which he wrote in a notebook belonging to his Cambridge period. Four of these are particularly worth examining here:

Words are like women; they yield less if you fall on them with violence than if you play on them with discrimination.

To express a common thought delicately is not to clothe a village girl in silk, but to make such a lady of her that silk is her proper clothing.

It is a point of difference between prose and poetry that prose demands perfection of form, and poetry can do without it.

There are a few common words—*rose, moon, star, love*—which are so beautiful both in themselves and in what they express that their presence insensibly heightens a bad piece of writing, but makes a good one more difficult to compose.

The commonplace books in which Strachey made entries when he was a young man also contain a number of quotations concerning style. One of his favorites was a maxim from the Chinese:

"Moderate your brilliance and most of your difficulties will disappear."

Throughout the years of his literary career Strachey maintained with all the power of strong conviction his belief that in history and biography, both of which should be considered arts, style was indispensable. In "Macaulay" he wrote: "What are the qualities that make a historian? Obviously these three—a capacity for absorbing facts, a capacity for stating them, and a point of view." And in "Gibbon" he went still further: "The style once fixed, everything else followed. Gibbon was well aware of this."

But with all his emphasis upon the importance of style, Strachey does not attempt to define it. He does not believe that it can be defined or understood through mechanical processes of analysis. Style partakes of art, and art is always magic in Strachey's thinking. The secret of style is therefore not to be discovered; it is of its very nature mysterious. Hidden potencies, for good or for evil, dwell within it. Even the most skillful writers may find these difficult to control and direct. Furthermore, style is a gift with which writers are born. It cannot be acquired, although it can be cultivated. Strachey discusses most of these ideas in an article which he contributed to the *Spectator* early in 1908:

> Style—like beauty and like genius—is one of those mysterious qualities which can be immediately perceived, but which cannot be defined. Pages of analysis and description will fail to convey the notion which becomes obvious at once from a paragraph by Swift or Sir Thomas Browne. If we examine the paragraph, if we split it up into the component parts— the sense, the sound, the rhythm, the balance, the arrangement—we shall find that the informing spirit of the whole, the style itself, has somehow or other slipped through our fingers and disappeared, like the principle of life in the chemical analysis of protoplasm. Thus there is no receipt for style; one has it or one has it not; and though, if one has it, there are aids—such as study and practice—towards the perfecting of it, yet there can be no doubt that its essence is a gift inborn.

Some writers—Walter Pater was one of them—seek through a lifetime, with all the laborious refinements of scholarship and taste, to achieve style, and in the end achieve only the imitation of it; while a Bunyan, tinkering in the highways, flows at will with the very perfection of language. Nor is the gift confined to those whose fame rests on their mastery of words. Nothing is more interesting than to watch the magic of style springing out unexpectedly from the utterances of great men of action, bringing an alien sweetness into the hard world of fact.[1]

Words fascinate and mystify Strachey. He is impressed by the indefinable powers which they carry with them; and he is also impressed, like a modern semanticist, by their trickiness. They seem to possess an individual independence and a spirit of life which make them a wonderful means of expression when they obey a master but which may enable them at times to enslave rather than to obey even such a great master as Shakespeare unless he maintains careful and constant guard:

> Perhaps of all the creations of man language is the most astonishing. Those small articulated sounds, that seem so simple and so definite, turn out, the more one examines them, to be the receptacles of subtle mystery and the dispensers of unanticipated power. Each one of them, as we look, shoots up into
>
> "A palm with winged imagination in it
> And roots that stretch even beneath the grave." [2]

Thus when words are combined in sentences, the interaction of words among themselves reveals everincreasing potencies, and sig-

1. "The Prose Style of Men of Action," *Spectator, 100* (Jan. 25, 1908), 141–2. See also "Gibbon"; "A New History of Rome," *Spectator, 102* (Jan. 2, 1909), 20–1; "The Praise of Shakespeare," *Spectator, 92* (June 4, 1904), 881; and "The Age of Spenser," *Spectator, 98* (March 23, 1907), 457–8.

2. Introduction to G. H. W. Rylands' *Words and Poetry* (New York, Payson and Clark, 1928). Collected in *Characters and Commentaries*.

nifications multiply rapidly. "In a single written sentence a hundred elusive meanings obscurely palpitate." [3] In this fact lies the opportunity of the skillful writer to gather, concentrate, clarify, and intensify meanings working in unity; but in it also lies the danger of meanings so relating themselves to meanings as to produce unintentional complication, obscurity, or delusion, or, what is worse, intentional deception.

For Strachey these dangers were illustrated near the end of the first World War by the way journalists and politicians juggled words and metaphors in order to discredit German efforts to bring about peace. These journalists and politicians had warned the public that the German peace-feelers were "peace traps." Strachey commented as follows:

> Let us look, first, at the meaning of the words. Words are queer things, possessed of queer properties, of which perhaps the queerest of all is their faculty of taking on a life of their own, independent of their creator, like the monster of Frankenstein. Man made words; but words, once made, live by their own force, assume new meanings and strange attributes, and may end by enslaving or even destroying their maker. Now there is a peculiarly subtle danger in words of the metaphorical kind. There is a curious fascination about them; they seem to come to one packed with meaning, and yet to reveal that meaning at a glance. And some metaphors are, indeed, glorious winged creatures, in whose keeping the spirit of man can pass in a flash beyond "the flaming bounds of space and time"; they are the very substance of the noblest of man's achievements—Poetry. But there is another species of metaphor, very different from the metaphor of the poet—a serpentine, insidious thing, or—for it seems natural to use a metaphor to describe a metaphor, just as one sets a thief to catch a thief—a trap. . . . If the good metaphor may be conveniently called the poet's metaphor, the bad one deserves the name of the journalist's. The essential characteristic of the journalist's metaphor is speciousness: under

3. *Ibid.*

a guise of brevity and vigor it, in fact, confuses, in order to insinuate suggestions which would have been rejected in any other shape. When a journalist states that the Germans are preparing a peace trap, he appears to be expressing, in a neat and forcible way, two facts, of which one is obvious— that the Germans are deceitful fellows, and of which the other may probably be true—that they are about to offer terms of peace. . . . Ministers nowadays are the humble pupils of journalists.[4]

Strachey believed that the good writer needed to be on guard not merely against obscurity, delusion, and deliberate deception but also against various other vices of language. He was aware of the ancient distinction between *words* and *things,* and although he was himself strongly susceptible to the spell of words as such, he condemned as stylistic decadence any tendency of a writer to enjoy words in themselves at the expense of the meaning which they should convey and to which they should always be subservient. Hence he deplored the fact that even Shakespeare, in the plays of his final period, subordinated interest in character to an indulgence of his love of rhetoric and the language of poetry.[5] Likewise, the eighteenth-century James Thomson fell far short of greatness in such a poem as *The Seasons* because he characteristically displayed a greater interest in words than in things, a vice which was fatal in a nature poet. Thomson also had other vices: he was much given to empty generalizations and to academic pomposity. He was far more interested in rhetoric than he was in the landscapes which he attempted to describe.[6]

Another vice of language was "fine writing," with its ornateness, its self-consciousness, its artificiality, its thoughtlessness, and its lack of taste, simplicity, sincerity, or force.[7] Still another was general carelessness, a failure to take pains with style and to make

4. "Traps and Peace Traps," *War and Peace,* June, 1918, pp. 269–70.
5. Introduction to Rylands' *Words and Poetry;* "Shakespeare's Final Period," *Books and Characters* (New York, Harcourt, Brace, 1922), pp. 55–6.
6. "The Poetry of Thomson," *Spectator, 100* (March 14, 1908), 421–2.
7. See particularly "The Swan of Lichfield," *Spectator, 99* (Dec. 7, 1907), 929–30; and "The Life of Henry Irving," *Spectator, 101* (Dec. 26, 1908), 1104.

it as good as possible. Strachey found this vice in many of the two-fat-volume biographies written in the Victorian period and in much of the work of academic historians. Another vice was that of wordiness, whether it was the orator's unrelenting and merciless flow of words, as illustrated by Macaulay's style; or the general diffuseness and resulting lack of true cogency to be found in Carlyle's letters and some of his other writings; or the seemingly endless outpouring of talk in one of Bernard Shaw's plays. Closely related was glibness, a smooth and oily utterance characteristic of those writers born with a talent for facile expression. Strachey found this vice in the writings of his godfather, the first Earl of Lytton ("Owen Meredith"): "One may imagine, at Lord Lytton's poetical christening, a bad fairy gliding in among the rest. The good ones were lavish with their gifts of charm and distinction, and imagination, and humor, and feeling; and then, after them all, came the witch with her deceitful present: 'Yes, my dear, and may you always write with ease!' The child grew up endowed with a fatal facility." [8] On the other hand, Strachey believed that it was possible to go too far in an effort to avoid wordiness, rhetoric, and "fine writing." A style which was cold, colorless, rigid, and severe and which used words as if their sole function was to be a part of a mechanical process was certainly not an ideal style. The writings of modern scholars were much too likely to reveal this shortcoming.[9] Even classicism, with the marvelous sharpness, the

8. "The First Earl of Lytton," *Characters and Commentaries* (New York, Harcourt, Brace, 1933), p. 111. On Macaulay Strachey wrote: "The style is the mirror of the mind, and Macaulay's style is that of a debater. The hard points are driven home like nails with unfailing dexterity; it is useless to hope for subtlety or refinement; one cannot hammer with delicacy. . . . From the time of Cicero downwards, the great disadvantages of oratory has been that it never lets one off. One must hear everything, however well one knows it, and however obvious it is." "Macaulay," *Portraits in Miniature* (New York, Harcourt, Brace, 1931), pp. 172, 173. Strachey wished that Carlyle could have kept in mind his own observation (borrowed from Shakespeare's *The Merry Wives of Windsor*, I, i): "*Pauca verba* is the only remedy we can apply to all the excesses and irregularities of the head and heart." "Some New Carlyle Letters," *Spectator, 102* (April 10, 1909), 577–8.

9. "Mr. Sidney Lee on Shakespeare," *Spectator, 97* (Dec. 1, 1906), 887–8; "A Frock-Coat Portrait of a Great King," *Daily Mail*, Oct. 11, 1927, p. 10; "Creighton," *Portraits in Miniature*, pp. 205 ff.

intellectual pith, and the lucidity which it was capable of achieving in the hands of a master like Voltaire, could carry its processes of selection so far that language became a cabined and confined thing. To Strachey language was a gorgeous living creature, subjected to control but still free and therefore capable of sudden outbursts of meaning and emotion and of surprises springing from the mysterious and unfathomable nature of words, alone and in conjunction. There was, however, another fault more serious than any of these. As a matter of fact, a writer might succeed in avoiding all the others and yet, if he were guilty of this fault, fall far short of achieving a great style. It had to do with what Strachey called "the supreme quality of style," namely a power of concentration which fused all the details and parts together into a unity which possessed organic life. Froude was to Strachey an example of a talented writer and historian who, with all his gifts, lacked the power to use language in such a way as to create a living unity.[10]

When we turn to the positive side of Strachey's thinking on style, we soon realize that there was not, to him, one perfect style to the exclusion of all others. Instead, there were many good styles. There was, for instance, the style of utmost simplicity in which adequacy was the ideal. This style reached its perfection when it became absolutely transparent so that substance seemed to be everything and style merely a medium of which the reader was scarcely conscious. It possessed no ornaments, and it provided no distractions. Strachey found an example of it in the poems of Mary Elizabeth Coleridge:

> It would be difficult to imagine a less ornamented style. The splendor of mere sound, the beauty of the unanticipated word, all the graces and arts of rhetoric and "fine writing,"— these things are banished from Miss Coleridge's verse, which produces its effects in a totally different way. For it produces them, not by means of the magic of expression, but simply and directly by means of what is expressed. This is a difficult art, and it is clear enough that the essential condition of its success is that there should be something worth expressing. If

10. "Froude," *Portraits in Miniature*, p. 201.

one has only commonplaces in one's mind, one must send them
forth in gorgeous raiment, or not at all; to show them to the
world naked and unadorned is simply to court derision.[11]

The style of Mrs. Inchbald in *A Simple Story* was similar; it was
"part and parcel of her matter." Strachey contrasted it with
Thackeray's, "mere ornament, existing independently of what
he has to say." [12] Strachey liked to compare this style at its best
to plate glass as he praised it in the works of such masters of
prose as Swift and Stendhal.

Somewhat related, but more elegant, refined, and highly polished, was the great tradition of prose style which the principles
of classicism had produced as they had influenced many of the
best French writers. In this style economy, precision, cleanness, "exquisite measure," and restraint were the qualities sought after.
It was a style which always gave Strachey pleasure and which
was an important influence on his own writing.

But at the opposite pole was another style for which Strachey
had almost equal admiration. If the prose of Swift and of French
classicism may be spoken of as Doric, this may be termed Gothic.
Both styles achieve unity and cogency, but the one through restraint, order, lucidity, and simplicity and the other through abundance, complication, mystery, and complexity. Strachey praised
the Gothic style wherever he found it skillfully used. Dostoievsky
had provided a brilliant example of it:

> No doubt the most obviously disconcerting of Dostoievsky's
> characteristics is his form. Most of his works are not only
> exceedingly long, but—at any rate on a first inspection—ex-
> tremely disordered. Even in *The Brothers Karamazov,* the
> last and most carefully composed of his novels, the construc-
> tion seems often to collapse entirely; there are the strangest
> digressions and the most curious prolixities. . . . His mind,
> by its very nature, did not move on the lines of judicious
> design and careful symmetry; it brought forth under the stress

11. "The Late Miss Coleridge's Poems," *Spectator, 100* (Jan. 4, 1908), 19–20.
12. Introduction to Mrs. Inchbald's *A Simple Story, Characters and Commentaries,* p. 127.

of an unbounded inspiration, and according to the laws of an imaginative vision in which the well-balanced arrangements of the ordinary creative artist held no place. Thus the more one examines his writings and the more familiar one grows with them, the more distinctly one perceives, under the singular incoherence of their outward form, an underlying spirit dominating the most heterogeneous of their parts and giving a vital unexpected unity to the whole. The strange vast wandering conversations, the extraordinary characters rushing helter-skelter through the pages, the far-fetched immense digressions, the unexplained obscurities, the sudden, almost inconceivable incidents, the macabre humor with its extravagant exaggerations—all these things, which seem at first little more than a confused jumble of disconnected entities, gradually take shape, group themselves, and grow at last impressive and significant. The effect is like that of some gigantic Gothic cathedral, where, amid all the bewildering diversity of style and structure, a great mass of imaginative power and beauty makes itself mysteriously felt, and, with its uncertain proportions and indefinite intentions, yet seems to turn by comparison even the purest and most perfect of classical temples into something stiff and cold.[13]

The great Russian's complexity, extravagance, vigor, and boldness suggested the Elizabethans to Strachey. The first step of any good critic attempting to evaluate such a style was to understand it for what it was. It would be a great mistake to appraise Marlowe, Webster, Donne, or Shakespeare strictly in terms of norms provided by classicism. One of Dr. Johnson's shortcomings as a critic of Shakespeare lay in the fact that he did not understand Shakespeare's "bold and imaginative use of words." [14] Beddoes, a later "Elizabethan" of the nineteenth century, had been unappreciated because critics of his day did not see that his idiom had much in

---

13. "Dostoievsky," *Spectator, 109* (Sept. 28, 1912), 451–2; "A Russian Humorist," *Spectator, 112* (April 11, 1914), 610–11. The second essay has been collected in *Characters and Commentaries.*

14. "Shakespeare on Johnson," *Spectator, 101* (Aug. 1, 1908), 164–5.

common with that of the earlier time.[15] And the same error led to the discrediting of even so great a style as that of Sir Thomas Browne. What could be more futile than to seek for simple constructions and homely words in the pages of Browne's prose? Yet Strachey found Edmund Gosse doing just that in his book on Browne: Strachey said that Gosse was attacking the central principle of Browne's style, "its employment of elaborate and gorgeous latinisms." Gosse was like a man who admired the beauty of a butterfly but did not care for the wings: "To the true Browne enthusiast, indeed, there is something almost shocking about the state of mind which would exchange 'pensile' for 'hanging' and 'asperous' for 'rough,' and would do away with 'digladiation' and 'quodlibetically' altogether. The truth is, that there is a great gulf fixed between those who naturally dislike the ornate, and those who naturally love it." [16]

Strachey was well aware that the writer who, like Browne, attempted to achieve his effects through freedom, vigor, and boldness encountered dangers to which writers who used restraint and simplicity were not exposed:

> And, if not the highest of all, Browne's peak is—or at least it seems from the plains below—more difficult of access than some which are no less exalted. The road skirts the precipice the whole way. If one fails in the style of Pascal, one is merely flat; if one fails in the style of Browne, one is ridiculous. He who plays with the void, who dallies with eternity, who leaps from star to star, is in danger at every moment of being swept into utter limbo, and tossed forever in the Paradise of Fools.[17]

W. E. Henley's writings were the work of one who had been unsuccessful in his use of novel constructions and queer words:

> His pages are crowded not only with words which are in themselves unusual, but with curious and unexpected verbal

15. "The Last Elizabethan," *Books and Characters,* pp. 253–4.
16. "A New Book on Sir Thomas Browne," *Speaker,* Feb. 3, 1906, p. 441; "Sir Thomas Browne," *Books and Characters,* pp. 37–8.
17. "Sir Thomas Browne," pp. 44–5.

combinations. . . . The far-fetched words and queer constructions not only catch our attention, they worry it. . . . Henley belonged to the romantic school, but he was not a master of its method. He could imitate the boldness and the singularity of the great romantics—their extravagance of tone, their strange and varied vocabulary—but he lacked the crowning art which with them lifts what would otherwise be merely an odd assemblage of heterogeneous details into the region of imperishable beauty. Great poetry, whatever else it may be, is always harmonious; and this truth is nowhere more apparent than in those writers who, like the major Elizabethans, succeed in blending together the most diverse elements into a single whole, so that their poetry resembles a varied landscape flooded with evening light.[18]

A self-conscious style seeking to be strikingly original and forceful could thus fail just as surely as an insipid, commonplace style without surprises and without vitality. As a matter of fact, Strachey manifested both his catholicity of taste and his sense of the practical in making considerable allowances for platitudes. It was not difficult to justify them in such a writer as Macaulay. "The path of wisdom," he wrote in his early days at Cambridge, "lies midway between a platitude and a paradox." [19] Only a very extreme style would attempt to be entirely new and altogether striking and unpredictable. Something needed to be given and deemed worthy of repetition if style were to be fully communicative and effective. Macaulay deserved praise because he had talent for combining an old truth with a new manner of expressing it: "Platitudes are, after all, the current coin of artists, critics, and philosophers; without them all commerce of the mind would come to a standstill; and a great debt is owing to those who, like Macaulay, have the faculty of minting fresh and clean and shining platitudes in exhaustible abundance." [20] Strachey's own frequent use of clichés, occurring on the same pages and in

18. "The Works of W. E. Henley," *Spectator, 101* (Aug. 8, 1908), 196–7.
19. In an unpublished paper entitled "Should We Have Elected Conybeare?" (dated Nov. 14, 1903).
20. "Macaulay's Marginalia," *Spectator, 99* (Nov. 16, 1907), 743.

the same paragraphs with words and constructions of striking originality and freshness, was without any doubt deliberate and was related to the principle by which he justified platitudes in Macaulay and condemned strenuous novelty in Henley.

If one were asked to name the qualities of style which Strachey admired most, one would think immediately of many of the qualities discussed above: economy, precision, restraint, cleanness, boldness, vigor, freshness, clearness, and simplicity. Perhaps more than in any of these qualities, however, he found delight in color and sound.

Two writers whom he praised for the color which he found in their styles were Bacon and Newman. Bacon as a man he did not admire; nevertheless, his was a "consummate mastery of the English language." He did not believe that Bacon could be judged by examining separate sentences. The sentences were interdependent; and each was a charming blend of idea and color: "The true charm of Bacon's writing cannot be revealed in single sentences; it lies in the elaboration, the interconnection, the orderly development, the gradual exposition of a series of subtle and splendid thoughts. Of modern writers, Montesquieu, perhaps, comes nearest to him, but Montesquieu lacks the rich coloring which distinguishes Bacon's style. It is this characteristic—this combination of color and thought—which gives Bacon his unique position among prose writers." [21] Newman's ideas, particularly those in the religious writings, had very little appeal for Strachey. Yet he admired Newman and enjoyed reading him because Newman was a literary artist: "He lived to write his *Apologia*, and to reach immortality, neither as a thinker nor as a theologian, but as an artist who has embalmed the poignant history of an intensely human spirit in the magical spices of words." [22] Newman's style reflected a delicate sensitiveness and the most subtle nuances of color: "He was a child of the Romantic Revival, a creature of emotion and of memory, a dreamer whose secret spirit dwelt apart in delectable mountains, an artist whose subtle

21. "Bacon as a Man of Letters," *Spectator, 101* (Oct. 24, 1908), 621–2.
22. *Eminent Victorians* (London, Chatto and Windus, 1926), p. 14.

senses caught, like a shower in the sunshine, the impalpable rain-
bow of the immaterial world." [23]

Possibly Strachey's love of sound was even greater than his
love of color. One explanation of the tremendous appeal which
the drama had for him was that it provided an opportunity for
him to listen to the music of words. For him faithfulness to the
integrity of sounds in the speaking of words was almost as important as faithfulness to meaning. He could not bear any trick
of voice or affectation of speech which violated the proper sound
of a word. He objected strenuously to the way in which many
actors in 1908 spoke Shakespeare's lines: "The hideous and bar-
baric utterance with which, in our ordinary theaters, actors attempt to reproduce the poetry of Shakespeare is nothing short of
a disgrace to the stage." [24] It was a great pity, he felt, that there
were not more actors with voices like that of Granville Barker.[25]
Sarah Bernhardt rose to supreme heights as an actress as she
demonstrated her ability to speak adequately the great lines
from Racine: "The words boomed and crashed with a superhuman resonance which shook the spirit of the hearer like a leaf
in the wind." [26] Much of the charm which Sir Thomas Browne's
prose had for Strachey lay in the sounds of its words. We have
Strachey's own statement concerning how much he enjoyed reading Browne aloud at Cambridge: "The present writer, at any
rate, can bear witness to the splendid echo of Browne's syllables
amid learned and ancient walls; for he has known, he believes,
few happier moments than those in which he has rolled the period
of the *Hydriotaphia* out to the darkness and the nightingales
through the studious cloisters of Trinity." [27] Milton was, of course,
one of the great masters of verbal sound. In his work there was
much worth reading for the sake of the sound alone:

> Milton, fond as he was of crowding a word with meanings,
> was equally fond of using words which have very little mean-

23. *Ibid.,* p. 13.
24. "Mr. Granville Barker," *Spectator, 100* (March 28, 1908), 499–500.
25. *Ibid.*
26. "Sarah Bernhardt," *Characters and Commentaries,* pp. 259–60.
27. "Sir Thomas Browne," p. 47.

ing at all. His catalogues of proper names are hardly more than processions of gorgeous sounds. . . . Who or what is "Bellerus old"? Probably nobody knows, and certainly nobody ought to care. . . . Let us not look up latitudes, nor search into history; let us listen to the mysterious music of the words, and be content. The truth is that only a poet is fit to be Milton's lexicographer.[28]

Comus was to Strachey "a play of prigs," with too much talk and too little action. Nevertheless, it was in large part redeemed by the exquisite melody of its verses. While watching a performance of the masque at Cambridge in 1908, the words of the old Cavalier in Scott's Woodstock came into Strachey's mind, and he wished to interrupt the play for a moment and speak them: " 'These verses flow sweetly, and sound in my ears like the well-touched warbling of a lute. . . . Repeat me them again, slowly and deliberately; for I always love to hear poetry twice, the first time for sound, the latter time for sense.' " [29] Part of Pope's greatness as a poet lay likewise in his mastery of verbal sounds. Through his "subtle and dexterous handling" of the heroic couplet, he had avoided monotony and had achieved "those fine shades and delicate gradations of sound and expression of which the secret is only known to the true artist." It was here, Strachey said, that Pope was supreme. And he asked: "Who can be surprised that Pope said he cared for sound more than anything else?" [30]

Strachey found this music lacking in the verses of Thomas Hardy, a poet whose genius he considered "peculiarly modern." He had great admiration for Hardy, with his "sardonic realism" and with his "ironic presentments of human relationships and human follies and human insignificance, in his sad and subtle scrutinies of the oddly interwoven grandness and futilities of ordinary life." His very harshness and clumsiness were a reflection of the modern temper and manner. "He speaks; he does not sing. Or rather, he talks—in the quiet voice of a modern man or

28. "Milton's Words," Spectator, 99 (Dec. 14, 1907), 991–2.
29. "Comus at Cambridge," Spectator, 101 (July 18, 1908), 94–5.
30. "Alexander Pope," Spectator, 103 (Nov. 20, 1909), 847–8.

woman, who finds it difficult, as modern men and women do, to put into words exactly what is in the mind. He is incorrect; but then how unreal and artificial a thing is correctness! He fumbles; but it is that fumbling that brings him so near to ourselves." [31] Strachey would certainly not have contended for a single moment that modern writers should avoid the influence of Hardy and return as far as possible to Tennyson's sweet melody. Yet his own writing was in the tradition which made much of euphony. He must have believed that even in a world in which noise, groping, awkwardness, and lack of harmony were prevalent in the thoughts and actions of men and were reflected in the very idiom through which they tried to communicate with one another there still could be great delight and profit in listening to the words of older writers whose prose as well as whose verses sang and that there might be further profit in attempting to keep alive their way of writing. He may have reasoned that if modern life and language threatened to become drab and unmelodious the artist clearly had the duty of using the means which he had at his disposal in order to enrich literature, as far as possible, and through literature life, by providing color and music in generous measure.

31. "A Short Guide to Thomas Hardy," *New Statesman,* March 11, 1916, pp. 551–2; "Mr. Hardy's New Poems," *Characters and Commentaries,* p. 181.

CHAPTER 13

Style in Action

FROM FIRST TO LAST Strachey's style was clearly marked, recognizably individual, and, in almost every sentence, impressive. His friends considered it important and were to some extent influenced by it while he was still at Cambridge; and the reviewers of his writings have nearly always treated it as noteworthy. Some of them have praised it very highly; others have pointed out what they considered faults.

At the time of his death, the *Spectator* spoke of him as "a writer's writer, like Mr. Max Beerbohm," and declared that the "careful perfection of his style was a wholesome influence in an age which provides too much dilapidated prose." [1] Beerbohm himself expressed great admiration for Strachey's style. "Here was a delicately effulgent master," he said, "a perfect master, of English prose." He added, however, that in his opinion Strachey was not a man of genius and explained that Strachey's artistry was too careful to be that of a genius: "Very exquisite literary artists seldom are men of genius. Genius tends to be careless in its strength. Genius is, by the nature of it, always in rather a hurry. Genius can't be bothered about perfection." [2] This is not the place, if there is one, to define genius. And an attempt to prove that Strachey was an unquestionable genius would be tedious, to say the least. Possibly, however, Sir Max's assumptions concerning the

1. Jan. 30, 1932, p. 139. The *Spectator* also says here: "It is many years since he wrote much for us, but we remember with some pride his early literary criticisms, particularly of French literature, that appeared in the *Spectator*."

2. *Lytton Strachey* (New York, Alfred A. Knopf, 1943), pp. 9–10.

nature of genius owe too much to romantic ideas which would
have it that in genius energy always excels discipline. Some allowance must certainly be made for the kind of genius that one
associates with Sophocles, Virgil, Racine, and Ben Jonson. This
very union of discipline and vigor in Strachey's style has brought
forth high praise from Clifford Bower-Shore: "In all his work
Strachey conveys the magic, the power, and the illimitable range
of the English language. His prose suggests far more than a
stimulation of associated ideas. . . . Strong and supple, disciplined and devoid of fervid rhetoric, it abounds in vigor coupled
with sensitive vitality." [3] Joseph Wood Krutch has expressed his
admiration for Strachey's combination of a good style with good
sense:

> To him one goes, not primarily for fact and not primarily
> for the most modern interpretations of either historical or
> other phenomena, but for the same literary delight which
> one seeks in Gibbon. Take up any one of his essays and one
> may be sure of several rare and agreeable things. One may
> be sure that there will be no windiness or absurdity, no
> extravagance, and no folly. One may be sure also that one
> will find said all that shrewdness, wit, and cultivated common
> sense can say. There will be a beginning, a middle, and an
> end, and no loose threads left dangling.[4]

Strachey was to P. M. Jack a writer who "could not write badly
and never wrote idly." As Jack studied the essays collected in
Characters and Commentaries, he came to the conclusion that
the style of the earlier ones was a little too obviously balanced
but that in the later ones Strachey's style improved and progressed
"from pattern to design." [5]

Most of those who have found fault with Strachey's style have

3. *Lytton Strachey: An Essay* (London, Fenland Press, 1933), p. 88. George
Dangerfield has written that Strachey was "by way of being a master of English prose." "Lytton Strachey," *Saturday Review of Literature, 18* (July 23,
1938), 3.
4. "Lytton Strachey," *Nation, 134* (Feb. 17, 1932), 200.
5. New York *Times Book Review,* Nov. 12, 1933, p. 2.

had in mind something like Jack's distinction between pattern and design. They have believed that Strachey did not entirely succeed in concealing the devices of rhetoric even in some of the later writings. Louis Kronenberger, for instance, although conceding that Strachey had erudition, irony, and even style, has said that Strachey's was not a great style. In his opinion, Strachey was a great rhetorician rather than a great stylist. "We see through rhetoric. We can only see *into* the finest natural prose." [6] Similarly, Prince Mirsky has complained that Strachey had "a dangerous mannerism of beginning and ending his articles with certain rhetorical flourishes." [7] Strachey's success in exploiting rhetoric, in the opinion of R. L. Mégroz also, fell short of completeness. According to Mégroz, however, in refusing to neglect rhetoric, Strachey set a salutary example to an age which had fallen into slovenly ways of writing prose: "Though he often lacked the power that would have justified his rhetoric, Lytton Strachey's rhetorical manner in an epoch when suspicion of the ornate has been carried past all reasonable bounds, will probably prove to be his chief, or at least his most influential and useful quality as a prose writer." [8]

Strachey's intention, we know, was to produce literary art. Although he believed and often said that art was magic, he certainly did not assume that magic comes into being without aids or means. His point was simply that to understand the aids and means was not to learn in full the secret of the magic. He himself drew extensively on the vast resources of craftsmanship that had been handed down to him in literary tradition. He would never have dreamed of arguing what some prose writers of today have assumed, namely that writing well is entirely an act of spontaneous intuition and that technique is not needed to further the purposes

6. "Lytton Strachey," *Bookman* (N.Y.), *71* (July 1930), 375–80.

7. D. S. Mirsky, "Mr. Lytton Strachey," *London Mercury,* 8 (June, 1923), 175–84.

8. Introduction to Bower-Shore's *Lytton Strachey,* n. 3, above. The curious may want to examine Hugh Kingsmill's parody of Strachey's style in "Joseph, from *Eminent Egyptians,*" *English Review,* 54 (April 1932), 399–404.

of art. His own writings were all produced in a workshop where care had been taken to arrange the materials in good order and where a great variety of tools were ready at hand. He would have probably been the first to admit that some of his writings showed flaws relating to craftsmanship—that occasionally his work appeared with the tool-marks still showing or that at times it smelled of the workshop.

It is interesting and profitable to examine Strachey's style in the light of the principles and practices of Wordsworth and Milton —two poets whom he greatly admired. In the preface to the *Lyrical Ballads* Wordsworth had had much to say about a literary art in which may be perceived "similitude in dissimilitude, dissimilitude in similitude," of the principle by which art is thought of as the product of a weaving process in which the fixed and constant warp becomes delightfully intermeshed with a variable woof. Wordsworth used this method, as Coleridge pointed out, again and again, so often that it became thoroughly characteristic of him. But Milton used it even more brilliantly. And to Strachey Milton was the supreme artist among English poets. His art had exemplified with great distinction the principle by which the union of sameness and variety and of law with freedom became an inexhaustible source of joy. No one who has read Strachey's writings thoughtfully can doubt that they were written with this principle in mind.

We cannot read Strachey, in the first place, without being impressed by the sameness which stamps itself upon every page. His sentences are all the product of a steadfast mind and a clear, definite purpose. It is not merely that his point of view is fixed and that his habits of expression are formed. It is not merely that he is obviously determined to say nothing that is not sensible. Fully as important are certain qualities of style, possibly to him ideals of style, which he never allows himself to forget. One of these is lucidity. We simply cannot imagine Lytton Strachey lapsing into obscurity or dallying lazily with the ambiguous.[9] Another

9. Leonard Bacon has written: "When you spoke of his book, hateful to say, you had to use words like *lucid* and *penetrating*. Wrong he might be, but

quality of style for which he constantly sought was penetration. He was not satisfied with mere exposition; there must also be revelation. Style must possess and stimulate insight. He also wished for precision, for diction that was clean, exact, and crisp. Another striking quality of style which he desired and which his writings possess in unusual measure is maturity. His is the kind of maturity that treats his readers as highly intelligent adults. It is not the false maturity of esoteric sophistication so common in the literary criticism of our day. Esoteric sophistication in style is motivated by the writer's desire to dazzle the reader and give the impression that he knows more than the reader knows or could ever possibly understand. The motivation from which the real maturity of Lytton Strachey's style arises is just the opposite. The relationship which he establishes with his readers is a friendly, democratic one. His allusions, his questions, and his insinuations are all phrased in such a manner as to flatter the reader's intelligence, and he never seems to lack confidence in his reader's ability to get the point. He is a reasonable man writing for reasonable men; and he assumes that while things are being talked about they may as well be discussed on the highest possible level.

Other qualities which Strachey desired in his style were color, humor, appeal to the ear, and appeal to the imagination. Humor he valued highly, both because he found it delightful in itself and because it provided his style with a highly effective balance wheel. Through the use of color, appropriate verbal sounds, and well-chosen images he was able to enrich his style, to increase its range, and to endow it with some of the potencies which are to be found in poetry.

All these qualities of style are woven into the warp of Strachey's style and give it constancy. Not to be overlooked also among such qualities is that of good form—the kind of good form which

---

he was never unclear in his life, and no one's eye has ever glanced more carelessly or easily right through a grindstone." "An Eminent Post-Victorian," *Yale Review,* N.S. *30* (Winter 1941), 311. And Guy Boas has also said: "That which he prized most in literature was lucidity." *Lytton Strachey,* English Association Pamphlet No. 93 (Nov. 1935), p. 7.

can result only from obedience to the generally accepted conventions of good writing. His writings show that he realized the importance of structure in the sentence, organization in the paragraph, and the outline in the essay or book. Likewise, his punctuation is almost always strictly conventional. He does not seem to have had great respect for that kind of cleverness which can display itself only at the expense of helpless comma rules. His interest in rhetoric and extensive exploitation of it are closely related to his general respect for the conventions of good writing. He wished to communicate as fully and to be as effective as possible, and in the principles of rhetoric he found a time-tested means conveniently at hand.

Thus Strachey assumed, as Milton, Wordsworth, and many other writers have done, that good writing should have a warp, qualities making for sameness running throughout the whole. But he also wished, as they did, for freshness and variety. He found equal delight in the uniformity of classicism and the variety of romanticism but highest delight in the union of the two. And he found plenty of opportunity for achieving variety without seriously violating uniformity. He did so by creating an interplay between long sentences and paragraphs and short sentences and paragraphs, between the simple and the compound or complex, between the commonplace and the singular, between the emphatic and the easy or relaxed, between the assertive and the insinuative or interrogative, between the serious and the playful, between the ponderous and the light, between the choppy and the smooth, between the rapid and the slow, between the vigorous and the delicate, between the whispered and the exaggerated, between the redundant and the restrained, and between lengthy ornate Latin expressions and short, simple Saxon words.

His skill is nowhere seen at better advantage than in some of his narrative passages. He enjoyed stories, particularly those which go to make up history, and he always told them well. His narrative style is nearly always vigorous, direct, economical, and vivid. It never loses its sense of direction or point; and it rarely misses an opportunity to gather humor along the way. It is admirable even in his extremely early writings. The following passage, dealing with the Electress Sophia and giving a rapid survey of events which in some hands would become extremely tedious, is from a review published in 1904:

> On the death of Mary, William was free to marry again, and there was no reason to expect that Anne's numerous progeny would all die before her. Yet William never remarried, and the death of the Duke of Gloucester in 1700 removed the last impediment to the succession of Sophia. In the same year another death hastened on what was now in any case inevitable. Charles II of Spain, after incredible delays, expired, bequeathing the whole of his vast possessions to the grandson of Louis XIV. In an evil hour Louis accepted the testament; the War of the Spanish Succession hove violently into sight; the whole of Europe was ranged upon opposing sides, and in the following year the Act of Settlement secured to England at once the alliance of Hanover and a Protestant dynasty.
>
> That Sophia herself never reaped what had been so miraculously sown is, perhaps, the most fitting end to the story. Lingering in Herrenhausen amongst her women and her swans, conversing with Leibnitz upon metaphysics and diplomacy, trudging daily the gravel paths about her orangery between the clipped hedges and the statues and the artificial lakes, she passed the final years of her life in retirement and in peace.[10]

The style here, early as it is, is neat and firm. It uses rhetoric without stiffness. It flows easily and freely and yet obeys the conventions. It satisfies the eye and pleases the ear. And a spark of humor runs up and down the lines. Not least important, it is obviously written for mature readers who already know the general facts about the history of Europe and the succession to the English throne and who know who Leibnitz is.

The same sense of historic significance and the same respect for the reader's intelligence, with perhaps greater restraint and correspondingly greater power of suggestion, go into the making

10. "The Electress Sophia," *Spectator, 92* (Jan. 9, 1904), 55–6.

of the following passage from *Queen Victoria,* in which the queen disciplines her grandson who will some day be Kaiser William II of Germany:

> She took a particular delight in her grandchildren, to whom she showed an indulgence which their parents had not always enjoyed, though, even to her grandchildren, she could be, when the occasion demanded it, severe. The eldest of them, the little Prince Wilhelm of Prussia, was a remarkably headstrong child; he dared to be impertinent even to his grandmother; and once, when she told him to bow to a visitor at Osborne, he disobeyed her outright. This would not do: the order was sternly repeated, and the naughty boy, noticing that his kind grandmama had suddenly turned into a most terrifying lady, submitted his will to hers, and bowed very low indeed.

The situation treated here is a dramatic one of a rather simple sort composed of a preparation, a complication, a climax, and a result. Its appeal is mainly to the historic sense. Strachey's narrative style is fully capable, however, of dealing with dramatic situations which are much more complex and which stir our emotions to much greater depths. The account of Prince Albert's death in *Queen Victoria* provides us with an example:

> Sometimes his mind wandered; sometimes the distant past came rushing upon him; he heard the birds in the early morning, and was at Rosenau again, a boy. Or Victoria would come and read to him "Peveril of the Peak," and he showed that he could follow the story, and then she would bend over him, and he would murmur "liebes Frauchen" and "gutes Weibchen," stroking her cheek. Her distress and her agitation were great, but she was not seriously frightened. . . . On the morning of December 14, Albert, just as she had expected, seemed to be better; perhaps the crisis was over. But in the course of the day there was a serious relapse. Then at last she allowed herself to see that she was standing on the edge of an appalling gulf. The whole family was

summoned, and, one after another, the children took a silent farewell of their father. "It was a terrible moment," Victoria wrote in her diary, "but, thank God! I was able to command myself, and to be perfectly calm, and remained sitting by his side." He murmured something, but she could not hear what it was; she thought he was speaking in French. Then all at once he began to arrange his hair, "just as he used to do when well and he was dressing." "Es ist kleines Fräuchen," she whispered to him; and he seemed to understand. For a moment, towards the evening, she went into another room, but was immediately called back; she saw at a glance that a ghastly change had taken place. As she knelt by the bed, he breathed deeply, breathed gently, breathed at last no more. His features became perfectly rigid; she shrieked one long wild shriek that rang through the terror-stricken castle—and understood that she had lost him for ever.

The appeal here is not so much to our sense of history as to our elemental humanity. We are in the presence of a great and horrible universal which Strachey's simple, unhurried, but relentless style compels us to face. A single pompous phrase would have destroyed the whole effect, and restraint rules every sentence up to the uncontrollable outbreak of anguish in the last. How unpretentious but how appropriate the rhythms of the sentences are! "The whole family was summoned, and, one after another, the children took a silent farewell of their father." "As she knelt by his bed, he breathed deeply, breathed gently, breathed at last no more." There is rhetoric here, but it is disciplined rhetoric completely subdued and serving inconspicuously as a means to an end. The passage is strong in terror and deeply moving in its tenderness. It would lose much without such details as Albert's memories of his boyhood, his careful arranging of his hair near the end, and the little German phrases of endearment which he and Victoria whisper to one another.

Strachey was too much interested in literary craftsmanship to ignore the possibilities of the paragraph. He did not, therefore, like many modern journalists and short-story writers, commit himself to the use of the short paragraph exclusively. It was not merely that addiction to the short paragraph meant that there could be no effective variety in the length of paragraphs. It was not merely that a sequence of paragraphs all of which were short would provide him with no opportunity for achieving emphasis, as he liked to do, by placing a short paragraph immediately after several extremely long ones. Much more important to Strachey was the consideration of what could be done on the inside of a paragraph which granted commodious length to its creator. He did not like, to borrow a figure from Coleridge, a series of short panting paragraphs but preferred one that could take a deep breath of thought. In long paragraphs a variety of patterns might be employed; emphatic constructions could be piled upon emphatic constructions like thunderhead clouds piled upon one another; heaviness could become more heavy through a process of accumulation; and rapidity would have room enough to run a delightful race. Climax could extend itself and gather emphasis. Cataloguing could be used effectively, as it is in Strachey's listing of the many possessions which the acquisitive and thrifty Victoria watched over in her old age. In the long paragraph, also, sentences could be displayed in families, bearing a family likeness and functioning in an organic unity, and yet revealing individual differences all the more obvious and interesting because of the very qualities in which each sentence shared. In short, long paragraphs gave Strachey an opportunity not to be found in a succession of short ones, that of achieving variety in many ways through the reconciliation of similitude and dissimilitude.

Strachey's interest in effective sentence construction, like his interest in all other matters pertaining to style, appeared early. Sentences with excellent patterns are to be found, as we have seen, in his parody of "Little Red Riding Hood," which may have been written as early as 1897. In his first published essays, likewise, beginning with "Two Frenchmen" (October 1903), the reader can select without any difficulty examples of almost every kind of sentence pattern. The following sentence dealing with Macaulay comes from "Horace Walpole," published in May 1904: "The criticism is written in the great reviewer's most trenchant style; it contains passages which stand, for clearness and brilliancy, on the level of his cleverest and most brilliant work; every other sentence is an epigram, and all the paragraphs go off like Catherine-wheels; everything is present, in fact, that could be desired, except the remotest understanding of the subject." This is an effective sentence, employing parallelism and balance, pauses and rhythm, arrangement and surprise. It vigorously praises Macaulay with a loud voice only at last to reduce him to nothing with a whisper. Many such sentences, highly interesting in terms of literary technique, are scattered through the early essays.

As we examine Strachey's sentences, in his later work as well as in the early essays, two facts impress us. One is the constant and persistent care with which he shaped almost every sentence that he wrote; the other is the great variety of patterns which he used. It would not be easy to prove that he preferred any device of sentence construction or any form of the sentence. His style flows so easily from sentence to sentence that one is scarcely conscious of the numerous shifts from device to device and from pattern to pattern. Here, as in dealing with paragraphs, he followed the principle of achieving variety within uniformity. Like all other masters of prose style, he accomplishes much by varying the length of his sentences. He does much, also, with parallelism and balance:

> It was not by gentle sweetness and womanly self-abnegation that she had brought order out of chaos in the Scutari Hospitals, that, from her own resources, she had clothed the British Army, that she had spread her dominion over the serried and reluctant powers of the official world; it was by strict method, by stern discipline, by rigid attention to detail, by ceaseless labor, by the fixed determination of an indomitable will.

> The modern reader of *Tom Brown's Schooldays* searches in vain for any reference to compulsory games, house colors, or cricket averages. In those days, when boys played games they played them for pleasure; but in those days the prefectorial

system—the system which hands over the life of a school to an oligarchy of a dozen youths of seventeen—was still in its infancy, and had not yet borne its fruit.

He also likes the periodic sentence, which uses both syntax and arrangement to create suspense and to throw emphasis upon what comes last:

> Nor, it is to be hoped, need any Englishman be reminded that the consequences of a system of government in which the arbitrary will of an individual takes the place of the rule of law are apt to be disgraceful and absurd.

> An uneasy suspicion gradually arose: it began to dawn upon the Roman authorities that Dr. Newman was a man of ideas.

> If Victoria had died in the early seventies, there can be little doubt that the voice of the world would have pronounced her a failure.

Strachey does not overwork the periodic sentence, however, and thus produce a style that is too strenuous; instead, he uses it occasionally against a context of sentences which have relaxed patterns.

Contrast is another device of which Strachey is fond. The following sentence combines it with cataloguing and parallelism: "Such were the daily spectacles of colored pomp and of antique solemnity, which—so long as the sun was shining, at any rate—dazzled the onlooker into a happy forgetfulness of the reverse side of the Papal dispensation—the nauseating filth of the highways, the cattle stabled in the palaces of the great, and the fever flitting through the ghastly tenements of the poor." He may combine contrast with balance and with the emphasis which can be given to a word by placing it at the end: "Voltaire was a scoundrel; but he was a scoundrel of genius."

Many modern writers are afraid to use repetition and as a result fall into one of the most irritating vices of style—into what Sir Arthur Quiller-Couch condemned under the name "the trick of elegant variation." They studiously avoid repeating any im-

portant word and seek self-consciously and strenuously for
synonyms. Strachey writes in the great tradition of style which
makes skillful repetition a virtue. In the following sentence
repetition is effectively combined with balance and with periodic
structure: "Henceforward female duty, female elegance, female
enthusiasm, hemmed her completely in; and her spirit, amid the
enclosing folds, was hardly reached by those two great influences,
without which no growing life can truly prosper—humor and
imagination." The repetition often goes far beyond the bound
of single sentences. Strachey likes to get hold of a word that suggests possibilities and, alertly catching it on the bounce, toss it
up in the air again and again, testing, as it were, its true weight.
Often, too, he will repeat a whole phrase or group of words
through sentence after sentence and paragraph after paragraph.
The repeated words may be a character tag, as they are in
"Florence Nightingale," when we hear more than once that "the
Bison was bullyable" and that Clough wrapped up parcels in
brown paper. This device is used in connection with Prince
Albert also; he had a habit, we are told many times, of making
a memorandum, whatever the occasion and however important
or unimportant it might be. Sometimes the repetition is for purposes of insinuation. In "Cardinal Manning" Strachey expresses
great curiosity about what was said at Manning's "mysterious interview" with Pope Pius IX three years before his coversion,
and then begins to ask again and again, "What did Pio Nono
say?" At times also repetition is used in the manner of the leit-
motif in comic opera. Such a term as the "Holy Ghost," used in
connection with King Philip of Spain or Cardinal Manning or
Gladstone or General Gordon, was sure in Strachey's hands to be
tossed in the air many times as though it were assumed that the
more it was tossed up the more ridiculous it became. The term
in itself seems to have amused Strachey, and it might almost be
thought of as his favorite comic character.

Even when he did not repeat it, Strachey was very fond of the
question as a device of style. Here, for one thing, was another
way of varying the sentence patterns and of relieving the montony
that might be produced by a series of affirmations. Strachey knew

that the occasional flashing of a question was a great help in keeping readers awake. But it was equally useful for purposes of insinuation and emphasis. Such are its uses in the following passage on Gladstone: "In the physical universe there are no chimeras. But man is more various than nature; was Mr. Gladstone, perhaps, a chimera of the spirit? Did his very essence lie in the confusion of incompatibles? His very essence?" Question presses upon question here, as often in Strachey's work, so that the point cannot be missed. Sometimes questions in a series may provide a summary and a transition, as in this passage from "General Gordon": "What should he do next? To what remote corner or what enormous stage, to what self-sacrificing drudgeries, or what resounding exploits, would the hand of God lead him now? He waited, in an odd hesitation." Strachey also used questions frequently to provoke thought and fresh evaluation of conventional ideas. In the following passage he wishes the reader to test the wisdom underlying the kind of strict moral instruction to which Victoria and Albert subjected the future Edward VII: "The experiment had never been made of letting Bertie enjoy himself. But why should it have been? 'Life is composed of duties.' What possible place could there be for enjoyment in the existence of a Prince of Wales?" Questions may also be very effective in the analysis of character, as in that of Prince Albert:

> Albert, certainly, seemed to be everything that Stockmar could have wished—virtuous, industrious, persevering, intelligent. And yet—why was it?—all was not well with him. He was sick at heart. . . . He was lonely, not merely with the loneliness of exile but with the loneliness of conscious and unrecognized superiority. . . . There was something that he wanted and that he could never get. What was it? Some absolute, some ineffable sympathy? Some extraordinary, some sublime success? . . . Who was there who appreciated him, really and truly? Who *could* appreciate him in England? And if the gentle virtue of an inward excellence availed so little, could he expect more from the hard ways of skill and force?

It would be an error to think of Strachey's use of questions as merely a mechanical device which he had discovered and learned to use with ingenuity. His questions spring from something fundamental in his mind. They are related to his admiration for science and to the great fascination which psychological probing had for him. He was himself clearly aware that his was an interrogative mind.

His mind was also one that delighted in expressing itself through the concrete and the specific. His extensive use of quotations is related to this fact. He realized their value in literary criticism and objected to discussions of literature that were limited to abstractions and generalities and that did not give examples of the literature being discussed. This fault was to be found in W. P. Ker's *Essays on Medieval Literature:* "The most penetrating discussion of literary work is never quite satisfactory unless it is supported by the testimony of the work discussed. It is like a descriptive catalogue of pictures without the pictures themselves." [11] It was possible, however, to carry a good thing too far. Judgment and consideration for the intelligent reader was needed in selecting passages to be quoted just as they were needed in all other matters concerning style. W. W. Greg's *Pastoral Poetry and Pastoral Drama* provided many quotations which were unnecessary: "Though there are many quotations which it is pleasant to meet, either because one knows them already or because one does not know them at all, it is somewhat distressing to have nothing taken for granted. That there is beautiful poetry in *Comus* is a proposition which hardly needs demonstration; and who wishes for a paraphrase of *Lycidas?*" [12]

This habitual preference for the specific and concrete became united with a marked dramatic instinct in the quotations which Strachey used in his biographical writing. He believed that his

11. "Medieval Studies," *Spectator,* 97 (Nov. 17, 1906), 786–7. It should be noted that in general Strachey praises Ker here as an extremely helpful guide for those who feel uncomfortable in studying the Middle Ages: "He has provided, so to speak, an express train to the Middle Ages; he has built a pleasant inn for the traveller in those inhospitable regions; and he has placed the windows so that they overlook the finest views."

12. "The Pastoral," *Spectator,* 97 (July 28, 1906), 132–3.

characters would soon let us know what they were if they were allowed to talk. If they were wise, their words would reflect their wisdom. If they were stupid or absurd, their words would give them away. Concerning Strachey's quotations from characters whom he does not like, F. L. Lucas has written: "He did not denounce his characters; he let them speak for themselves. The resulting laughter was usually deserved." [13] The skill with which Strachey could use quotations to make those who speak the words appear ridiculous is shown in the following passage from "Voltaire and Frederick the Great." Although the passage is short, in it three people speak, and all three become absurd: "As for La Mettrie, he made his escape in a different manner—by dying after supper one evening of a surfeit of pheasant pie. 'Jesus! Marie!' he gasped, as he felt the pains of death upon him. 'Ah!' said a priest who had been sent for, 'vous voilà enfin retourné à ces noms consolateurs.' La Mettrie, with an oath, expired; and Frederick, on hearing of this unorthodox conclusion, remarked, 'J'en suis bien aise, pour le repos de son âme.' " In *Queen Victoria* the reader can have little doubt about King William's simple-mindedness after Strachey provides us with the following account of his religious conversion: "For many years his Majesty had been a devout believer. 'When I was a young man,' he once explained at a public banquet, 'as well as I can remember, I believed in nothing but pleasure and folly—nothing at all. But when I went to sea, got into a gale, and saw the wonders of the mighty deep, then I believed; and I have been a sincere Christian ever since.' " Nothing could give a better impression of the banality which often characterized Queen Victoria's utterances than such quotations as the following: " 'Albert said,' she noted next day, 'that the chief beauty of mountain scenery consists in its frequent changes.' " " 'We were always in the habit,' wrote Her Majesty, 'of conversing with the Highlanders—with whom one comes so much in contact in the Highlands.' " Those who know the specious nature of the reasoning in Paley's *Evidences of Christianity* learn much about Manning's shortcomings as a logician from this quotation: "He read Paley's *Evidences*. 'I took in the whole argument,' wrote

13. "Lytton Strachey: An Artist in History," *Observer,* Jan. 24, 1932, p. 5.

Manning, when he was over seventy, 'and I thank God that nothing has ever shaken it.' " Possibly Manning's relation to Newman may have been less difficult than Strachey represents it as being. But the following quotation from a letter to Manning leaves no doubt in the mind that Newman himself did not consider it a happy one. "I can only repeat what I said when you last heard from me. I do not know whether I am on my head or my heels when I have active relations with you. In spite of my friendly feelings, this is the judgment of my intellect." Readers who have been slow to accept Strachey's view of General Gordon as a brave man tragically led to his destruction by a muddled mind and love of glory will be likely to concede that the argument is clinched in this quotation from Gordon himself shortly before his death: "What holes do I not put myself into! And for what? So mixed are my ideas. I believe ambition put me here in this ruin." The antithesis between Strachey's almost unrestrained sense of humor and Dr. Arnold's complete lack of humor comes into sharp focus in this quotation: " 'Nowhere,' said Dr. Arnold,' nowhere is Satan's work more evidently manifest than in turning holy things to ridicule.' " Quotations, however, are tricky and may suggest to the reader questions about the author who selected them as well as throw light on the person whose words they are. The last quotation, taken with the other evidence which Strachey provides, is certain to give the impression that Dr. Arnold lacked humor; but, at the same time, it may cause the reader to begin wondering just where the line should be drawn in the exercise of one's sense of humor, to ask whether or not there are some things which should not be laughed at, and to question whether or not Strachey always kept within the proper limits. We know that he had limits, but they were formulated in terms of the practice exemplified by the great tradition of satire and in terms of humanistic values and not in terms of respect for "holy things." Even so, a religious reader may wonder whether Strachey allowed his sense of humor too much scope.

But Strachey did not write for religious readers, not for the conventional sort at least. And in all fairness to him, it is well to note that his quotations are not always used for the purpose of ridicule. In *Queen Victoria,* for instance, although there are numerous quotations which do not spare the queen, there are also some very significant ones which reflect great credit upon her. Her strength of character, her courage, and her political foresight are all clearly indicated in this one: "Not once, not twice, but many times she held over his head the formidable menace of her imminent abdication. 'If England,' she wrote to Beaconsfield, 'is to kiss Russia's feet, she will not be a party to the humiliation of England and would lay down her crown.'" We stand in awe of her sense of what is fitting, her tenderness, and her admirable humanity as we read this passage treating the death of Disraeli:

> When she knew that the end was inevitable, she seemed, by a pathetic instinct, to divest herself of her royalty, and to shrink, with hushed gentleness, beside him, a woman and nothing more. "I send some Osborne primroses," she wrote to him with touching simplicity, "and I meant to pay you a little visit this week, but I thought it better you should be quite quiet and not speak. And I beg you will be very good and obey the doctors."

Although in Strachey humor is never far away from such passages, they do not suffer from the fact. Strachey had learned from great predecessors, including Chaucer and Shakespeare, that in human life the serious, the admirable, the sad, the holy, and the ridiculous often dwell near one another. He knew that great men often may appear ridiculous, that amusing things may happen at funerals, and that the behavior of both the congregation and the preachers in churches may be very funny indeed.

If he had been a religious man, certainly he would have thought of God as possessing the attribute of humor. He would have reasoned that that Being who created a world in which there is so much to laugh at must have had the power to laugh and to enjoy laughter. He could not approve of Florence Nightingale's conception of God: "She could not bear to smile or to be gay, 'because she hated God to hear her laugh, as if she had not repented of her sin.'" Strachey, like Fielding, found the world full of humor which, like manna from Heaven, had only to be discovered in order to be enjoyed. Much of the humor in his writings is of this kind: the slapstick of the mountainous Hume, at a party of laughing young ladies, attempting to sit in a chair much too weak and suddenly subsiding to the ground, and of old Lord Rolle tripping over his mantle and falling down the steps at Victoria's coronation; the delightfully eccentric ghost which he found in Aubrey's *Miscellanies* who would answer no questions but disappeared "with a curious Perfume and most melodious Twang"; and the intrinsically absurd incidents in the lives of Doctors North and Colbatch. This is not to say that Strachey does not use style to heighten the humor of what was already funny. For instance, he tells us that Colbatch's formidable antagonist, the great classical scholar Richard Bentley, dealt with his opponents "as if they had been corrupt readings in an old manuscript."

There are many passages in his writings, such as the two given below, in which the humor lies almost entirely in the style. The first deals with the Catholic Council which met to formulate the doctrine of Papal Infallibility:

> For two months the Fathers deliberated; through fifty sessions they sought the guidance of the Holy Ghost. The wooden seats, covered though they were with Brussels carpet, grew harder and harder; and still the mitred Councillors sat on. The Pope himself began to grow impatient; for one thing, he declared, he was being ruined by the mere expense of lodging and keeping the multitude of his adherents. "Questi infallibilisti mi faranno fallire," said his Holiness.

In the second Strachey combines Florence Nightingale's interest in sanitation, her interest in work, and her interest in God:

> Yet her conception of God was certainly not orthodox. She felt toward Him as she might have felt towards a glorified sanitary engineer; and in some of her speculations she seems hardly to distinguish between the Deity and the Drains. As one turns over these singular pages, one has the impression

that Miss Nightingale has got the Almighty too into her clutches, and that, if He is not careful, she will kill Him with overwork.

The kinds of humor to be found in Strachey's works are greatly varied. Much of it springs from irreverence toward objects which custom, convention, and orthodoxy have accepted as holy. Some rises from incongruity or a ridiculous hodge-podge of details. Some is based on pure absurdity, an utter and complete violation of common sense. Much of it exploits with great skill the device of bathos, a quick sinking from the lofty to the commonplace. And much of it is rooted in irony, an irony which is the product of close, philosophical observation of human affairs, with their strange quirks and unpredictable twists.

The humor of irreverence appears in many of Strachey's writings long before the time of *Eminent Victorians*. It would be difficult to find a more lively example of it than that given by the following taken from an essay published in April 1905, "Voltaire's Tragedies":

> But lo! when the Governor spoke, it was seen at once that an extraordinary change had come over his mind. He was no longer proud, he was no longer cruel, he was no longer unforgiving; he was kind, humble, and polite; in short, he had repented. Everybody was pardoned, and everybody recognized the truth of Christianity. And their faith was particularly strengthened when Don Gusman, invoking a final blessing upon Alzire and Zamore, expired in the arms of Don Alvarez.

This is a shocking passage to those orthodox Christians who insist that it makes religious conversion appear ridiculous. Actually Strachey is not ridiculing Christian conversion so much as he is Voltaire, who had used this highly improbable situation as the ending to one of his plays, and the eighteenth-century French audiences which applauded such endings. Likewise, it is not God that Strachey satirizes in dealing with Florence Nightingale, Cardinal Manning, General Gordon, and King Philip of Spain, but

ridiculous thinking about God, used for purposes of rationalizing
or for cloaking the ego, and ridiculous behavior related to such
thinking.

Often Strachey's humor is based not nearly so much on dis-
respect as on incongruity. Such is the humor with which, in "General Gordon," a Chinaman named Hong, a religious fanatic who
had announced that he was the younger brother of Jesus, is treated:
"His mission was to root out Demons and Manchus from the face
of the earth, and to establish *Taiping,* the reign of eternal peace.
In the meantime, retiring into the depths of his palace, he left
the further conduct of earthly operations to his lieutenants, upon
whom he bestowed the title 'Wangs' (kings), while he himself,
surrounded by thirty wives and one hundred concubines, devoted
his energies to the spiritual side of his mission." To what great
lengths a hodge-podge of incongruity may sometimes go in the life
of a human being we discover in Strachey's brilliant sentence
dealing with the death of King Philip of Spain: "And so, in
ecstacy and in torment, in absurdity and in greatness, happy,
miserable, horrible, and holy, King Philip went off, to meet the
Trinity." The style here is a veritable whirlwind of clashing con-
cepts and frenzied rhythms fanning the spirit of the deceased Philip
into a confused cloud of chaff and floating straws and blowing it
upward toward the sky.

Strachey's humor based on the purely absurd also provides his
style with opportunities which are not missed. In the following
passage Strachey makes a sly thrust in the direction of the philosopher A. N. Whitehead, whom he had not learned to respect too
highly at Cambridge, in the course of elaborating upon what he
considers an absurdity:

> In the sight of God, we used to be told, a thousand years are
> as a day; possibly; but notions of the deity are not what they
> were in the days of King David and Sir Isaac Newton; Evolu-
> tion, the Life Force, and Einstein have all intervened; so
> that whether the dictum is still one to which credence should
> be attached is a problem that must be left to Professor White-
> head (who has studied the subject very carefully) to determine.

However that may be, for mortal beings the case is different. In their sight (or perhaps one should say their blindness) a thousand years are too liable to be not as a day but as just nothing.[14]

Bathos, with its sudden descent from the sublime to the ridiculous, is one of Strachey's favorite devices.[15] He was thoroughly familiar with its use for comic purposes in such writers as Pope and Byron. He used it frequently and nearly always with great brilliance. With it he ridicules, in "Cardinal Manning," the mysticism of Newman and Keble and what he considers the religious vagaries of Hurrell Froude and W. G. Ward:

[Newman and Keble saw] a whole universe of spiritual beings brought into communion with the Eternal by means of wafers.

The sort of ardor which impels more normal youth to haunt Music Halls and fall in love with actresses took the form, in Froude's case, of a romantic devotion to the Deity and an intense interest in the state of his own soul. He was obsessed by the ideals of saintliness, and convinced of the supreme importance of not eating too much.

. . . W. G. Ward, a young man who combined an extraordinary aptitude for *a priori* reasoning with a passionate devotion to Opéra Bouffe.

Bathos enlivens the style of the miniatures. The following passage treats John Aubrey, who had gone to the Continent to seek relief from disappointments in love and literature: "He sought distractions abroad, but without success. '1664, in August,' he noted, 'had a terrible fit of spleen, and piles, at Orléans.' " With bathos, likewise, Strachey emphasizes the contrast between Bacon's lofty professions of purpose and his extravagance: "Weeks passed, months passed, and still the Attorney-Generalship hung in the wind, and the regeneration of mankind grew dubious amid a mountain of unpaid bills." In *Queen Victoria* Strachey does not

14. "The Life, Illness, and Death of Dr. North," *Portraits in Miniature* (New York, Harcourt, Brace, 1931), pp. 30-1.
15. Boas considers this Strachey's best stylistic device.

like Baroness Lehzen, a pompous, pretentious, managing woman. With bathos he reduces her to her proper stature: "The pastor's daughter, with all her airs of stiff superiority, had habits which betrayed her origin. Her passion for caraway seeds, for instance, was uncontrollable." Similarly, in his treatment of Prince Albert, Strachey plunges from Albert's interest in music and painting to his interest in a method of converting sewerage into agricultural manure.

Another device which Strachey uses often, irony, does not always achieve a comic effect. Frequently, Strachey's purpose in employing it is that of suggesting a philosophical pondering of the strange ways in which human affairs unfold. Queen Victoria, for instance, stubbornly opposes Prince Albert, Uncle Leopold's candidate for her hand, as long as he is in distant Germany and is to be thought of in the abstract; then she sees him and forgets all the points in the reasoning with which she has opposed him; she melts, suddenly and completely. In "General Gordon" irony calls attention to one form of cultural intolerance and narrowness: "Though he was too late to take part in the capture of the Taku Forts, he was in time to witness the destruction of the Summer Palace at Pekin—the act by which Lord Elgin, in the name of European civilization, took vengeance upon the barbarism of the East." [16] In *Elizabeth and Essex* the implications of some of the irony are darkly tragic. In sending her lover Essex to his death, Elizabeth feels moving within her the spirit of her father, who had had his own wives executed: "Yes, indeed, she felt her father's spirit within her; and an extraordinary passion moved the obscure profundities of her being, as she condemned her lover to her mother's death. In all that had happened there was a dark inevitability, a ghastly satisfaction. . . . The wheel had come full circle." [17] Tragic, too, is the ironic picture of Sir Walter

16. The Strachey family's traditional defense of Warren Hastings rested in part on their belief that he was a tolerant, enlightened colonial administrator who, unlike Macaulay, did not wish to impose Western culture on the people of India but who desired rather to see that they were educated in a manner that would develop their own indigenous culture.

17. Freud's theories concerning father-daughter relationships have certainly influenced Strachey here.

Raleigh at a window silently watching the execution of Essex. There are times, however, when Strachey's sharp sense of the ridiculous does find its way into his irony. It is a definite undercurrent in this treatment of the Chinese diplomatist Li Hung-Chang:

> It was Gordon who gave him his first vision of Europe. Nothing could be more ironical. The half-inspired, half-crazy Englishman, with his romance and his fatalism, his brandy-bottle and his Bible, the irresponsible knight-errant whom his countrymen first laughed at and neglected, then killed and canonized—a figure straying through the perplexed industrialism of the nineteenth century like some lost "natural" from an earlier Age—this was the efficient cause of Li Hung-Chang's illumination, of his comprehension of the significance of Europe, of the whole trend of his long, cynical, successful, worldly-wise career.

Satirical humor likewise motivates the irony in Strachey's treatment of Clough's search for health, peace of mind, and religious faith: "He had determined to seek the solution of his difficulties in the United States of America. But, even there, the solution was not forthcoming." Thus irony, with its marked possibilities for variation, served Strachey admirably not only for comic purposes but for the more general purpose of suggesting change and dissimilarity which could be significantly and effectively related to a background of uniformity in style.

Strachey's faith in this principle helps to explain much that we discover in an examination of his choice of words. He had, we know, an almost Elizabethan ability to enjoy words for the sake of themselves; but we also know that he realized the dangers which went with this enjoyment and that he kept guard constantly over his own style to prevent words from becoming an end in themselves. Even so, we do not feel that his words lose all their freedom or all the charm which they often manifest in their separate existence. Strachey's style attempts to reconcile the independent charm of the word with its more important function in a context. Thus it demonstrates that words may, if properly managed, provide a variety of their own at the same time that

they serve to further the purpose which runs uniformly throughout the whole piece of writing.

A fondness for long words of classical origin soon makes itself
manifest after one begins to read Strachey. These words reflect his
delight in French literature, in Sir Thomas Browne's prose, and
in the diction which characterized much of the literature of eighteenth-century England. Such words as *intensity, lucid, pellucid,
lurid, curious, singular, vitriolic, extraordinarily, astonishing,
virulence, sardonic, peccant, villatic, salubrious, dithyrambic,
vituperation, volubility* are among his favorites. Some, like *lurid,
astonishing,* and *extraordinarily,* used with vividness and emphasis
in mind, are perhaps overworked. Others, like *intensity* and *lucid,*
may suggest qualities which Strachey prized very highly. Most
of them are good, mouth-filling words, pleasant to come upon
occasionally as one reads, particularly as one reads aloud. Many
of them wear the delightful glitter of the ornate and in both their
finery and their length serve as effective foils to the short, homely
words which Strachey also likes to use. There is a rare instinct
by which skillful writers combine the big words, with their commodious length, their fullness of meaning, and their grand attire,
with the inconspicuous vigor and forthrightness of numerous hard-
working, unassuming little words. Strachey praised this instinct
as he found it in the prose of Lincoln, who combined "the charm
of decoration with the most direct force"; [18] and he sought to
achieve its quality in his own work.

Edmund Wilson and others have accused Strachey of being
terribly given to clichés.[19] In a sense their accusation is well

18. "The Prose Style of Men of Action," *Spectator, 100* (Jan. 25, 1908),
141–2. Strachey compares Lincoln with Cromwell and Bunyan and speaks
of him as "another great Puritan." Lincoln's style is "full, like Cromwell's, of
reminiscences of the Bible; but it has more of the beauty and less of the
sternness of the Biblical manner."

19. "Lytton Strachey," *New Republic,* Sept. 21, 1932, pp. 146–8. But Wilson
also declares Strachey to be "one of the best writers of his time—one of
the best English writers in English." Raymond Mortimer has written: "Mr.
Strachey writes, as Sir Joshua painted, in the grand manner. Sonorous epi-
thets and Gibbonian polysyllables reverberate through his pages. His style
is full of metaphors, but they are almost always intended to convey not an

grounded. It would be hard to excuse Strachey for writing that Michelet "shows us the spectacle of the past in a series of lurid lightning-flashes." [20] Appropriate though it is to Michelet, the whole statement is stale and unimpressive. It may easily break up into the cliché *spectacle of the past,* the overworked word *lurid,* and the metaphor *shows by lightning flashes,* excellent when it was fresh in the hands of Lord Jeffrey and Coleridge and applied to Carlyle's *French Revolution* and Shakespeare's *King Lear,* but too vigorous and picturesque to be repeated.

Strachey does not, however, fall into unjustifiable triteness often. Although he likes upon occasion to use words, phrases, and even longer groups of words which have been repeated many times, he knows well the significance of a context. He has learned thoroughly Wordsworth's great teaching that the value and effectiveness of words is dependent chiefly on their relation to other words. We gain some insight into his methods from a passage in "Voltaire and Frederick the Great" where he skillfully introduces two often-told stories which he wants to use:

> Thus the two famous and perhaps mythical sentences, invariably repeated by historians of the incident, about orange-skins and dirty linen, do in fact sum up the gist of the matter. "When one has sucked the orange, one throws away the

image but an idea. . . . He frequently uses the most exhausted clichés as the simplest instruments at hand to communicate a fact. . . . He is inclined to let his words lose their independent life." "Mrs. Woolf and Mr. Strachey," *Bookman* (N.Y.), *68* (Feb. 1929), 625–9.

20. *Landmarks in French Literature* (New York, Henry Holt; London, Thornton Butterworth, 1912), p. 233. Gamaliel Bradford wrote in his journal on November 28, 1928: "The Strachey *Queen Victoria* and the *Essex* . . . overwhelm me with absolute despair. What is the use of my even pretending to write when there are men of such genius as that, with whom I can no more pretend to compete than I could with Shakespeare or Tacitus?" But he also wrote the next day that he had gradually come to feel that Strachey's superiority was "not so crushing after all." One of Strachey's imperfections, he said, had to do with style: "He falls into *clichés* such as I hope I have long since eschewed; as, for example, 'The time was ripe,' and numerous others." *The Journal of Gamliel Bradford,* ed. Van Wyck Brooks (Boston and New York, Houghton Mifflin, 1933), pp. 478, 479.

skin," somebody told Voltaire that the King had said, on being asked how much longer he would put up with the poet's vagaries. And Frederick, on his side, was informed that Voltaire, when a batch of the royal verses were brought to him for correction, had burst out with "Does the man expect me to go on washing his dirty linen for ever?" Each knew well enough the weak spot in his position, and each was acutely and uncomfortably conscious that the other knew it too.

Those who are critical even of this passage may argue that merely labeling material as old does not make it fresh. The answer is that Strachey uses more than a label here: he uses a vital context, and this context indicates that there is good reason why the stories have been often told and deserve to be told again.

It would be useless to deny that he uses many expressions which some strict critics consider highly questionable. He shows us Voltaire "spoiling for a fight" and determined to "settle the hash" of one of his enemies. He speaks of Frederick II's "high-falutin pathos." He tells us that Uncle Leopold "was very well aware on which side his bread was buttered" and that, further-more, he "wanted to have a finger in every pie." Queen Victoria "beat about the bush" before telling Lord Melbourne of her pro-posal to Albert. When she married Albert, she was not in the habit of "playing second fiddle." Albert and Victoria "had some hankerings" for the match of Prince Leopold with Queen Isabella. In many of the rivalries and antagonisms around the throne of Queen Elizabeth, it was often "touch and go." There was "some-thing fishy" about Dr. Lopez. The queen herself, "having polished off King James," proceeded to deal with more difficult matters. On occasion, she "mounted her high horse." And there were times when "all went swimmingly" in the affairs of Madame de Lieven, who also liked to have "a finger in every pie."

Although Strachey's use of such groups of words may not be justifiable always in terms of context, his intention is clear and his practice can in general be defended. In the first place, such expressions are often merely current coin in vernacular speech or are idiomatic; hence to repeat them is no more objectionable than to repeat single words generally accepted and used. In the second place, he enjoyed, as Chaucer, Shakespeare, and Fielding did, the spicy flavor and the vitality of an occasional colloquial or even slang expression. Furthermore, he knew that such expressions, when skillfully employed, are useful in enabling even a lofty style to maintain contact with the earth and to suggest that, in all its soaring, it has not forgotten the great C-Major of life. He did not wish his style to be effeminate or anemic. His ideal of style, we know, was not that of Walter Pater. He did not admire unrelieved propriety, unrelieved subtlety, unrelieved intellectualism, or unrelieved efforts to achieve freshness. Neither did he admire a style which was altogether rough and masculine. He was not willing to go all the way with Hemingway and be completely unacademic, rugged, and muscular. But for the purposes of relief somewhat manly, stock-in-trade expressions often served him well. They relaxed a style which might otherwise become too close. In style, as in football, the close formation must in general be maintained but occasionally spaces must open up to permit the quick thrust forward. Strachey's informal expressions were also the woof for his own respect for propriety, for his own subtlety, for his own intellectualism, for his own exquisite taste, and for his own talent in producing fresh and memorable phrases.

That he had marked talent for turning phrases is beyond question. It is demonstrated again and again on every page that he wrote. He tells us in "Florence Nightingale" that the principal doctor "was lost in the imbecilities of a senile optimism," that fortunately Florence "possessed the art of circumventing the pernicious influences of official etiquette," that on one occasion she proceeded in her efficient, straightforward way to get things done while "the miserable 'Purveyor' stood by, wringing his hands in departmental agony," and that Sidney Herbert was happiest when he was enjoying his peaceful country home, Wilton, "the majestic house standing there resplendent in the summer sunshine, among the great cedars which had lent their shade to Sir Philip Sidney." In *Queen Victoria* we are told that Lady Caroline Lamb "whirled with Byron in a hectic frenzy of love and fashion," that "a queen's

husband was an entity unknown to the British Constitution," and
that on Victoria's birthday Disraeli produced "an elaborate con-
fection of hyperbolic compliment." It is needless to multiply
examples of this gift, clear enough to all who have read Strachey.

Strachey's fondness for nicknames also arises in part from his
realization of the value of occasional informality. He knew too
that nicknames are nearly always picturesque and may often suggest through metaphor significant traits of characters. But many
of Strachey's imitators have got in trouble as they have attempted
to follow him in the use of nicknames and of other stylistic devices which suggest informality. Freedom in the use of the informal requires, we know, corresponding taste, judgment, and
skill; and unfortunately Strachey's imitators have often lacked
these. His imitators have also attempted to follow him in using
vivid details, seemingly trivial to the unobservant, to suggest
important associations and to give the style concreteness. But
here again they have frequently failed because they have not been
guided by the principle of variety which Strachey kept in mind.
He knew when to give details and when to give a concise, general
statement, when to employ elaboration and when to use restraint,
when to confine himself to the language of abstraction and when
to appeal to the senses. Considerations of brevity he never forgot.
He did not like realistic novels packed with details—details which
cluttered the mind or filled it with tedium.

That his style possesses poetic qualities has been observed almost from the beginning of his literary career. The pleasure which
he found in reading poetry and in writing it is reflected in his
prose. If there are many times when his style appeals chiefly to
our fundamental sanity, our common sense, and our sense of reality,
there are many others when it appeals just as strongly to our
imagination and to our sense of beauty. His mind was well supplied with figures, and he was skillful in selecting those which
would do his work best. Leonard Bacon has well said: "He could
always reveal what was new in the old, what was old in the new.
His illumination lit like a magnesium flare whole armies of
analogies that had slept peacefully in the dark of the mind, and

now sprang up as at some sudden alarm." [21] And Bower-Shore
has written of the manner in which Strachey's style assumed form
and shape as it came forth, "calling up a train of glorious images,
rich in their impressive solemnity." [22] His images, however, are
often far from solemn and may give off sparks of irrepressible
humor. The habit of analogy seems to have been fixed upon him
from the time when he first began to write, and excellent figures
are to be found in his early work. The two which follow are taken
from the *Spectator* reviews: "[Spenser's *Faerie Queene*] bore within
it no fiery seed of new and unexpected life; for there is little that
lives in it, though there is much that dreams. A less bracing poem
was never written. In its softness, its charm, its languor, its long
elaboration of luxurious ease, it resembles nothing so much as an
enormous featherbed." [23] It is a good image, amusing enough to
give some relief to those who have had to read Spenser against
their will and soft enough not to jar too severely the rabid readers
of the poet. "Light verse may be described as the millinery of
literature. Its most characteristic qualities are precisely those
of a lady's hat: it is charming, gay, graceful, and it does not last." [24]
Although some light verse does last, a vast amount of it does not;
and furthermore we must not expect an analogy to be fitting at
all points.

Two of Strachey's best and most fully elaborated figures are
to be found in "Voltaire and Frederick the Great." One deals with
Frederick's clumsy and futile efforts to write, under the tutorage
of Voltaire, verse highly polished in the best French style:

> The spectacle of that heavy German Muse, with her feet
> crammed into pointed slippers, executing, with incredible
> conscientiousness, now the stately measure of a Versailles
> minuet, and now the sprightly steps of a Parisian jig, would

21. "An Eminent Post-Victorian," p. 313.

22. *Lytton Strachey*, pp. 100–1.

23. "The Age of Spenser," *Spectator, 98* (March 23, 1907), 457–8. A review of J. J. Jusserand's *A Literary History of the English: From the Renaissance to the Civil War, 1.*

24. "Light Verse," *Spectator, 102* (Feb. 20, 1909), 304–5.

be either ludicrous or pathetic—one hardly knows which—
were it not so certainly neither the one nor the other, but
simply dreary with an unutterable dreariness, from which the
eyes of men avert themselves in shuddering dismay.

The second deals with Voltaire himself in his confused and not
always happy relation to Frederick: "At times, in this Berlin
adventure, he seems to resemble some great buzzing fly, shooting
suddenly into a room through an open window and dashing fran-
tically from side to side; when all at once, as suddenly, he swoops
away and out through another window which opens in quite a different direction, towards wide and flowery fields; so that perhaps
the reckless creature knew where he was going after all."
    When we look for figures in Strachey's longer works, they ap-
pear in great abundance. In *Eminent Victorians,* although Florence
Nightingale has been called a swan, she is more like an eagle and
can be a tigress; Lord Panmure is a bison with its head down,
and Sidney Herbert is a stag, a comely, gallant creature; Dr. Hall,
who has "worried his way to the top of his profession," is a rough
terrier of a man; Manning is also an eagle, a cruel, unscrupulous,
predatory bird; Newman is usually a dove, although once in an
uncomfortable situation he is a thoroughbred harnessed to a four-
wheeled cab. In *Queen Victoria* we are told that the Napoleonic
harrow passed over Saxe-Coburg and are thus spared many details.
The comparison of Victoria to a small smooth crystal pebble becomes a fundamental image which reappears from time to time
throughout the book with accumulating meaning and increasing
complexity. When the prince consort dies, the British Constitution,
"dropping the dead limb with hardly a tremor, continued its
mysterious life as if he had never been." The most memorable
and most fully exploited figure in *Elizabeth and Essex* is that
repeated again and again as a symbol of Bacon's nature—a serpent:
"A serpent, indeed, might well have been his chosen emblem—
the wise, sinuous, dangerous creature, offspring of mystery and
the beautiful earth." Queen Elizabeth, in a manner appropriate
to the days of Drake and Raleigh, is compared to a ship: "Such
was her nature—to float, when it was calm, in a sea of indecisions,

and, when the wind rose, to tack hectically from side to side."
King Philip's figure is also appropriate and picturesque: "The
spider of the Escurial had been spinning cobwebs out of dreams."
There are many other effective figures in these books. The frequency with which they appear helps to explain why the imagination never sleeps as one reads Strachey and why, through the
mysterious economy characteristic of its workings, the books give
one the impression of being both copious narratives and masterpieces of brevity.

The poetic quality of Strachey's style is also due in considerable
part to its appeal to the ear. Here again Strachey is guided by considerations of appropriateness. Many of his passages have a delightful music which both wins the reader and holds him. But
Strachey can employ cacophony as skillfully as he does euphony;
and he is very fond of onomatopoeia in working with both. Alliteration is one of his favorite devices. We note the repetition
of f's and p's in the following passage: "The Miss Nightingale of
fact was not as facile fancy painted her. She worked in another
fashion, and towards another end; she moved under the stress of
an impetus which finds no place in the popular imagination. A
Demon possessed her. Now demons, whatever else they may be,
are full of interest." The passage labors and is strenuous, as it
is intended to be. The explosive p's warn us that we are in the
presence of restless, dangerous, pent-up power, and the f's are like
escaping steam. In the following passage Strachey combines a
succession of s's with hard c's and the assonance of short i's for
the purpose of onomatopoeia—to suggest the crisp sound made
when paper is cut: "He would snip with scissors the pages of
ancient journals, and with delicate ecclesiastical fingers drop unknown mysteries into the flames." Rough sounds and turbulent
noises, t's, p's, and hard c's, are appropriate in a passage which
tells us of the quick, intensified struggle through which Prince
Leopold gained dominancy over the young Victoria: Leopold
was now "to try his hand at the task of taming a tumultuous
Princess. Cold and formal in manner, collected in speech, careful in action, he soon dominated the wild, impetuous, generous
creature by his side." Strachey does not like Madame St. Laurent

in *Queen Victoria;* therefore when she has finished playing her petty part he hisses her off the stage with a series of sibilants: "The subsequent history of Madame St. Laurent has not transpired." We suspect both a snicker and a giggle at the expense of the young Victoria to lurk beneath the sounds in the following passage: "The Princes shared her ecstasies and her italics between them; but it is clear enough where her secret preference lay." Appropriately light and airy are the sounds in this sentence: "Eugénie, cool and modish, floated in an infinitude of flounces by her side." The shriveled skin and the slow, painful walking of old age are suggested by the sounds of this sentence: "Lord John Russell dwindled into senility; Lord Derby tottered from the stage." The actions and schemes of human beings are frequently distasteful and ugly. There are times when they may be described in words which echo the sounds of fighting cats, irritable, scratching, and spitting: "The apartments at Kensington were seething with subdued disaffection, with jealousies and animosities virulently intensified by long years of propinquity and spite." Strachey is perhaps too fond of alliteration, and at times it becomes self-conscious and a distraction in his hands. There are times also when his sounds seem to be introduced purely for the sake of themselves or of the pleasure which comes from turning a neat phrase. When Strachey writes, "The time had come for the Crystal Palace to be removed to the salubrious seclusion of Sydenham," we are impressed much more by the ostentation of the style than by its appropriateness or by the fact which it conveys. Even so, blessed be the phrase-makers, for they rescue us just when the dull words of a host of work-a-day writers have almost convinced us that reading, and listening, were not intended to be a joy.

Not merely alliteration and assonance but stresses, rhythms, and pauses are important in Strachey's prose. An abnormal sentence pattern, with stresses and pauses which break it up and produce the effect of choppiness, may be used in contrast with a sentence of smooth continuity: "Happy, certainly, she was; and she wanted everyone to know it. Her letters to King Leopold are sprinkled thick with raptures." The opening rhythms here are slow, deliberate, and emphatic; and then the passage picks up speed and races toward the word "raptures." Likewise, a style which is intended to be slow, laborious, and heavy may become more so through the use of pauses: "England lumbered on, impervious and self-satisfied, in her old intolerable course." Note how the following passage treating Cecil in *Elizabeth and Essex* varies its stresses and pauses to throw emphasis where it should be and to make sure that the reader digests the meaning as he goes along.

> While he labored, his inner spirit waited and watched. A discerning eye might have detected melancholy and resignation in that patient face. The spectacle of the world's ineptitude and brutality made him, not cynical—he was not aloof enough for that—but sad—was he not a creature of the world himself? He could do so little, so very little, to mend matters; with all his power and all his wisdom he could but labor, and watch, and wait. What else was possible? What else was feasible, what else was, in fact, anything but lunacy? He inspected the career of Essex with serious concern.

Here, as almost always in Strachey's writing, the principle of contrast helps to produce life and variety. Not only do pauses work in harmony with motion forward and stresses with unemphasized sounds, but repetitions with fresh words, questions with conclusions, and roughness with smoothness.

If we seek for a passage that combines most of the best qualities of Strachey's style, we can scarcely do better than to choose a piece of character analysis in "General Gordon" which treats Sir Evelyn Baring, later Lord Cromer. It lacks humor, but it has an excellent variety of sentences, skillful use of rhetoric, effective images, and cadences and sounds which please the ear:

> When he spoke, he felt no temptation to express everything that was in his mind. In all he did, he was cautious, measured, unimpeachably correct. It would be difficult to think of a man more completely the antithesis of Gordon. His temperament, all in monochrome, touched in with cold blues and indecisive greys, was eminently unromantic. He had a steely colorlessness, and a steely pliability, and a steely

strength. Endowed beyond most men with the capacity of foresight, he was endowed as very few men have ever been with that staying-power which makes the fruit of foresight attainable. His views were long, and his patience was even longer. He progressed imperceptibly; he constantly withdrew; the art of giving way he practiced with the refinement of a virtuoso. But, though the steel recoiled and recoiled, in the end it would spring forward. His life's work had in it an element of paradox. It was passed entirely in the East; and the East meant very little to him. It was something to be looked after. It was also a convenient field for the talents of Sir Evelyn Baring.

This a restrained style and a firm one. It proceeds deliberately and with marked sureness of phrase to set forth its intended meanings. Yet, though it is controlled and kept within the framework of conventional linguistic practices, it is not rigid, it is not colorless, it is not without life. The bright woof shows in every sentence; the loom weaves freely; the magic shuttle is at work.

CHAPTER 14

Reputation and Influence

WE KNOW that the power to influence which the general public associated with Strachey's books beginning with the publication of *Eminent Victorians* was felt by his friends to be strong even in his Cambridge days. It was both intellectual and personal. Sir Desmond MacCarthy, one of those early friends, has attributed it to superior culture, wit, emotional courage, and intellectual ardor. He believes that the courage and the intellectual intensity were particularly important.[1] Another of these early friends, Leonard Woolf, has spoken of it as coming "from the very core of his character" and of its strength to persist in Strachey's personal relationships throughout his life.[2] Evidence that it impressed strangers as well as friends is to be found in a statement by Sir J. D. Beazley, the classical scholar and authority on Greek antiquities, who visited Cambridge in 1904 and met Keynes and Strachey. He said that at the time he thought them the two cleverest men he had ever met and that years later as he looked back he still thought that they were the two cleverest men he had ever met.[3] Keynes was himself susceptible to this power in Strachey, as he found it associated with a sympathetic understanding of other people and with a sharp and intelligent questioning

1. "Lytton Strachey: The Art of Biography," *Sunday Times,* Nov. 5, 1933, p. 8. A review of *Characters and Commentaries.*
2. "Lytton Strachey," *New Statesman and Nation, 3* (Jan. 30, 1932), 118. Cf. the testimony of another friend, Francis Birrell, in "Lytton Strachey," *Revue Hebdomadaire,* July 23, 1932, p. 405.
3. R. F. Harrod, *The Life of John Maynard Keynes* (New York, Harcourt, Brace, 1951), pp. 91-2.

of society and its institutions.[4] It was a power which established
confidence. Long before Strachey became famous, his friends
believed that he would become a writer and were sure that he
would distinguish himself. This attitude is likewise reflected in a
letter which his cousin, St. Loe Strachey, wrote in 1909, in which
he said that Lytton Strachey, though still young and not well
known, was "one of the very ablest" of the younger critics, that
he knew his Dryden and Congreve as well as he did his Shakespeare and the Elizabethans, and that all competent judges who
knew his work were loud in its praise.[5]

Related to this power as both his friends and his readers had
grown familiar with it was the shock which came to them when he
died. To them, his death suddenly created a horrible vacuum
which it seemed impossible to fill. Vincent Sheean has written: "To
the friends of Lytton Strachey his recent death must have been
like an earthquake, shattering the ordinary structure of existence.
For he was the center of it, the focus. As he governed a conversation without expenditure of words, so he influenced the minds of
those who knew him without doing much toward that end."[6]
His readers had a corresponding feeling. Guy Boas has written:
"He had the grace, in every sense, to love and salute the highest
when he saw it, and to give exquisite pleasure to his contemporaries, so that when he died it seemed to those that loved
his art that one of the brightest lights of the generation had
suddenly gone out."[7] The New York *Times* commented on the
day after his death: "Lytton Strachey should have died hereafter,
not in his prime. . . . To this generation he has given plenty
of pleasure."[8]

We know, on the other hand, that Strachey had numerous

4. *Ibid.*

5. Quoted in Cyril Clemens, *Lytton Strachey* (Webster Groves, Mo., International Mark Twain Society, 1942), pp. 8–9.

6. "Lytton Strachey: Cambridge and Bloomsbury," *New Republic,* 70 (Feb.
17, 1932), 19–20.

7. *Lytton Strachey,* English Association Pamphlet No. 93, Nov. 1935, p. 21.

8. Jan. 22, 1932, p. 18. An editorial. It was strongly attacked in a letter
signed H. I. Crawford and printed on Jan. 25 (p. 16) as evidence of a tendency in the *Times* to "praise the good and disparage the excellent."

critics during his lifetime and that even before his death something of a general reaction to his fame had set in. His fame had
reached its climax with the publication of *Queen Victoria* in
1921. The essay on "Pope," published in 1925, had much in it
of a controversial nature. And *Elizabeth and Essex* was a disappointment to many readers. Even though in the brilliant miniatures of the latest years the public still found the delightful qualities
which it expected in Strachey, works of impressive length and
importance seemed to be no longer forthcoming. Strachey himself, although considering various subjects for long biographies
to be written in the future, was giving a great part of his time to
editing the *Greville Memoirs*. The world in general seemed to
be undergoing momentous changes. The stock market crash came
in 1929; the problem of Germany seemed more than ever un-
settled and dangerous; an ominous restiveness began to assert
itself with new vigor in the Japanese. *Eminent Victorians,* with
the spirit which had engendered and acclaimed it at the end of
the first World War, began to seem far away. People were beginning to wonder whether the skepticism which immediately
followed that war and prevailed for some years afterward had
been of any real help in setting the world in order. Matters were
beginning to be extremely grim and serious; laughter seemed
out of place. Security began to seem more and more important,
far more important than the free exercise of the critical faculty.
Concerning the reaction to Strachey's reputation, George Dangerfield wrote in the *Saturday Review of Literature* in 1938:

> Lytton Strachey died in 1932, and even then his reputation,
> for a brief while so bright, had begun to grow dim. Today
> his books are rarely mentioned without condescension. . . .
> Contemporary opinion regards him, if at all, as a kind of
> meteor, hurrying across the skies to extinction, and leaving
> behind it an unsavory smell . . . of sulphur. . . . He is
> known as a man who peered under the sofas and poked into
> the closets of history, solely in order to discover the evidences
> of dust and moth.[9]

9. *18* (July 23, 1938), 3.

In the Rede Lecture at Cambridge for 1943, Sir Max Beerbohm remarked ironically that even though Strachey had not been a great writer his gifts and his repute had amply sufficed "to ensure reaction against him very soon after the breath was out of his body." [10] The sales of his books have not been great in recent years. And the reviews of the new English edition of his works in six volumes (1948) by no means indicate that a reaction to the reaction has set in.

Yet the tides of opinion in their ebbing and flowing are not easy to measure or evaluate. Just what does it mean, for instance, in terms of Strachey's general reputation, that a master's thesis, "The Development of Lytton Strachey's Biographical Method," [11] was submitted to the faculty of the University of Chicago in 1929; or that selections from Strachey have been included in numerous anthologies which college students have been required to use as textbooks steadily from the time of *Eminent Victorians* to the present day? Has Strachey become a "classic," of interest only to the academic mind? And is it true that even within university walls the historians have rejected him and left him entirely in the hands of enthusiastic but immature young instuctors in English and their not-so-enthusiastic and even more immature freshmen and sophomores? Has the fate which Bernard Shaw dreaded and for many years skillfully fended off in his dealings with publishers of textbooks claimed Lytton Strachey for its victim? And was his sudden rise to fame but a sulphurous meteor which soon rightly disappeared? Was the taste of the public which applauded *Eminent Victorians* and *Queen Victoria* an unhealthy one? The problem in dealing with Strachey's reputation is to discover what discriminating readers have thought of his works, whenever they have appeared and whatever the drift of the general opinion may have been at the time.

Let us investigate the indictment against him. As early as 1919 Sir Edmund Gosse complained that Strachey was not only careless in handling facts but also too much inclined to appeal to a taste

10. *Lytton Strachey* (New York, Alfred A. Knopf, 1943), p. 14.
11. By Marjorie H. Thurston, now a member of the English Department of the University of Minnesota.

that was rooted in cheapness and superficial thinking. The Victorian age, he asserted, was after all a very great one; a wholesale attack on it meant a failure to discriminate. Strachey lacked sympathy and imaginative insight. His characters were like puppets "observed from a great height by an amiable but entirely superior intelligence." And his attitude became particularly dangerous when it concerned spiritual matters. The Victorians themselves "carried admiration to the highest pitch." But they had a regard for distinctions and discriminated in what they admired. Strachey's readers were neither enthusiastic nor capable of determining values: "Such violence of taste is now gone out of fashion; every scribbler and dauber likes to believe himself on a level with the best, and the positive criterion of value which sincere admiration gave is lost to us. Hence the success of Mr. Lytton Strachey." [12]

Even Strachey's irony, according to Lloyd R. Morris, praised as highly as it had been, was not good irony but was instead "the instinctive, desperate gesture of an austere and celibate intelligence trapped in a single illicit relation with sentimentality." [13] E. G. Clark complained of Strachey's indelicacy and bad taste, and described his prose as morbid.[14] Claude W. Fuess also explained Strachey's success in terms of his willingness to satisfy readers who were reacting against the idealism of the Victorians and of the first World War:

Strachey's books, especially the *Queen Victoria,* came on the market at precisely the right moment and, even in competition with prose fiction, held their own in the bookstalls. At the opening of what has been called the "Jazz Age," he

12. "The Agony of the Victorian Age," *Some Diversions of a Man of Letters* (New York, Scribner's, 1919), pp. 313–36. Gosse praises here what he takes to be a very different attitude toward the Victorians found in the Earl of Asquith's Romanes Lecture at Oxford, 1918, which, while giving generous praise to *Eminent Victorians,* was the work of one who was able to rise above his subject and "gazing at the Victorian Age, as it recedes, he declared it to have been very good."
13. "The Skepticism of Mr. Strachey," *Outlook, 131* (Aug. 23, 1922), 681–2.
14. "Mr. Strachey's Biographical Method," *Catholic World, 129* (May, 1929), 129–35.

catered to a generation which rejoiced at smartness, irreverence, and cynicism, and which liked to see the garments of
authority stripped from schoolmasters and generals and car-
dinals and monarchs.[15]

The serious implication of such criticism is that the taste to which
Strachey appealed was shallow, uninformed, and by its very nature
ephemeral. There can be little doubt that a fairly widespread
acceptance of this assumption has done great damage to his reputation since the time of his death.

It has also been assumed by some of his critics that the "point
of view" which he insisted upon maintaining was extremely narrow, rigid, and cocksure. Leonard Bacon has written: "Actually,
he was fastened like a limpet to the prejudice of his time and his
class, make it 1905 and Trinity College, Cambridge. . . . And
he was not infrequently to be found upon a spiritual pedestal."
Strachey's, Bacon added, was as much a pedestal as Macaulay's.[16]
Edmund Wilson found something decidedly disagreeable about
"the curious catty malice" with which "the high-voiced old Bloomsbury gossip gloated over the scandals of the past as he ferreted
them out in his library." And he objected to Strachey's treatment
of women. Strachey seemed to take pleasure in seeing them hu-
miliated. And he "almost invariably picked unappetizing subjects
and seemed to make them more unappetizing still." [17] Bacon,
James Truslow Adams, Frank Swinnerton, and Harold Nicolson
all have asserted their belief that truly excellent biographies do
not come into being through the method which they assumed
Strachey used, namely, that of beginning with a preconception of
character and then proceeding simply to elaborate on that. Adams
declared that Strachey's influence here was little short of disastrous.[18] Swinnerton said that such a method rose from the smug-
ness and lack of imagination likely to be found in Cambridge men:
"Cambridge is a very much larger place than Bloomsbury, and

15. *Saturday Review of Literature, 8* (Feb. 6, 1932), 501.
16. "An Eminent Post-Victorian," *Yale Review,* N.S. *30* (Winter 1941), 316.
17. *New Republic, 72* (Sept. 21, 1932), 146–8.
18. "New Modes in Biography," *Current History, 31* (Nov. 1929), 258.

yet a place to which Bloomsbury owes both its best names and a certain devastatingness of mind little touched by the curious gift of imagination. Imagination I take to be the faculty by means of which one enters into the minds of others, and is not surprised to find them full of good things." The Cambridge man, he continued, "is impervious to outside suggestion. He knows best." [19] Nicolson, although granting that Strachey's works had some very high merits, said that "any personal thesis on the part of the biographer" was destructive of "pure" biography. "Boswell had no thesis, nor had Lockhart: they worked wholly on the inductive method." [20]

Throughout the years, likewise, beginning with Gosse's objections to the representation of Cromer in *Eminent Victorians,* critics have continued to complain that Strachey did not have a sufficient respect for facts. G. B. Harrison made a point of this in his review of *Elizabeth and Essex.*[21] The obituary notice in the *Spectator,* while it contained much praise, asserted: "But I should define his supreme talent as that of the historical novelist. . . . So far from being a realist, he was a glutton for the romantic." [22] F. A. Simpson protested that Strachey was guilty of both carelessness and falsification in his treatment of Manning. "Great, in fact, as were his merits as an artist, he suffered as an historian from the defect that in the last resort he did not care enough for truth." [23] In reviewing the new British edition of Strachey's complete works (1948), James Pope-Hennessy objected vigorously to what he assumed to be Strachey's disregard for facts. He quoted with approval Lord Rosebery's remark to another Victorian statesman that Strachey's *Queen Victoria* was "quite a readable

19. *The Georgian Scene* (New York, Farrar and Rinehart, 1934), 344–5.
20. *The Development of English Biography* (London, Hogarth Press, 1933), p. 153. Nicolson also wrote, in "Prince Albert," *Observer* (London), March 20, 1949 (a review of Roger Fulford's *The Prince Consort*), that the ironical school of biography, "as initiated by Froude, perfected by Lytton Strachey, and popularized by Guedalla," was on the decline and that it was now assumed that in general biography should be constructive and not destructive.
21. "Elizabeth and Her Court," *Spectator, 141* (Nov. 24, 1928), 177.
22. Jan. 30, 1932, p. 139.
23. *Spectator, 122* (Jan. 7, 1944), 7–8.

work of fiction." Pope-Hennessy granted that the style of Strachey's works still sparkles but found in them a texture which, after the passing of years, "shows thin." Strachey deliberately wrote what he knew to be untrue, he said, and was "unjust to himself and disloyal to his own remarkable gifts." His sin was that of "treating biography, that ornament of English literature, as though it were a vehicle for working off personal spite and airing private jokes." His influence was therefore decidedly vicious: "He initiated a new school of English biography, and by his imaginative, vindictive and entirely personal way of dealing with his material, he unwittingly did the biographical writing of the inter-war period very considerable harm." In many respects the two fat volumes of Victorian biography were preferable to the works of the new school: "The stodgiest of the Victorian tomb-biographies are crammed with varied facts and many letters, and if one reads them one never goes unrewarded away. The same cannot be said of contemporary biography, and for this state of affairs Lytton Strachey must shoulder much of the blame." [24]

Pope-Hennessy's attack raises the question of the extent to which a writer is responsible for what his imitators do. It goes without question that Strachey's imitators have been many and that a number of them have been guilty of extremely bad writing. Very few of them, if any, have risen to his level. Guy Boas was not far from wrong when he wrote in 1935 that among the imitators only Harold Nicolson and Francis Hackett have derived "virtue and not damage from him," [25] although a word might be said in favor of Philip Guedalla and perhaps one or two other biographers in the new school. Simpson has stated succinctly the reason why imitation of Strachey has frequently resulted in cheapness and decadence: "His virtues were all his own, while his faults were fatally easy to copy and surpass." [26] As early as 1929 Strachey's friend Raymond Mortimer sensed the great risk which his imitators ran. Both Strachey and Virginia Woolf, he said, were highly individual writ-

24. *Spectator, 133* (Feb. 25, 1949), 264.
25. *Lytton Strachey*, p. 15.
26. Quoted by Desmond MacCarthy in "Lytton Strachey," *Sunday Times,* Jan. 16, 1949, p. 3.

ers, and for that reason any effort to imitate them literally would
certainly become disastrous. He was alarmed at the imitations
which had already appeared: "Already we are being snowed under
by biographies whose authors attempt to compensate for their lack
of scholarship by cheap sneers, undergraduate epigrams and picturesque inventions." [27] Unfortunately, the more unusual a successful writer is, the more likely he is to have imitators who cannot
distinguish between his merits and faults, or their own. The imi-
tative mind does not often know its limits. But should we hold a
writer responsible for the inferior works of his imitators? If so,
Shakespeare himself must carry an extremely heavy burden of
guilt which has accumulated through the centuries in the productions of lesser dramatists. And the indictment against Donne, Milton, Wordsworth, Goethe, Tennyson, James Joyce, Yeats, and T. S.
Eliot would be a very serious one indeed. The value of a writer's
influence can be determined not by what bad writers but by what
good ones owe to him. Only the good writers can discover what is
truly good in the original and at the same time, through the force
of their own individualities, make a use of it that is fresh, impressive, and not servile.

Let us now turn, therefore, to what has been pointed out as
good in Strachey's work and ask ourselves whether it is really good
and whether its influence on good writers may be of value. As we
do so, we are certain to observe that the unfavorable and the favorable commentators more than once simply contradict one another.
Strachey's reputation has suffered from too many offhand judgments on both sides. And it has been too often forgotten that,
with Strachey as with Swift, a lucid style and a light touch do not
infallibly indicate a lack of depth and complexity.

The essays in *Books and Characters* (1922) and *Characters and
Commentaries* (1933) earned considerable praise for Strachey as a
literary critic. On May 18, 1922, the London *Times* highly commended his interpretation of Racine, called attention to his rare
sense of justice, and spoke of his delight in the hidden quality of
things which most people have forgotten how to understand.[28]

27. "Mrs. Woolf and Mr. Strachey," *Bookman* (N.Y.), *68* (Feb. 1929), 625.
28. P. 16.

In October of the same year Lawrence Gilman, writing for the *North American Review,* also gave high praise to Strachey the critic.[29] J. M. Murry's review of *Books and Characters* in the *Nation and Athenaeum* glowed with admiration and was in complete sympathy with the praise given in the *Times.*[30] After the publication of *Characters and Commentaries,* P. M. Jack wrote in the New York *Times* that, although Strachey was generally on the opposite side and appeared to be a little perverse at times, he had a faculty for sharpening the reader's critical sense and often proved to be right. Furthermore, such criticism was a delight to read: "We doubt if another miscellany of this sort could possess half the wit and distinction of style that we find here." [31] These comments are fairly representative of those which have found merit in Strachey's critical writing. Although his reputation as a critic has never been as great as that which he enjoyed for some time as a biographer, it has lost less ground through the passing of years. It has always suffered much more from indifference and neglect than from open attack.

As late as 1937 Edgar Johnson praised Strachey's sense of values and the largeness of his point of view: "In Strachey the old Elizabethan lion refines down to a cat, cunning, cruel, swiftly ferocious, but retaining some of the old lion-hatred of smallness, nastiness, hypocrisy, pomposity, and sentimentalism. The lion singles out the enemy to be destroyed; it is the cat, however, that plays slyly and patiently with the victim." [32] Previously, André Maurois had spoken of him not only as an iconoclast using the method of irony but also as a highly gifted writer working in the tradition of the great humorists and as "a very deep psychologist." [33] At the time of Strachey's death, F. L. Lucas said that the popular conception of him magnified his purely negative qualities far too much. It had become a poor travesty of the truth:

29. Pp. 553–60.
30. June 3, 1922, pp. 346–7.
31. Nov. 12, 1933, *Book Review,* p. 2.
32. *One Mighty Torrent: The Drama of Biography* (New York, Stackpole, 1937), p. 509.
33. "The Modern Biographer," *Yale Review,* N.S. *17* (Jan. 1928), 231–45.

Public figures inevitably come to stand in the public gaze stiffly sculptured in a single pose; that is so simple, and the reality is too complex. And so to the ordinary man Lytton Strachey seemed the incarnation of modern irreverence, the heartless cynic, the smiler with the knife; an Old Man of the Mountain conducting posthumous assassinations; the denying Mephistopheles of the mysterious Satanic world of "Blooms-bury," tossing a plump Queen Victoria on the spikes of the Albert Memorial. . . . How that charming and mischievous smile would have flitted across his face, could he but have read what the last few days have said of him, sitting on his veran-dah facing the Berkshire downs in that house he had so filled with his personality.[34]

Beerbohm said that to call Strachey a "debunker" was both vulgar and silly.[35] Almost no analysis has been made, however, of either the basis of his satire or the positive side of his philosophy. Today, as at the time of his death, he is in the popular mind simply one of the leaders among the writers who reacted against Victorianism and a biographer who very entertainingly ridiculed the queen and some of her subjects.

Recently such distinguished writers as E. M. Forster and F. L. Lucas have come to his defense when he was under formidable attack. Forster answered Bertrand Russell, who in a radio broad-cast had said that as a disciple of G. E. Moore, Strachey had "de-graded his ethics into advocacy of a stuffy girls'-school sentimental-izing" and implied that Strachey, far from being a great man, was very eccentric, affected, and specious-minded. His style, Russell complained, often suggested Macaulay's. Lord Russell admitted,

34. "Lytton Strachey: An Artist in History," *Observer,* Jan. 24, 1932, p. 5. Arthur Waugh wrote in a letter to the *Spectator,* Jan. 30, 1932, p. 146: "He was the citizen of an intellectual republic which was breaking free from the tyranny of hypocrisy and pretence; and, if he showed himself at times over-satisfied at his superiority to the weaknesses of the preceding generation, he was never blind to the risks and penalties of revolution. He stood at the parting of the ways, looking before and after; there was as much tenderness in his retrospect as hope in his outlook."

35. *Lytton Strachey,* p. 15.

however, that when he had read *Eminent Victorians* in prison he had laughed so loudly that an officer had felt compelled to remind him that a prison was a place of punishment. Forster's published letter in reply said in part:

> It is true that Strachey was clever, although not as clever as Lord Russell, and it is also true that cleverness alone cannot make a man great. But there was more than cleverness in his case. There was the passion which shone through his work and made it vivid. There was his admirable style—it never reminded me of Macaulay's though I should not have sneered at it if it had. There was a certain historical power; the accuracy of *Queen Victoria* has, I believe, not been seriously impugned; *Elizabeth and Essex* is inaccurate but is in other ways his greatest work. There was, of course, his sense of humor, and, equally important but frequently forgotten, there was his fondness for fun. He liked playing about, and if people discussed such a vast subject as Life not genuinely but in terms of hot air he would instantly play the fool. There was indeed a natural gaiety in him—a gaiety which supported Lord Russell as a prisoner but is evidently of no use to him as an O.M.[36]

Lucas defended Strachey in a letter published in the *Times Literary Supplement* for June 10, 1955. He objected to the phrase "the consciously artistic, meretricious skill of Lytton Strachey and his followers," which a *Times* reviewer had used in discussing R. H. Super's *Walter Savage Landor* (May 27, 1955). Lucas professed to be "puzzled by this curious linking of 'artistic' and 'mere-

36. See the *Listener, 43* (July 17, 1952), 97–8; and July 24, 1952, p. 142. It does seem a pity that Lord Russell, professing to love the free mind as a philosopher and having been in a position throughout the years to acquire the truth concerning Strachey, should make statements as ill natured and illiberal as those in his radio talk were. His personal dislike of Strachey reached back through the years, and Strachey, as he met Russell from time to time, sensed it. He wrote in a letter of May 27, 1919: "Garsington was terribly trying. . . . Bertie worked his circular saw as usual. I've never been able to feel at ease with him, and I can only suppose that he dislikes me—pourquoi?"

tricious,' " and asked, "Must we shrink from anything 'artistic' in biography?" Then he gave Strachey eloquent praise:

> Were Strachey alive, he could have defended himself better than I can; though he would doubtless have disdained to, on Buffon's principle—*"Il faut laisser ces mauvaises gens dans l'incertitude."* But though there may be some errors in *Eminent Victorians* which Strachey's admirers must regret; though he may have had a bad influence on fools; though, like Voltaire, he was too brilliant to be always patient, and too passionate in his hate of bigotry and brutality to be always impartial—none the less I should be surprised if many biographies of our century lived as long as *Queen Victoria,* or as some of the vignettes in *Books and Characters* and *Portraits in Miniature.* He stood for reason, grace and style, in an age not, I think, overwell endowed with any of them; and though to the intelligent his excellences should continue to speak for themselves, it would be a pity if the younger generation were even temporarily deterred from reading him by this sort of exaggerated innuendo.

All in all, there has been fairly general agreement about the service which he has rendered to biography in three respects. First, he taught and demonstrated that biography should have good proportions and judicious selection. Second, he taught and demonstrated that a biography should be written in good style. Third, he taught and demonstrated that the characters in a biography should be made to live again. Thus he did much to check a deplorable drift in biographical writing toward the careless, the pedantic, the wooden, and the tedious. At the same time, according to Maurois, some of the English universities were hostile toward him in his lifetime because, even though he had showed himself a man of erudition skilled in sniffing out details, he had denied that history was a science and had "made so bold as to reinstate Clio among the Muses." [37] To Maurois, he was "a model of composition, of

37. *Prophets and Poets,* trans. Hamish Miles (New York and London, Harper, 1935), p. 215.

style, and likewise of poetry." [38] Strachey did not succeed in bringing to an end the writing of long, multi-volume biographies. Such works, relating to Lincoln, Jefferson, Lee, Washington, Shelley, Dickens, Carlyle, and many other subjects continue to appear. Many of them are the product of the soundest research methods and the highest scholarship which our age can provide. We can be duly grateful for their fullness and trustworthiness. We can also be grateful because, unlike many of the copious Victorian works in the life-and-letters category, they have full indexes. But in many instances we can also be grateful for obvious painstaking about form and style such as did not characterize the two fat Victorian volumes. And for this improvement Strachey deserves at least part of the credit. Let us hope that both kinds of biography will continue to be written. They are really complementary. But the genuinely meritorious artistic biography, such as is represented by Strachey's best works, will always be comparatively rare.

That Strachey has also had an international influence, both in America and in countries where English is not spoken, is certain. Among the translations have been that of *Queen Victoria* into German (1925), by Hans Reisiger, and into Spanish (1934); that of "General Gordon" into German, also by Reisiger, published in the *Neue Rundschau,* June–August 1931; that of the same work into French, by J. Dombasle, published in the *Revue des deux mondes,*

38. Foreword to Clemens, *Lytton Strachey.* Fuess wrote of Strachey: "His standards were high, his scholarship was scrupulous, and his style was a delight." *Saturday Review of Literature,* p. 502. The review of the new British edition of Strachey's works in the *Times Literary Supplement,* June 17, 1949, p. 396, was in the main critical but conceded that one of Strachey's merits was his ability to communicate excitement. MacCarthy makes the interesting statement, in "The Style of Lytton Strachey," *Sunday Times,* Feb. 9, 1936, p. 8, that he quite definitely prefers Lytton Strachey's works to *The Coming Struggle for Power* by John Strachey, son of Lytton Strachey's cousin St. Loe Strachey. For other favorable comments on Strachey, see Edwin Muir, "Lytton Strachey," *Nation and Athenaeum, 37* (April 25, 1925), 102–4; Oliver Warner, "The Art of Mr. Lytton Strachey," *Bookman* (London), *80* (June 1931), 157; Stephen Gwynn, "Lytton Strachey," *Fortnightly Review, 137* (March 1932), 387–8; Clifford Bower-Shore, *Lytton Strachey: An Essay* (London, Fenland Press, 1933), p. 88; and Joseph Wood Krutch, "Lytton Strachey," *Nation, 134* (Feb. 17, 1932), p. 200.

April 15–May 1, 1932; and that of "Florence Nightingale" into German, also by Reisiger, published in the *Neue Rundschau,* October, December 1932.[39] I have not made a thorough study of the translations and believe that a number of others may be added to the list. Just how much influence the translations have had, however, cannot be stated without further research.

The really important question concerning Strachey's reputation is whether his books retain their vitality, their power to please, and their timeliness when reread after a period of intervening years. No test of a work's permanent virtues can take the place of a close and thoughtful rereading. When the new American edition of *Queen Victoria* appeared in 1949, a well-known and highly reputable critic, Ben Ray Redman of the *Saturday Review of Literature,* submitted it to this test. The significance of his report, quoted in part below, is not to be doubted:

> I returned to Lytton Strachey's *Queen Victoria* with some doubts, wondering whether I would find it as excellent as it had seemed more than twenty-five years ago, but the doubts were unwarranted. It survives triumphantly as a work of art, skillfully composed of facts and circumscribed by truth. Witty without ostentation, probing without cruelty, it makes Victoria's character—with all its absurdities—an object of intense interest, and one from which it is impossible to withhold respect. We cannot help laughing at her ridiculous moments, but we cannot help admiring her dogged virtues, among which the simple power of survival was so largely responsible for her place in history. Strachey has arranged and manipulated the threads and incidents of her career with dexterity and economy.[40]

I can only observe that my own experience, with this book and with many of Strachey's other writings, has confirmed Redman's high opinion of Strachey's work. I read the biographical works with great pleasure soon after they were first published, even

39. See also Günther Köntges, *Die Sprache in der Biographie Lytton Stracheys* (Marburg-Lahn, 1938).

40. Oct. 29, 1949, p. 21.

though I have very little of the iconoclast or the satirist in my temperament. After Strachey's death his works were dismissed from my mind almost completely until the time of the second World War. Then, in the midst of an intensified routine imposed by the war, I sought relief in reseach, as far as time allowed, and desired a subject which would be "light" and amusing. Strachey's works seemed to meet the requirement. They also seemed, at first, an ideal subject for a work which was to have critical balance, with plenty of opportunity for adverse comment such as would make the words of commendation more convincing. Having resolved to make the fullest use of this opportunity, I began rereading. But in going through the books again and again, as this study required, I found many times that I was disarmed and that weapons which I had intended to use for attack were taken away from me. What I had considered faults as I had thought of Strachey in the abstract or remembered his works after a lapse of years simply were not there when the works were carefully re-examined. I had to be just even if as a result the quality of nice balance in my judgments was seriously threatened. To some degree, of course, an experience similar to this is common among scholars as they work with their subjects. Nevertheless, I have worked with other subjects and, speaking comparatively, must testify to Strachey's unusual power to win the reader who returns to him with an open mind. Others can test this power for themselves.

It is only thus that the permanent worth of his writings can be determined. Both the unfavorable and the favorable comments which critics have made should be considered, but the final verdict is not to be arrived at by subtracting the one from the other or by attempting to reconcile the two. It is obvious that the opinions of one superior critic on either side may far outweigh all the others. And even his opinions may be misleading unless we consider them in constant and repeated reference to Strachey's books.

In attempting to make my final appraisal of his work, I have kept in mind this principle. What I have considered his shortcomings I have indicated as I encountered them. What will last in his work I have likewise indicated. It may be summarized here briefly. Strachey is, I believe, a true classic of English prose whose permanent reputation is in little danger. His writings will be highly valued in the future as they have been in the past for the steadfast love of art and beauty which they reflect; for the ideal of order which they embody in an age of confusion; for the marked respect for literature underlying them and for the guidance and increased delight which they give to others who wish to read the best books; for a superb style equally effective in biography and criticism; for an unshakable conviction concerning the incalculable value of friendship, an intense interest in people as individuals, an unusual insight into their lives, and a deep power of sympathy for them; for the complete faith which he consistently shows in the free mind; for a constant loyalty to truth, both scientific and humane; and for an unfailing sense of humor compounded of both laughter and sanity. Discerning readers will always be refreshed and strengthened by the hygiene of laughter and the iron vein of courage to be found throughout his works. His mind and spirit were invincible. He knew what it was to be buffeted by life, and no one was more sharply aware of the shortcomings of his age than he was. But for him it was not enough that the artist should know the life of his time and reflect it in his art. He must also rise above it and dominate it, as Homer, Shakespeare, and Milton had done. Great art thus became a victory. The defeatism and confusion which have characterized much of the writings of our century never gained the slightest foothold in Strachey's domain. His eyes were often sad with knowledge, but within the fortress of his mind there was never any thought of surrender. He did not write for those who have timid intellects or who are afraid to exercise all their faculties. Such persons will continue to be shocked by him, as they have been shocked by Chaucer and Fielding. But it seems safe to predict that as long as the liberal humanistic tradition is allowed to flourish there will be many readers who will find in the works of Lytton Strachey a sure source of strength and delight.

A CHRONOLOGICAL CHECK LIST OF
LYTTON STRACHEY'S WRITINGS

THE LIST BELOW contains all of Strachey's published writings which I have been able to find and some of the unpublished ones. His unsigned contributions to the *Spectator* are included, even though some of these may be the product of collaboration with the editor or some other member of the staff. Strachey's writings for the *Spectator* have been identified partly through the help of James Strachey and partly through the use of a marked file of that journal. The following symbols are used for convenience of reference: *BC, Books and Characters* (1922); *PM, Portraits in Miniature and Other Essays* (1931); *CC, Characters and Commentaries* (1933); *BE, Biographical Essays* (1948); *LE, Literary Essays* (1948). This list is an expansion of my "A Chronological Check List of Lytton Strachey's Writings," *Modern Philology, 44* (Feb. 1947), 189–92.

"The Monk. 600 A.D." *Cambridge Review, 22* (Feb. 14, 1901), 181. A poem signed "Selig," anagram for Giles.

"Ningamus Serta Rosarum." *Cambridge Review, 22* (in the addition to the issue of June 5, 1901), xiii. Signed "G.L.S." Reprinted in *Euphrosyne: A Collection of Verse* (Cambridge, Elijah Johnson, 1905), p. 11. A poem.

"Warren Hastings." An unpublished essay submitted for the Greaves Prize. Finished Sept. 26, 1901.

"Ely: An Ode." In *Prolusionae Academical* (Cambridge, Cambridge University Press, 1902), pp. 9–15. A poem which has the strophes, antistrophes, and the epode of the Pindaric ode. Won the Cambridge Chancellor's Medal for English Verse in 1902. Recited in the Senate House, June 10, 1902.

"After Herrick." *Cambridge Review, 23* (Supplement following p. 388, June 12, 1902), xi. Signed "G.L.S." A poem.

"The Cat." (same Supplement), p. xxii. Signed "G.L.S." Reprinted in *Euphrosyne*, p. 68. A poem.

"From the Persian." *Cambridge Review, 24* (Feb. 5, 1903), 168. Signed "G.L.S." A poem.

"Two Frenchmen." *Independent Review, 1* (Oct. 1903), 185–9. Collected in *CC* and *LE.*

"The Electress Sophia." *Spectator, 92* (Jan. 9, 1904). A review of A. W. Ward, *The Electress Sophia and the Hanoverian Succession.*

"The Wrong Turning." *Independent Review, 2* (Feb. 1904), 169–73. Collected in *CC* and *LE.* A review of Austin Dobson, *Fanny Burney.*

"Horace Walpole." *Independent Review, 2* (May 1904), 641–6. Collected in *CC* and *BE.* A review of Mrs. Paget Toynbee, *The Letters of Horace Walpole.*

"The Praise of Shakespeare." *Spectator, 92* (June 4, 1904), 881–2. A review of *The Praise of Shakespeare: An English Anthology,* ed. C. E. Hughes.

"Shakespeare's Final Period." *Independent Review, 3* (Aug. 1904), 405–18. Collected in *BC* and *LE.* Originally written for and read to the Sunday Essay Society, Nov. 29, 1903. This society then met every week in Professor Bevan's rooms, Trinity College, Cambridge.

"Land and Sea Pieces." *Spectator, 93* (Aug. 27, 1904), 294–5. A review of A. E. Legge, *Land and Sea Pieces.*

"Newman." *Spectator* (supplement), *93* (Oct. 1, 1904), 457. A review of William Barry, *Newman.*

"Warren Hastings, Cheyt Sing, and the Begums of Oude." A long typewritten thesis, unpublished, completed in 1905. Strachey was disappointed in the hope that this thesis would earn him a fellowship at Cambridge.

"English Letter Writers." In *CC* James Strachey dates the composition 1905. First published in *CC,* also in *LE.*

"Shakespeare's Sonnets." *Spectator, 94* (Feb. 4, 1905), 177–8. A review of H. C. Beeching's edition of Shakespeare's sonnets.

"The Tragedies of Voltaire." *Independent Review, 5* (April 1905), 309–19. Collected as "Voltaire's Tragedies" in *BC* and *LE.*

"Shakespeare's Marriage." *Spectator, 95* (July 29, 1905), 153–4. A review of J. W. Gray, *Shakespeare's Marriage.*

"John Lyly." *Speaker, 13* (Dec. 9, 1905), 236. An unsigned review, identified by James Strachey, of J. D. Wilson, *John Lyly.*

"Forgotten Poets." *Spectator, 96* (Jan. 27, 1906), 115–16. A review of George Saintsbury, *Minor Poets of the Caroline Period,* Vol. *1.*

"Sir Thomas Browne." *Independent Review, 8* (Feb. 1906), 158–69. Collected in *BC* and *LE.*

"A New Book on Sir Thomas Browne." *Speaker, 13* (Feb. 3, 1906), 441. An unsigned review, identified by James Strachey, of Edmund Gosse, *Sir Thomas Browne.*

"Andrew Marvell." *Spectator, 96* (April 14, 1906), 582–3. A review of Augustine Birrell, *Andrew Marvell.*

"The Poetry of Blake." *Independent Review, 9* (May 1906), 215–26. Collected in *BC* and *LE.*

"The Lives of the Poets." *Independent Review, 10* (July 1906), 108–13. Collected in *BC* and *LE.*

"The Value of Poetry." *Spectator, 97* (July 21, 1906), 93–5. A review of J. C. Collins, *Studies in Poetry and Criticism.*

"Versailles." *Speaker, 14* (July 28, 1906), 387. Collected in *CC.* A review of J. E. Farmer, *Versailles and the Court under Louis XIV.*

"The Pastoral." *Spectator, 17* (July 28, 1906), 132–3. A review of W. W. Greg, *Pastoral Poetry and Pastoral Drama.*

"Mademoiselle de Lespinasse." *Independent Review, 10* (Sept. 1906), 345–56. Collected in *CC* and *BE.*

"Not by Lockhart." *Speaker, 15* (Oct. 20, 1906), 82–3. An unsigned review, identified by James Strachey, of Andrew Lang, *Sir Walter Scott* and of G. L. G. Norgate, *Life of Sir Walter Scott.*

"Medieval Studies." *Spectator, 97* (Nov. 17, 1906), 786–7. A review of W. P. Ker, *Essays on Medieval Literature.*

"Mr. Sidney Lee on Shakespeare." *Spectator, 97* (Dec. 1, 1906), 887–8. A review of Sidney Lee, *Shakespeare and the Modern Stage, with Other Essays.*

"The First Earl of Lytton." *Independent Review, 12* (March 1907), 332–8. Also in *Living Age, 253* (April 20, 1907), 153–6. Collected in *CC* and *LE.*

"The Age of Spenser." *Spectator, 98* (March 23, 1907), 457–8. A review of J. J. Jusserand, *A Literary History of the English People from the Renaissance to the Civil War.*

"Provincial Letters." *Spectator, 98* (April 13, 1907), 574–5. A review of *Provincial Letters and Other Papers* by the author of *Pages from a Private Diary.*

"Shakespeare's First Editors." *Spectator, 98* (June 22, 1907), 979–80. A review of T. R. Lounsbury, *The First Editors of Shakespeare.*

"Lady Mary Wortley Montagu." *Albany Review, 1* (Sept. 1907), 708–16. Collected in *CC* and *BE.*

"Rothiemurchus." *Spectator, 99* (Oct. 5, 1907), 464. A review of the Rev. Hugh Macmillan, *Rothiemurchus.*

"Shakespeare and Water." *Spectator, 99* (Oct. 5, 1907), 462. A review of A. S. G. Canning, *Shakespeare Studied in Six Plays.*

"Molière." *Spectator, 99* (Oct. 26, 1907), 612–13. A review of A. R. Waller's translation, *The Plays of Molière.*

"The Last Elizabethan." *New Quarterly, 1* (Nov. 1907), 47–72. Collected in *BC* and *LE.*

"Cambridge." *Spectator, 99* (Nov. 2, 1907), 668–9. A review of J. W. Clark, *Cambridge.*

"Mr. Walkley on the Drama." *Spectator, 99* (Nov. 16, 1907), 776–7. A review of A. B. Walkley, *Drama and Life.*

"Macaulay's Marginalia." *Spectator, 99* (Nov. 16, 1907), 743. A review of Sir G. O. Trevelyan, *Marginal Notes by Lord Macaulay.*

"Sir Henry Wotton." *Spectator, 99* (Nov. 23, 1907), 821–2. A review of Logan Pearsall Smith, *The Life and Letters of Sir Henry Wotton.*

"The Mollusc." *Spectator, 99* (Nov. 30, 1907), 867–8. The first of a series of articles on the drama which Strachey signed "Ignotus."

"The Swan of Lichfield." *Spectator, 99* (Dec. 7, 1907), 929–30. A review of E. V. Lucas, *A Swan and Her Friends.*

"Milton's Words." *Spectator, 99* (Dec. 14, 1907), 991–2. A review of Laura E. Lockwood, *Lexicon to the English Poetical Works of John Milton.*

"French Poetry." *Spectator, 99* (Dec. 21, 1907), 1051–2. A review of John C. Bailey, *The Claims of French Poetry* and of *The Oxford Book of French Verse,* ed. St. John Lucas.

"L'Art Administratif." *Spectator, 99* (Dec. 28, 1907), 1093–4. A review of William Archer and H. Granville-Barker, *A National Theater: Scheme and Estimates.* Signed "Ignotus."

"The Late Miss Coleridge's Poems." *Spectator, 100* (Jan. 4, 1908), 19–20. A review of Mary E. Coleridge, *Poems.*

"Old Masters at Burlington House." *Spectator, 100* (Jan. 11, 1908), 61–2. Done in collaboration with Duncan Grant. Signed "Z."

"The International Society." *Spectator, 100* (Jan. 18, 1908), 97–8. Signed "Z."

"The Prose Style of Men of Action." *Spectator, 100* (Jan. 25, 1908), 141–2. A subleader, probably done in collaboration with St. Loe Strachey.

"Mr. Beerbohm Tree." *Spectator, 100* (Feb. 1, 1908), 185–6. Signed "Ignotus."

"Elizabethanism." *Spectator, 100* (Feb. 8, 1908), 213–14. A subleader.

"The Sicilians." *Spectator, 100* (Feb. 29, 1908), 336–7. Signed "Ignotus."

"Coleridge's *Biographia Literaria.*" *Spectator, 100* (March 7, 1908), 376–7. A review of J. Shawcross' edition.

"The Poetry of Thomson." *Spectator, 100* (March 14, 1908), 421–2. A review of G. C. Macaulay, *James Thomson.*

"Wordsworth's Letters." *Spectator, 100* (March 21, 1908), 460–1. A review of William Knight, *Letters of the Wordsworth Family.*

"Mr. Granville Barker." *Spectator, 100* (March 28, 1908), 499–500. Signed "Ignotus."

"Shakespeariana." *Spectator, 100* (April 4, 1908), 536–7. A review of W. G. Boswell-Stone, *Shakespeare's Holinshed* and of other Elizabethan works.

"The Age of Louis XIV." *Spectator, 100* (April 11, 1908), 577–8. A review of *The Age of Louis XIV,* Vol. 5 of *The Cambridge Modern History.*

"Modern Poetry." *Spectator, 100* (April 18, 1908), 622–3. A review of Walter Jerrold, *The Book of Living Poets.*

"Shakespeare on the Stage." *Spectator, 100* (April 25, 1908), 669–70. Signed "Ignotus."

"Seventeenth-Century Criticism." *Spectator, 100* (May 2, 1908), 706. A review of J. E. Spingarn, *Critical Essays of the Seventeenth Century.*

"The Grandiloquence of Wordsworth." *Spectator, 100* (May 9, 1908), 746–7. A review of N. C. Smith, *The Poems of William Wordsworth.*

"King Lear." *Spectator, 100* (May 23, 1908), 830–1. A review of the Malone Society reprint, *The History of King Leir, 1605.*

"The Shakespeare Memorial." *Spectator, 100* (May 23, 1908), 820–1.

"Three Frenchmen in England." *Spectator, 100* (May 30, 1908), 866–7. A review of J. C. Collins, *Voltaire, Montesquieu, and Rousseau in England.*

"The Poetry of Racine." *New Quarterly, 1* (June 1908), 361–84. Collected as "Racine" in *BC* and *LE.*

"Three New Plays." *Spectator, 100* (June 6, 1908), 899–900. Signed "Ignotus."

"The Poetry of T. E. Brown." *Spectator, 100* (June 13, 1908), 938–9.

"Elizabethan Drama." *Spectator, 100* (June 20, 1908), 975–6. A review of F. E. Schelling, *Elizabethan Drama, 1558–1642.*

"Coquelin." *Spectator, 100* (June 27, 1908), 1029–30. Signed "Ignotus."

"Milton." *Spectator, 101* (July 4, 1908), 9–10.

"Comus at Cambridge." *Spectator, 101* (July 18, 1908), 94–5.

"America in Profile." *Spectator, 101* (July 25, 1908), 132–3. A review of Charles Whibley, *American Sketches.*

"Shakespeare on Johnson." *Spectator, 101* (Aug. 1, 1908), 164–5. A review of Walter Raleigh, *Johnson on Shakespeare.*

"The Works of W. E. Henley." *Spectator, 101* (Aug. 8, 1908), 196–7. A review of *The Works of William Ernest Henley,* Vols. *1–4.*

"The Guides." *Spectator, 101* (Aug. 15, 1908), 232. A review of Col. G. J. Younghusband, *The Story of the Guides.*

"Tragedy Old and New." *Spectator, 101* (Aug. 22, 1908), 266. A review of C. E. Vaughan, *Types of Tragic Drama* and of A. H. Thorndike, *Tragedy.*

"The Shakespeare Apocrypha." *Spectator, 101* (Aug. 29, 1908), 298–9. A review of C. F. Tucker Brooke, *The Shakespeare Apocrypha.*

"Mr. Barrie's New Play." *Spectator, 101* (Sept. 26, 1908), 444–5. A review of *What Every Woman Knows.* Signed "Ignotus."

"An Anthology." *New Quarterly, 1* (Oct. 1908), 603–10. Also in *Living Age, 259* (Nov. 21, 1908), 477–81. Collected in *CC* and *LE.*

"A Poet on Poets." *Spectator, 101* (Oct. 3, 1908), 502–3. A review of A. C. Swinburne, *The Age of Shakespeare.*

"Mr. Yeats's Poetry." *Spectator, 101* (Oct. 17, 1908), 588–9. A review of *The Collected Works in Verse and Prose of William Butler Yeats.*

"FitzGerald and 'Posh.' " *Spectator, 101* (Oct. 24, 1908), 635. A review of James Blyth, *Edward FitzGerald and "Posh."*

"A Mirror for Gentlefolks." *Spectator, 101* (Oct. 24, 1908), 630–1. A review of A. S. Palmer, *The Ideal of a Gentleman.*

"Bacon as a Man of Letters." *Spectator, 101* (Oct. 24, 1908), 621–2.

"Lady Epping's Lawsuit." *Spectator, 101* (Oct. 31, 1908), 673–4. A review of H. H. Davies' play. Signed "Ignotus."

"Introduction to Mrs. Inchbald's *A Simple Story.*" London, Henry Frowde, October, 1908. Collected in *CC* and *LE.*

"The Admirable Boileau." *Spectator, 101* (Nov. 7, 1908), 735–6.

"The Political Wisdom of Burke." *Spectator, 101* (Nov. 14, 1908), 774. A letter to the editor. Signed "Z."

"The Italian Renaissance." *Spectator, 101* (Nov. 22, 1908), 838–9.

"Mr. Hawtrey." *Spectator, 101* (Nov. 28, 1908), 880–1. Signed "Ignotus."

"John Milton." *Spectator, 101* (Dec. 5, 1908), 933–4. An article for the three hundredth anniversary of Milton's birth.

"Some New Plays in Verse." *Spectator, 101* (Dec. 12, 1908), 998–9.

"Music and Men." *Spectator, 101* (Dec. 19, 1908), 1059–60. A review of C. V. Stanford, *Studies and Memories.*

"A Play for Children." *Spectator, 101* (Dec. 26, 1908), 1098–9. A review of Graham Robertson, *Pinkie and the Fairies.* Signed "Ignotus."

"Some Napoleonic Books." *Spectator, 101* (Dec. 26, 1908), 1100–1.

"The Life of Henry Irving." *Spectator, 101* (Dec. 26, 1908), 1104. A review of Austin Brereton's book on the subject.

"A New History of Rome." *Spectator, 102* (Jan. 2, 1909), 20–1. A review of Guglielmo Ferrero, *The Greatness and Decline of Rome,* Vols. *3* and *4.*

"The Poetry of William Barnes." *Spectator, 102* (Jan. 16, 1909), 95–6. A review of *Select Poems of William Barnes,* ed. Thomas Hardy.

"The Age of Corneille." *Spectator, 102* (Jan. 30, 1909), 182–3. A review of Arthur Tilley, *From Montaigne to Molière.*

"The Shakespeare Problem." *Spectator, 102* (Jan. 30, 1909), 185. A review of H. C. Beeching, *William Shakespeare, Player, Playmaker, and Poet.*

"The Author of *Hudibras.*" *Spectator, 102* (Feb. 6, 1909), 224–6. A review of *Samuel Butler: Characters and Passages from the Notebooks,* ed. A. R. Waller.

"Light Verse." *Spectator, 102* (Feb. 20, 1909), 304–5.

"Jonathan Swift." *Spectator, 102* (Feb. 27, 1909), 341–2. A review of *The Prose Works of Jonathan Swift,* ed. Temple Scott, Vol. *12.*

"The Follies." *Spectator, 102* (Feb. 13, 1909), 262–3. Signed "Ignotus."

"Caran d'Ache." *Spectator, 102* (March 6, 1909), 371–2.

"Elizabethans Old and New." *Spectator, 102* (March 13, 1909), 420–2.

"Mr. Galsworthy's Plays." *Spectator, 102* (March 27, 1909), 498–9. Signed "Ignotus."

"Canning and His Friends." *Spectator, 102* (March 27, 1909), 499–500. A review of Captain Josceline Bagot's book on the subject.

"Some New Carlyle Letters." *Spectator, 102* (April 10, 1909), 577–8. A review of *The Love Letters of Thomas Carlyle and Jane Welsh,* ed. Alexander Carlyle.

"Alexander Pope." *Spectator, 103* (Nov. 20, 1909), 847–8. A review of George Paston, *Mr. Pope: His Life and Times.*

"Warren Hastings." *Spectator, 104* (March 12, 1910), 429–30. A review of *Selections from the State Papers of the Governors-General of India,* ed. G. W. Forrest, Vols. *1* and *2*.

"The Rousseau Affair." *New Quarterly,* 2 (May 1910), 147–57. Collected in *BC,* where it is erroneously dated 1907; also in *BE.*

Landmarks in French Literature. ("Home University Library.") New York, Henry Holt & Co.; London, Williams & Norgate, 1912. First published in England on Jan. 12.

"Dostoievsky." *Spectator, 109* (Sept. 28, 1912), 451–2. A review of *The Brothers Karamazov,* trans. Constance Garnett.

"Madame du Deffand." *Edinburgh Review,* 217 (Jan. 1913), 61–80. Collected in *BC* and *BE.* The first publication signed "Lytton Strachey."

"The Poetry of John Donne." *Spectator, 110* (Jan. 18, 1913), 102–3. A review of H. J. C. Grierson, *The Poems of John Donne.*

"Avons-nous changé tout cela?" *New Statesman,* Nov. 22, 1913, pp. 204–6. Collected in *CC.*

"The Old Comedy." *New Statesman,* Dec. 6, 1913, literary supplement. Collected in *CC* and *LE.*

"Henri Beyle." *Edinburgh Review,* 219 (Jan. 1914), 35–52. Collected in *BC* and *LE.*

"Bonga-Bonga in Whitehall." *New Statesman,* Jan. 17, 1914, pp. 459–60. Collected in *CC.*

"A Russian Humorist." *Spectator, 112* (April 11, 1914), 610–11. A review of Dostoievsky, *The Idiot* and *The Possessed,* trans. Constance Garnett. Collected in *CC* and *LE.*

"A Victorian Critic." *New Statesman,* Aug. 1, 1914, pp. 529–30. Collected in *CC* and *LE.*

"Voltaire and England." *Edinburgh Review,* 220 (Oct. 1914), 392–411. Collected in *BC* and *BE.*

"Mr. Hardy's New Poems." *New Statesman,* Dec. 19, 1914, pp. 269–71. Collected in *CC* and *LE.*

"Voltaire and Frederick the Great." *Edinburgh Review,* 222 (Oct. 1915), 351–73. Collected in *BC* and *BE.*

"French Poets through Boston Eyes." *New Statesman,* March 4, 1916, pp. 524–5. Collected in *CC.*

"A Short Guide to Thomas Hardy."*New Statesman,* March 11, 1916, pp. 551–2. A review of Harold Child, *Thomas Hardy.*

"A Sidelight on Frederick the Great." *New Statesman,* Jan. 27, 1917, pp. 397–9. Collected in *CC* and *BE.*

"An Adolescent." *New Statesman*, March 31, 1917, pp. 613–15. Collected in *CC* and *BE*.

"A Statesman: Lord Morley." *War and Peace*, Feb. 1918, pp. 190–1. Collected in *CC* and *BE*.

"Rabelais." *New Statesman*, Feb. 16, 1918, pp. 473–4. Collected in *CC* and *LE*.

"A Diplomatist: Li Hung-Chang." *War and Peace*, March 1918, pp. 208–10. Collected in *CC* and *BE*.

"Militarism and Theology." *War and Peace*, May 1918, pp. 249–50. Collected in *CC*.

Eminent Victorians. London, Chatto & Windus; Garden City, N.Y., Garden City Pub. Co., 1918. First published in England on May 9.

"Traps and Peace Traps." *War and Peace*, June 1918, pp. 269–70.

"The Claims of Patriotism." *War and Peace*, July 1918, pp. 292–3. Collected in *CC*.

"The Character of Lord Cromer." *Times Literary Supplement*, July 4, 1918, pp. 313–14. A letter to the editor, in reply to Sir Edmund Gosse's letter with the same title (*ibid.*, June 27, 1918, p. 301).

"Lady Hester Stanhope." *Athenaeum*, April 4, 1919, pp. 131–3, 166–7. Also, under title "Un-Victorian Victorian," in *Living Age, 301* (May 17, 1919), 409–14; and, as "Curious History of Lady Hester Stanhope," in *Golden Book, 22* (July 1935), 76–81. Collected in *BC* and *BE*.

"Mr. Creevey." *New Republic, 19* (June 7, 1919), 178–81; *Athenaeum*, June 13, 1919, pp. 453–5; *Living Age, 302* (July 19, 1919), 158–62. Collected in *BC* and *BE*.

"Shakespeare at Cambridge." *Athenaeum*, June 20, 1919, p. 501. Collected in *CC* and *LE*.

"Voltaire." *Athenaeum*, Aug. 1, 1919, pp. 677–8; *New Republic, 20* (Aug. 6, 1919), 14–16. Collected in *CC* and *BE*.

"Walpole's Letters." *Athenaeum*, Aug. 15, 1919, pp. 744–5; *Living Age*, Sept. 27, 1919, pp. 788–91. Collected in *CC* and *BE*.

"Suppressed Passages in Walpole's Letters." *Athenaeum*, Sept. 5, 1919, p. 853. Signed "L.S." Letter to the editor.

"Happiness." *Atlantic Monthly, 125* (April 1920), 489–90. Also in *New Statesman and Nation, 13* (June 26, 1937), 1045–6. A poem.

"Dizzy." *Woman's Leader, 12* (July 16, 1920), 543. Collected in *CC* and *BE*.

Queen Victoria. London, Chatto & Windus; New York, Harcourt,

Brace & Co., 1921. Also published serially in *New Republic, 26–27* (March 30–June 8, 1921), 127–9, 153–5, 181–2, 225–9, 259–63, 285– 9, 318–23, 347–9, 375–7; 15–18, 42–4. First published in England in April.

Books and Characters, French and English. London, Chatto & Windus, May 1922; New York, Harcourt, Brace & Co., June 1922. Contains a dialogue attributed to Voltaire which Strachey says has never been printed before.

"Sarah Bernhardt." *Nation and Athenaeum, 33* (May 5, 1923), 152–3; *Century Magazine, 106* (July 1923), 468–70. Collected in *CC* and *BE.*

"Charles Greville." *Nation and Athenaeum, 33* (Aug. 11, 1923), 593–4; *New Republic, 35* (Aug. 15, 1923), 325–7. Collected in *BE.*

"John Aubrey." *Nation and Athenaeum, 33* (Sept. 15, 1923), 741–2; *New Republic, 36* (Oct. 10, 1923), 176–8. Collected in *PM* and *BE.*

"Congreve, Collier, and Macaulay." *Nation and Athenaeum, 34* (Oct. 13, 1923), 56–8; *New Republic, 36* (Nov. 21, 1923), 335–6. Collected as "Congreve, Collier, Macaulay, and Mr. Summers" in *PM* and under original title in *LE.*

"Sir John Harington." *Nation and Athenaeum, 34* (Nov. 17, 1923), 271–2; *New Republic, 37* (Nov. 28, 1923), 12–13. Collected in *PM* and *BE.*

"The Sad Story of Dr. Colbatch." *Nation and Athenaeum, 34* (Dec. 22, 1923), 459–60; *New Republic, 37* (Dec. 26, 1923), 115–16. Collected in *PM* and *BE.*

"The Abbé Morellet." *Nation and Athenaeum, 34* (Jan. 26, 1924), 602–3; *New Republic, 37* (Feb. 13, 1924), 306–7. Collected in *PM* and *BE.*

"Muggleton." *Nation and Athenaeum, 35* (July 26, 1924), 534–5; *New Republic, 39* (July 30, 1924), 265–7. Collected in *PM* and *BE.*

"Madame de Sévigné's Cousin." *Nation and Athenaeum, 36* (Oct. 4, 1924), 14–15; *New Republic, 40* (Oct. 8, 1924), 141–2. Collected in *PM* and *BE.*

"James Boswell." *Nation and Athenaeum, 36* (Jan. 31, 1925), 609– 10; *New Republic, 41* (Feb. 4, 1925), 283–5. Collected in *PM* and *BE.*

"Mary Berry." *Nation and Athenaeum, 36* (March 21, 1925), 856–8; *New Republic, 42* (April 1, 1925), 152–4. Collected in *PM* and *BE.*

"Pope." (Leslie Stephen Lecture for 1925.) Cambridge, Cambridge University Press, 1925. First edition, June 1925. Reprinted in *CC* and *LE*.

The Son of Heaven. A play, two performances of which were given at the Scala Theater, London, July 12 (Sunday) at 8:15 P.M., and July 13 at 2:30 P.M. Performed for the benefit of the London Society for Women's Service. (For the complete cast, see the London *Times*, July 14, 1925, p. 12. See also reviews by J. C. Squire, *London Mercury*, Aug. 1925, pp. 422–3; and Desmond MacCarthy, *New Statesman*, July 18, 1925, p. 394.) Revived by Vera Bowen for a run of three weeks at the New Lindsey Theater, London, in May 1949. Unpublished.

"The Eighteenth Century." *Nation and Athenaeum, 39* (May 29, 1926), 205–6; *New Republic, 47* (June 16, 1926), 110–12. Collected in *CC* and *BE*.

"The Life, Illness, and Death of Dr. North." *Nation and Athenaeum, 40* (Feb. 19, 1927), 694–5; *New Republic, 50* (March 9, 1927), 67–9. Collected in *PM* and *BE*.

"A Frock-Coat Portrait of a Great King." *Daily Mail,* Oct. 11, 1927, p. 10. A review of Sir Sidney Lee, *King Edward VII,* Vol. 2.

Letter to the London *Times,* Nov. 12, 1927, p. 8. Insists on the publication of the complete *Greville Memoirs*.

"Hume." *Nation and Athenaeum, 42* (Jan. 7, 1928), 536–8. Collected in *PM* and *BE*.

"Gibbon." *Nation and Athenaeum, 42* (Jan. 14, 1928), 565–7. Collected in *PM* and *BE*.

"Macaulay." *Nation and Athenaeum, 42* (Jan. 21, 1928), 596–7. Collected in *PM* and *LE*.

"Carlyle." *Nation and Athenaeum, 42* (Jan. 28, 1928), 646–8. Collected in *PM* and *BE*.

Introduction to G. H. W. Rylands, *Words and Poetry*. London, Hogarth Press, 1928; New York, Payson & Clark, 1928. Reprinted in *CC* and *LE*.

Elizabeth and Essex: A Tragic History. London, Chatto & Windus, Dec. 1928; New York, Harcourt, Brace & Co., 1928. Published serially, with omissions, in *Ladies' Home Journal, 45* (Sept. 1928), 6–7; (Oct. 1928), 9–10; (Nov. 1928), 16–17; (Dec. 1928), 17.

"Obscenity in Literature." *Nation and Athenaeum, 44* (March 30, 1929), 108. Letter to the editor. A reply to Gilbert Murray, who had objected to obscenity in modern literature.

"Mandell Creighton." New York *Herald Tribune Books,* May 28,

1929, pp. [1], 6; *Life and Letters* (London), 2 (June 1929), 409–16. Collected as "Creighton" in *PM* and *BE*.

"One of the Victorians." *Saturday Review of Literature, 7* (Dec. 6, 1930), 418–19; *Life and Letters, 5* (Dec. 1930), 431–8. Collected as "Froude" in *PM* and *BE*.

"Madame de Lieven." *Saturday Review of Literature, 7* (April 18, 1931), 748–9; *Life and Letters, 6* (April 1931), 247–58. Collected in *PM* and *BE*.

"The Président de Brosses." *New Statesman and Nation, 1* (April 11, 18, 1931), 250–1, 281–2; *New Republic, 66* (April 22, 1931), 267–70. Collected in *PM* and *BE*.

Portraits in Miniature and Other Essays. London, Chatto & Windus, May 1931; New York, Harcourt, Brace & Co., 1931.

Characters and Commentaries. London, Chatto & Windus, Nov. 1933; New York, Harcourt, Brace & Co., 1933. Edited with a preface by James Strachey. Contains an unfinished essay, "Othello," hitherto unpublished, reprinted in *LE*.

"The Two Triumphs." *Saturday Review of Literature, 16* (June 19, 1937), 4. A poem.

"The Two Triumphs," "The Haschish," "Happiness." *New Statesman and Nation, 22* (June 26, 1937), 1045–6.

Editor, with Roger Fulford, of *The Greville Memoirs, 1814–1860.* 8 vols. London, Macmillan & Co., 1938. First complete and un-expurgated edition. Fulford says in the preface that Strachey started work on this edition in 1928. "The notes are almost all Mr. Strachey's—though here and there it has been found possible to add to them in the light of information published since his death."

The Collected Works. 6 vols. Landmarks in French Literature. Eminent Victorians. Queen Victoria. Elizabeth and Essex. Biographical Essays. Literary Essays. London, Chatto & Windus, 1948.

INDEX

Abercrombie, Lascelles, 28 n.

Adams, Henry, 30, 140

Adams, J. T., 205 n., 342

Addison, Joseph, 156

Albany Review, 28 n.

Albert, Prince, 50, 186 n., 226 f., 231, 233, 234-5, 309-10, 314, 315, 324, 328

Alexandria, 14

Allenswood, 10, 111

American language and literature, 30, 122, 245-7, 325; "America in Profile," 360

Antonines, 141

Aphorisms, 51 n., 64, 186 n., 187 n., 200, 287

Apostles, "Conversazione Society," 18-19, 62

Archer, William, 28 n., 75

Ariosto, Lodovico, 255

Aristophanes, 11, 160 n., 172

Aristotle, 135, 176

Armstrong, Archie, 185

Arnold, Matthew, 44 n., 51 n., 53, 57, 72, 74 n., 83, 156 f., 173-7, 269; "A Victorian Critic," 58 n., 173 n.

Arnold, Dr. Thomas, 58, 169 f., 176-7, 203 n., 204 n., 211, 217, 220-1, 223, 253, 318

"L'Art Administratif," 75 n., 101 n., 124 n.

Asquith, the Earl of Oxford and, 37, 38 n., 214, 341 n.

Aubrey, John, 247, 320, 323; "John Aubrey," 56 n., 194, 262

Austen, Jane, 29, 128

"Avons-nous changé tout cela?" 70 n., 178 n.

Bach, J. S., 162

Bacon, Francis, 30, 43, 66-7, 155, 162, 204, 237, 242-3, 298, 323, 332; "Bacon as a Man of Letters," 360

Bacon, Leonard, 136 n., 205, 256, 305 n., 330, 342

Bagot, Capt. Joscelin, 260

Bailey, J. C., 75 n., 121, 129

Baines, Frank, 103

Balfour, Mr., 19 n.

Balzac, Honoré de, 117 f., 124, 274-5

Baring, Maurice, 78, 101

Barker, H. Granville. *See* Granville-Barker

Barkway, Lumsden, Bishop of St. Andrews, 18

Barnes, William, 29 f., 195 n.; "The Poetry of William Barnes," 183-4

Barrie, J. M., 30, 104, 142; "Mr. Barrie's New Play," 101 n., 102

Bartet, Jeanne Julia, 107

Beaumont and Fletcher, 17, 80, 96

Beazley, J. D., 337

Beddoes, T. L., 29, 273, 275; "The Last Elizabethan," 84, 98-9

Beeching, H. C., 80, 88

Beerbohm, Sir Max, 34 n., 38, 43, 97 n., 204 n., 238, 302-3, 340, 347

Bell, Clive, 18, 19 n., 37, 38-9, 140, 213

Bell, Vanessa, 38 and n.

Bellay, Guillaume du, 116

Belloc, Hilaire, 28 n.

Date Due